Medical Malpractice
The Duke Law Journal Symposium

Medical Malpractice

The Duke Law Journal Symposium

Duke Law Journal

Ballinger Publishing Company • Cambridge, Massachusetts
A Subsidiary of J.B. Lippincott Company

 This book is printed on recycled paper.

Copyright © 1977 by Duke Law Journal. All rights reserved. No part of this publication may be reproduced, stored in a retrieval system, or transmitted in any form or by any means, electronic mechanical photocopy, recording or otherwise, without the prior written consent of the publisher.

International Standard Book Number: 0-88410-701-9

Library of Congress Catalog Card Number: 76-49822

Printed in the United States of America

Library of Congress Cataloging in Publication Data
Main entry under title:

  Medical malpractice.

  Includes bibliographical references.
  1. Insurance, Physicians' liability—United States—Addresses, essays, lectures. 2. Physicians—United States—Malpractice—Addresses, essays, lectures. 3. Medical personnel—United States—Malpractice—Addresses, essays, lectures. I. Duke law journal. [DNLM: 1. Malpractice. 2. Insurance, Liability—United States. W44 M4883]
KF1220.M2M4   346'.73'033   76-49822
ISBN 0-88410-701-9

Contents

Preface vii

Chapter One
Some Social Aspects of the Medical Malpractice Dilemma
David Mechanic 1

Chapter Two
The Relationship Between Medical Malpractice and Quality of Care
Robert H. Brook, Rudolf L. Brutoco and Kathleen N. Williams 19

Chapter Three
"Medical Adversity Insurance"—Has Its Time Come?
Clark C. Havighurst 55

Chapter Four
The Insurance of Medical Losses
Richard S.L. Roddis and Richard E. Stewart 107

Chapter Five
A Proposal to Improve the Cost to Benefit Relationships in the Medical Professional Liability Insurance System
Myron F. Steves, Jr. 131

Chapter Six
Medical Malpractice Litigation Under National Health Insurance: Essential or Expendable?
George J. Annas, Barbara F. Katz and Robert G. Trakimas 161

Chapter Seven
The Medical Malpractice Standard of Care: HMOs and Customary Practice
Randall Bovbjerg 201

Chapter Eight
Comment
An Analysis of State Legislative Responses to the Medical Malpractice Crisis 241

Preface

The term "medical malpractice" has become an increasingly familiar—and sometimes frightening—one to patients, doctors and insurers. In recent months, the spectre of physician strikes, astronomical damage awards, soaring liability insurance premiums, and allegations of poor-quality medical care have stirred debate in state legislatures, the Congress, the press and scholarly journals. The medical malpractice crisis is real, and the problems which created that crisis remain with us.

Much has been written on the subject. But because the issue is so large and has an impact on so many widely divergent interests, no recent publication has integrated scholarly treatments of all major facets of this critical problem in one package. Similarly, numerous publications have catalogued the efforts of state legislatures to deal with rising malpractice insurance premiums, but no attempt to analyze the legal and practical implications of those changes has been available. In this volume, the *Duke Law Journal* brings together the thoughts of leading writers on the medical, legal, insurance and sociological aspects of the medical malpractice dilemma. Among the articles that follow are an explanation of the problems which have beset medical liability insurers, written by former insurance commissioners of New York and California; a discussion of the potential effect of changes in the present malpractice system on the quality of medical care, prepared by three Rand Corporation researchers; original pieces on the malpractice problem in the context of the emerging Health Maintenance Organization (HMO) and National Health Insurance; an overview of the sociological phenomena which have contributed to the crisis situation; and two major proposals for changes in our system of compensating the victims of therapy-induced injury.

In addition, the staff of the *Journal* has surveyed and reviewed the numerous state enactments and proposals addressing the medical malpractice problem, has distilled from those documents the major categories of change implemented, and has discussed the efficacy and legal validity of each in a way which, it is hoped, will be helpful to those charged with finding a solution to the current crisis.

The *Duke Law Journal* is indebted to Professor Clark C. Havighurst, Director of Duke University's Program on Legal Issues in Health Care, for his guidance and the financial assistance he provided through Grant No. HS01539 from the National Center for Health Services Research, United States Department of Health, Education and Welfare.

Medical Malpractice

The Duke Law Journal Symposium

SOME SOCIAL ASPECTS OF THE MEDICAL MALPRACTICE DILEMMA

DAVID MECHANIC*

Current medical malpractice problems are symptomatic of deeper issues in the practice of medicine, in our system of social insurance, and in the fabric of our society. The noisy manifestations of the malpractice debate—complaints about staggering increases in the insurance premiums physicians pay in certain vulnerable specialties[1] or about contingent fees of attorneys[2]—are perhaps some of the least important aspects. As is true of many other problems, the symptoms are more easily treated than the basic malady, but symptomatic treatment at best buys time to examine, to reflect, and to consider more basic long-term approaches.

A great deal has been written about malpractice, but pertinent data to answer many obvious questions are not readily available. Thus, it becomes difficult to distinguish the speculative but plausible hypothesis from the true state of affairs. This Article can do little to remedy this basic shortcoming, since I have no new data to clarify issues where they have become obfuscated. My objectives, however, are to define the basic issues underlying the malpractice dilemma, to clarify some common concepts that are amenable to research, and to suggest certain hypotheses that deserve examination.

Medical malpractice litigation is said to perform two important functions: (1) to deter physicians from lax, careless, or negligent behavior;[3] and (2) to compensate patients injured as a consequence of the negligence of the hospital, physician, or ancillary health care

---

* Professor of Sociology and Director, Center for Medical Sociology and Health Services Research, University of Wisconsin—Madison.

The author appreciates the helpful comments of Lawrence Friedman in the preparation of this Article.

THE FOLLOWING CITATION WILL BE USED IN THIS ARTICLE:

U.S. DEP'T OF HEALTH, EDUCATION AND WELFARE, REPORT OF THE SECRETARY'S COMMISSION ON MEDICAL MALPRACTICE (1973) [hereinafter cited as MEDICAL MALPRACTICE REPORT].

1. *See* N.Y. Times, Jan. 8, 1974, at 1, col. 6; *id.*, June 1, 1975, at 1, col. 1; *cf.* J. O'CONNELL, ENDING INSULT TO INJURY: NO-FAULT INSURANCE FOR PRODUCTS AND SERVICES 41-42 (1975).

2. *See* MEDICAL MALPRACTICE REPORT 18.

3. J. O'CONNELL, *supra* note 1, at 42-44; Brown, *Social Resource Allocation Through Medical Malpractice*, 6 WILLAMETTE L.J. 235, 242 (1970).

personnel.[4] As to the first function, it is assumed that the threat of possible malpractice litigation encourages prudent behavior beyond that which is learned in the training of the health professional. Particularly in the case of the hospital, such a threat is believed to result in greater attention to risks with low probability (such as those due to inadequate safety precautions, the unavailability of specialized equipment which is needed infrequently, or inadequate supervision of personnel). It is not clear what proportion of malpractice claims or dollars awarded is related to such problems,[5] but it is assumed that since hospitals are rated by risk, there is an incentive operating to avoid malpractice claims.[6]

Although physicians are not usually rated by risk beyond the nature of their specialized fields, it is assumed that the stigma associated with a malpractice judgment is a significant deterrent to carelessness. It is not obvious, however, that physicians perceive malpractice claims as stigmatizing, and it appears that some feel merely harassed and persecuted by the claims. Some very fragmentary and inadequate data suggest that physicians may have sympathy for a colleague who is sued, and may refer patients to such a colleague to ensure that he does not suffer financially from malpractice litigation.[7] Perhaps the most troublesome aspect of having a malpractice claim made against a physician is the anxiety, lost time, and uncertainty that may be involved. Even when such claims are rejected, and physicians vindicated, being sued is an unpleasant and disruptive experience. Thus, the costs to the physician must be weighed not only in terms of the awards actually made, but in terms of the total costs of becoming entangled in such an incident. A claim made against a conscientious physician may cause him considerable suffering and may distract him from his best efforts.

The second generally accepted function of the malpractice mechanism is to compensate persons who suffer injury as a result of errors in treatment. But medical malpractice suits are at best a capricious and inequitable means of compensation. While some claimants obtain very large awards, others suffering from equally serious injuries receive no compensation at all. If our social insurance system were more satisfactory, and provided ample compensation for necessary

---

4. Brooke, *Medical Malpractice: A Socio-Economic Problem From a Doctor's View*, 6 WILLAMETTE L.J. 225, 226 (1970).
5. MEDICAL MALPRACTICE REPORT 5-12.
6. *Id.* at 41-42.
7. Schwartz & Skolnick, *Two Studies of Legal Stigma*, 10 SOCIAL PROB. 133, 138-39 (1962).

medical costs and for disability resulting in dependence, the malpractice issue would be a less important concern for us. Although there would still be a need to deal with compensation for pain and suffering resulting from negligence, this is probably the aspect of malpractice having the least social significance. Because we do not have an adequate system of health care insurance, and because assistance for the disabled and dependent is modest, the manner in which the medical malpractice mechanism compensates victims of negligence looms more significant.

Hypotheses Concerning the Growth of Medical Malpractice Litigation

In recent decades medical science and technology have experienced dramatic growth, accompanied by increasing specialization and subspecialization of medical care and a larger and more heterogeneous mix of health care manpower.[8] Public expectations concerning the performance of the medical sector have also grown, stimulated by the mass media's treatment of impressive developments in medical technology and knowledge. All of these changes—as I shall attempt to illustrate—contribute both to the probability that errors will occur and to the probability that patients, becoming cognizant of errors, will make claims against physicians.

Increasingly, physicians have available a more powerful technology for evaluating and treating disease, but a technology that also can cause havoc when incorrectly applied. The traditional practitioner, with his little black bag, was able to affect disease in only a modest way, but his possibilities of doing harm were also more limited than at present. Given the complex technology that physicians now command, human error having important adverse consequences is inevitable even when physicians are fully qualified, careful, and prudent. More important is the fact that, unlike the errors of his predecessors, the errors of a modern physician have great capability for harm. Even a small lapse in judgment or attention in the application of a complex and risky treatment or diagnostic procedure may have major consequences for the patient in terms of pain experienced or resultant disability. While we all might agree that in the use of high-risk procedures (such as heart catheterization or particular types of biopsies) a certain probability of adverse events is to be expected, the physician has no assurance that a malpractice claim will not be made

---

8. *See generally* H. GREENFIELD, ALLIED HEALTH MANPOWER: TRENDS AND PROSPECTS (1969).

against him when such adverse consequences occur, nor that a finding of fault will not result.

The uncertainty experienced by the physician results, in part, from the ambiguity of medical standards and the unknown criteria for a finding of malpractice. The occurrence of adverse events varies a great deal among physicians and hospitals, and depends both on the quality of the professionals and on the types of cases involved; it has been demonstrated repeatedly that teaching hospitals in general provide higher quality care than proprietary hospitals.[9] The fact that variations in performance exist does not imply that those with poorer performance are guilty of malpractice; yet it remains unclear what standard of medical practice will be perceived by judge or jury as below the acceptable minimum. The determination is arrived at through the process of an adversary proceeding in which claimant and defendant marshal various evidence to sustain their positions. Given the nature of this process, it is quite possible that adverse effects, which may be reasonably anticipated in at least some cases where complex diseases are treated with dangerous medical techniques, may be seen by juries as instances of malpractice.

The problem is made especially difficult in that the existence of a given probability of adverse events does not mean that when such events occur they are not a result of errors. For example, we can predict quite reliably the approximate deaths and injuries due to automobile accidents in the coming month. We know, given our system of highways, the construction of automobiles, human error in driving, variable weather conditions, and the like, that in the aggregate a certain rate of accidents is inevitable. This does not mean that in any particular accident we cannot specify that the proximate cause of the injury was the error of one of the parties involved. Similarly, while statistically it may be inevitable that a gastroenterologist, in inserting gastroscopes in thousands of patients' stomachs, will pierce the wall of an individual's stomach, in any instance in which the stomach is injured it may be due to momentary negligence or an error of judgment on the part of the physician. While we recognize that there are errors in all human activities, and thus it is unjust to stigmatize the physician in such cases, it still may be fair to compensate the injured patient.

An element in the apparent increase in malpractice awards is the unwillingness of hospitals, physicians, and insurers to contest small

---

9. Goss, *Organizational Goals and Quality of Medical Care: Evidence from Comparative Research on Hospitals*, 11 J. HEALTH & SOCIAL BEHAVIOR 255 (1970).

claims, even when their merits are dubious, because of the costs of prolonged litigation.[10] There is a tendency to agree to small settlements to avoid the harassments of litigation. It has been alleged that awareness of this among lawyers encourages litigation that would not have been pursued had defensive efforts been more persistent. In conjunction with certain other incentives for litigation, including the contingent fee and the absence of a requirement to pay costs in an unsuccessful suit, it is not surprising that malpractice litigation occurs more commonly in the United States than in other countries where these incentives do not exist.[11] Depending on one's perspective, however, the American system may be thought superior in providing poor litigants a fair opportunity to seek redress under circumstances in which they feel they have been injured. The inhibition of such litigation in many countries may reflect too strong a bias in favor of the authority of the medical profession.

The emerging medical organization that has accompanied growing medical knowledge and technology has also probably contributed to increased litigation. As a larger number of people are involved in a patient's care, the risks of errors in communication and follow-up treatment are very much increased. Similarly, the fragmentation of care leads to an erosion of the relationships between doctors and patients and of the quality of communication and trust.[12] Thus, misunderstandings between doctor and patient are more likely to occur, and patients are less likely to develop loyalty and commitment to a physician. When things go wrong they are more likely to feel that he is blameworthy, and are more likely to consider litigation.

Evidence for this point of view is at best fragmentary. One study in California found that patients who sued doctors reported that the doctors had been unresponsive and had insisted on large payments despite adverse results.[13] Some additional support comes from a study of consumer attitudes conducted by the Temple University Institute of Survey Research.[14] In this national study involving

---

10. *See* Sagall, *Medical Malpractice: Are the Doctors Right?*, 10 TRIAL 59 (July/Aug. 1974). *But see* Keeton, *Compensation for Medical Accidents*, 121 U. PA. L. REV. 590, 596 (1973).

11. *See* Addison & Baylis, *The Malpractice Problem in Great Britain*, in MEDICAL MALPRACTICE REPORT Appendix 854; Welsh, *Medical Malpractice in Canada*, in MEDICAL MALPRACTICE REPORT Appendix 849.

12. *See generally* D. MECHANIC, THE GROWTH OF BUREAUCRATIC MEDICINE (1976).

13. R. BLUM, THE MANAGEMENT OF THE DOCTOR-PATIENT RELATIONSHIP (1960); R. BLUM, THE PSYCHOLOGY OF MALPRACTICE SUITS (1957).

14. Peterson, *Consumers' Knowledge of and Attitudes Toward Medical Malpractice*, in MEDICAL MALPRACTICE REPORT Appendix 658.

1,017 interviews, the surveyors found that while respondents had favorable attitudes toward the technical competence of physicians, most people felt that relationships with doctors had deteriorated over the last twenty years.[15] A subgroup of respondents reported that either they or members of their families had suffered a negative medical care experience. Persons reporting such negative experiences were more likely to report also that today's doctors maintained poor doctor-patient relationships.[16] Major reasons given for the view that physicians have become less dedicated were that they are too interested in money, that they are less accommodating and more difficult to reach, and that they are more impersonal or inconsiderate.[17] Although it is impossible to infer causal relationships from correlational findings, these data are at least consistent with the hypothesis that deteriorating and impersonal doctor-patient relationships contribute to the malpractice problem.

Still another factor in the rise of litigation is the changing character of both the medical and legal communities. Until relatively recently it was difficult to litigate a malpractice case successfully because of the unavailability of medical testimony.[18] Increasingly, American medicine has become more fragmented, and medical testimony is more accessible to patients and their attorneys.[19] Physicians now more commonly concede that they have a responsibility to testify for a patient who they believe has been wronged. Similarly, it appears that lawyers are more willing to accept malpractice work, and firms have emerged that specialize in this area.[20] It has been alleged that receptivity among lawyers to malpractice litigation increased following the implementation of no-fault automobile insurance. Any serious test of that allegation would require a comparison of data obtained over time from states with and without no-fault automobile insurance. It seems more likely that growing litigation in the medical area is a result of a variety of factors, including the increased availability of medical testimony. Lawyers tend not to accept malpractice work unless medical corroboration is available.[21] Finally, all of these

---

15. *Id.*
16. *Id.* at 678.
17. *Id.* at 668.
18. 3 A. AUERBACH, HANDLING ACCIDENT CASES 9-10 (1960); M. GROSS, THE DOCTORS 520 (1966).
19. MEDICAL MALPRACTICE REPORT 36-37.
20. *See, e.g.,* Waxman, *A Health Care Slide,* 11 TRIAL 24 (May/June 1975). *See generally* Frankel, *Medico-Legal Communications,* 6 WILLAMETTE L.J. 193, 218 (1970).
21. Dietz, Baird & Berul, *The Medical Malpractice Legal System,* in MEDICAL MALPRACTICE REPORT Appendix 99.

changes are concurrent with growing sophistication among consumers, increasing acceptance of consumer rights, and greater accessibility to legal services.

There is little question that the growth of medical technology and its dramatic achievements have done a great deal to increase popular expectations of the possibilities of medical treatment. People often expect miracles, but they are less tolerant of the dangers associated with the use of new techniques. Evidence from other areas of medical care research suggests that when patients have unrealistic expectations about their medical treatment, they feel more angry and dissatisfied with their care and pose more difficult problems of medical management and social adjustment.[22] It seems reasonable to extrapolate from such studies the principle that public expectations—to the extent they are unrealistic—contribute to growing disappointment in experience and to greater expressions of dissatisfaction, thus contributing to malpractice litigation.

Perhaps most basic—but also more vague—is a growing sense of distrust in contemporary American society. Trust is the glue that cements human relationships, that allows us to proceed—though inadequately informed—with some confidence that the claims made by others are reliable. We live in a period in which all claims are increasingly scrutinized, and it is more common to see the motives and sincerity of people challenged. With the increasing complexity of technology and social organization, there is an enormous proliferation of rules, regulations, and contracts that help to define rights and obligations. Yet even in the most bureaucratic context, written rules are but a small fraction of the necessary understandings required to carry out activities. Flexibility and discretion are necessary for effective performance, and these must depend to some extent on trust. As trust becomes more unstable, efforts are made to formulate more and more rules to govern behavior, but the proliferation of rules, and the difficulty of writing them in a way that will achieve the desired ends, result in inefficiencies and tendencies toward manipulation. In short, when the level of distrust becomes too high, social institutions are threatened, and an attempt to impose further rules and regulations will prove an inadequate remedy.

It is difficult to assess to what extent current malpractice difficulties reflect growing distrust of physicians. Certainly, available evi-

---

22. *See* I. JANIS, PSYCHOLOGICAL STRESS (1958). *See also* Egbert, Battit, Welch, *et al.*, *Reduction of Postoperative Pain by Encouragement and Instruction of Patients*, 270 NEW ENG. J. MED. 825 (1964).

dence continues to support the assertion that physicians are highly regarded by the public and continue to occupy a privileged status among American occupations.[23] But the medical profession in recent years has been subjected to a barrage of criticisms, both from outside and from within, that has contributed to some loss of trust and confidence. With unfavorable mortality and morbidity statistics, misuse of human subjects in experimentation, dominance and control in the profession's self-interest, and profiteering and chicanery on the part of a few physicians in public programs, the public has been given considerable basis for insecurity. And this has occurred at the same time that the public has become, in some sense, more dependent on medical care for general social sustenance due to the erosion of other social institutions such as the church, the kinship group, the neighborhood, and the family. The public seems to share a strange ambivalence about medical care—characterized by high and often unreasonable expectations, a strong sense of dependency, and a critical attitude. It is precisely when people expect too much that they are most likely to suffer bitter disappointment.

None of the foregoing should be taken to mean that medicine—and the way it is practiced—has made no contribution to the growing sense of dissatisfaction. Certainly there have been abuses, and the thrust of medical organization has not been toward the preservation of close doctor-patient relationships, educational dialogues between practitioners and patients, or the humanization of medical services. While physicians are often kind and helpful, their priority has been the absorption of new technologies and their efficient application, and not medical practice as a broader social endeavor. But even if their priorities had been different, it is not clear that the problems we now face could have been avoided. The malpractice crisis, in part, reflects the larger society of which it is a part, and it may be that there is only a limited amount that physicians can do to alleviate it.

The Epidemiology of Medical Malpractice Litigation

Although it is difficult to locate current data on the occurrence of malpractice claims, the estimates from the Secretary's Commission on Medical Malpractice will serve our purposes. Patients tend to be naive about the possibilities and dangers of medical treatment, and lack any clear standard by which to decide whether the physician behaved negligently. Thus patients may use a variety of standards such

---

23. A. REISS, JR., OCCUPATIONS AND SOCIAL STATUS (1961).

as bad outcome, apparent irregularities in the physician's behavior, or advice of friends or relatives as clues to the possibility that they have suffered a wrong. Desire to take some action against a physician may result as much from superficial clues, which the patient associates with a bad outcome, as from any objective medical circumstance. Or, conceivably, the motivation for a complaint may result as much from a desire for retribution for what the patient feels is callous and inhumane behavior on the part of the physician as from any seriously negative outcome. We know too little about how medical encounters that are eventually litigated compare with ordinary medical encounters.

Once a patient has come to believe that negligent behavior has occurred, he is likely to make inquiries, discussing his experiences with relatives and friends. If he is to make a claim he must find a lawyer willing to pursue the case, and this too will depend on whether he finds an appropriate legal pathway. He may be discouraged by his initial contact with a lawyer who is uninterested in such a case or views the grievance as either inappropriate or unprofitable to pursue. The ability to make successful contact with a suitable lawyer probably depends both on the patient's sophistication and social network and on the characteristics of the bar in the region in which he lives.

On the basis of data from twenty-six of the largest malpractice insurance carriers, the staff of the Commission on Medical Malpractice estimated that a malpractice incident was reported or alleged by physician or patient for one of every 158,000 patient visits.[24] A claim was made for one of every 226,000 visits.[25] Only one in ten claims ever reached trial, and one half of the payments made in response to claims in 1970 were for less than $2,000.[26] Although the dollar amounts have escalated somewhat in the past few years, the basic point still holds true that the vast majority of awards are relatively small.

A contentious issue is whether too many malpractice suits are being filed. Many physicians feel that litigation is often mischievous and unduly encouraged by a variety of incentives that are not present in other countries.[27] Among the procedures often discouraged else-

---

24. MEDICAL MALPRACTICE REPORT 12. *See also* Rudov, Myers & Mirabella, *Medical Malpractice Insurance Claims Files Closed in 1970,* in MEDICAL MALPRACTICE REPORT Appendix 1.
25. MEDICAL MALPRACTICE REPORT 12.
26. Rudov, Myers & Mirabella, *supra* note 24, at Appendix 21.
27. *See* N.Y. Times, June 2, 1975, at 53, col. 4; J. O'CONNELL, *supra* note 1, at 39.

where are the contingent fee, the doctrine of *res ipsa loquitur*, the use of juries, and the absence of the requirement that the loser pay the winner's litigation costs.[28] It is important to recognize, however, that the United States differs in fundamental ways from some of the other countries with which it is compared. American culture encourages an attitude less acceptant of authority, and more willing to challenge it, than almost any other country in the world. We also have a very heterogeneous population, a wide variety of alternative value systems and life styles, and extremely effective national systems of communication. The population is highly mobile geographically, and people's ties with neighborhoods and communities are weak. Moreover, American medicine is more complex, more heterogeneous, more technologically developed, and more uneven in quality than that of most comparably developed nations. Americans are also more likely to have high expectations of their medical care, and probably have better access to lawyers. Thus, regardless of incentives for litigation inherent in the legal system, the conditions exist, particularly in urbanized areas, for a demanding and aggressive stance toward the medical care system. In England, and perhaps in other countries, patients are more docile and more accepting of whatever care they are given.[29]

If we had an adequate definition of "fault," we could determine through investigation those cases in which injury resulted from negligence, and compare them with malpractice claims filed and awards actually made. In the absence of such data some indirect indication of whether too many claims are being made can be obtained through surveys of lawyers and patients. The national Malpractice Commission surveyed lawyers who reported that they accepted approximately one in eight claims among clients alleging malpractice.[30] About half of the claims rejected by the lawyers were attributed to a lack of liability. Before lawyers accepted a malpractice case they usually required evidence that there was a reasonable possibility of malpractice, corroborated by a physician's opinion. Attorneys reported that malpractice claims took more time to litigate than other negligence work, and felt that they were turning down worthy claims because the stakes were too small in relation to the required work.

The Temple University survey, referred to earlier, provides some data from a consumer perspective. About two fifths of the 1,017

---

28. *See* Addison & Baylis, *supra* note 11, at Appendix 860; Welsh, *supra* note 11, at Appendix 851-53.

29. *See* Mechanic, *General Medical Practice in England and Wales: Its Organization and Future*, 279 NEW ENG. J. MED. 680 (1968).

30. Dietz, Baird & Berul, *supra* note 21, at Appendix 99-101.

respondents reported that either they, their spouses, or their dependents had suffered negative medical care experience within the past ten years.[31] Such reports, of course, reflect only the perceptions of the respondents, and provide no indication of the degree of malpractice involved. But it is interesting that only thirty-seven respondents, or eight percent of respondents reporting adverse experiences, indicated that legal advice was considered.[32] Only fourteen respondents took the matter up with a legal adviser, and six made a claim of malpractice. Of these, two later withdrew the claim without settlement, two settled before trial, and two claims were still in process at the time of the study.[33] Thus it appears that very few of the grievances experienced lead to claims of negligence.

These two studies provide some indirect indication that the number of claims made against physicians is not excessive, given the extent to which patients perceive grievances and the extent to which lawyers feel that claims of negligence have some merit. Moreover, physicians working in the area of quality assurance have reported that serious errors occur frequently and that a large proportion of hospital records show major errors of omission or commission.[34] While only some of these errors may result in serious adverse consequences for the patient, any of them potentially can become an issue in a malpractice suit. Lawyers apparently feel that too much work is involved in pursuing small claims, and in any case the costs of initiating litigation would leave litigants with very little compensation. Indeed, one of the major problems with the existing malpractice mechanism is the very high administrative costs and the modest compensation left for the litigant.[35] A countervailing tendency, as suggested earlier, may be the willingness of defendants to settle small suits quickly to avoid their nuisance value, thus encouraging such claims. But it is likely that the deterrent against small claims is the more powerful one.

The Problem of Defensive Medicine

One of the most confused areas involved in the malpractice discussion concerns the allegations of defensive medicine. Physicians

---

31. Peterson, *supra* note 14, at Appendix 668-75.
32. *Id.* at Appendix 674-75.
33. *Id.* at Appendix 675.
34. MEDICAL MALPRACTICE REPORT 10.
35. *Id.* at 34; MEDICAL MALPRACTICE: A DISCUSSION OF ALTERNATIVE COMPENSATION AND QUALITY CONTROL SYSTEMS 17 (D. McDonald ed., Center for the Study of Dem. Inst., 1971).

have been vocal in their claims that the current malpractice situation encourages them to engage in protective maneuvers that are expensive but have relatively little value.[36] Some state that the growing litigation induces them to use expensive, and sometimes risky, diagnostic procedures to provide a record protecting them against liability, should their behavior be at issue. To the extent that this occurs, it unnecessarily inflates the costs of medical care. Other physicians claim that the threat of litigation forces them into a defensive posture when performing certain procedures or treating certain types of injuries associated with high rates of litigation. In neither case is there much hard evidence that defensive medicine significantly distorts the process of medical care.

Professor Hershey[37] has tried to narrow the issue by defining defensive medicine as a "deviation from what the physician believes is sound practice and which is generally so regarded, induced by a threat of liability."[38] The key phrase here is "generally so regarded," the content of which is difficult to define. The core of the difficulty in making sense of defensive medicine is the looseness and ambiguity of medical standards. Presumably, defensive medicine occurs because physicians feel that they are vulnerable to charges of negligence when they fail to perform certain "unnecessary" tests or procedures such as a skull x-ray following head trauma. Physicians would be vulnerable if they did not use such procedures because other physicians, competent in their specialty, may testify in malpractice cases that the performance of such procedures is essential for an appropriate assessment of the patient's injury. Since physicians find it difficult to agree about many aspects of diagnosis and treatment, the physician who wishes to follow a less elaborate course of evaluation and treatment may feel that he becomes vulnerable in the event of a claim against him. Allegedly, this leads to the use of unnecessary procedures.

The purpose of standards is to bring the practice of each physician to a minimal norm of acceptable practice. To the extent that a standard is established when there is considerable disagreement, the standard induces persons to practice differently from the way they would in its absence. For those who agree with the standard, it is seen as

---

36. MEDICAL MALPRACTICE REPORT 14; Project, *The Medical Malpractice Threat: A Study of Defensive Medicine*, 1971 DUKE L.J. 939, 942; *cf.* Ribicoff, *Medical Malpractice: The Patient Versus the Physician*, 6 TRIAL 10-27 (Feb./Mar. 1970) (discussing the phenomenon of "negative" defensive medicine).

37. Hershey, *The Defensive Practice of Medicine, Myth or Reality*, 50 MILBANK MEMORIAL FUND Q. 69 (1972).

38. *Id.* at 72.

a definition of appropriate care; for those who see the standard as unrealistically high, conformity constitutes defensive medicine. In short, arguments about defensive medicine inevitably reflect disagreements and confusion about the practice of medicine itself.

If defensive medicine were as great a problem as many physicians allege, one might expect certain regional variations in practice. For example, one would suppose that in states or localities with high rates of litigation, physicians in particular specialties would be much more likely to use certain procedures in dealing with problematic cases than would comparable physicians in low-litigation areas. Although there are no large-scale studies of the question, one attempt to examine this hypothesis found little evidence in its support, and suggested that varying patterns of physician behavior are more likely to reflect local norms and professional customs than the threat of litigation.[39] Although it is no doubt true that some physicians order tests and procedures which they feel are unnecessary due to their fear that a lack of such testing may lead to liability, the fact may be that these tests and procedures should be done. The real issue is one of standards, and in this area medicine is in a muddle. As a result, there are some crucial issues of defensive medicine, but they are different from the examples physicians usually cite.

Most of what is regarded as acceptable community practice is based on judgments of medical process and not of outcome. Up to now physicians have been trained in and have practiced within the philosophy that Victor Fuchs has called the "technologic imperative,"[40] namely, to the extent that a procedure can possibly be helpful to the patient, it should be done. These judgments are made without serious consideration of their cost-effectiveness. Thus, certain practices that are based entirely on process judgments have become normative, even in some cases where outcome studies raise serious questions about the value of the procedure. Such norms defining customary practice make it very difficult for a physician to act solely on the basis of the research literature when this literature is not consistent with custom.

Take, for example, the proliferation of intensive coronary care units. While many physicians believe such units to be of value in saving lives, controlled trials fail to support this belief, at least for many

---

39. Project, *supra* note 36, at 959-60.
40. Fuchs, *The Growing Demand for Medical Care,* 279 NEW ENG. J. MED. 190 (1968).

common cardiac incidents.[41] But, given the climate of physician opinion and customary practice, a medical group would feel extremely vulnerable to malpractice claims if it departed from the use of coronary intensive care despite a belief that such care is unnecessary and expensive. Also, when there is division in the medical community concerning the value of a given procedure, a prudent physician is likely to lean toward doing too much, since physicians involved in a malpractice trial might be able to make a more convincing case to a jury that the procedure should have been undertaken. Since the outcome of a contest between adversaries is in doubt when the medical situation is unclear, the uncertainty is likely to reinforce the technologic imperative.

From a purely economic point of view, an important question about the existing malpractice mechanism is the extent to which it increases the total aggregate costs of medical practice by reinforcing conservative decisions. As resources for medical care become more limited relative to the increasing technological possibilities, medical planners will have to develop means to establish priorities and to determine which procedures truly enhance outcome. Whether they will do so through government-promulgated standards, through local standards developed by Professional Standards Review Organizations (PSROs) or peer review groups, through consumer participation and input, or some combination of all three, is not clear.[42] What is required, however, is a mechanism for legitimizing the standards adopted so that professionals who conform to them can feel relatively safe from negligence claims. Such standards, however, should also reflect cost-effective practice so that they do not further reinforce the technologic imperative and the trend of increased medical care costs.

The Distributive Effects of Malpractice Litigation: Who Bears the Risk?

The existing malpractice mechanism is an inequitable way of compensating persons who suffer adverse consequences as a result of negligence. It is inequitable because the awareness of medical error,

---

41. Mather, Pearson, Read, et al., *Acute Myocardial Infarction: Home and Hospital Treatment*, 3 BRIT. MED. J. 334 (1971). See also A. COCHRANE, EFFECTIVENESS AND EFFICIENCY: RANDOM REFLECTIONS ON HEALTH SERVICES (1972).

42. One recent Note suggests that the due process clause requires that extensive procedural safeguards be used in making any decision concerning allocation of scarce medical resources. Note, *Due Process in the Allocation of Scarce Lifesaving Medical Resources*, 84 YALE L.J. 1734 (1975). The procedural implications of such a position, if accepted by the courts, would be considerable.

the process of making a claim, and the amount of compensation paid are not congruent with the adversities suffered by patients due to negligence. Compensation tends to be much influenced by a variety of social, psychological, and personal factors. Moreover, the true costs involved in bringing and contesting claims are substantial, and only a modest proportion of the money awarded constitutes actual compensation to the litigant. While no-fault insurance has been advocated for the medical care area, such a proposal leaves unsolved the difficult problem of distinguishing adverse outcomes resulting from negligence from those that are the product of the natural development of the patient's condition or that result unavoidably from high-risk therapy. Many medical measures are dangerous, but are used to forestall even greater adverse consequences related to an illness. Under the existing tort system the adversary process reaches the necessary decisions as to which incidents can be said to flow from physician error as opposed to other causes. Under a no-fault system, other fact-finding and decision-making techniques would be necessary.

While this paper does not deal with alternatives to malpractice, such as arbitration or mediation, it is relevant to consider some underlying questions concerning alternative decision-making devices. Many physicians, alarmed by increasing malpractice rates, advocate no-fault insurance in the hope that such a mechanism would be less expensive than the present system.[43] While it certainly seems plausible that a no-fault system would substantially reduce the middle-man costs associated with extensive litigation, it does not follow that an effective no-fault system would be less expensive; indeed, it may be far more costly. Unless the administration of such a system were quite conservative, it might require that many more patients be compensated.

First, a no-fault system may generate more claims since the inhibition against charging one's doctor with personal negligence may be relieved by the no-fault definition. Second, it is conceivable that under a no-fault system physicians may be more willing to inform patients that they have been injured as a result of medical treatment, and encourage them to seek compensation. Third, a no-fault system might foster a moral obligation on the part of the medical care system to compensate injured patients even when these patients have not become aware of the cause of their problems or have failed to make a claim because of ignorance, timidity, passivity, or whatever. Such

---

43. N.Y. Times, Feb. 8, 1974, at 12, col. 1. *But see* J. O'CONNELL, *supra* note 1, at 73-74 (discussing unexpected costliness of no-fault medical coverage).

an approach would be far more equitable than simply compensating patients who are aggressive enough to pursue their claims; however, it would also be very expensive.

The class of adverse events most difficult to deal with under a no-fault system is that involving the use of high-risk techniques. A certain degree of error, as noted earlier in this Article, is inevitable, particularly in the use of complex medical procedures. Some have argued that patients must assume such risks since they are an inevitable part of the treatment process. But the patient may be in the poorest position to assume the risk of inevitable medical errors. As a result of such errors the patient may suffer serious injury, prolonged disability, and increased costs of medical care and dependence. It would be reasonable to share the risks of such costs with others using the same medical care system, but who luckily escape the inevitable error. If a procedure results in one adverse event in a thousand, the person who suffers that event is left with the total cost of the error. It would seem fairer to distribute the cost among the patients who benefit from the procedure. Though this would be a heavy burden for a system replacing malpractice, it would not be an unreasonable one. Many of the costs could be assumed by increased health insurance coverage and disability compensation.

A no-fault system would protect medical personnel and institutions against allegations that the inevitable errors result from their negligence and incompetence. We do not know whether the existing fault mechanism has a deterrent effect, but to the extent that it does, a no-fault system might neutralize it. On the basis of the data that I have studied on physician behavior, I am somewhat skeptical of the theory that the threat of malpractice actions has a major deterrent effect upon the technical work of physicians, although it may well have a greater effect on the services that hospitals make available and on their supervisory procedures. But the interpersonal aspect of doctor-patient relationships is subtle, and moving to a no-fault system may conceivably have more important effects on such relationships than on technical performance.

In the traditional practice of fee-for-service medicine, the fact that the patient pays a fee gives him some modest influence in the relationship. As competition among doctors for patients declines, this influence is less potent, but the fact that a fee is involved affects the orientation of both patient and physician to some extent.[44] Increas-

---

44. E. FREIDSON, PROFESSION OF MEDICINE: A STUDY OF THE SOCIOLOGY OF APPLIED KNOWLEDGE (1970).

ingly, as patients have moved from fee-for-service to prepaid contexts they have suffered some erosion of their influence unless they are particularly aggressive. In prepaid settings, physicians seem more oriented to the standards of their colleagues than to the demands of patients.[45] Also, they are more likely to think of the typical patient as "trivial" in the prepaid situation and take him somewhat for granted.[46] Similarly, patients in prepaid contexts are more likely to complain about the physician's lack of interest in them, his inflexibility, and the feeling that they are being treated like "charity cases."[47] This may be a reaction particularly associated with patients who grew up in a fee-for-service context and then changed to a prepaid plan, and it may be less of a problem for future generations who are more receptive to bureaucratic treatment. Increasingly, however, the patient has less leverage in his personal transactions with the physician.

One of the remaining sources of power for the patient is his ability to threaten or initiate malpractice litigation when he feels that his interests have been abused. Although patients rarely do so, the remote threat may to some extent control the bounds of physician behavior. The use of a malpractice threat as a means of stating a grievance may be a latent and undesirable aspect of the present system, but it may also be one of the last sources of the patient's power in his relationship with the physician, the clinic, or the hospital. Other means of increasing patients' involvement in their care have received a great deal of discussion, but few have been attempted on a major scale.[48] Such techniques include complaint mechanisms, consumer participation in decision-making groups, regular opportunities for changing health programs (as in dual choice and re-enrollment), and the use of ombudsmen. While these are relatively uncertain substitutes for the power of the fee (and possibly also for the latent malpractice threat), they hold promise for the future.

The key point is that the malpractice problem is but a symptom of more basic problems in the organization and provision of health care and social services. An effective substitute for the existing system must be sensitive to the changing balance of power between

---

45. *See* N.Y. Times, Jan. 11, 1973, at 1, col. 1; *id.* at 22, col. 2.

46. Mechanic, *Patient Behavior and the Organization of Medical Care*, in INSTITUTE OF MEDICINE, ETHICS OF HEALTH (National Academy of Sciences 1973).

47. Tessler & Mechanic, *Consumer Satisfaction with Prepaid Group Practice: A Comparative Study*, 16 J. HEALTH & SOCIAL BEHAVIOR 95 (1975).

48. *See* N.Y. Times, April 8, 1973, at 25, col. 1 (suggesting creation of federal agency to monitor quality of patient care under Medicaid and Medicare).

patients and physicians, and must contain adequate channels for patients who feel wronged or harmed to state their grievances and to receive fair consideration. It is the development of such an alternative system that will require our long-term efforts.

THE RELATIONSHIP BETWEEN MEDICAL MALPRACTICE AND QUALITY OF CARE†

ROBERT H. BROOK,* RUDOLF L. BRUTOCO,** AND
KATHLEEN N. WILLIAMS***

INTRODUCTION

Medical malpractice claims are increasing at a rate of about ten percent per year.[1] Seven chairmen of neurosurgery departments in leading New York hospitals have a combined total of twenty-five malpractice suits filed against them, seeking an aggregate total of $6.3 million.[2] In 1960, total malpractice premiums in the United States were $60 million; by 1975, the total will be about $1 billion.[3] Many insurance companies have stopped providing professional liability coverage and some physicians have been temporarily unable to obtain malpractice insurance at any price.

California, although perhaps at the frontier of the medical malpractice issue, is not atypical. The number of claims per 100 physician policy years there has increased from about twelve in 1968-69 to about twenty-five in 1975.[4] In 1974-75, six jury awards in California were for over a million dollars each; in the state's entire history, there have been only sixteen awards of over a million dollars each.[5] Rates for malpractice insurance increased by 400 percent

---

* M.D., Sc. D.; Assistant Professor of Medicine, UCLA; Senior Staff Health Services Researcher, The Rand Corporation, Santa Monica, Calif.
** Schools of Medicine and Public Health, UCLA; Consultant, The Rand Corporation, Santa Monica, Calif.
*** M.A.; Graduate Fellow, The Rand Corporation, Santa Monica, Calif.
† The research reported in this Article was performed pursuant to a grant from the U.S. Department of Health, Education and Welfare, Washington, D.C. The opinions and conclusions expressed herein are solely those of the authors, and should not be construed as representing the opinions or policy of any agency of the United States Government.
 1. *Liability Versus Protection*, MED. ECON., Oct. 29, 1973, at 93.
 2. *Evidence Suggests Causes of Professional Liability Problem*, 2 COMMENTARY, No. 5, at 2 (Med. Liability Comm'n, July 1975).
 3. *Now Doctors Charge Insurers With Malpractice*, BUSINESS WEEK, Aug. 4, 1975, at 40; *cf.* Steves, *Medical Malpractice In Perspective*, 28 CPCU ANNALS 209, 215 (1975).
 4. *State by State Survey Finds Professional Liability Woes in Many Regions*, AM. MED. NEWS, Feb. 24, 1975, at 9.
 5. *Id.*

between 1968 and 1970, and in Southern California, physicians in high-risk specialties such as orthopedics or neurosurgery may have premiums in the $30,000 range.[6] In other states, such as Ohio, rate increases as high as 750 percent in one year have been requested.[7] Physicians, in turn, are turning the malpractice issue back on itself. Suits have been filed against insurance companies charging that they are conspiring to limit the availability of malpractice insurance, thus making it easier for these companies to sell policies which contain provisions favorable to them.[8] A Florida orthopedic surgeon has filed a $3 million suit against two former patients and their attorneys, who had previously sued him for alleged malpractice.[9] Physicians have also begun to strike for legislative intervention to solve the malpractice crisis.[10] These strikes have resulted in economic chaos, if not potential ruin, for some hospitals, and at least temporary dislocations in the usual pattern of obtaining medical care for some people.

In response to these pressures from all sides, legislation which would affect some aspect of malpractice has either been introduced in the legislature or is in preparation in all but three states—Virginia, Wyoming, and Mississippi.[11] In addition, four federal bills are pending for consideration by the Congress.[12] Much of the proposed legislation would radically alter the malpractice system, the principle elements of which include: (1) patient responsibility to recognize when an injury has occurred; (2) patient responsibility to determine whether that injury might be due to negligence; (3) patient responsibility to approach the legal system to determine if he should receive a settlement for the injury which has occurred; and (4) resolution of the claim through the tort system, which pits the physician and his insurance company against the patient and his lawyer.

Some of the arguments for or against changes in the malpractice system are concerned with the impact of the present and future systems

---

6. See note 58 *infra*.
7. Curran, *Malpractice Insurance: A Genuine National Crisis*, 292 NEW ENG. J. MED. 1223 (1975).
8. *Now Doctors Charge Insurers With Malpractice*, *supra* note 3, at 40.
9. Rosenberg, *He Sued His Malpractice Accusers Right Back—For $3,000,000*, MED. ECON. Dec. 8, 1975, at 69.
10. L.A. Times, Jan. 9, 1976, § 1, at 1, col. 2; *id.*, Dec. 30, 1975, § 1, at 1, col. 2; N.Y. Times, June 15, 1975, § 4, at 6, col. 1; *id.* June 2, 1975, at 1, col. 1; *id.*, May 4, 1975, § 4, at 3, col. 2. The American Medical Association House of Delegates officially approved the use of "slowdowns." Altman, *A.M.A. Backs Doctors Curbing Service*, N.Y. Times, June 18, 1975, at 81, col. 1.
11. See note 93 *infra*.
12. See note 118 *infra*.

on the quality of medical care provided, and this Article is addressed to that issue. Specifically, the Article is divided into three parts: (1) consideration of quality-of-care constructs, including the art-of-care, technical care, quality-of-care assessment, and quality-assurance programs; (2) the relationship of malpractice to quality of care, with emphasis on insurance premiums and on availability of physicians; and (3) the development of policy and research suggestions for understanding and/or altering the present malpractice system.

QUALITY-OF-CARE CONSTRUCTS

Interest in measuring the quality of medical care and then using the results of this assessment to improve the quality of care delivered is at least 100 years old. Florence Nightingale studied the medical facilities available to the British Army during the Crimean War[13] and developed a simple reporting system to highlight the unsafe conditions which existed in army field hospitals. Her work indicated that changes in sanitary conditions in these hospitals could produce dramatic reductions in case-fatality rates. In order to promote changes, she developed widely published charts which graphically depicted the high death rate of soldiers in these hospitals.

In 1908, Ernest W. H. Groves, a surgeon at the Bristol General Hospital, issued a plea for the uniform registration of results of operations.[14] In pursuit of this goal, he conducted a survey of the fifty British hospitals with over 200 beds, receiving replies from twenty-seven hospitals. Results of the survey showed that there was a forty-four percent operative mortality from radical operations for malignant diseases of the stomach, a twenty-four percent mortality from prostatectomies, and a nine percent mortality from appendectomies. The personnel in the hospitals which responded to his questionnaire considered it desirable and feasible to institute a system for routinely recording results of operations, but little came of this sentiment.[15]

A few years later in the United States, Ernest A. Codman, a surgeon at the Massachusetts General Hospital, attempted to determine

---

13. F. NIGHTINGALE, *Proposal for Improved Statistics of Surgical Operations*, in NOTES ON HOSPITALS 171 (3d ed. 1863).
14. Groves, *A Plea for Uniform Registration of Operation Results*, 2 BRIT. MED. J. 1008, 1008-09 (1908). The basis for Groves's plea was:
> If . . . a surgeon makes a specialty of some disease or operation and tabulates all his own results, or another by chance has some notable successes and records them, or the author of a textbook collects published records of various writers and summarizes them, is it not obvious that such collection of figures will represent the best and not the average results? *Id.* at 1008.
15. *Id.*

whether patients were well treated by instituting a follow-up system at the hospital.[16] The objective of this system was to raise his own level of performance by examining all the patients on whom he had operated, one year after their operations. After being thoroughly frustrated in these efforts, he resigned his position as a professor of surgery and started his own hospital in which he instituted a follow-up system. Each patient on whom he had operated was recalled a year later and his health reassessed in terms of the original objectives of the initial operation. From this assessment, Codman determined whether his original diagnosis was correct, whether his operation was a technical success, whether the patient benefited from the operation, and whether he had produced untoward iatrogenic effect by operating on this patient.[17]

Despite this century-old interest in quality of care, there is little agreement on a precise definition of quality of care; how to measure it; what, if any, deficiencies exist in the care provided; and how, if necessary, to improve it. The quality-of-care problem takes on a special significance in the midst of the current medical malpractice crisis. Yet despite the absence of an agreement on any precise definition of quality of care, its measurement, and how to improve it, certain generic principles are relevant to the discussion which will follow.

Art-of-Care

Any definition of quality of care must contain at least two constructs: the art-of-care provided and the technical aspect of the care provided. The art-of-care refers to what Professor Donabedian[18] would call the management of the social, economic, and cultural aspects of the physician-patient relationship. Increasing the art-of-care would result in: (1) adoption by the patient of a life style conducive to

---

16. Codman, *The Product of a Hospital*, 18 SURGERY, GYNECOLOGY & OBSTETRICS 491 (1914). Expressing his concern over the quality of care, Codman lamented:

> One might say that the instruction of the students is irrespective of the results to the patients, but let us suppose, in surgery, for example, that all the operations which have been watched by these students have been misdirected efforts at the cure of disease, and the students have learned to do something which is not worth while and does not really improve the patient. The product of the hospital in this case, even as regards student instruction, would be nil—even worse than nil. We are, therefore, referred again to the classification of disease and the results to the patients, because a student would naturally wish to receive his instruction at a hospital where the treatment was shown to be of benefit to the patient. We may, then, say that the product of the hospital in medical education, like the product in the number of cases treated, depends on whether or not the cases are well treated.... *Id.* at 492.

17. E. CODMAN, A STUDY IN HOSPITAL EFFICIENCY: THE FIRST FIVE YEARS (1916).

18. Donabedian, *Promoting Quality Through Evaluating the Process of Patient Care*, 6 MED. CARE 181 (1968).

longevity; (2) increased compliance by the patient with regimens for controlling asymptomatic or mildly symptomatic chronic disease; (3) willingness on the part of the patient to discuss "sensitive" symptoms and health problems with the physician; and (4) utilization of health services in a timely manner so that symptoms or problems would be dealt with at a stage when they can be cured or ameliorated.

Valid measures for assessing the art-of-care are just now being developed.[19] Thus, there is a dearth of information on how the art-of-care varies as a function of physician or medical care system characteristics. For instance, the question of whether an internist or family practitioner provides a higher level of art-of-care cannot be answered by available information. Likewise, no information is available to answer the question of whether the physician-patient relationship has deteriorated in the last decade.[20] Clearly, the belief that malpractice suits have increased because the doctor-patient relationship has deteriorated can be neither confirmed nor denied by objective information.

Technical Care

Measurement of the technical aspect of care concerns whether (1) the diagnosis was adequately established; (2) therapy was appropriate; (3) diagnostic and therapeutic procedures were applied in an efficient manner; (4) medical technology was reasonably exploited; and (5) appropriate professional measures and facilities were used. Numerous research or quasi-research studies have assessed or evaluated the technical aspects of care;[21] most of these have reported substantial deficiencies in the care provided. Examples include the following cases: anemia was not recognized or treated in forty-five percent of the anemic children being cared for at a Children and Youth project which was providing "comprehensive" care; one half of these children were anemic at the end of the study.[22] One eighth of all hospital admissions of Teamsters Union family members in New York City were considered medically unnecessary, and two fifths of those admitted received only

---

19. *See* Ware & Snyder, *Dimensions of Patient Attitudes Regarding Doctors and Medical Care Services*, 13 MED. CARE 669, 670 (1975).

20. *But cf.* Mechanic, *Some Social Aspects of the Medical Malpractice Dilemma*, 1975 DUKE L.J. 1179, 1183-84.

21. *See, e.g.*, BROOK, QUALITY OF CARE ASSESSMENT: A COMPARISON OF FIVE METHODS OF PEER REVIEW (1973) (DHEW Publication No. HRA-74-3100).

22. Starfield & Sheff, *Effectiveness of Pediatric Care: The Relationship Between Processes and Outcome*, 49 PEDIATRICS 547 (1972).

fair or poor care.[23] Only one fourth of patients with severe gastrointestinal symptoms who presented themselves to the emergency room of either a university[24] or a city hospital[25] were judged to have received a level of care which met even minimum standards. One third of North Carolina's general practitioners were found to be delivering a poor or marginal level of care.[26] Fifty-one percent of a sample of Ontario physicians and twenty-six percent of a sample of Nova Scotia physicians were found to be practicing medicine of satisfactory quality.[27] Examination of the quality of care given by Hawaiian physicians demonstrated deficiencies in both the hospital and ambulatory settings; provision of good care would have required increasing the taking and recording of medical histories and physical examinations, performing more laboratory tests, and providing more follow-up care.[28]

Technical care, therefore, has been shown to be deficient regardless of how it is paid for, who provides it, or in what setting it is provided. In the absence of adequate mechanisms and finances to assess and improve the quality of care provided, this situation should not be unexpected.

Quality-of-Care Assessment

Quality-of-care assessment is hampered by methodologies and problems of real policy relevance. Quality of care can be assessed by three different variables: structural, process, or outcome. Structural variables are innate characteristics of facilities and physicians, such as whether a poison chart is posted in an emergency room, or the age

---

23. R. TRUSSELL, M. MOREHEAD & J. EHRLICH, THE QUANTITY, QUALITY AND COSTS OF MEDICAL AND HOSPITAL CARE SECURED BY A SAMPLE OF TEAMSTER FAMILIES IN THE NEW YORK AREA 21, 25 (1962).

24. Brook, Berg & Schechter, *Effectiveness of Non-emergency Care Via an Emergency Room: A Study of 166 Patients with Gastro-intestinal Symptoms*, 78 ANNALS OF INTERNAL MED. 333, 337 (1973).

25. Brook & Stevenson, *Effectiveness of Patient Care in an Emergency Room*, 283 NEW ENG. J. MED. 904, 907 (1970).

26. Peterson, Andrews & Spain, *An Analytical Study of North Carolina General Practice 1953-1954* (pt. II), 31 J. MED. EDUC. 1 (No. 12 1956).

27. Clute, *The Quality of General Practice*, in GENERAL PRACTITIONER 262-340 (1963).

28. B. PAYNE & T. LYONS, METHOD OF EVALUATING AND IMPROVING PERSONAL MEDICAL CARE QUALITY: OFFICE CARE STUDY (Am. Hosp. Ass'n, In Press); B. PAYNE & T. LYONS, METHOD OF EVALUATING AND IMPROVING PERSONAL MEDICAL CARE QUALITY: EPISODE OF ILLNESS STUDY (Am. Hosp. Ass'n, In Press). Simple calculations on data from these studies suggest that the number of ambulatory procedures might need to be doubled and the number of inpatient procedures increased by one half to meet reasonable standards of good care.

or board certification status of the physician. Process variables refer to what a physician or other health provider does to or for a patient, such as whether a cardiogram is ordered for a patient with crushing chest pain. Outcome variables are those concerned with what happens to a patient and are measured by mortality, morbidity, disability, and psychosocial functioning.

The purpose of the medical care system is to improve the health of people, a goal which is not necessarily synonymous with either raising the qualifications of health care providers or increasing the number of services provided. The most valid assessment of quality of care is gained through outcome information. Regulation of the medical care system, however, depends upon information which can be collected inexpensively; to date, this has meant relying on structural and process information which can be obtained from routine reports, insurance claims forms, or the medical record. Collection of outcome information usually requires arranging for a follow-up interview with the patient, an extremely expensive procedure. Unfortunately, many structural and process items used to assess care have been shown not to be valid, *i.e.* not related to improvement in patient health. For example, physicians who are specialists, who graduated high in their medical school classes, who attend continuing education courses, or who subscribe to (and read) journals are not necessarily better physicians.[29] Comprehensive care clinics do not necessarily provide better technical care than do hospital outpatient clinics.[30] The only two structural variables which consistently seem to relate to better quality of care are whether the physician is a "modal" specialist and whether he is young.[31] In some, but not all, studies, board-certified physicians performed better than their noncertified colleagues.[32]

Similarly, much of what is known about which processes of care are related to improved health is based on conventional wisdom, and tests

---

29. *See* Peterson, Andrews & Spain, *supra* note 26, at 71, 83, 88.
30. Morehead, Donaldson & Seravalli, *Comparisons Between OEO Neighborhood Health Centers and Other Health Care Providers of Ratings of the Quality of Health Care*, 61 AM. J. PUB. HEALTH 1294, 1306 (1971).
31. B. PAYNE & T. LYONS, EPISODE OF ILLNESS STUDY, *supra* note 28. The term "modal specialist" refers to treatment of a patient by a physician who is trained to treat the specific problem the patient has. For example, the modal specialist for a child with a kidney stone is a urologist, and not a family practitioner.
32. *See* R. TRUSSELL, M. MOREHEAD & J. EHRLICH, *supra* note 23, at 45-46, 83 table 34; B. PAYNE & T. LYONS, EPISODE OF ILLNESS STUDY, *supra* note 28; R. BROOK & K. WILLIAMS, EFFECT OF THE NEW MEXICO PEER REVIEW SYSTEM ON COST AND QUALITY OF MEDICAL CARE: A REVIEW OF THE IMPACT OF THE NEW MEXICO EXPERIMENTAL MEDICAL CARE REVIEW ORGANIZATION ON MEDICAL CARE DELIVERED TO THE MEDICAID POPULATION, 1971-1973 (Rand Corporation, To Be Published).

of conventional wisdom sometimes produce disturbing results. For instance, not all women with breast cancer necessarily need a radical mastectomy;[33] treatment of adult onset diabetes with oral hypoglycemic agents probably does more harm than good;[34] some groups of patients who have acute heart attacks may, on the average, have a higher probability of survival when treated at home than when treated in a modern coronary care unit;[35] and many women with varicose veins will obtain an equally acceptable cosmetic result with less morbid complications when treated with a simple outpatient procedure than with the conventional operation which requires hospitalization.[36] Yet all the more aggressive procedures are still standard accepted therapy, and likely would be the benchmark by which acceptable quality of care would be judged in any national medical care review system.

Regulation on the basis of structural or process information must be done carefully. No matter what variable (structural, process, or outcome) is used in quality assessment, deficiencies in care will be found, but the level of those deficiencies will vary considerably as a function of the assessment method used.[37] If quality-of-care assessment on the basis of process data differs markedly from assessment on the basis of outcome data, acceptance of the former as a basis for taking steps to improve care might lead to large increases in the amount of money spent on personal medical care without a corresponding improvement in the health of the American people.[38]

---

33. *See* Meier, *Statistics and Medical Experimentation,* 31 BIOMETRICS 511, 515-16 (1975).

34. The University Group Diabetes Program, *A Study of the Effects of Hypoglycemic Agents on Vascular Complications in Patients with Adult Onset Diabetes,* 19 DIABETES Supp. 2 (1970). The UGDP study suggests that the specific hypoglycemic used—tolbutamide—raises the incidence of cardio-vascular illness in diabetic patients. The study, however, did not extend its findings to include other hypoglycemic agents.

35. Mather, Pearson & Reed, *Acute Myocardial Infarction: Home and Hospital Treatment,* 3 BRIT. MED. J. 334 (1971).

36. Chant, Jones & Weddell, *Varicose Veins: A Comparison of Surgery and Injection/Compression Sclerotherapy,* 2 LANCET 1188 (1972); Piachaud & Weddell, *Cost of Treating Varicose Veins,* 2 LANCET 1191 (1972).

37. For a study demonstrating this variance, see Brook, *supra* note 21. Using process and outcome data, Brook assessed the quality of care delivered to 296 patients with either an ulcer in the stomach or duodenum, hypertension, or a urinary tract infection. Process assessment indicated that twenty-three percent of patients received acceptable care, but outcome assessment indicated that sixty-three percent of patients received acceptable care. *Id.* at iii. The truth undoubtedly lies somewhere in between, and the decision of how care should be improved is dependent upon which number is accepted. *Id.*

38. *See id.* at 57.

Quality-Assurance Programs

Attempts to assess quality of care have been confined largely to research endeavors. In the last two years, however, two major quality-assurance programs have been developed.[39] The first is the Professional Standards Review Organization (PSRO) program, which has been established to review and improve the quality and efficiency of hospital care given to Medicare and Medicaid recipients.[40] The second is the Physician Evaluation Performance (PEP) program of the Joint Commission on the Accreditation of Hospitals, which requires the performance of process and outcome audits for the maintenance of hospital accreditation.[41]

Both programs contain similar features: (1) review of hospital care only; (2) selection of a few diagnostic categories for audit; (3) local determination by physicians of the diagnostic categories for audit and of the criteria and standards against which care will be audited; (4) reaudit to determine if deficiencies have been corrected; and (5) reporting of results to an external body—the federal government or the Joint Commission. Both PSRO and PEP have virtually excluded the public from any real role in quality assurance. For instance, in order to implement the PSRO program, the United States has been divided into 203 areas. In each of these areas a group composed solely of physicians has the right to organize the PSRO, with the public excluded from any role at the local level. Determination of whether local PSROs and PEPs work is left mostly to imagination, since the system by which PSROs and PEPs are evaluated is weak.[42] It is too early to tell whether either one or both of these programs will contribute to improving the health of the American people.

Relationship of Malpractice to Quality of Care

Facts about the operation of the present medical malpractice system are sparse. Those that both relate to the quality-of-care issue and are consistent among observers of the malpractice system are even more sparse. Nevertheless, certain facts which are germane to an

---

39. Because of their very recent implementation, it is of course too early to predict whether either one or both of these programs will contribute to improving the health of the American people.

40. 42 U.S.C. §§ 1320C-1 to C-19 (Supp. III 1973). *See* Office of Professional Standards Review, PSRO Program Manual (1974) (HEW Publication).

41. *See* C. Jacobs & N. Jacobs, The PEP Primer: The JCAH Performance Evaluation Procedure for Auditing and Improving Physician Care (1974).

42. R. Brook & A. Avery, Quality Assurance Mechanisms In the United States: From There To Where? 15 (Rand Corp. Paper Series, P-5520, Oct., 1975).

examination of the relationship between malpractice and the quality of medical care can be identified.

Malpractice premiums have increased dramatically in the last few years, and even larger increases have been proposed.[43] This increase in premiums has paralleled a rise in the number of malpractice claims, and there are predictions that every practicing physician will be sued at least once in his lifetime.[44] Premiums vary substantially by area of the country,[45] and are set principally according to the amount and type of surgery a physician does.[46] Certain surgical specialists and anesthesiologists pay much higher premiums than internists or pediatricians, and are the targets of many more malpractice claims.[47]

Malpractice premiums are, in general, not experience-rated at the individual physician level.[48] A physician who practices part-time is likely to have a premium similar to one who practices full-time; a pediatrician who sees 100 patients per day probably will have the same premium as one who sees ten patients per day; and a physician with a malpractice claim pending will have the same premium as one who

---

43. In Ohio, increases of 750 percent in a year have been proposed. Curran, *supra* note 7, at 1223-24.
44. *Liability Versus Protection*, MED. ECON., Oct. 29, 1973, at 93.
45. *State by State Survey, supra* note 4. *See* Steves, *A Proposal to Improve the Cost to Benefit Relationships in the Professional Liability Insurance System*, 1975 DUKE L.J. 1305, 1319.
46. A general practitioner, pediatrician, or internist who does not perform even minor surgery may have a premium one-seventh that charged an orthopedic surgeon. Kendall & Haldi, *The Medical Malpractice Insurance Market*, in MEDICAL MALPRACTICE REPORT Appendix 494, 505. Specialists in the areas of orthopedic surgery, neurosurgery, anesthesiology, and obstetrics-gynecology have the highest premiums. *Cf.* Steves, *supra* note 45, at 1316-17 & n.65.
47. A survey of medical malpractice incidents in Maryland during the decade from 1960 to 1970 revealed that slightly more than half of the malpractice claims were associated with four high-risk specialties: general surgery, eighty-six claims; obstetrics-gynecology, sixty-eight claims; anesthesiology, thirty-six claims; and thoracic surgery, nine claims. These specialists, however, comprised only one fourth of the physician membership insured under the program being studied. Evans, Hemelt & Olsson, *A Survey of Professional Liability Incidence in Maryland*, in MEDICAL MALPRACTICE REPORT Appendix 623; Pabst, *Comments on the Maryland Professional Liability Survey*, in MEDICAL MALPRACTICE REPORT Appendix 632.

An examination of all claims closed throughout the United States in 1970 substantiated these findings concerning the skewed distribution of malpractice claims. Rudov, Myers & Mirabella, *Medical Malpractice Insurance Claims Files Closed in 1970*, in MEDICAL MALPRACTICE REPORT Appendix 1. For example, anesthesiologists produced 7.9 percent of the malpractice claims, but represent 3.6 percent of the U.S. physician pool; orthopedic surgeons produced 8.8 percent of the claims, but represent only 3.2 percent of the pool. Similar figures for internists are 6.9 and 14.0 percent, respectively, and for pediatricians 2.3 and 6.0 percent. *Id.* at 16.
48. *See* Kendall & Haldi, *supra* note 46, at 533-34.

does not. Further, the likelihood of a physician being sued does not vary markedly with personal or professional characteristics, with the exceptions of specialty and area of the country in which he practices. For instance, age, board certification, urban versus rural practice, and foreign medical training seem to have little bearing on the frequency of involvement in litigation.[49] It also appears that the likelihood of a physician being sued more than once is related as much to chance as to his being a poor physician.[50] Finally, the probability of being sued varies with the practice site in which care was given: a higher percentage of malpractice incidents occurs within a hospital treatment setting than during office visits.[51]

---

49. Examination of malpractice claims closed in 1970 indicated that sixty percent of the physicians involved in a claim were board-certified; the age distribution of physicians who were sued did not differ from that of the U.S. physician population as a whole. Rudov, Myers & Mirabella, *supra* note 47, at 16-17.

Examination of 3,166 physicians insured under the Maryland Med-Chi program from 1960 to 1970 indicated that of the 322 physicians sued, forty-nine percent were board-certified. Board-certified physicians were just as likely to be sued multiple times as were nonboard-certified physicians. Furthermore, urban physicians were only slightly more likely to be sued than were rural physicians. Fifteen percent of the claims were against graduates of foreign, non-English-speaking medical schools, but nineteen percent of the physicians had been educated in such schools. Thus, physicians who were older, not board-certified, or foreign trained—characteristics which have been associated in some studies with the provision of a lower level of quality of care—do not appear to account for a larger proportion of malpractice claims than would be expected by chance alone. Evans, Hemelt & Olsson, *supra* note 47, at 626-27; Pabst, *supra* note 47, at 634. This conclusion is weakened somewhat by the manner in which the data from the studies quoted above were analyzed. When the relationship between age or board certification and the number of malpractice claims was determined, specialty was not taken into account. Specialty is highly correlated with the number of malpractice claims. If specialty also has a high correlation with age or board certification status, then a significant relationship between age or board certification status and the number of malpractice claims could have been missed.

50. Of the 3,166 physicians insured under the Med-Chi program in Maryland from 1960 to 1970, 2,844 (ninety percent) were not sued; 276 (nine percent) were sued once; and forty-six physicians (1.4 percent) were sued more than once each for a total of 105 times. Evans, Hemelt & Olsson, *supra* note 47, at 624, 630; *see* Pabst, *supra* note 47, at 633-34. Chance would predict that twenty-one physicians would have had more than one claim filed against them. *Id.* at 634. If the analysis which produced the number twenty-one had corrected for the variation in suit by specialty, then the deviation from chance would have been even less. Generalization of the results of this one-state study is dangerous, however. More studies are required before definitive conclusions can be drawn.

51. Seventy percent of the malpractice incidents in Maryland between 1960 and 1970 occurred in hospitals, with fourteen percent occurring in emergency rooms, and twenty-nine percent took place in physicians' offices. Evans, Hemelt & Olsson, *supra* note 47 at 629-30. Hospital accreditation did not protect the hospital from being sued, since ninety-one percent of the hospitals which settled a malpractice claim in 1970 were JCAH-accredited. Rudov, Myers & Mirabella, *supra* note 47, at 17.

Facts from the patients' perspective are equally revealing. For example, a study of a sample of medical records of patients hospitalized at two typical community hospitals indicated the following: among 23,750 patients discharged during one year, 1,780 patient injuries occurred; 517 of these injuries resulted from negligence; and thirty-one malpractice claims were filed against the hospital or medical staff.[52] Since detection of injury was dependent upon its having been noted in the medical record, the actual injury and negligence figures may have been higher.

These data become more meaningful in light of principles established in other studies. For instance, it would appear that the negligence resulting in the 517 injuries for which claims could have been filed was based on improper treatment in 445 (eighty-six percent) of the cases and on failure to diagnose properly in seventy-two (fourteen percent) of the cases. Forty percent of the claim incidents result in eventual payment to the claimant. Although the median payment has been small ($2,000), three percent of claims will exceed $100,000.[53] Of all patients who suffer an injury in a hospital, 0.7 percent are compensated; of all patients who suffer a hospital injury due to negligence, 2.4 percent are compensated. These figures, coupled with the fact that only eighteen to twenty percent of the premium dollar is returned to the patient,[54] indicate that the current malpractice restitution system is not particularly effective or rewarding.

Any examination of the interaction between malpractice issues and quality of health care that ventures beyond the facts noted above must be based largely on logic because of the sparsity of reliable data. The malpractice system seemingly could affect quality of care in three principal ways: (1) premium differentials could influence the types of physicians available in various areas of the country; (2) unsuccessful defense of a malpractice claim could lead to direct sanctions against a health care provider or facility; and (3) the atmosphere of the malpractice crisis, even in the absence of a claim, could affect the

---

52. Pocincki, Dogger & Schwartz, *The Incidence of Iatrogenic Injuries*, in MEDICAL MALPRACTICE REPORT Appendix 50.

53. Rudov, Myers & Mirabella, *supra* note 47, at 1.

54. Welch, *Medical Malpractice*, 292 NEW ENG. J. MED. 1372, 1375 (1975). Data published in a 1969 Senate subcommittee report indicated that approximately twenty-seven cents of the premium dollar reached the patient in 1968. *Report of AMA Board of Trustees to 1969 AMA Convention*, in SENATE SUBCOMM. ON EXECUTIVE REORGANIZATION TO THE COMMITTEE ON GOVERNMENT OPERATIONS, 91ST CONG., 1ST SESS., MEDICAL MALPRACTICE: THE PATIENT VERSUS THE PHYSICIAN 1001-02 (Comm. Print 1969). Other estimates place the percentage return to the patient as high as thirty-eight percent. *See id.* at 10 (Introductory statement of Sen. Ribicoff).

physician-patient relationship. Before discussing each proposed effect in detail, however, it is necessary to place the whole issue in some historical perspective.

Forty years ago, the primary function of the medical care system was the compassionate caring for patients. Malpractice resulting from an injury caused by improper therapy was almost an impossibility, since most therapies were placebos and capable neither of alleviating a disease nor of causing harm. Today, due to advances in the biomedical sciences, another function of medical care must also be considered: efficient delivery to the entire population of efficacious medical services that result in cure or control of disease and maintenance or improvement of health. Unfortunately, new therapies—antibiotics, intensive care units, radical surgical procedures, anti-neoplastic drugs—which do improve the health of the American people are also capable of producing serious iatrogenic disease. The effectiveness of these therapies is determined in part by the methods and manner by which they are applied, in short, by the level of quality of care. The apparently paradoxical situation which obtains today—namely, improvement in the health of the American people due to better medical care accompanied by an increase in malpractice claims—is not too difficult to explain: modern medicine has increased the physician's chance of doing harm, and the probabilistic nature of medical treatment alone would suggest that malpractice claims would dramatically increase. Variation in physician performance or choice of therapy, which in 1935 was relatively meaningless, today can have serious consequences in terms of patient well-being. This variation, coupled with the rising public expectation of increased longevity fostered by the biomedical revolution, renders the health care atmosphere even more conducive to the filing of malpractice claims.

Given this historical relationship between quality of care and the malpractice issue, the central question of this Article can be posed. In the absence of the present restitution system for medical malpractice, would the quality of medical care and (thereby) the health level of the American people increase more or less than it would if the present malpractice system were kept in place? A direct and simple answer to this question is impossible, but approximations can be obtained by looking at possible effects of the malpractice system on quality.

Malpractice Premiums and Availability of Physicians

Given both that the amount of malpractice premiums will continue to rise dramatically and that differentials in premiums will continue to occur as a function of physician characteristics, several major system effects might be hypothesized:

1. Decrease in the number of applicants to medical school;
2. Decrease in the number of physicians who specialize in high-risk specialties (*e.g.*, orthopedics);
3. Migration of physicians from areas in the country with high premiums to those with low premiums;
4. Decrease in the number of part-time practicing physicians;
5. Decreases in the performance of surgery or special procedures;
6. Increase in the cost of care;
7. Decrease in the number of young physicians who go directly from training into solo fee-for-service practice; and
8. Increase in physician slowdowns or strikes which will either temporarily or permanently make medical care unavailable.

Each of these hypothetical effects merits some comment.

Application Rate to Medical School. In the near future, primary care physicians in private fee-for-service practice may be paying $5,000 to $10,000 for malpractice insurance; this would be the lower end of the premium scale. It is unlikely that this premium level, in and of itself, would cause the number of applicants to medical school to drop.[55] Whether some or many students enter medical school for economic reasons is debatable. Not debatable, however, is the fact that these "high" premiums on the average represent a very small percentage (five to ten percent) of the physician's *gross* salary.[56] On the whole, physicians will remain at the top of the economic ladder, regardless of the level of malpractice premiums. During hard economic times, the M.D. degree is the only degree which guarantees job stability; this fact alone will continue to lead a large excess of highly qualified applicants to medical school. High malpractice premiums (at least at the levels

---

55. The number of applicants for admission to the 1974-75 term in United States medical schools was 42,624, an increase of 2,118 over the previous year. Crowley (ed.), *Medical Education in the United States 1974-75*, 234 J.A.M.A. 1333, 1337 table 8 (1975). The number of students applying has increased 122 percent in the last ten years, *id.* at 1336, although the most recent increase is not so large as the previous year's gain of 4,371 applicants, *id.* at 1337 table 8.

56. The average gross income for all physicians during 1973 has been estimated at almost $84,000. CENTER FOR HEALTH SERVICES RESEARCH AND DEVELOPMENT, AM. MED. ASS'N, PROFILE OF MEDICAL PRACTICE 195 table 66, and 204 table 75 (1974). Net income for the same period was estimated at approximately $50,000. *Id.* at 195 table 66. The estimates were based on approximately 3,000 observations. Average net income was based only on those physicians reporting a profit.

now being proposed in Southern California) will not cause or aggravate a "physician shortage," if such a phenomenon indeed exists.[57]

Training of Physicians in High-risk Specialties. In Southern California, by 1976, the premium differential between a surgeon and an internist may be $30,000.[58] One might argue that this discrepancy would lead to the training of fewer medical school graduates as surgeons, but there is no evidence that this outcome would occur. If it did, it would be socially beneficial. In this country many surgical procedures are performed unnecessarily, and the amount of surgery performed in any geographic area is related to the number of surgeons in that area.[59] On the other hand, the number of physicians willing to give first contact primary or family care is in short supply.[60] Moreover, the differential in income between surgeon and primary care physician is usually greater than the differential in malpractice premiums,[61] and for those physicians who choose to specialize in surgery for purely economic reasons, the economic rationale remains. The differential in malpractice claims creates an incentive in the right direction (*i.e.* away from surgery), but that incentive is not strong enough to reduce the number of physicians who are being trained in oversupplied specialties.

Physician Migration. Other things being equal, differentials in insurance premiums by geographic area could have an effect on quality by causing physician migration from areas of excess physician supply to those which are undersupplied or vice versa. The net effect of such migration is not likely to be observed, however, because of the large size of premium areas[62] and the difficulty of taking account of all other

---

57. To the extent that physicians are able to pass on the high cost of insurance to patients, the impact on entry into the profession would, of course, be even smaller.

58. The Insurance Services Office rates for California would require a premium payment of $6,074 by an internist who performs no surgery for $100,000/300,000 policy limits. The same coverage for certain surgeons—gynecology, hand, head and neck, plastic—would cost $37,066, according to the ISO ratings. INSURANCE SERVICES OFFICE, PHYSICIANS, SURGEONS AND DENTISTS PROFESSIONAL LIABILITY MANUAL (Jan. 1, 1976, Revision) (California P.S. & D. Rates, Seventh Reprint).

59. *See* Bunker, *Surgical Manpower: A Comparison of Operations in the United States and in England and Wales,* 282 NEW ENG. J. MED. 135 (1970); Lewis, *Variations in the Incidence of Surgery,* 281 NEW ENG. J. MED. 880 (1969).

60. *But cf.* Crowley, *supra* note 55, at 1365-66; Wall Street J., Oct. 31, 1975, at 1, col. 1.

61. The average gross income for surgeons during 1973 has been estimated at approximately $97,000, CENTER FOR HEALTH SERVICES, *supra* note 56, at 191 Table 62, and 201 Table 72, some $18,000 more than the estimated 1973 gross income of the general practitioner, *id.*

62. In California, for example, the ISO rates apply to the entire state, with no geographic differentiation. INSURANCE SERVICES OFFICE, *supra* note 58. Virginia, by con-

factors. A doctor practicing in an inner city area where there is an undersupply of physicians, for example, is likely to pay the same malpractice premium as one who practices in the oversupplied suburbs of the same city,[63] meaning that little incentive exists for him to remain in the inner city and implying that quality might well suffer in that situation. Even in the instance of a premium differential favoring the inner city, the motivation for leaving may be so strong as to outweigh the relatively trivial incentive (for staying) of lower malpractice insurance costs.

Discouragement of Part-Time Practice. Malpractice premiums that are not adjusted to reflect decreased risk exposure in part-time practice could force many part-time physicians out of practice, and thus decrease the availability of care. Insofar as these physicians have characteristics that are associated with being less technically competent, such as being older or simply not doing enough procedures to remain competent, then their removal from practice would raise the level of care provided. Unfortunately, the characteristics of physicians who choose to work part-time has not been systematically documented. Many physicians may steadily practice until they die at some advanced age; others may practice only sporadically over a large part of their careers. Thus, on average, discouragement of part-time practice may be a positive result of high malpractice premiums. On the other hand, the practice of medicine by competent, young, female physicians and by academic physicians, many of whom see patients on a part-time basis, would also be eliminated. Other less discriminatory means should be found to accomplish the objective of removing from practice the incompetent part-time practitioner.

Performance of Surgery by Primary Care Physicians. Premium differentials between primary care specialists who do not perform surgery and those who do are large. For instance, in 1976 the general practitioner in Southern California who does not do surgery may have a premium of about $7,000; one who does may have a premium of about $21,000. An internist in the same area may pay about $5,000; if he does bronchoscopy, his premium may increase to about $10,000.[64]

---

trast, is divided into three rating territories. BUREAU OF INSURANCE, STATE CORP. COMM'N (Virginia), MEDICAL MALPRACTICE INSURANCE IN VIRGINIA: THE SCOPE AND SEVERITY OF THE PROBLEM AND ALTERNATIVE SOLUTIONS 13 (1975).

63. *See, e.g., id.* (Nov. 1, 1975, Revision) (New York P.S. & D. Rates, Third Reprint) (indicating that ISO rates for New York City and suburban Nassau County are identical).

64. The figures in the text are based on personal communications between the authors and insurance officials in California. The most recent published ratings of the

Since general practitioners do surgery less frequently than surgeons, this premium disparity could make surgery by general practitioners unprofitable. To make it profitable, practitioners could choose to increase either the amount of surgery they do or the prices they charge. But the surgery market in many areas is becoming saturated, and prices for surgery are likely to be fixed by surgeons and fiscal intermediaries. It is improbable, then, that general practitioners will be able to increase either the amount or price of their surgery. High malpractice premiums thus may increase the likelihood that surgery will be done by surgeons instead of general practitioners. If surgery performed by family practitioners is of poorer quality than that performed by surgeons (this is the accepted belief), then the quality of care will rise as general practitioners are drawn out of the surgical market.

The performance of special procedures is another matter. A specialist in pulmonary disease may be called upon to do only about thirty bronchoscopies a year. If he receives $200 per bronchoscopy, then his gross receipts would be $6,000. His net receipts would be less than the additional malpractice premium he must pay.[65] The incentive would be either to do more—presumably unnecessary—bronchoscopies, or to stop doing them. Either result is bad. In the first case, patients will be subjected unnecessarily to risky procedures, and in the latter a necessary procedure may become relatively unavailable, at least in some communities or facilities.

Cost of Care. Physicians faced with rising malpractice premiums will likely try to pass that cost on to their patients. A primary care physician seeing twenty patients a day for 200 days per year has 4,000 patient visits. If his premium increases $5,000 for that year, he may well increase his office visit by $1. This is not an insignificant increase. Where groups of patients such as the poor who are eligible for Medicaid are involved, the desire on the part of the physician to raise fees may be particularly burdensome, for the reason that fee schedules are deter-

---

Insurance Services Office indicate that a Southern California general practitioner who performs no surgery would pay a $6,074 annual premium in 1976 for $100,000/300,000 malpractice coverage, plus additional charges for corporate or partnership liability or employment status. A general practitioner performing certain minor procedures—including angiography, arteriography, catheterization, and needle biopsy—would pay $18,216. The annual premium for an internist who does not perform surgical procedures also would be $6,074 for $100,000/300,000 coverage, while the internist who does minor surgery would pay $11,121 for the same protection. INSURANCE SERVICES OFFICE, *supra* note 58. The ISO ratings, of course, are not binding on insurance companies, which must seek state approval for rates.

65. The added premium of $5,000, see note 64 *supra* and accompanying text, would almost surely exceed the physician's net income from $6,000 in revenue.

mined by the state, and not by the physician. Thus, the option of raising fees is not really open to those physicians who practice in areas with large numbers of Medicaid patients. In order to maintain income, those physicians could move to non-Medicaid areas, refuse to take Medicaid patients, see more patients more quickly, increase the number of procedures ordered, or raise fees to non-Medicaid patients. All these options would have a deleterious impact on the general level of medical care, by reducing the availability of care to those who need it most or by decreasing the quality of care provided.

Entrance to Solo Practice. High malpractice premiums may make it harder for young physicians to enter solo fee-for-service practice. Physicians just entering practice might of necessity take positions in group practices or Health Maintenance Organizations (HMOs), even if such positions were not the desired career paths. This result could be viewed as an infringement on the right of a physician to practice medicine in the setting of his choice. At present, there is no evidence to suggest that such a result will occur; nevertheless, if it did, the effect on quality might well be positive. HMOs probably deliver slightly better care, on the average, than does the fee-for-service system.[66] High malpractice premiums, then, might increase the competitive advantage of HMOs vis-à-vis the fee-for-service system.[67]

Physician Strikes. Finally, the possibility remains that many physicians may stop or curtail providing services in protest against high premiums.[68] Why physicians have chosen to strike on this issue is unclear. Other equally important cost issues—the rising prices of a hospital day, a medical instrument, or a drug, for example—have been ignored. Physician strikes are likely to generate onerous solutions to the malpractice crisis, ones requiring greater government regulation of physicians—an outcome strenuously opposed in the past by organized medicine.[69] In the short run, the most important effect of high mal-

---

66. *See* Shapiro, Williams, Yerby, *et al., Patterns of Medical Use by the Indigent Aged Under Two Systems of Medical Care,* 57 AM. J. PUB. HEALTH 784 (1967); Shapiro, Weiner & Densen, *Comparison of Prematurity and Perinatal Mortality in a General Population and in the Population of a Prepaid Group Practice Medical Care Plan,* 48 AM. J. PUB. HEALTH 170 (1958).

67. For a general discussion of HMOs and the malpractice issue, see Bovbjerg, *The Medical Malpractice Standard of Care: HMO's and Customary Practice,* 1975 DUKE L.J. 1375.

68. See note 10 *supra.*

69. *See, e.g.* Association of Am. Physicians & Surgeons v. Weinberger, 395 F. Supp. 125 (N.D. Ill. 1975), *appeal dismissed sub nom.* Association of Am. Physicians & Surgeons v. Mathews, 44 U.S.L.W. 3304 (U.S. Nov. 18, 1975) (unsuccessful constitutional challenge of PSRO legislation).

practice premiums on quality may be that of causing physician strikes, and consequently making care unavailable to many people in time of need. Long-range solutions to the problems of malpractice need to be designed, but the current crisis must be controlled before it produces substantial harm.

In summary, the direct effects of the increasing cost of malpractice premiums on the quality of national medical care appear to be minor and somewhat unpredictable. Minor changes that favor improved quality, such as decreasing the number of family practitioners who do surgery or decreasing the number of part-time physicians, may occur. On the other hand, some necessary procedures may become less readily available, and care in general may become less available to disadvantaged members of society. On balance, changes in current malpractice premium-setting should be formulated without considering the potential effects discussed above, because those effects involve fundamental questions about health care delivery which should be addressed on their own merits and because the relationship between higher premiums and those effects is ambiguous at best.

Disciplinary Actions Against Physicians

A major effect of the current malpractice system on quality of care could occur after the resolution of a malpractice claim, in the form of disciplinary action (or inaction) against either a physician or hospital by some official organization. To examine this contention, three principal factors need to be considered. First, results from analysis of data collected even five years ago may be irrelevant. Second, contemplated disciplinary actions can vary widely, from loss of license, to suspension or restriction of licensure, to mandated continuing education. Third, no longer will a small subgroup of physicians be identified by malpractice insurance claims; thus, disciplining physicians on the basis of their having been sued turns into the more generic issue of disciplining physicians in general. Data from a study performed in Maryland[70] indicated that only ten percent of the physicians in that state were sued in the decade from 1960 to 1970. In the past decade a physician's being sued was a relatively rare event; however, the figure for the decade from 1975 to 1985 could be fifty to seventy-five percent, a number which could translate a rare event into a common phenomenon.

Disciplinary Measures Past and Present. Disciplinary actions in the past have been few in number, especially at the level of state

---

70. Evans, Hemelt & Olsson, *supra* note 47, at 623; *see* Pabst, *supra* note 47, at 632.

licensure boards, where disciplinary measures range from notices of deficiency to license revocations. Prior to this year, physicians in all but three states were licensed for life; five additional states have enacted relicensure provisions during the 1975 legislative sessions.[71] In the last ten years, 0.66 percent of physicians in the United States had difficulty with licensing boards; about one half of these physicians suffered a major disciplinary action such as suspension of licensure.[72] Most disciplinary actions are for drug or alcohol abuse, unethical behavior, or advertising infractions; only rarely is such a proceeding initiated on grounds of medical incompetence or malpractice.[73] Only eighteen states have statutes in effect which specifically mention professional incompetence as justification for removal of a medical licensure.[74]

State medical societies have not been involved significantly in physician discipline. Their actions are not public, and only rarely are the consequences severe; ultimate punishment would be expulsion from the society. As recently as 1965, only nine state medical societies even specified incompetence as a reason for disciplining a member.[75] And in 1969, only fourteen physicians in the United States were expelled from their respective state medical societies; another fourteen were suspended.[76]

Extent of Disciplinary Action. In the past ten years, perhaps 0.1 percent of United States physicians have been disciplined on the grounds of medical incompetence. Between 1969 and 1973, seven states with a physician population totaling 23,000 reported no disciplinary action whatsoever.[77] At the other extreme, California disciplined 0.58 percent of its physicians, while in the five states with the most physicians other than California, 0.11 percent were disciplined.[78]

Estimates of the number of medically incompetent physicians

---

71. See notes 105-08 *infra* and accompanying text. *See generally* Derbyshire, *Better Licensure Laws for Better Patient Care*, HOSP. PRACTICE 152-56, 158, 164 (Sept. 1972).
72. Derbyshire, *Medical Ethics and Discipline*, 228 J.A.M.A. 59, 61 (1974).
73. *Id.*
74. Derbyshire, *Disciplining the Incompetent Physician*, HOSP. PRACTICE 140-47 (June 1971). *See also* Kansas State Bd. of Healing Arts v. Foote, 200 Kan. 477, 436 P.2d 828 (1968) (court sustained board's revocation of medical license for incompetence even though statute did not state incompetence as grounds for revocation).
75. Derbyshire, *What Should the Profession Do About the Incompetent Physician?*, 194 J.A.M.A. 119 (1965), discussed in Derbyshire, *supra* note 74, at 140.
76. Derbyshire, *supra* note 74, at 141.
77. Derbyshire, *supra* note 72, at 61.
78. *Id.*

range from three to five percent.[79] Thus, the current system disciplines one thirtieth to one fiftieth of the incompetent physicians.[80] Clearly, all disciplinary systems, including the malpractice system, have not been very effective in dealing with the problem of incompetent practice.

There is little hope that the malpractice system will contribute to a solution of this important problem. Even if licensure boards were to conduct routine reviews of those doctors who lost malpractice claims, the use of this information as a screening device for instituting disciplinary actions would be very inefficient and possibly misleading, since ever greater numbers of physicians are being sued. Eventually, the state licensure board might be reviewing virtually all physicians. Furthermore, the social stigma of being sued will decrease as the percentage of doctors being sued increases. Finally, in the absence of other information concerning a physician's practice, analysis of malpractice claims is unlikely to be a useful mechanism through which physicians could be disciplined. This function should be part of a quality assurance system which will generate extensive data about the nature and quality of a physician's practice. The addition of information about malpractice claims to these data would be redundant. In any event, the crucial issue is not the collection of data, but whether the quality assurance system will use that data to improve care or, if necessary, discipline physicians.

The Effect of the Malpractice System on the Doctor-Patient Relationship

Most of the arguments that relate changes in the current malpractice system to changes in the level of quality provided focus on altering the doctor-patient relationship. Alterations which have been postulated to occur are: (1) increased responsibility of the health care provider for assurance of adequate patient outcomes; (2) performance of more laboratory procedures and tests to verify or correct clinical judgments; (3) discouragement of the use of innovative procedures;

---

79. Nelson, *Incompetent Doctors: Few Lose License*, L.A. Times, July 21, 1975, at 1, col. 1. A recent study indicated that six percent of the physicians who were treating Medicaid patients in New Mexico gave forty percent of the injections judged to be medically inappropriate. R. BROOK & K. WILLIAMS, *supra* note 32.

80. If three percent of physicians are incompetent and only 0.1 percent are disciplined, then a simple division yields the result that 3.3 percent, or one thirtieth, of incompetent physicians actually are disciplined. With the five percent estimate of incompetence as the divisor, the same division yields a result of two percent, or one fiftieth.

(4) increased use of consultants; (5) discouragement of the delegation of responsibility, for instance to physician assistants; (6) a raised level of caution manifested by increased medical recordkeeping; and (7) development of a suspicious and adversary environment between patient and doctor.

That each of these statements is value-laden is obvious. Virtually, all the positive statements could be written in a negative formulation and vice versa. Both facts and an explicit value system are needed if an adequate understanding of the impact of malpractice on the doctor-patient relationship is to occur. Unfortunately, there is a dearth of information available on the subject.[81]

The central features of many of the points raised above involve the notion of defensive medicine. Modern medical science has produced an ever increasing number of costly procedures and tests which can in some cases supply vital medical information and are for the most part harmless. A skull X-ray series for a child with a possible head injury is an example. The issue at hand is whether these tests are performed to protect against malpractice suits or to benefit the patient. Some data suggest that virtually no procedures are done to protect against malpractice,[82] but former Secretary of Health, Education and Welfare Caspar Weinberger has stated that $3 to $7 billion may be spent on defensive medicine which is of no benefit to the patient.[83] An adequate answer to this question will depend on knowledge of the sensitivity and specificity of the tests or procedures being considered and on the value the public places on correct diagnosis or identification of all conditions or diseases. In any event, any further significant jumps in malpractice premium levels may well render previous research and interpretations irrelevant, because the situation in that circumstance would simply not be comparable to the present. It seems reasonable to predict that so-called defensive medicine may indeed rise as a consequence of additional increases in malpractice premiums of the magnitude of increases to date.

Use of Tests, Procedures, and Consultants. Consider, for instance, a cancer screening test. Assume that the prevalence of the cancer in the population is one in a hundred, the sensitivity of the test (the ability of a test to detect a disease if it is present), is 0.99, and the specificity of the test (the ability of a test to determine that the person does not have the disease given that the disease is absent) is

---

81. *See* Bernzweig, *Defensive Medicine,* in MEDICAL MALPRACTICE REPORT Appendix 38.
82. *Id.* at 39-40; Project, *The Medical Malpractice Threat: A Study of Defensive Medicine,* 1971 DUKE L.J. 939.
83. Weinberger, *Malpractice—A National View,* 32 ARIZ. MED. 117 (1975).

also 0.99.[84]

The following table indicates what would happen if the screening test were applied to 10,000 people:

Test Result	True Result		Total
	Disease Present	Disease Absent	
Disease present	a	b	a + b
Disease absent	c	d	c + d
Total	a + c = 100	b + d = 9900	10,000

Sensitivity = a/(a + c) = a/100 = 0.99
a = 99; c = 1

Specificity = d/(b + d) = d/9900 = 0.99
b = 99; d = 9801

For every person who actually has the disease (cell a above), an additional "victim" would be identified, who does not have the disease (cell b); that is, one true positive would be identified for each false positive. One person who actually has the disease would be missed (cell c). If it were desirable to identify *every* person who has the disease, then the 9802 people in whom the disease was declared absent must be rescreened. The prevalence of the disease in this smaller population is 1/9802 or 0.0001; the results of the rescreening are as follows:

Test Result	True Result		Total
	Disease Present	Disease Absent	
Disease Present	a	b	a + b
Disease Absent	c	d	c + d
Total	a + c = 1	b + d = 9801	9802

Sensitivity = a/(a + c) = a/1 = 0.99
a = 1; c = 0

Specificity = d/(b + d) = d/9801 = 0.99
b = 98; d = 9703

Applying the test to this population twice would result in the identification of 100 true positives, zero false negatives, and 197 false positives. In order to decide whether the second application of this test to a population is worth the cost, society must place a value on the desirability of detecting every patient with the disease; the value of the harm done to patients falsely labeled as positive must be compared to the good done to those labeled as true positives. Physicians, regardless of the "malpractice crisis," are trained to err on the side of aggressive management of patients; in the face of uncertainty, they prefer to act,

---

84. The three statistics chosen represent a very favorable screening situation. Virtually all tests are neither so specific nor sensitive; prevalence of the disease is usually on the order of one in a thousand.

not to wait. Determination of whether this represents "good" or "bad" defensive medicine must await a value judgment by society. Without an explicit value judgment, some people will argue that dual application of the hypothesized screening test is evidence of the harmful effects of the malpractice issue on quality of care, and other observers will take the opposite view.[85]

The malpractice situation is even more complex than that illustrated by the application of a no-risk screening test to the population. Modern therapeutics have produced potent medicines and procedures (*e.g.*, certain cancer chemotherapies, bone marrow transplants) which may, at great monetary cost, extend the life of a few while producing little benefit to many. How should these therapies be applied? If they are not considered by a physician, is a malpractice claim justified? If they are used and produce harm in some patients, as they certainly must, is a malpractice claim justified? Unless society develops an explicit system to address these questions, value judgments concerning the relationship between malpractice and the level of quality of care delivered will be difficult to make in the future.

In the past few years, physicians have begun to set process criteria which describe what they should do to the patient in order to deliver good care. When these criteria have been applied to actual medical practice, the number of procedures performed (including X-rays) appears to be inadequate by a factor of two or three.[86] From the viewpoint of the malpractice issue, no evidence supports the contention that procedures which otherwise have no social value are performed simply for the sake of avoiding malpractice suits. On the other hand, evidence to support the notion that the threat of malpractice litigation increases the performance of useful procedures is also absent, at least in part because changes in physician behavior are difficult to accomplish and require concerted effort.[87] Substantial improvements in physician behavior are certainly not produced by the *threat* of malpractice sanctions; otherwise major deficiencies in medical practice would not continue to be identified in quality-of-care studies.

Medical Recordkeeping. Some observers have suggested that the threat of malpractice suits has led to increased medical recordkeeping

---

85. The system-wide consequences of defensive medicine should not be too easily dismissed, especially as they relate to higher costs, patient well-being, misallocation of funds or manpower, and general system performance in the face of scarce resources. Research is needed to address these issues within today's malpractice environment, if realistic appraisals and predictions are desired about the situation tomorrow.

86. *See* B. PAYNE & T. LYONS, OFFICE CARE STUDY, *supra* note 28; B. PAYNE & T. LYONS, EPISODE OF ILLNESS STUDY, *supra* note 28.

87. *See* Williamson, Alexander & Miller, *Continuing Education and Patient Care Research: Physician Response to Screening Test Results*, 201 J.A.M.A. 938, 942 (1967).

and thereby to a better quality of care.[88] No studies have been performed to support this opinion. Clearly the value of greater record-keeping is related to the use of this information in future patient management. Recording information just as a protection for court proceedings is a waste of expensive physician time. Unfortunately, the threshold beyond which recording findings becomes wasted effort is unknown. Moreover, evidence suggests that the critical element in medical care delivery may be the reliability with which a history is taken and physical findings are elicited;[89] the *recording* of information then becomes of secondary importance.

A definitive answer to whether the malpractice system leads to better quality of care by way of increased recording of medical information must await studies which determine the value of this additional information. The results of these studies probably will indicate that detailed recording of information produces little patient benefit. Thus, this malpractice effect will be one of decreasing slightly the efficiency of the medical care system.

Traditional Doctor-Patient Relationship. Finally, it is asserted that the malpractice situation is aggravating the dissolution of the "traditional" doctor-patient relationship. Again, in the absence of data to test this assertion, one can only argue that all institutions of society are in a state of decay—whether they be marriage, the family, or government. The times suggest that, even in the absence of the the malpractice crisis, the conventional doctor-patient relationship (authority figure versus dependent figure) would be deteriorating; in the future, the status of the patient and the physician may be more nearly equal. Disappearance of the conventional doctor-patient relationship, whether or not aggravated by the malpractice crisis, may be a social good which will lead to a greater willingness by the patient to assume more responsibility for his own health.

In summary, there is little information available to answer the question of the effect of the current or future malpractice system on the quality of medical care. Furthermore, even if such information were available, its interpretation would be impossible until society determines what amount of health it wants at what price. In the absence of such information, rhetoric which supports either side of the issue will be heavy, but its impact on policy, one hopes, will be minimal.

---

88. Roemer, *Controlling and Promoting Quality in Medical Care*, 35 LAW & CONTEMP. PROB. 284, 297 (1970). *But cf.* Lyons & Payne, *The Relationship of Physicians' Medical Recording Performance to Their Medical Care Performance*, 12 MED. CARE 463 (1974); R. BROOK & A. AVERY, *supra* note 42, at 27.

89. Koran, *The Reliability of Clinical Methods, Data and Judgments* (pts. 1-2) 293 NEW ENG. J. MED. 642, 695 (1975).

POLICY AND RESEARCH IMPLICATIONS

The discussion above is characterized by a marked lack of data. Indeed, any relationship between the malpractice crisis and deterioration or improvement in quality of care is established mainly through inappropriate generalization from sparse data and deductive reasoning, except insofar as malpractice is a crystal-clear reflection of poor quality of care in general. The impact of the threat of a malpractice claim on improving the level of quality of care appears to be miniscule when compared to the impact of other factors in the medical care system which dictate the level of quality of care provided. Similarly, no evidence substantiates the assertion that the threat of a malpractice claim seriously impairs the level of patient care provided. The immediate conclusion, then, is that in resolving the malpractice crisis of the 1970s, considerations other than quality should be given a much heavier weight.

Nevertheless, some tentative conclusions can be advanced which permit suggestions for research studies and policy to be made. First, the issue of sanctioning the physician should be separated from that of compensating the patient. A fair system for compensating the patient must be developed, whether that be through a no-fault insurance system,[90] an arbitration mechanism, or through some form of life or disability insurance. Second, separation of physician sanction from patient compensation should be done carefully, so that resolution of the first issue does not lead to a distortion of the quality of care provided. Third, the opportunity that the present malpractice crisis provides for increasing the accountability of the medical care system, especially physicians and hospitals, should not be squandered; physician insistence on having the government involved in solving a medical care delivery problem is not likely to occur again in the near future.[91] Unfortunately, early attempts by state legislatures and the federal government to solve the malpractice crisis may have worsened the quality-of-care problem.[92]

---

90. For discussions of the feasibility of nonfault compensation systems for medical accidents, *compare* O'Connell, *No-Fault Insurance for Injuries Arising from Medical Treatment: A Proposal for Elective Coverage*, 24 EMORY L.J. 21 (1975), *with* Keeton, *Compensation for Medical Accidents*, 121 U. PA. L. REV. 590 (1973).

91. It should be recognized that this Article addresses a rather narrow issue with respect to malpractice, namely the performance and accountability of physicians. This emphasis should be placed in context, however, and acknowledgement made of the need for other parties to be held equally accountable in the malpractice environment. The quality assurance movement is a viable force in medicine today, and a variety of peer review mechanisms have been established throughout the country; the time is here for the legal profession, the insurance industry, and other principals (*e.g.*, politicians) of the malpractice issue to bring the same discipline to bear on their own activities.

92. Early legislation duplicates various activities of PSROs and of some new bodies

QUALITY OF CARE

All but three state legislatures have dealt with the malpractice issue in 1975.[93] Twenty-eight states have enacted laws; thirty-eight states have established special malpractice study commissions to prepare legislation for 1976 sessions.[94] An examination of these bills reveals an effort by state legislators to improve the quality of medical care provided as they modify the malpractice system in favor of the physician by, for example, decreasing physician liability or limiting the award size. Laws in ten states require all malpractice claims (or, in some cases, awards and settlements) to be reported to appropriate state boards, the insurance committee, or the legislature.[95] Michigan,[96] Ohio,[97] Nevada,[98] Florida,[99] and Oregon[100] have enacted legislation which requires health care providers, screening panels, medical societies, and hospital review committees to report instances of possible malpractice, questionable professional conduct, or professional incompetence to the state licensing board. This requirement is intended to precipitate an investigation when reports of sufficient urgency or num-

---

created at the state level. This will undoubtedly lead to jurisdictional confusion, with overlapping of responsibility in some areas and neglect of tasks in others. To promote the highest possible care, a more streamlined approach is clearly needed, implying a consolidation of efforts at one level or another.

93. According to a survey conducted by Rudolf L. Brutoco, one of the authors of this Article, in 1975, the three states which had not taken some legislative steps in the medical malpractice area were Virginia, Wyoming, and Mississippi.

94. See Table I. For a general discussion of the state legislative response to the current malpractice crisis, *see* Comment, *An Analysis of State Legislative Responses to the Medical Malpractice Crisis,* 1975 DUKE L.J. 1417.

95. Act of Mar. 3, 1975, Act 306, § 1, [1975] Ark. Gen. Acts; Medical Injury Compensation Reform Act, § 2.3, [1975] West's Cal. Legis. Service No. 9, at 3771, 3775-78 (codified at CAL. BUS. & PROF. CODE §§ 801(a), 802, 803, 805); Medical Malpractice Reform Act of 1975, ch. 75-9, § 5, [1975] West's Fla. Sess. Law Service No. 1, at 7, 10-11 (codified at FLA. STAT. ANN. § 768.133(2)); IND. ANN. STAT. § 16-9.5-6(1) (Burns Supp. 1975); Ch. 241, [April 9, 1975] Kan. Sess. Laws 647-48; Pub. Act No. 44, § 1, [1975] West's Mich. Legis. Service No. 1, at 95, 95-96 (codified at MICH. COMP. ANN. § 500.2477); Ch. 302, § 6, [1975] Nev. Stat. (codified at NEV. REV. STAT., tit. 3 (1973)); Act of May 21, 1975, ch. 109, § 2, [1975] McKinney's Sess. Law Service of N.Y. No. 4, at 134, 135 (codified at N.Y. INS. LAW § 335); Act of Sept. 13, 1975, ch. 796, § 10, [1975] Ore. Laws (codified at ORE. REV. STAT. § 743); Health Care Services Malpractice Act, Act 111, §§ 401, 702(c), [1975] Purdon's Pa. Legis. Service No. 2, at 296, 299, 303 (codified at PA. STAT. ANN. tit. 40, §§ 1301.401, 1301.702(c)).

96. Pub. Act No. 106, § 1, [1975] West's Mich. Legis. Service No. 3, at 196 (codified at MICH. COMP. LAWS ANN. § 338.109a) (osteopaths); Pub. Act No. 107, § 11a, [1975] West's Mich. Legis. Service No. 3, at 197 (codified at MICH. COMP. LAWS ANN. § 338.1811a) (physicians); Pub. Act No. 111, § 12(4), [1975] West's Mich. Legis. Service No. 3, at 220 (codified at MICH. COMP. LAWS ANN. § 331.442) (hospitals).

97. Act of July 28, 1975, [1975] Page's Legis. Bull. No. 3, at 174, 182 (codified at OHIO REV. CODE ANN. § 4731.22(C)(2)).

98. Ch. 303, § 9(1), [1975] Nev. Stat. (codified at NEV. REV. STAT. § 630.9(1)).

99. Medical Malpractice Reform Act of 1975, ch. 75-9, § 12, [1975] West's Fla. Sess. Law Service No. 1, at 15 (codified at FLA. STAT. ANN. § 458.1201(1)(p)).

100. Ch. 796, § 6(2), [1975] Ore. Laws (codified at ORE. REV. STAT. § 677).

ber about one health care provider are received. (Indeed, some states, e.g., Massachusetts,[101] statutorily require that all "complaints relating to the proper practice of medicine" be investigated.) Such communications are confidential and individuals making these reports are protected by law from liability, as are members of the review committee. Patient grievance mechanisms also are being implemented in some states. Colorado, for instance, requires an investigation of any sworn complaint for reasonable cause.[102] Eleven states have substantially broadened the basis for disciplinary actions by including substandard or incompetent care as sufficient cause for disciplining a physician.[103]

The range of disciplinary actions available to state licensure boards has also been increased. Previously, probation, suspension, and revocation of license were the basic means of punishment. Certain state boards can now fine a health care provider, require specific additional schooling, issue public reprimands, or restrict a provider's practice to specified areas of competency (e.g., a practitioner could be prohibited from performing surgery or specific surgical procedures).[104] The availability of these less drastic disciplinary measures is important because the existence of only relatively severe sanctions has led to the tendency to take no action at all except in the most extreme cases. Oregon has empowered the Board of Medical Examiners to suspend

---

101. Act of June 19, 1975, ch. 362, § 3, [1975] Adv. Legis. Service No. 5, at 316 (codified at MASS. ANN. LAWS ch. 112, § 5).

102. H.B. 1557, § 2 (Colo. 1975).

103. Medical Injury Compensation Reform Act, § 16, [1975] West's Cal. Legis. Service No. 9, at 3786 (codified at CAL. BUS. & PROF. CODE § 2361(c)); H.B. 252, § 1 (Colo. 1975); Medical Malpractice Reform Act of 1975, ch. 75-9, § 12; West's Fla. Sess. Law Service No. 1, at 15 (codified at FLA. STAT. ANN. §§ 458.1201(m), (o), (p)); IND. ANN. STAT. § 16-9.5-6(2) (Burns Supp. 1975); Act of June 19, 1975, ch. 362, § 3, [1975] Adv. Legis. Service No. 5, at 316 (codified at MASS. ANN. LAWS ch. 112, § 5(c)); Pub. Act No. 143, § 1, [1975] West's Mich. Legis. Service No. 3, at 288 (codified at MICH. COMP. LAWS ANN. § 338.1811(2)(i)); Ch. 303, § 18, [1975] Nev. Stat. (codified at NEV. REV. STAT. § 630.030); Act of May 21, 1975, ch. 109, § 30, [1975] McKinney's Sess. Law Service of N.Y. No. 4, at 154-55 (codified at N.Y. EDUC. LAW § 6509(2)); N.C. GEN. STAT. 90-14(6) (Adv. Legis. Service No. 5, 1975); Act of July 28, 1975, [1975] Page's Legis. Bull. No. 3, at 174, 182 (codified at OHIO REV. CODE ANN. § 4731.22(B)(6)); ch. 796, § 2, [1975] Ore. Laws (codified at ORE. REV. STAT. §§ 677.190(15), (16)).

104. Medical Injury Compensation Reform Act, § 22, [1975] West's Cal. Legis. Service No. 9, at 3787 (codified at CAL. BUS. & PROF. CODE § 2372.5); Medical Malpractice Reform Act of 1975, ch. 75-9, § 12, [1975] West's Fla. Sess. Law Service No. 1, at 15 (codified at FLA. STAT. ANN. § 458.1201(3)(a)); Act of June 19, 1975, ch. 362, § 3, [1975] Adv. Legis. Service No. 5, at 316 (codified at MASS. ANN. LAWS ch. 112, § 5) (reprimand); Act of July 28, 1975, [1975] Page's Legis. Bull. No. 3, at 174, 181 (codified at OHIO REV. CODE ANN. § 4731.22(B)); ch. 796, § 3, [1975] Ore. Laws (codified at ORE. REV. STAT. § 677.205(2)(e)); Health Care Services Malpractice Act, Act No. 111, § 901, [1975] Purdon's Pa. Legis. Service No. 2, at 305-06 (codified at PA. STAT. ANN. tit. 40, § 1301.901).

the physician's license temporarily without a hearing when permitting the physician to continue to practice medicine would constitute an immediate danger to the public,[105] thereby preventing in the most extreme case the occurrence of additional injury during the process of formal litigation and hearings. In 1971, New Mexico became the first state to require continuing education and periodic relicensure.[106] Eight states now require post-licensure education, ranging from fifteen to fifty hours per year.[107] Six states have passed laws which require physicians to take a competency examination upon demand by the licensing board.[108]

At the federal level, the Kennedy-Inouye bill[109] contains several intended quality assurance provisions, including: the establishment of national licensure and relicensure standards;[110] the requirement of PSRO review of participating physicians;[111] the evaluation of practitioners who lose a large number of malpractice claims;[112] the requirement of concurring consultation for any elective surgery;[113] and the

---

105. Ch. 796, § 3, [1975] Ore. Laws 250, *amending* ORE REV. STAT. § 677.205(3).

106. Act of Mar. 24, 1971, ch. 135, § 1, [1971] N.M. Laws 396 (codified at N.M. STAT. ANN. § 67-5-3(E) (1974)), *amending* N.M. STAT. ANN. § 67-5-3 (1953).

107. Medical Injury Compensation Reform Act, § 11, [1975] West's Cal. Legis. Service No. 9, at 3779-80 (codified at CAL. BUS. & PROF. CODE § 2101.6); Pub. Act No. 79-1136 (H.B. 1964) (Ill. 1975); KAN. STAT. ANN. § 65-2809 (1972) (education requirement at the discretion of the State Board of Healing Arts); ANN. CODE MD. § 43-128(c) (Supp. 1975) (education requirement at the discretion of the State Board of Medical Examiners); Act of June 13, 1975, Pub. Act No. 112, § 1, [1975] West's Mich. Legis. Service No. 3, at 221 (codified at MICH. COMP. LAWS ANN. § 338.1810(7)); N.M. STAT. ANN. § 67-5-3(E) (1974); Act of July 28, 1975, [1975] Page's Legis. Bull. No. 3, at 174, 182 (codified at OHIO REV. CODE ANN. § 4731.281(A)); Act of July 23, 1975, ch. 37, § 10, [1975] West's Wis. Legis. Service No. 1, at 41-42, *as amended*, Act of Oct. 2, 1975, ch. 79, § 4, [1975] West's Wis. Legis. Service No. 2 at 434 (codified at WIS. STAT. ANN. § 655.017). Twelve state medical associations and five specialty societies have established continuing education requirements for maintenance of membership. Ruhe, *Recent Events of Special Interest to Medical Education*, 234 J.A.M.A. 1326, 1327 (1975).

108. Medical Injury Compensation Reform Act, § 22, [1975] West's Cal. Legis. Service No. 9, at 3787 (codified at CAL. BUS. & PROF. CODE § 2372.5(a)) (competency exam after the completion of additional training); Ch. 303, § 20, [1975] Nev. Stat. (codified at NEV. REV. STAT. § 630.140(2)); N.C. GEN. STAT. 90-14(11) (Adv. Legis. Service No. 5, 1975); Act of July 28, 1975, [1975] Page's Legis. Bull. No. 3, at 174, 182 (codified at OHIO REV. CODE ANN. § 4731.22(B)(16)); Act of Sept. 13, 1975, ch. 796, § 7, [1975] Ore. Laws (codified at ORE. REV. STAT. § 677.——); Act of Apr. 5, 1975, ch. 61, § 3(2), [1975] Wash. Legis. Service No. 1, at 84 (codified at WASH. REV. CODE ANN. § 18.72.275). The competency examinations in California, Nevada, North Carolina, and Oregon test a doctor's medical knowledge and skills; those in Ohio and Washington examine his mental and physical competence to practice medicine.

109. S. 215, 94th Cong., 1st Sess. (1975) (National Medical Injury Compensation Insurance Act of 1975).

110. *Id.* § 1731.

111. *Id.* § 1725.

112. *Id.* § 1707(b).

113. *Id.* § 1704(c)(3).

establishment of provider responsibility for informing patients of adverse results, on the threat of personal liability.[114]

This survey of the laws which have been passed or are pending in state legislatures and the Congress produced the expected results. Emphasis is on reporting instances of incompetency, continuing education and relicensure, and broadening the effectiveness of state licensure boards. In many ways these legislative actions foster a piecemeal approach to quality assurance. In part they duplicate the activities of the PSRO and PEP and, except for the Kennedy-Inouye proposals, do little to strengthen them. Relicensure and educational activities will improve care only if deficiency in cognitive knowledge is the major problem in the delivery of better health care. If a physician's habits and behavior, such as his willingness to see a patient in the middle of the night, are more important in determining quality than attending courses, the impact of the relicensure procedures on quality is likely to be severely limited. Mandatory continuing education, which usually contains material of more interest to the educator than to the practicing physician, and relicensure requirements may lead to the mastery of material which is not relevant to the practicing physician or is quickly forgotten.[115]

Tabulation and reporting of the number of physician-specific malpractice events are also not likely to improve the quality of medical care. In the absence of knowledge about the physician's case mix or the number of patients he treats, the physician malpractice claim rate will be virtually useless. Substantial time and money would be spent in investigating such incidents, and this expenditure of resources would likely duplicate the work being performed by whatever quality assurance system exists in the area, such as PSRO. If malpractice claims must be reported, they should be reported directly to the PSRO, where the data at least would be concentrated in the hands of one organization which could then generate physician profiles.[116] These profiles would be used to determine if the malpractice incident is an aberration or represents a typical pattern of practice.

One state bill[117] and several federal bills[118] propose the establish-

---

114. *Id.* §§ 1705(c)(1)-(2).

115. *See* Brown & Uhl, *Mandatory Continuing Education: Sense or Nonsense*, 213 J.A.M.A. 1660, 1661, 1667 (1970).

116. The PSRO would know the number of patient care activities of each physician.

117. S.B. 2873 (Wash. 1975). Other proposals, *e.g.*, A.B. 926 (Cal. 1975); H.B. 3251 (Ore. 1975), would have established administrative mechanisms for compensating the victims of iatrogenic injuries, but would have retained negligence as the determinant of provider liability.

118. *See, e.g.*, S. 215, 94th Cong., 1st Sess. (1975); H.R. 4881, 94th Cong., 1st Sess. (1975); H.R. 5183, 94th Cong., 1st Sess. (1975).

ment of a no-fault insurance system. The system would identify events that more often than not are due to physician negligence and would compensate patients who have suffered these events without their having to prove physician negligence. A record would be kept of the number of physician-specific compensated events, and this record could be used as a quality-of-care measure. Again the utility of this measure is limited without the simultaneous collection of data which describe the physician's patient care activities.[119]

Research Opportunities

It would have been desirable to have more information to support the conclusions stated above. Even at this late date in the policy debate over malpractice, it would be useful to conduct studies to determine, in a more precise manner, the relationship between malpractice and quality of care. Basic epidemiologic information about the incidence and prevalence of poor physician practice and how it relates to physician characteristics is sorely needed. Studies determining the impact of a large malpractice claim on the patterns of practice in an area could easily be done. For instance, emergency care provided to injury victims could be studied in selected sites. Within a couple of years, at least one large malpractice suit would probably occur in one or more of these sites. Following such a suit, the quality of emergency care could be reassessed to determine the effects, if any, of the malpractice suit. Similarly, studies could be designed which would examine the change in physicians' practices when they move from a high-malpractice situation to a low-malpractice situation, or vice versa. For example, what changes occur when doctors leave military practice where the malpractice claim rate is low and enter the fee-for-service system where it is high? What happens when doctors move either into or out of a prepaid group practice which has a low level of malpractice claims, or into or out of the fee-for-service system which has a higher level of malpractice claims? Finally, perhaps the most important question on which research is desperately needed involves the relationship between the commission of events which would be legally compensable vis-à-vis the general level of quality of care that a provider

---

119. The no-fault insurance system could produce one major paradoxical effect as the definition of a compensable event is broadened. Suppose a patient with terminal cancer seeks treatment from a physician. If this patient died from his disease, his family would not be compensated. If, however, he were treated with powerful drugs which perhaps could be beneficial but were not in this case, and this treatment regimen produced or hastened death, then the patient has suffered a compensable event and his family would be awarded restitution. Since the future economic stability of the family is considered by many physicians when decisions about the care to be given to a terminal patient are made, the pressure would be on the physician to make some deaths that would occur anyway appear to be compensable events.

renders. Research which answers these questions could greatly facilitate the development of a system for compensating patients which would both provide justice to the patients who have suffered untoward events and increase the level of quality of care rendered to all patients, even those who have not suffered untoward events.

Concluding Remarks

Up to this point, the conclusions reached are of little use to policymakers. They suggest that more research is needed and that proposed changes in the malpractice system which would include relicensure and mandatory education are likely to be expensive and produce little alteration in the quality of medical care. What then should be done to take advantage of the current crisis and increase the accountability of the medical care system?

The answer lies in trading off improvements in the entire approach to medical malpractice protection[120] with fundamental alterations of the current quality assurance system in the United States, the PSRO. When the law containing PSRO was passed, many compromises were necessary in order to gain some cooperation by the medical profession.[121] These compromises make the PSRO system both less public and less accountable than it could be. Furthermore, they limit the depth and breadth of the quality assessment activities that the PSRO is permitted to perform. In place of building an expensive duplicate quality assurance system based on reporting malpractice claims or on relicensure, the current PSRO quality assurance system should be made more accountable by altering it in the following ways:

1. Local PSROs should have elected public members, and these public members should observe, if not participate in, the technical review of quality of care; without such public participation bad care can too easily be hidden.[122]

2. The authority of PSROs should be extended to include the review of care given to all patients whether or not their care is financed by the federal government; Medicaid and Medicare patients should not be the only ones to benefit from a quality assurance program.

---

120. To reiterate, these improvements could take the form of significantly lower malpractice premiums (however accomplished), medical panel arbitration of claims, ceilings on physicians' liability (with optional patient self-coverage for higher amounts), or some combination of the above.

121. *See* 3 U.S. CODE CONG. & AD. NEWS 4989 (1972); STAFF OF SENATE COMM. ON FINANCE, 93D CONG., 2D SESS., BACKGROUND MATERIAL RELATING TO PROFESSIONAL STANDARDS REVIEW ORGANIZATIONS (PSRO's) (Comm. Print 1974); *cf.* Gosfield, *Consumer Accountability in PSROs*, 6 U. TOLEDO L. REV. 764, 770-75 (1975).

122. *See* Gosfield, *supra* note 121, at 798.

3. The authority of PSROs should be extended to cover the review of ambulatory as well as hospital care.

4. The results of the quality audits should be made available to the public by PSRO area, hospital, and if necessary, by physician or at least by a physician characteristic—such as age or board certification status.[123]

5. Standards and criteria of care should be set nationally instead of locally; otherwise Americans in different medical care areas will be receiving different levels of care.

6. Licensed physicians should be required to participate actively and without compensation in the peer review activities of the PSRO; otherwise their license should be revoked.[124]

7. The effectiveness of the PSRO in altering the quality of care in its community should be determined by means of an external audit prepared by an agency such as the National Center for Health Statistics of the Department of Health, Education and Welfare; without such an audit the validity of the PSRO's results cannot be substantiated.

8. The PSRO should be given the authority to revoke the license of a physician.[125]

In the long run, improving the quality of care depends on increasing the public awareness of the medical care system and of what is required to maintain one's health. This will necessitate access to information which to date has remained hidden from public view. If the present malpractice crisis produces legislation which alters the PSRO system to accomplish these objectives, that outcome will go a long way toward improving the quality of care delivered and thus the health of the American people.[126] Unfortunately these rather sweeping alterations in the PSRO program by themselves may not increase the health of the American people, unless the public demonstrates its interest in improving its health by vigorously monitoring the program through its elected representatives.

---

123. *See id.* at 775-89. This suggestion assumes that such analyses would be placed in proper context, so that hospitals or physicians caring for more acutely ill patients are not penalized.

124. Of course, physician time will not be without cost as perceived by the medical care system. It is imperative that physician time for peer review not be considered a "reimbursable" professional activity, but rather a professional responsibility akin to attending grand rounds or keeping abreast of the medical literature.

125. For a detailed description of current quality assurance activities in the United States, see R. BROOK & A. AVERY, *supra* note 42.

126. For the argument that the development of PSROs will make the malpractice suit superfluous as a quality control device, see Simmons & Ball, *PSRO and the Dissolution of the Malpractice Suit*, 6 U. TOLEDO L. REV. 739 (1975).

Table — November 1975
SELECTED CHARACTERISTICS OF STATE AND FEDERAL MALPRACTICE BILLS WHICH RELATE TO QUALITY OF CARE

State[c]	Characteristic[a,b]									
	1	2	3	4	5	6	7	8	9	10
Alabama	----	----	----	----	----	----	----	----	----	----
Alaska	----	----	----	----	----	----	----	----	----	----
Arizona	----	----	----	----	----	----	----	----	----	P
Arkansas	L	----	----	----	----	----	----	----	----	----
California	L	L	L	L	L	L	L	L	----	P
Colorado	----	----	L	L	----	----	----	----	----	----
Connecticut	----	----	----	----	----	----	----	----	----	----
District of Columbia	----	----	----	----	----	----	----	----	----	----
Delaware	----	----	----	----	----	----	----	----	----	----
Florida	L	L	----	L	L	----	----	----	----	L
Georgia	----	----	----	----	----	----	----	----	----	----
Hawaii	----	----	P	----	----	----	----	----	----	----
Idaho	----	----	----	----	----	----	----	----	----	L
Illinois	----	----	----	----	----	----	----	L	----	P
Indiana	L	----	----	L	----	----	----	----	----	----
Iowa	----	----	----	----	----	----	----	----	----	L
Kansas	L	----	----	----	----	----	E	E	----	----
Kentucky	----	----	----	----	----	----	----	----	----	----
Louisiana	----	----	----	----	----	----	----	----	----	L
Maine	----	----	----	----	----	----	----	----	----	----
Maryland	----	----	----	----	----	----	E	E	----	----
Massachusetts	----	----	L	L	----	----	L	----	----	----
Michigan	L	L	E	L	L	----	----	L	----	----

[a] Action in 1975: P = Proposed
L = Enacted into Law
E = Existing

[b]Legend
1. Requires all malpractice claims and/or settlements to be reported to governmental agency
2. Requires reporting of repeated or gross malpractice and/or professional incompetence and/or disciplinary actions to State Board by screening panels, medical societies, or hospital review committees
3. Quality assurance boards established, or state licensing boards charged with increased responsibility for on-going monitoring of provider performance
4. Broadens basis for disciplinary action against health care providers
5. Provides for restriction of practitioners' license
6. Provides for competency examinations for continued licensure at State's discretion
7. Periodic relicensure
8. Requires continuing education
9. Requires PSRO review of services of participating providers
10. Specifies criteria for informed consent

QUALITY OF CARE

State[c]	1	2	3	4	5	6	7	8	9	10
Minnesota	P	----	----	----	----	----	----	----	----	----
Mississippi	----	----	----	----	----	----	----	----	----	----
Missouri	----	----	----	----	----	----	----	----	----	----
Montana	----	----	----	----	----	----	----	----	----	----
Nebraska	----	----	----	----	----	----	----	----	----	----
Nevada	L	L	L	L	L	L	----	----	----	L
New Hampshire	----	----	----	----	----	----	----	----	----	----
New Jersey	----	----	----	----	----	----	----	----	----	----
New Mexico	----	----	----	----	----	----	E	E	----	----
New York	L	----	L	L	L	----	----	----	----	L
North Carolina	----	----	----	P	P	P	----	----	----	P
North Dakota	----	----	----	----	----	----	----	----	----	----
Ohio	----	L	L	L	L	L	L	L	----	L
Oklahoma	----	----	----	----	----	----	----	----	----	----
Oregon	L	L	L	L	L	L	----	----	----	P
Pennsylvania	L	----	L	----	L	----	----	----	----	P
Rhode Island	----	----	----	----	----	----	----	----	----	----
South Carolina	----	----	----	----	----	----	----	----	----	----
South Dakota	----	----	----	----	----	----	----	----	----	----
Tennesee	----	----	----	----	----	----	----	----	----	L
Texas	P	----	----	----	----	----	----	----	----	----
Utah	----	----	----	----	----	----	----	----	----	----
Vermont	----	----	P	P	P	----	----	----	----	P
Virginia	----	----	----	----	----	----	----	----	----	----
Washington	----	----	P	P	----	P	----	----	----	----
West Virginia	----	----	----	----	----	----	----	----	----	----
Wisconsin	----	----	----	----	----	----	----	L	----	----
Wyoming	----	----	----	----	----	----	----	----	----	----
Federal										
S. 215	P	----	----	----	----	----	P	----	P	----
S. 432	P	----	----	----	----	----	P	----	P	----
S. 188	----	----	----	----	----	----	----	----	----	----
HR 1600	P	----	----	----	----	----	----	----	----	----

[c]Statutes enacted or proposed in 1975 in survey: Act of Mar. 3, 1975, Act 306, [1975] Ark. Gen. Acts; H.B. 2418 (Ariz. 1975); Medical Injury Compensation Act, [1975] West's Cal. Legis. Service No. 9, at 3776; COLO. REV. STAT. ANN. §§ 12-36-117 (1)(p) and 12-43.5-101 to 103; FLA. STAT. ANN. §§ 458, 768 (Supp. 1976); S.B. 1389 (Hawaii 1975); IDAHO CODE ch. 41 (Supp. 1975); Pub. Act No. 79-1136 (H.B. 1964) (Ill. 1975); IND. ANN. STAT. tit. 16, § 16-9 et seq. (Burns Supp. 1975); H.F. 803, [1975] Iowa Legis. Service No. 3; Act of Apr. 9, 1975, ch. 241, [1975] Kan. Sess. Laws 647-48; Pub. Act No. 529 (H.B. 636, (La. 1975)); MASS. ANN. LAWS ch. 112, § 5 (Supp. 1976); MICH. COMP. LAWS ANN. §§ 331.422, 338.109, 338.1810 (Supp. 1976); H.F. 1803 (Minn. 1975); NEV. REV. STAT. §§ 630.003 et seq. (1975); Act of May 21, 1975, ch. 109, [1975] McKinney's Sess. Law Service of N.Y. No. 4, at 134; N.C. GEN. STAT. 90-14(6) (Supp 1975); OHIO REV. CODE ANN. § 4731 et seq. (Page Supp. 1976); ORE. REV. STAT. §§ 677 et seq. (Supp. 1976); PA. STAT. ANN. tit. 40, § 1301 (Supp. 1976); TENN. CODE ANN. §§ 23-3401 to 3421 (Supp. 1975); S.B. 635 (Tex. 1975); S. 170, 171 (Vt. 1975); WASH. REV. CODE ANN. §§ 18.72 et seq. (Supp. 1976); WIS. STAT. ANN. § 655 (Supp. 1976).

"MEDICAL ADVERSITY INSURANCE"—
HAS ITS TIME COME?

Clark C. Havighurst*

In 1972, prior to the onset of the recent crisis in medical malpractice insurance and the resulting widespread reappraisal of patients' legal rights and malpractice remedies, this writer participated in the formulation of a blueprint for "medical adversity insurance" (MAI), which was published as "a no-fault approach to medical malpractice and quality assurance."[1] The MAI proposal was not a finished product, however, and it was not ready for serious legislative or professional consideration when the current problems arose and made the field suddenly fertile for substantive and procedural change. Indeed, it was presented less as a proposal for immediate adoption than as a theoretically sound model for further study and as a conceptual benchmark for evaluating both the fault system and existing quality-assurance mechanisms. Now, however, MAI has been given enough additional substance to qualify it for policy makers' attention.

The original MAI proposal was highly specific about the scheme's mechanics but sketchy about the coverage of the no-fault insurance which it contemplated that providers would purchase for the benefit of their patients. The emphasis on mechanical details in the original presentation no doubt obscured the essentials of the MAI idea, namely (1) advance specification of a limited list of automatically compensable events, carefully drawn up by medical experts under some form of public supervision, and (2) design of the insurance scheme

---

* Professor of Law and Director, Program on Legal Issues in Health Care, Duke University. Work on this Article was supported by grant number HS01539 from the National Center for Health Services Research, U.S. Department of Health, Education and Welfare. Sue Rankin, Class of 1978, Duke University School of Law, assisted ably in the research, particularly in developing the tentative list of compensable events included in Part III.

THE FOLLOWING CITATIONS WILL BE USED IN THIS ARTICLE:

U.S. Dep't of Health, Education and Welfare, Report of the Secretary's Commission on Medical Malpractice (1973) [hereinafter cited as Medical Malpractice Report];

Havighurst & Tancredi, *"Medical Adversity Insurance"—A No-Fault Approach to Medical Malpractice and Quality Assurance*, 51 Milbank Memorial Fund Q. 125 (1973), *reprinted in* 613 Ins. L.J. 69 (1974) [hereinafter cited as Havighurst & Tancredi, with page references to both sources].

1. Havighurst & Tancredi.

to keep providers in some measure financially accountable for the results of treatment in order to preserve and strengthen their incentives to avoid medical accidents and obtain better medical results. This Article concentrates on these essentials, attempting to be more specific about MAI's coverage, without reiterating or debating the compensation scheme's details.[2] It also attempts to place the MAI proposal in the perspective of the on-going debate concerning the law of medical malpractice and the quality of medical care.[3]

I. THE FAULT SYSTEM DISCREDITED

A. *The Standard Arguments Against the Fault System*

The arguments for scrapping the fault system as the vehicle for dealing with medical injuries are quite persuasive. Indeed, even the conventional wisdom bears scrutiny rather well. The most frequently noted adverse consequences of the system as it is currently structured and administered may be listed as follows:

(1) *the very high legal and administrative costs* involved in claims processing and fault-finding;[4]
(2) *the psychic and time costs* to physicians occasioned by charges of professional negligence and by the litigation process used to evaluate such charges;

---

2. Under the original proposal, no-fault insurance would indemnify all medical expenses and all wage losses, subject to a minimum and maximum per week. *Id.* at 128, 71-72. It was suggested that some allowance might be made for severe pain and suffering on the basis of a formula rather than attempting to individualize such damages or ignoring them altogether. *Id.* at 128-29, 72. (On the proposed treatment of collateral sources, see text accompanying notes 110-12 *infra*.) Discovery of claims would be assured by requiring providers, as a condition of relief from malpractice claims, to disclose the existence of claims against an MAI fund. *Id.* at 130, 73. Although it was suggested that policies not be cancellable, *id.* at 131, 74, it now seems unnecessary to make this an explicit requirement. Subrogation of the insurer to claims against such third parties as drug manufacturers and blood banks was contemplated as a means of strengthening the incentives of other actors in the system. *Id.* at 141, 81.

3. Any advocate of policy change cannot be altogether comfortable when his argument is based almost exclusively on theory. Yet the potential complexity of MAI is such that only physicians can translate the concept into practical terms and prepare the plan for definitive assessment. Thus, this Article can only stress the rather powerful logic behind MAI and urge intensive investigation of its practical merit. Most importantly, it argues for evaluation of MAI on its own terms rather than under some other premise, and much of the discussion is devoted to examining the premises of participants in the malpractice/quality-of-care debate.

4. *See* Steves, *A Proposal to Improve the Cost to Benefit Relationships in the Medical Professional Liability Insurance System*, 1975 DUKE L.J. 1305.

(3) *the antagonisms unleashed*, not only between doctors and patients but also between doctors and lawyers—or, more importantly, between doctors and the law itself, which physicians find arbitrary, incapable of drawing realistic distinctions, and responsive only to emotion and the crasser human instincts;

(4) *"defensive" medical practice*, defined as either (*a*) the use of diagnostic and other resources primarily for the purpose of protecting the physician against a successful malpractice claim rather than the patient against an adverse medical result or (*b*) the refusal to provide needed care or to adopt desirable new methods out of a concern that exposure to liability would be increased;[5] and

(5) *the haphazard incidence of claims*, which seem, like lightning, to strike largely at random,[6] suggesting that (*a*) many injuries go uncompensated, (*b*) a vast amount of negligence goes unpoliced, and (*c*) due process and the established legal merit of a malpractice claim are insufficient guarantees, in view of the system's failure to treat all like things similarly, of the fairness of a judgment against an individual provider.[7]

Any benefits of the fault system which could offset the foregoing disadvantages must be found in improvements in the quality of care that are stimulated by provider apprehensions about potential claims and liability. But, even if potential tort liability does perform a substantial quality-assurance function in the health care system,[8] the costs

---

5. *See, e.g.*, Bernzweig, *Defensive Medicine*, in MEDICAL MALPRACTICE REPORT Appendix 38; Hershey, *The Defensive Practice of Medicine, Myth or Reality?*, 50 MILBANK MEMORIAL FUND Q. 69 (1972); Project, *The Medical Malpractice Threat: A Study of Defensive Medicine*, 1971 DUKE L.J. 939-48; Address by Potchen, Twine & Roberts, A Dynamic Systems Analysis of Defensive Medicine, Medical Malpractice Crisis Conference (U. of Md. School of Law, Nov. 21-22, 1975).

6. *See* MEDICAL MALPRACTICE REPORT 23; Peterson, *Consumers' Knowledge of and Attitudes Toward Medical Malpractice*, in MEDICAL MALPRACTICE REPORT Appendix 658, 665-93 (survey indicated many people had had "negative medical care experiences" without pursuing legal remedies); Brook, Brutoco & Williams, *The Relationship Between Medical Malpractice and Quality of Care*, 1975 DUKE L.J. 1197.

7. Physicians are particularly disturbed that claims appear to be occasioned less by variations in the technical quality of the care received than by such factors as the patient's personality and circumstances, the doctor's "bedside manner," the lawyer's interest in the claim, and chance disclosure of the existence of actionable negligence. See also text accompanying note 13 *infra*. The unscientific character of both the fact-finding process and the means of establishing the legal standard of care also contribute to perceptions of unfairness. *See, e.g.*, Child, *Lawyers, Doctors and Medical Malpractice: A Surgeon Reacts*, in MEDICAL MALPRACTICE 43 (Shapiro, Steingold & Needham eds. 1965).

8. There is substantial doubt about whether the hazard of malpractice claims con-

of the current system's dysfunctional aspects are still so great as to compel attention to the possibility that the objectives sought could be achieved more cheaply or more effectively by other means.

The legislative deliberations precipitated by the recent malpractice crisis have not focused extensively on the possibility of a new departure.[9] Instead, the legislatures have been primarily concerned with shoring up the fault system, the insurance component of which was rapidly breaking down.[10] In attempting to make insurable a set of risks which was becoming uninsurable, policy makers initially confined themselves to addressing the current system's defects, and only recently has attention been directed to the possibility of eliminating or de-emphasizing the fault factor in compensating for injuries.[11] As one proposal for doing this, the MAI scheme also calls attention to the need either to maintain and perhaps strengthen the quality-assurance function of the injury-compensation system or to replace it with something at least equally effective. The MAI proposal should be helpful to ob-

---

tributes to improving the quality of care. *See* Brook, Brutoco & Williams, *supra* note 6, at 1220; Ball, PSRO, Malpractice Litigation, and Defensive Medicine, Medical Malpractice Crisis Conference (U. of Md. School of Law, Nov. 21-22, 1975). The possibility remains, however, that doctors' responses to the malpractice threat, including the phenomenon of defensive medicine, see text accompanying note 5 *supra*, contribute to better technical care than would be obtained if there were no sanctions for poor-quality care other than professional sanctions.

Another type of qualitative benefit may flow from physicians' perception that lawsuits are less likely to be initiated if the patient has not been personally offended during treatment. *See* Pabst, *Comments on Medical Opinion Survey of Physicians' Attitudes on Medical Malpractice*, in MEDICAL MALPRACTICE REPORT Appendix 83, 84 (citing "poor communications" as the chief cause of the malpractice problem); Mechanic, *Some Social Aspects of the Medical Malpractice Dilemma,* 1975 DUKE L.J. 1179; Peterson, *supra* note 6. This may lead the physician to be more respectful of the patient's feelings, cultivating "bedside manner" as a means of avoiding lawsuits. Consumer groups and others have been hesitant to see patients' malpractice rights curtailed because of the lack of other means of holding providers accountable for the care provided. *E.g.*, Wolfe, *The Real Victim*, TRIAL 26 (May/June 1975) ("Thus far, unfortunately, malpractice litigation has clearly been the only form of protest in which the consumer has had any reasonable chance at redress for grievances."). *See also* Thompson, Lupton & Feldesman, *Patient Grievance Mechanisms in Health Care Institutions*, in MEDICAL MALPRACTICE REPORT Appendix 758. On MAI's impact on this problem, see note 49 *infra*.

9. While radical, the Kennedy-Inouye no-fault bill, S. 215, 94th Cong., 1st Sess. (1975), was offered primarily for discussion purposes. See text accompanying notes 31-33 *infra*.

10. *See* Comment, *An Analysis of State Legislative Responses to the Medical Malpractice Crisis,* 1975 DUKE L.J. 1417.

11. These possibilities have been actively considered by the following, among others: National Conference on Medical Malpractice; Conference on the Medical Malpractice Crisis (U. of Md. School of Law, Nov. 21-22, 1975); ABA Commission on Medical Professional Liability; American Insurance Association All Industry Committee; and New York Special Advisory Panel on Medical Malpractice. See also note 9 *supra*.

B. Outcome Assessment Versus Process Standards

The MAI scheme also points up some additional arguments, more fundamental than the foregoing pragmatic ones, which can be advanced against continued reliance on the fault system. Thus, it reflects the attention which reformers in the health field have recently focused on the advantages of assessing the quality of medical care on the basis of actual outcomes—that is, in terms of resulting patient health—rather than on the basis of "process"—that is, the individual steps actually taken in treating the patient.[12] Although malpractice claims occur only where there has been a bad outcome, the fault system is in no other respect outcome-oriented. For one thing, only a very small proportion of unsatisfactory outcomes produce claims, and fortuitous factors—for example, doctor or patient personality traits, the degree to which the patient's hardship is mitigated by collateral sources of financial protection, and the patient's possible ignorance that negligence rather than bad luck accounted for his injury—are perhaps more important determinants of claims initiation than a bad outcome itself.[13] A bad outcome is therefore by no means a sufficient condition for a malpractice lawsuit, though it is obviously a necessary one. It may nevertheless still be true that the malpractice suit is the only appreciable external check on the quality of outcomes currently operating in the health care system.[14]

---

12. *See, e.g.,* A. Cochrane, Effectiveness and Efficiency—Random Reflections on Health Services (1972); P. Ellwood, P. O'Donoghue, W. McClure et al., Assuring the Quality of Health Care (1973); Williamson, *Outcomes of Health Care: Key to Health Improvement*, in Methodology of Identifying, Measuring and Evaluating Outcomes of Health Service Programs, Systems, and Subsystems 75 (C. Hopkins ed. 1970); Brook & Appel, *Quality of Care Assessment: Choosing a Method for Peer Review*, 285 New Eng. J. Med. 1323 (1973); Ball, *supra* note 8, at 11-16.

13. See notes 6-7 *supra* and accompanying text.

14. *See* Carlson, *Health Manpower Licensing and Emerging Institutional Responsibility for the Quality of Care*, 35 Law & Contemp. Prob. 848, 859-62 (1970). Carlson, however, appears to regard malpractice claims as more of a check on outcomes than they are in fact, and neglects to classify hospital tissue review committees as another outcome-oriented control. More recently, Professional Standards Review Organizations (PSROs) have been formed for the purpose of regulating the quality of care with some expectation that they will engage in outcome assessment and studies of cost-effectiveness. 42 U.S.C. § 1320c (Supp. III, 1973). *See* Havighurst & Blumstein, *Coping With Quality/Cost Trade-offs in Medical Care: The Role of PSROs*, 70 Nw. U.L. Rev. 6 (1975); Ball, *supra* note 8, at 38.

The legal standard of care employed under the fault system to judge provider negligence tends to focus attention on process rather than on outcome. Because liability is seldom automatic,[15] but depends on a showing that the doctor departed from accepted practice or omitted some customary diagnostic or therapeutic measure, physicians are compelled to do what other doctors do, and they depart from common practice only at their peril.[16] Certain kinds of "defensive" medicine reflect the effort of many physicians to reduce their legal exposure by erring on the side of doing too much rather than too little; their excesses may aid not at all in the patient's physical recovery but are instead intended solely to forestall his financial recovery in the event of an unsatisfactory result. Although physicians also frequently complain of the hazard of "cookbook" medicine under process-oriented regulatory controls,[17] the process standards enforced by the fault system are even more pernicious, since they do not make clear where the physician may safely stop and seem to require that everything possible be done. Moreover, because the fault system is administered by lawyers, judges, juries, and partisan experts, all exercising hindsight, physicians have no confidence that realistic standards will in fact be applied. They therefore operate on the worst-case hypothesis and protect themselves as best they can. There is surely a warrant for those reform proposals which would alter administrative arrangements under the present system to improve fault-finding processes,[18] thereby strengthening doctors' confidence that their conscientious efforts will not be penalized unless demonstrably deficient by reasonable standards.

---

15. *See generally* Louisell & Williams, Res Ipsa Loquitur—*Its Future in Medical Malpractice Cases*, 48 CALIF. L. REV. 252 (1960); McCoid, *The Care Required of Medical Practitioners*, 12 VAND. L. REV. 549, 605-32 (1959).

16. *See* 1 D. LOUISELL & H. WILLIAMS, MEDICAL MALPRACTICE ¶¶ 8.04-.06 (1973); McCoid, *supra* note 15, at 558-75, 581-85. The doctrine that adherence to custom in medical practice constitutes due care has long been buttressed by the maxim that a practitioner "experiments at his peril" with unusual methods. Carpenter v. Blake, 60 Barb. 488 (N.Y. Sup. Ct. 1871), *rev'd on other grounds*, 50 N.Y. 696 (1872); Slater v. Baker, 95 Eng. Rep. 860 (K.B. 1767). Such "experimentation" is of course justified if an innovative treatment offers the patient's best hope and informed consent is obtained. A. HOLDER, MEDICAL MALPRACTICE LAW 102-03, 249-54 (1975). More broadly, noncustomary practices may be approved if they are the chosen methods of a legitimate "school of practice" or of a "respectable" or "reputable" minority of practitioners. *Id.* at 44-45; 1 D. LOUISELL & H. WILLIAMS, *supra*, ¶ 8.04; W. PROSSER, HANDBOOK OF THE LAW OF TORTS 163 (4th ed. 1971); Bovbjerg, *The Medical Malpractice Standard of Care: HMOs and Customary Practice*, 1975 DUKE L.J. 1375; McCoid, *supra* note 15, at 565.

17. *E.g.*, Frederick, *"Cookbook Medicine": A New Tome Stirs Debate*, MED. WORLD NEWS, July 28, 1975, at 61, *discussing* AMA, MODEL SCREENING CRITERIA TO ASSIST PROFESSIONAL STANDARDS REVIEW ORGANIZATIONS (1975); *AMA Urges Medical Injury Compensation*, AM. MED. NEWS, Jan. 13, 1975, at 1.

18. *See* Comment, *State Legislative Responses, supra* note 10.

But, even if the fault system could be substantially improved, perhaps by employing arbitration or screening panels in the assessment of claims, only a few of the foregoing concerns would have been addressed, and none would have been fully resolved. Moreover, there would remain a strong basis for doubt that the legal standard being applied was in fact the socially appropriate one. Although it may seem paradoxical in light of a widely perceived need to improve the quality of medical care in the United States, the standard of care employed in malpractice suits, based as it is on customary processes and not on outcomes, is probably too high in many respects.[19] Professional standards, lacking scientific evidence of efficacy and cost-effectiveness, dictate many substantial expenditures which return little benefit and may on some occasions increase hazards.[20] It is a chronic problem in health care that many physicians' decisions taken in the name of the quality of care fail to advance that object either at all or enough to justify the costs entailed, thereby wasting societal resources and perhaps diverting them from more pressing health care needs.[21]

In nonmedical settings, the use of prevailing custom as a guide in assessing negligence is justifed if that standard has been determined by reasonably dependable market forces—that is, by buyers and sellers making private decisions with respect to the desirability of added increments of safety.[22] Where a safety measure thus generally agreed

---

19. This is not to deny that bad care may sometimes be customary. In some jurisdictions a perception of this state of affairs has led to a narrowing of the customary practice doctrine, based upon Judge Learned Hand's reasoning in The T.J. Hooper, 60 F.2d 737 (2d Cir. 1932). *E.g.*, Darling v. Charleston Community Memorial Hosp., 33 Ill. 2d 326, 211 N.E.2d 253 (1965), *cert. denied*, 383 U.S. 946 (1966); Favalora v. Aetna Cas. & Sur. Co., 166 So. 2d 299 (La. App. 1962); Incollingo v. Ewing, 282 A.2d 206 (Pa. 1971); Helling v. Carey, 83 Wash. 2d 514, 519 P.2d 981 (1974). *See* Note, *Comparative Approaches to Liability for Medical Maloccurrences*, 84 YALE L.J. 1141, 1146-50 (1975). Although custom-set standards may be either too low or too high by objective measures, this Article stresses mainly the excessive care which doctors may seek to take when their decision-making lacks financial constraints. *See* Bovbjerg, *supra* note 16, at 1396.

20. *See, e.g.*, A. COCHRANE, *supra* note 12; U.S. PUBLIC HEALTH SERVICE, FORWARD PLAN FOR HEALTH FY 1977-81, at 144-61 (DHEW Pub. No. 05-76-50074, 1975); Neuhauser, *The Future of Proprietaries in American Health Services*, in REGULATING HEALTH FACILITIES CONSTRUCTION 233-37 (C. Havighurst ed. 1974). These sources supply exhaustive further references.

21. See notes 23-24 *infra* and accompanying text. *See generally* Havighurst & Blumstein, *supra* note 14, at 9-20.

22. *See* Posner, *A Theory of Negligence*, 1 J. LEGAL STUDIES 29, 32-33 (1972). Although consumer ignorance can frequently be advanced to counter the presumption in favor of market-determined standards, this argument should not be too readily accepted, particularly since markets cater not to the average customer but to the marginal one, who is frequently better informed. Of course, custom would be an inappropriate guide

upon by buyers and sellers has been omitted by a seller, the buyer's right to sue supplies a useful opportunity to correct, after the fact, a kind of market failure occasioned, it is presumed, by the buyer's ignorance. With respect to medical care, however, custom and practice among practitioners may be a poor guide to appropriate safety-promoting conduct because consumers make few purchasing decisions. Not only are treatment decisions largely delegated to doctors, but, because third parties pay most of the bills, cost is taken into account to only a very limited extent; the physician's fiduciary responsibilities, which at one time included a duty to look out for the patient's pocketbook, are now largely directed to getting the maximum medical benefit for his patient, regardless of the cost.[23] Indeed, it is to a large extent the availability of third-party payment which allows the physician to incur the high costs involved in defensive medicine, which, by definition, is undertaken more for the benefit of the provider than for the good of the patient.[24] In these circumstances, prevailing custom and practice, even if that standard could be perfectly implemented in practice, would be an inappropriate standard. Departure from the fault system and its process-oriented standards would therefore be a positive step from the standpoint of health policy in general. One of MAI's prime features is its shift of emphasis from process to outcome.

C. *From Fault to No-Fault*

Because the fault system is dysfunctional in so many respects, alternatives to it must be seriously considered. One alternative is of course simply to repeal altogether the patient's right to sue a negligent physician, and some substantial limitations on that right have recently been imposed in some states in the form of (1) absolute dollar limits on recoveries permitted[25] and (2) revised statutes of limitations which arbitrarily cut off claims for undiscovered injuries.[26] Such piecemeal

---

for establishing duties toward individuals who were not parties to a contractual relationship with the alleged tort-feasor. *See id.* at 36-38. On the admissibility of evidence of custom, see generally Darling v. Charleston Community Memorial Hosp., 33 Ill. 2d 326, 211 N.E.2d 253 (1965); McCoid, *supra* note 15, at 558-75.

23. *See* Havighurst & Blumstein, *supra* note 14, at 13-15, 25-30.

24. *See* Project, *supra* note 5, at 942, 946. It is worth observing that the MAI scheme would not limit health care spending except insofar as unproductive defensive medicine was obviated. See note 112 *infra*. Cost control would have to be achieved by other means, since providers, under MAI or otherwise, have little incentive to seek the optimal level of spending. See notes 48 & 93 *infra*.

25. *See, e.g.,* IDAHO CODE § 41-4103 (Supp. 1975); IND. ANN. STAT. § 16-9.5-2-2 (Burns Supp. 1975). *See generally* Comment, *State Legislative Responses, supra* note 10, at 1418-25.

26. *See, e.g.,* FLA. STAT. ANN. § 768.28 (Supp. 1975); IND. ANN. STAT. § 16-9.5-3-1. *See generally* Comment, *State Legislative Responses, supra* note 10, at 1429-36.

repeals are troublesome in much the same sense that wholesale repeal of patients' tort remedies would be, but they have been tolerated primarily out of a desire to maintain the insurability of physicians' liability risks. Aside from measures couched in this expediency, however, repeal of the fault system without introduction of a substitute compensation mechanism has not been seriously proposed. Attention is therefore directed to "no-fault" compensation plans.

II. THE NO-FAULT NOTION AS APPLIED TO MEDICAL CARE: THE FUNCTION OF DETERRENCE

A. *Compensation or Deterrence as the Goal?*

The medical profession usually responds positively to proposals for a no-fault compensation system for medically caused injuries to patients. This response originates in large part in doctors' anticipation that a no-fault scheme would relieve them not only of the psychic and other burdens of malpractice claims and lawsuits but of financial responsibility as well. Thus, in his statement dissenting from the 1973 Report of the Health, Education and Welfare Secretary's Commission on Medical Malpractice, Dr. Charles A. Hoffman, then president of the American Medical Association (AMA), endorsed a compensation plan which would require employers to insure their employees against medical injuries.[27] Such a plan contrasts sharply, however, with another type of no-fault proposal, which would continue to require providers to bear at least some of the accident costs arising out of the care they render but would dispense with extensive factual inquiries and with fault-finding in individual cases. An essential basis for distinguishing among no-fault plans, therefore, is the extent to which the plan internalizes costs by imposing them in some meaningful way on the providers responsible for the care or externalizes them by passing them on to the public through government or some other third party unrelated to the health care transaction.

How one feels the costs of medical injuries should be borne depends largely on whether one focuses primarily on the need to compensate the injured patient or also considers it important to motivate providers to avoid compensable outcomes. Dr. Hoffman, stressing only the urgency of compensation for the injured, notes that the "economic need of patients injured in the course of their health care is just as great

---

27. MEDICAL MALPRACTICE REPORT 113, 127-30 (C. Hoffman, dissenting statement). *See also* Editorial, AM. MED. NEWS, Jan. 13, 1975, at 4.

regardless of whether the injury was caused by malpractice or whether it was an unavoidable risk inherent in the care."[28] But, because the victims of medical accidents are in no way a needier class than persons who are the victims of disease in general or of other types of accidents, a no-fault medical compensation system cannot be recommended solely on the ground that it would provide compensation for injuries which are now uncompensated.

A better ground for preferring a no-fault scheme is that it is a way of eliminating the problems caused by the existing system while not denying compensation to those who qualify for it now. Indeed, Dr. Hoffman's plan to compensate for medical injuries (including unavoidable events attending recognized risks)—while ignoring for compensation purposes other accidental injuries as well as the disease which brought the patient into the health care system in the first place—can best be defended not as a benefit to patients but as a means of totally eradicating the malfunctioning system of malpractice litigation. Many observers would be reluctant, however, to see problems generated by the law of medical malpractice "solved" by exonerating the negligent physician and eliminating altogether whatever incentives for better-quality care tort law may introduce. Attention is thus focused on compensation systems which, while removing malpractice cases from the courts and avoiding extensive fault-finding, could nevertheless preserve or strengthen the system's quality-enhancing incentives.

The MAI scheme reflects a strong preference for maintaining the tort system's function—however poorly performed it may now be[29]—of deterring medical accidents by inducing close attention to the myriad ways in which they can be prevented or their incidence reduced. It is this reliance on the deterrent effect of financial responsibility for accidents which distinguishes the no-fault approach of MAI from no-fault auto insurance, under which individuals must insure themselves and their passengers against injury but, at least below a certain threshold, have little or no financial responsibility for harm done to others. Because the public and their legislatures would probably be more reluctant to absolve physicians from the consequences of their failures than they were to allow unsafe drivers to escape liability to third persons,[30]

---

28. MEDICAL MALPRACTICE REPORT 127-28 (C. Hoffman, dissenting statement).
29. See note 8 *supra*.
30. For one thing, physicians are readily identified as a special, privileged class seeking exoneration from responsibility for the harms they cause by professional incompetence. *E.g.*, Starr, *The Doctor's Discomfort: Malpractice*, NEW REPUBLIC, June 28, 1975, at 16. "Unsafe drivers" are not so clearly personified or recognized as special pleaders in the debate over auto no-fault. Moreover, they may seem less blameworthy than the negligent physician and less subject to meaningful sanction under the fault sys-

legislative action to supersede the fault system for dealing with medical injuries may be difficult to obtain unless either MAI-type incentives or quality-assurance measures of other kinds are introduced.

B. *Deterrence Versus Governmental or Professional Quality Controls*

Many observers, but particularly physicians, reject the notion that incentives generated by legal liability for harms can help to improve the quality of medical care. Senator Daniel Inouye, in introducing a no-fault bill which would shift financial responsibility for medical injuries from individual providers to the federal government,[31] expressed the widely held belief:

> I believe that good doctors practice good medicine in spite of, not because of the threat of malpractice, and that they will continue to do so after the threat is lessened. Conversely, it is questionable whether a deficient or careless doctor can be made to practice good medicine by an external threat. In his case, it is more important that we identify him and take steps to prevent him from endangering the health and lives of his patients.[32]

Senator Inouye's bill, co-sponsored by Senator Edward Kennedy, would impose substantial new regulatory controls on physicians who elected to participate in the projected government-run no-fault insurance program.[33] The proposal points up the likelihood that legislative moves to establish a no-fault scheme without a deterrence feature will carry with them stiff substitute controls of the kind which are highly threatening to doctors.[34]

The standard response of the medical profession to the asserted need for increased quality assurance is to look only to professional controls and to resist reliance on either governmental controls or incentives supplied by the fault system or any conceivable substitute for it. Dr. Hoffman's statement referred to above,[35] while not conceding any significant necessity for strengthened quality assurance, reflected the

---

tem. Finally, licensing and policing efforts may seem substantially more effective in curbing highway than medical accidents, in part because the enforcement mechanisms are under more effective public control in one case than in the other. Despite these reasons for exonerating negligent drivers, no state has done so completely, suggesting that physicians cannot hope to escape continued exposure to liability of some kind.

31. S. 215, 94th Cong., 1st Sess. (1975).
32. 121 CONG. REC. S414 (1975) (remarks of Senator Inouye).
33. S. 215, 94th Cong., 1st Sess. § 1704 (1975).
34. State legislative efforts are revealing a similar expectation of greater submission to public control as a price of malpractice relief. *See* Brook, Brutoco & Williams, *supra* note 6, at 1223-27.
35. See text accompanying notes 27-28 *supra*.

AMA position that peer review is the only appropriate mechanism for achieving whatever quality control is required; his proposal that patients' protection against medical injuries be purchased by their employers was obviously designed to place the costs not on government, which would be induced to interfere further in medical practice, but on parties who were not well situated to introduce or press for quality controls of any kind. Others have suggested that patients insure themselves through a kind of "patient flight insurance," which would be purchased on entry into the hospital or automatically tacked onto every hospital bill.[36] Such risk-shifting proposals and others seeking to reduce or eliminate the malpractice threat to doctors are nearly always accompanied by an obligatory call for strengthened professional controls over the quality of care.[37]

The view that controls—governmental or professional, as the case may be—are more efficacious than incentives in maintaining the quality of care is difficult to test empirically, but it is theoretically unsound for at least one reason. Controls necessarily operate by establishing a minimum level which all providers must meet, and they supply no pressure to exceed that minimum. Incentives, on the other hand, operate on all providers all of the time, encouraging maximum attention to obtaining improved results even on the part of the very best physicians and hospitals. The pressure is thus for *performance*, not merely for *compliance* with minimal standards which, whether set by professional groups themselves or by a government bureau inevitably linked by the ties of political influence to organized providers, are unlikely to embody very high aspirations. Controls will inevitably be based primarily on process norms, some of them perhaps validated by outcome studies but all of them hard to change, hard to apply, and hard to reconcile with professional independence.[38]

The preference for controls and against incentives is traceable in the thinking of both Senator Inouye and Dr. Hoffman to an abiding faith in professionalism and ethics as an adequate guarantor of high-quality performance by all but a small minority of physicians, which is presumed to be amenable to governmental or professional policing. Popular as it is among physicians, this "bad-apple" theory, in addition

---

36. *See, e.g.*, HEALTH POLICY ANALYSIS PROGRAM, THE MALPRACTICE ISSUE IN WASHINGTON STATE 87 (Nov. 1975).
37. *E.g.*, Editorial, *supra* note 27.
38. *See* Havighurst & Blumstein, *supra* note 14, at 25-30; Havighurst & Bovbjerg, *Professional Standards Review Organizations and Health Maintenance Organizations: Are They Compatible?*, 1975 UTAH L. REV. 381, 401-04; Note, *Comparative Approaches, supra* note 19, at 1160-63.

to attributing all problems to the "other guy," has a slightly elitist ring, suggesting that physicians as a class are worthy of society's trust and that specific guarantees of their good performance can be dispensed with, except around the fringes.[39] Although Senator Inouye and Dr. Hoffman would obviously have many differences, the common ground between them is a shared belief that incentives are not a useful mechanism of social control in this important area.[40]

Senator Inouye and Dr. Hoffman to the contrary, however, it is not necessary to cast any aspersion on the average doctor's ethics or motives to suggest that financial incentives may be a useful adjunct to his sense of professional responsibility. One can even concede that a

---

39. *See, e.g.,* Editorial, *supra* note 27. Reliance on professionalism and ethics to compensate for consumer ignorance and uncertainty is practically essential in an industry like medical care. Arrow, *Government Decision Making and the Preciousness of Life,* in ETHICS OF HEALTH CARE 33 (L. Tancredi ed. 1974); Arrow, *Uncertainty and the Welfare Economics of Medical Care,* 53 AM. ECON. REV. 941, 949-51, 965-66 (1963). This is not to say, however, that opportunities for supplying additional checks on professional performance should be passed by. *Cf.* Goldfarb v. Virginia State Bar, 421 U.S. 773 (1975) (applying the antitrust laws to the legal profession). For a case adopting the elitist view to limit the force of the antitrust laws in the field of education, see Marjorie Webster Jr. College, Inc. v. Middle States Ass'n of Colleges & Secondary Schools, Inc., 432 F.2d 650 (D.C. Cir.), *cert. denied,* 400 U.S. 965 (1970).

40. The common ground between government and the medical profession is apparently large enough to support PSROs, which are extensive peer-review efforts mandated by statute and subjected to extensive federal oversight but controlled and operated by local practitioners. See note 14 *supra. See generally* Havighurst & Blumstein, *supra* note 14. PSROs are being heavily relied upon to control cost and assure the quality of care under federal financing programs, and they provide a base for an effective argument that extension of PSRO review to all care would obviate all other quality controls. *See* Simmons & Ball, *PSRO and the Dissolution of the Malpractice Suit,* 6 U. TOLEDO L. REV. 739 (1975).

It is noteworthy that another view widely shared in both government and the profession is that consumer sovereignty, advertising, private entrepreneurial initiative, and competition have no substantial place in the social control of the health care industry. *But cf.* Complaint, *In re* AMA, No. 9064 (F.T.C., Dec. 22, 1975). Just as in the case of quality assurance, the cost controls which must substitute for market incentives are unlikely to work well and are highly distasteful to physicians. *See* McClure, *The Medical System Under National Health Insurance: Four Models That Might Work and Their Prospects,* 1 J. HEALTH POL., POLICY & LAW — (1976). Because the medical profession cannot hope to preserve the status quo indefinitely against the demand for stronger government controls, it might be better advised to opt for restoration of a functioning marketplace with limited regulatory oversight as a means of preserving professional independence. Above all, this means accepting health maintenance organizations (HMOs) as active, independent competitors in a market conducive to their operation. *See id.*; Havighurst & Blumstein, *supra* note 14; Havighurst & Bovbjerg, *supra* note 38. On the subversion of HMOs by a combination of Congressional liberals and the AMA, revealing the confluence of views on the undesirability of allowing markets to function, see Starr, *The New Medicine: An Experiment Designed to Fail,* NEW REPUBLIC, Apr. 19, 1975, at 15; Starr, *The Undelivered Health System,* 42 PUB. INTEREST 66 (1976).

highly developed sense of ethics is a hallmark of the profession—I personally believe that it is—, yet recognize that this ethical sense is not distributed in precisely equal proportions. For the physician who feels no overwhelming ethical responsibility to maintain his competence or to limit his practice so as to honor the principle that he should "first, do no harm,"[41] it is highly likely, contrary to Senator Inouye's suggestion, that financial incentives will be quite meaningful.

As to even the above-average doctor, his no doubt strongly felt ethical obligation is to do what he was taught in medical school and what he sees other doctors doing for their patients; he is probably largely content to know that he is doing the best he knows how under frequently difficult circumstances. Yet there is lacking in his consciousness an awareness of how his results compare with the results achieved by other doctors. He has little feedback of information which might put him on notice that his efforts are misdirected, that improvements are possible, and that his best is not quite good enough. But with financial incentives based on the quality of outcomes and with claims experience supplying a convenient basis for comparing his performance with that of other physicians, such a physician would be induced to re-examine his methods, to seek advice and continuing education, to follow up with patients to check compliance with regimens and to discover new problems, and, finally, to limit his practice to those problems which he is most capable of handling successfully.

The recent Study on Surgical Services for the United States (SOSSUS) illustrates the medical profession's approach to solving quality-of-care problems. A plea is made for developing a "reliable data base for quantifying surgical excellence," a step said to be necessary "[i]f good surgeons are to be encouraged to operate more and poor ones less or not at all; if good hospitals are to be expanded, mediocre ones improved, and poor ones closed."[42] It is reasonable to expect, however, that a system of outcome-oriented incentives would achieve these goals far sooner than methods such as those contemplated in the SOSSUS report.[43] Not only is it unnecessary to wait for a definitive

---

41. Physicians are familiar with the principle *primum non nocere*: "First, do no harm." This appears to trace back to Hippocrates. *See* 1 HIPPOCRATES 165 (Loeb Library ed. 1923).

42. AMERICAN COLLEGE OF SURGEONS & AMERICAN SURGICAL ASS'N, SURGERY IN THE UNITED STATES 192 (1975) (SOSSUS Report).

43. For an expression of government's concurrence on the means to be adopted, see FORWARD PLAN FOR HEALTH, *supra* note 20, at 23:

[I]t is the shared responsibility of health professionals and government to provide a reasonable basis for confidence that action will be taken both to assess

"data base,"⁴⁴ but it is also unnecessary to implement inevitably debatable quality standards by applying specific sanctions against powerful professionals whose resistance to outside interference is legendary. Perhaps the profession can proceed against a tiny minority of incompetents who allegedly give the profession a bad name, but there is no way that across-the-board direct controls over surgeons and hospitals can ever be finely tuned to achieve overall effectiveness.⁴⁵ Only an unobtrusive, nonpolitical system of rewards and penalties can hope to achieve the worthy objectives specified in the SOSSUS report. Unfortunately, the gap between stating these objectives and realizing them by the means specified is so great that one may be forgiven for suspecting that the surgeons are more interested in demonstrating their good intentions than in measurably improving the fraternity's performance.

---

whether services meet professionally recognized standards and to correct any deficiencies that may be found. Quality assurance is thus not a guarantee of performance, much less of satisfactory results, but an iterative process that leads to improved health care quality. The quality assurance process consists of the following steps:
  i. Developing and disseminating knowledge regarding the efficacy, safety, and cost of medical procedures;
  ii. Developing and disseminating knowledge regarding methods of assessing and improving the quality of health care interventions, and
  iii. Establishing organizational and administrative entities that can use the information from steps 1 and 2 to assess and, through a variety of mechanisms, improve the quality of performance, and which can contribute to the development of new information.

44. *See also id.* (noting major deficiencies in the "knowledge" required for quality assurance). It is reasonable to expect that the research studies needed to enlighten the profession on quality-related matters would be more aggressively pursued by professional groups such as PSROs and the SOSSUS sponsors if providers had a direct financial stake in improving outcomes. The MAI system itself would supply valuable data on outcomes and, even more important, would feed it back, in the form of higher or lower costs, to individual providers for immediate action.

45. Most observers maintain faith that the obstacles to effective management of the system's quality can somehow be overcome, but there is recognition that much remains to be done:
  Methodologies for assessing health care quality and methods for influencing provider performance are still primitive and need further development and critical examination. Without a sound methodological underpinning, quality assurance activities cannot ensure accountability for provider performance, nor can the relationship between medical practice (process) and patient benefit (outcome) be adequately documented.
  . . . [I]t will not be possible to assure quality without an administrative structure to see to it that the practice is aligned with theory. *Id.* at 23-24.

It is fair to say that hardly any responsible person in the health care system recognizes any alternative to the peer-review method of quality assurance. It is far from clear, however, that the entire $110 billion health care enterprise can be centrally managed by expanding a mechanism which has so far had its only pronounced success at the institutional level and which is heavily dependent on providers' commitment and acceptance to make it function well.

C. What Providers Stand to Gain From an Outcome-Oriented Incentive System

Although providers will probably resist adoption of MAI or any other incentive-oriented quality-assurance mechanism, they may in fact have something to gain from it. As previously noted, it seems unlikely that substantial relief from malpractice suits will be granted without adoption of new quality-assurance measures to compensate for the loss of the perceived quality-enhancing benefits of the fault system. Physician accountability has become a watchword among reformers, and most mechanisms for increasing it should seem substantially more threatening to physicians than MAI. Even if extensive legislative relief from the malpractice burden is obtained, the special treatment thus accorded to doctors—"class legislation" it is being called in some places—will be charged up against them in the political ledger, to be balanced later on. On the other hand, if providers were willing to stand behind their work to the limited extent contemplated by MAI, the seemingly inexorable pressure for increased intervention in their decision-making might be reduced. The profession's political image would be improved, and, if MAI worked well, a persuasive case could even be made for rolling back some existing regulation.[46]

The outcome-oriented character of the MAI approach should also have particular appeal to providers. Concerned about "cookbook" medicine and defensive practice, they should respond positively to a quality-assurance mechanism which addresses results alone and pays little or no attention to how they were achieved. Although no imputation of fault should arise from payment of an MAI claim, the provider may well be induced to examine both his conscience and his methods by the reminder that reasonable expectations of a good outcome have been disappointed. But professional independence would remain inviolate, and providers could adopt whatever methods seemed to them, in the exercise of their scientific learning and professional judgment, most likely to be beneficial. All visible indications are that physicians value their independence highly. MAI, by offering physicians the only responsible basis on which their right to exercise independent professional judgment can be preserved, challenges them to reveal whether they in fact value simply their present nonaccountability for most bad outcomes.[47]

The incentives needed to make MAI work could probably be established without imposing on providers financial costs which seemed

---

46. See note 133 *infra*.
47. See notes 6-8 *supra* and accompanying text.

punitive. Indeed, a provider's cost flowing from the occurrence of a compensable outcome should probably be viewed more as a firm reminder than as a punishment, and certainly no provider should face the possibility of being wiped out by a run of bad luck. Although arriving at the appropriate level of direct provider responsibility would be difficult,[48] the program must appear to achieve substantially increased accountability if it is to inhibit the trend to ever-stricter controls. It does not seem necessary, however, that it be even as threatening to the average physician as the malpractice system seems to be. It should, of course, seem substantially fairer to physicians than the prevailing system and reasonably consistent with recognized professional obligations. Fortunately, it seems probable that these conditions can be met in a plan which, by reducing administrative costs, increases the number of dollars available for compensating patients and allows expanding the number of injuries for which compensation will be paid.

D. *Supplying Incentives Under MAI*

The central tenet of the MAI scheme is that financial incentives supplied by liability rules can be a major guarantor of good-quality medical care. Because of liability insurance and insurer rating practices, such financial incentives are an insignificant factor under the fault system, which appears to rely primarily on stigmatization and the unpleasantness of the litigation process to frighten providers into avoiding claims. Because MAI dispenses with most of the *in terrorem* effect of the fault system, it must deter accidents by introducing more effective financial incentives.[49] The mechanics of supplying effective in-

---

48. Incentives for good care would not necessarily be too weak under MAI even if substantially less than the full cost of accidents were borne by the responsible providers, since providers are not usually in a position of balancing the saving from preventive measures against the cost of taking them. See note 93 *infra*. The argument for deterrence under MAI is therefore not the same as that offered for strict liability in other areas—namely that optimizing behavior will be induced. *See generally* G. CALABRESI, THE COSTS OF ACCIDENTS 135 *et seq.* (1970); Calabresi & Hirschoff, *Toward a Test for Strict Liability in Torts*, 81 YALE L.J. 1055 (1972); Note, *Comparative Approaches, supra* note 19, at 1150-57 (discussing the applicability of tort theory to the malpractice problem without clear recognition of the impossibility of achieving optimal deterrence with present financing mechanisms). For a fuller discussion of this aspect of MAI and particularly its potential impact on inducing optimal performance by HMOs, see Havighurst & Tancredi 159-63, 94-96.

49. One possible qualitative loss from reducing physicians' malpractice fears could not be made up under MAI. Although MAI makes providers accountable for technical results, the narrowing of the patient's discretion about whether to initiate a malpractice lawsuit might reduce providers' incentives to cultivate good relationships with patients. See note 8 *supra*. Nevertheless, malpractice law is alleged to affect doctor-patient relations adversely in other respects, and the expanding physician supply, new grievance pro-

centives are potentially complex.[50]

The original MAI proposal contemplated that highly individualized experience rating in setting MAI premiums would serve to provide the desired incentives for quality assurance. The assumption was that some of the cost of each compensable outcome could be charged in some relatively direct way to the insured provider and to those other participants in the health care system who might be able to influence the frequency of such events, perhaps through strengthened peer-review efforts.[51] This approach, while rational as an incentive-preserving mechanism, involves some departure from established insurance principles, which are primarily concerned with the likelihood of future occurrences and not with distributing the costs of past events. Indeed, the primary purpose of liability insurance in general has been to relieve responsible parties of the costs associated with insured events, thus weakening incentives to avoid them. Although insurers in other areas have revealed some concern with accident avoidance, malpractice insurers have shown little interest in using rates either for deterrent purposes or as a recoupment measure even if desirable incentives for claims reduction would result.[52] One hopes that the actuaries called upon to implement MAI could be induced to take an active interest in doing more than passively assembling the funds to pay future claims.

---

cedures, and greater emphasis on consumer choice and advertising could also offset any loss which might be feared. The law of informed consent, which would not be affected by MAI, might also play an important continuing role. *See, e.g.,* Canterbury v. Spence, 464 F.2d 772 (D.C. Cir.), *cert. denied,* 409 U.S. 1064 (1972); Cobbs v. Grant, 8 Cal. 3d 229, 502 P.2d 1, 104 Cal. Rptr. 505 (1972); Note, *Restructuring Informed Consent: Legal Therapy for the Doctor-Patient Relationship,* 79 YALE L.J. 1533 (1970).

50. The costs borne by providers must have a direct impact and not be passed through to some third party. Although doctors are thought by some to be free to pass costs on to their patients, there are substantial limits to their ability to recoup in this fashion, and no physician would be wholly indifferent to his costs. It is clear that providers should not be able automatically to treat their actual premium costs or cost-sharing outlays as expenses for purposes of determining fees under fee schedules or cost-related reimbursement; rather, the average outlay for providers similarly situated should be so treated, leaving the provider free to profit from any lower premium resulting from good past experience and exposed to a loss from higher premiums. If the tax laws should continue to permit a business deduction for actual insurance premiums and payments under cost-sharing provisions, INT. REV. CODE OF 1954 § 162, the government would, in effect, share the cost of a provider's poor performance. Under these circumstances, a substantially larger premium or cost-sharing obligation would be required to make incentives meaningful.

51. *See* Havighurst & Tancredi 129-30, 140, 162-63; 72-73, 80, 96.

52. The random incidence of claims, see notes 6-7 *supra,* under the present system suggests that past claims may be poor indicators of future ones and that it would not be rational to set premiums in relation to experience. Practice appears to be that premiums are raised only after several claims. *See* Steves, *supra* note 4 at 1322; Roddis & Stewart, *The Insurance of Medical Losses,* 1975 DUKE L.J. 1281.

The mandatory and highly detailed experience rating contemplated in the original MAI proposal would require legislation and administrative oversight to achieve the fine-tuning visualized.[53] While an alternative possibility would be simply to define the events which must be covered and allow insurers to develop their own rating categories, this approach might fail to yield meaningful incentives. Not only have malpractice insurers not been accustomed to much individualizing of premiums, but actuarial considerations, dictating that rates be set only for large, non-self-selected groups, give the market some natural monopoly characteristics. Moreover, insurance regulation reinforces the monopolistic pattern and further retards the kind of competitive pricing innovation required to make MAI effective. Despite these reasons for fearing that insurers acting alone in implementing the no-fault model might not greatly strengthen provider incentive, one characteristic of MAI offers hope: the larger number and increased predictability of insured events under MAI would facilitate experience rating,[54] thus perhaps allowing meaningful incentives to be achieved without regulation which was unduly disruptive of existing insurance practices.

If experience rating could not be expected as a spontaneous development, a possible means of creating quality-assurance incentives in an MAI program without extensive interference with the insurance industry would be simply to impose a share of the cost of each claim directly on the responsible providers through some kind of deductible or coinsurance requirement. The possibilities are limitless, but appropriate incentives could probably be achieved without imposing large costs on individual providers. For example, the insured provider might be made responsible for, say, ten percent of each claim up to $50,000, with such amounts to be reimbursed to the insurer as part of future premiums over a five-year period. An alternative, or additional, mechanism would be a deductible under which an insured physician would pay the first, say, $10,000 of claims in any year and would profit by that amount if he avoided all compensable events. Cost-sharing arrangements might differ for different events, perhaps taking effect only after a certain number of claims had been paid and thus reflecting the degree to which a certain number of such events were thought to be unavoidable.

---

53. Different experience-rating formulae were contemplated for different events, so that incentives could be tailored to the needs of the particular case. *See* Havighurst & Tancredi 140, 80.

54. See notes 6-7 *supra* and accompanying text. Experience rating is deemed feasible in workmen's compensation when premiums exceed $500 per year. NAT'L COMM'N ON STATE WORKMEN'S COMPENSATION LAWS, REPORT 98 (1972).

It is possible that insurers providing no-fault coverage would voluntarily offer policies with coinsurance or deductible features.[55] These features would reduce premiums and would be attractive to those providers who anticipated few claims and therefore saw an advantage in limited self-insurance. If the insurance industry appeared insufficiently competitive to produce this self-insurance option spontaneously, it might be made mandatory by legislation or by state insurance regulation.

The mechanism for establishing a reasonable set of incentives for accident deterrence cannot be specified without further study of the insurance industry, the available techniques for distributing costs, and the advantages and difficulties of tailoring the impact to fit particular cases. As to some situations at least, it seems likely that regulatory attention would be desirable to fine-tune incentives and to assure that insurance rating practices did not neglect deterrence. Legislation to establish MAI should charge the administrators with responsibility for developing a reasonable deterrence feature through the use of such regulatory powers as were necessary to make it work both fairly and effectively.

III. THE NO-FAULT NOTION AS APPLIED TO MEDICAL CARE: COMPENSABLE EVENTS

A. *The Complexities of Identifying Compensable Events*

Several examinations of the prospects for employing no-fault concepts to relieve the medical malpractice crisis have concluded that the problems confronted in identifying compensable events are extremely great, perhaps insuperable.[56] The chief problem is that many variables, including patient idiosyncrasies, may determine the effects of a given medical treatment and the extent of any injury, so that many bad results can be as easily regarded as incidents of the patient's presenting condition as attributed to a "medical injury." Unless the no-fault scheme is to be simply a social insurance plan indemnifying as many losses as possible, some notion of preventable harm seems needed to identify compensable events.[57] Unfortunately, attention to prevent-

---

55. However, such spontaneous cost-sharing provisions would probably not produce the same incentives for peer review contemplated in the MAI proposal. Havighurst & Tancredi 139-40, 162; 80, 96.

56. MEDICAL MALPRACTICE REPORT 101; Roth & Rosenthal, *Non Fault Based Medical Injury Compensation Systems,* in MEDICAL MALPRACTICE REPORT Appendix 450; Note, *Comparative Approaches, supra* note 19; Keeton, *Compensation for Medical Accidents,* 121 U. PA. L. REV. 590, 615 (1973). Carlson, *Conceptualization of a No-Fault Compensation System for Medical Injuries,* 7 LAW & SOC'Y REV. 329 (1973).

57. The cost of a program to compensate all "medical injuries" or all iatrogenic injuries would be considerable. Two studies conducted for the HEW Secretary's Commis-

ability would open up questions very similar to those involved in applying the fault system (suggesting that "no-fault" would be a misnomer) and would invite second-guessing of almost any outcome less than full recovery. To avoid such inquiries, proposals for comprehensive no-fault coverage have drawn the line defining compensability on the basis of whether the cause of any bad result is to be found in the patient's disease or in the medical care system itself. Iatrogenicity is thus the key to such comprehensive no-fault plans.[58]

The apparent necessity under a comprehensive no-fault system for determining the cause of every resulting condition has led Professor Robert Keeton to question the advantage of such a system over the present one.[59] He suggests that the administrative cost in time and money of determining causation, when added to over-all cost increases due to an increase in the number of claims, may not be worth the gains in the form of a diminished threat to the reputations of physicians and standardization of compensation payments. The vast amount of litigation spawned by the "work-relatedness" of injuries under workmen's compensation serves as a warning against leaving too many factual issues open to dispute.[60]

Despite the foregoing reasons for despair over the prospects for a no-fault system, the MAI proposal offered a tentatively hopeful view.

---

sion on Medical Malpractice revealed that substantial percentages (8.5 percent and 7.6 percent, respectively) of hospitalized patients suffer some medical injury. *See* Boyden, *Medical Injuries Described in Hospital Patient Records*, in MEDICAL MALPRACTICE REPORT Appendix 41 (declining to state the 8.5 percent figure in part because the sample was not necessarily unbiased); Pocincki, Dogger & Schwartz, *The Incidence of Iatrogenic Injuries*, in MEDICAL MALPRACTICE REPORT Appendix 50, 55.

58. The studies by Boyden, *supra* note 57, and Pocincki, Dogger & Schwartz, *supra* note 57, both applied a causation test, as would the compensation schemes proposed by S. 215, 94th Cong., 1st Sess. (1975). See note 60 *infra*. *See generally* MEDICAL MALPRACTICE REPORT 113 (C. Hoffman, dissenting statement); and Roth & Rosenthal, *supra* note 56.

59. Keeton, *supra* note 56. Professor Keeton is not unfriendly to the no-fault idea, only unconvinced of its utility in this particular setting. Moreover, he was writing before the MAI proposal was published.

60. *See generally* 1 A. LARSON, THE LAW OF WORKMEN'S COMPENSATION ch. III (1972). Some inkling of the administrative fact-finding burden which would be entailed by an open-ended no-fault scheme can be gained from the language of the Kennedy-Inouye no-fault bill, S. 215, 94th Cong., 1st Sess. (1975). This bill would provide "compensation for loss from any injury suffered as a result of health care services provided by an insured . . . ." *Id.* § 1711(a). The bill further specifies that "an injury 'results' from the provision of health care services when it is more probably associated in whole or in part with the provision of such services than with the condition for which such services were provided." *Id.* § 1721(8). If the draftsmen did not really intend to make all evidence of possible intervening causes inadmissible, *see, e.g.*, Havighurst & Tancredi 147-49, 85-87, the final phrase should read "than with some other cause." In either event, it is not clear how patients' idiosyncracies would affect compensability.

It suggested that case-by-case adjudication of medical injuries and exposure to unmanageable costs could be avoided if a highly specified list of compensable injuries were developed in advance and incorporated in an insurance policy covering only those injuries, leaving other adverse outcomes to be handled under traditional doctrines and procedures, however they might be modified. Ideally, the list of events compensable under the MAI policy would be developed in such a way that each event would be readily recognizable when it occurred, with no occasion for further inquiry as to its etiology.[61] An event would be added to the list if medical opinion indicated that the event was usually or frequently—though by no means invariably—avoidable under good-quality medical care and that the frequency of the event could be expected to diminish if providers' attention were directed more strongly to the quality of the outcomes being achieved. Not all malpractice cases would be removed from the courts under this plan, but many would be.[62] Moreover, the list would be lengthened over time, beginning with the most obvious occurrences and later expanding to cover outcomes which, though seldom the subject of a lawsuit, were deemed avoidable in many instances.

Although the original MAI plan tentatively suggested some injuries for inclusion on the list of compensable events, its primary emphasis was on the analytics of list compilation. It stressed the necessity for fairness in not including events which in the contemplation of providers are very often unavoidable, although it argued the legitimacy of including some unavoidable events wherever necessary to eliminate a causation issue or to achieve another practical objective. Providers were urged to recognize that, while avoidability of an event is a factor in its inclusion on the list and the major goal of the system is to prevent avoidable events, the system nevertheless remains a "no-fault" scheme since blame is not in fact assessed in specific cases. Although physicians may resist the strict liability notion of automatic payment for outcomes which are sometimes unavoidable, it is in fact the inclusion of some unavoidable events in the listed outcomes which would shelter the provider from any imputation of fault whenever a patient suffers a compensable harm. There are thus positive advantages to providers, as well as to patients, from including some unavoidable events within the coverage of the compensation scheme. Even so, physicians (and others) contemplating MAI continually slip back into equating liability

---

61. *See* Havighurst & Tancredi 143-50, 83-88 (detailed illustration of the process of listing an event—hepatitis contracted within six months following a blood transfusion—in such a way as to exclude debate over causation).

62. See note 107 *infra*.

with blame, revealing that getting people to accept fully the notion of liability without fault requires considerable re-education.[63]

The criteria for listing an event as compensable would include several other factors in addition to the event's relative avoidability and the ease with which its occurrence or nonoccurrence could be established in specific instances. One complex issue is presented by the need to guard against the danger that making an adverse outcome of one course of treatment compensable would distort rather than improve treatment decisions, perhaps by causing providers to select a less appropriate treatment mode because of a reduced likelihood of a compensable outcome.[64] The ability of various providers engaged in the treatment process to take direct or indirect action to prevent or minimize harm would also have to be considered in deciding whose MAI policy should cover a particular event.[65]

Another factor which would undoubtedly enter into the specification of compensable events is the need of patients for compensation, which would be small wherever the main expense was medical costs largely covered under other programs.[66] However, adherence to the principles of MAI would caution against excluding at least highly avoidable events from compensation on this ground, since it would mean losing an opportunity for injury deterrence. The saving to the MAI program from excluding such events might be much less than the continued cost of avoidable injuries to other public and private financing programs.

---

63. Perhaps the best way to conceptualize liability without fault is to recognize that a loss has already occurred and that it is a legitimate social issue whether the loss should be left where it falls, subject to any insurance which the victim may have obtained, or should be shifted by legal means to someone else. The social cost of shifting the loss can only be justified if some offsetting benefit appears, but such a benefit may be found in improved incentives. Thus, it may not be at all difficult to justify placing the risk on a hospital or physician, either of which is almost always in a better position than the patient to minimize the risk by direct action or by inducing different behavior by the patient or by other participants in the treatment. See CALABRESI, *supra* note 48; Calabresi & Hirschoff, *supra* note 48. Physicians are already exposed to various kinds of vicarious liability—under the doctrines of *respondeat superior*, "borrowed servant," and the "captain of the ship"—based on similar principles. See note 89 *infra*. Despite the clear legitimacy of the no-fault liability principle, the MAI proposal nevertheless expresses a concern for physicians' perception of fairness and would push the bounds of liability only as far as quality gains were reasonably in prospect. See Havighurst & Tancredi 135-39, 77-79.

64. See text accompanying notes 99-106 *infra*.

65. See text accompanying notes 97-99 *infra*.

66. See text accompanying notes 110-15 *infra*. Malpractice claims are probably less likely to occur where the patient bears no out-of-pocket financial loss. Viewing MAI primarily as an answer to the problem of malpractice claims would therefore dictate its coverage of other areas first.

Expected dollar cost is probably an inevitable additional factor in listing compensable events, since introducing compensation where it is not now paid would be expensive. Although the theory of MAI would not admit cost as a legitimate consideration,[67] it probably could not be ruled out as a practical matter in a functioning program.

B. *Progress in Developing a List of Compensable Events*

The suggested compensable events in the original MAI proposal were merely illustrative of possibilities.[68] The only set of events carefully considered at that time was blood transfusion reactions.[69] Although the MAI proposal contemplated extensive professional investigation of numerous events which were candidates for the list, no professional groups have taken up the project, and it has not been possible to involve physicians extensively in subsequent investigations. The results of further specification efforts are therefore still highly tentative.

Our recent efforts toward compiling a definitive list of compensable events have concentrated on anesthesiology and general surgery.[70] The approaches taken in these two areas have differed substantially, and the differences are useful in illustrating the possibilities and flexibility of MAI.

1. *General Surgery*

Compensable outcomes for general surgery have been tentatively specified both with respect to surgery of all kinds and with respect to specific procedures.[71] The proposed list of compensable events in this area is as follows:

---

67. See text accompanying notes 109-12 *infra*.
68. Havighurst & Tancredi 134, 76.
69. These were deemed appropriate for compensation under a hospital-purchased MAI policy even in the case of certain hepatitis reactions which were neither clearly avoidable nor clearly caused by the transfusion. *Id*. at 143-50, 83-88.
70. The original proposal addressed orthopedics injuries. *Id*. at 133-35, 75-76. *See also* Tancredi, *Identifying Avoidable Adverse Events in Medicine*, 12 MED. CARE 935 (1974).
71. The list was compiled by reviewing the most common surgical complications and considering them in light of the following questions:
   1. To what extent is the incidence of this complication related to the technical skill, judgment, or attentiveness of the surgeon?
   2. Is this complication a clinically distinct entity? Can its existence be readily substantiated?
   3. How early in the postoperative period is this complication detectable?
   4. How costly are the sequelae of this complication?
   5. Would an incentive to minimize the occurrence of this complication bias the choice of treatment in unfortunate ways?

The primary source consulted was MANAGEMENT OF SURGICAL COMPLICATIONS (3d ed. C. Artz & J. Hardy 1975).

The most obvious candidates for a list of compensable events are those which courts

General

1. Foreign bodies acquired intraoperatively
2. Burns acquired intraoperatively
3. Injury resulting from severance of an indwelling plastic catheter[72]
4. Neurological deficit resulting from intramuscular injection
5. Injury resulting from mistaken identity
6. Injury resulting from inadvertent intravascular injection of local anesthetic
7. Postoperative wound dehiscence in noncarcinomatous patient under age forty-five[73]
8. Tetanus infection subsequent to treatment of wound
9. Severe reaction to administration of tetanus antitoxin

   [On irreversible neurological damage or death following intraoperative cardiac arrest or spinal anesthesia, see *Anesthesiology* below.]

Procedure-specific

Parathyroid surgery or thyroidectomy

10. Permanent recurrent laryngeal nerve damage[74]

---

would treat under the doctrine of *res ipsa loquitur*; there seems little to be said for case-by-case litigation of claims based upon foreign bodies acquired intraoperatively (#1), burns acquired intraoperatively (#2), surgical procedures erroneously performed on the wrong patient (#5), and a hemolytic reaction to a blood transfusion (#25, *see also* Havighurst & Tancredi 144, 83).

72. The relative avoidability of this complication is illustrated by the striking diminution of its incidence as practitioners have become more aware of the technical mistake which creates the difficulty. "Such occurrences can be minimized by careful attention to the management of the catheter and the catheter site as well as the utilization of radiopaque catheters and the careful measurement of the length of the catheter before insertion and after removal." Moncrief, *Complications of Parenteral Fluid Therapy*, in MANAGEMENT OF SURGICAL COMPLICATIONS, *supra* note 71, at 68, 75.

73. "Studies have shown that a few surgeons will have many wounds with dehiscence and others will have extremely few. Surgical technique is important." Hunt, *Wound Complication*, in MANAGEMENT OF SURGICAL COMPLICATIONS, *supra* note 71, at 21, 25. A number of technical errors are known to increase the likelihood of dehiscence. Other variables, such as age and condition of the patient and the type of operation performed, also affect the incidence of this complication. Restricting compensability to patients under forty-five would help to screen out the effects of the principal variables that lie beyond the surgeon's control.

74. "In the hands of competent surgeons experienced in exposing the recurrent laryngeal nerves, permanent nerve injury occurs in less than 1 per cent of cases." Hardy, *Complications of Thyroid and Parathyroid Surgery*, in MANAGEMENT OF SURGICAL COMPLICATIONS, *supra* note 71, at 291, 300. Technical skill and attentiveness are probably

11. Postoperative hypoparathyroidism exceeding two weeks' duration[75]

Thyroidectomy or tonsillectomy
12. Death in the immediate postoperative period[76]

Cholecystectomy
13. Injury to common bile duct[77]

Venous stripping
14. Injury from inadvertent stripping of femoral artery

Gastrointestinal procedures
15. Inadvertent gastroileostomy[78]
16. Duodenal stump leakage following gastric resection[79]
17. Instrumental perforation of esophagus[80]

---

the key variables determining the incidence of the complication. Permanent abnormal phonation and serious respiratory obstruction are the sequelae involved.

75. If all four parathyroid glands are inadvertently removed during surgery, hypocalcemic tetany will result, and lifelong drug therapy will be necessary to compensate for the activity of the removed glands. "In a review of 600 cases of thyroid surgery . . . 17 (2.8 per cent) cases of transient postoperative hypocalcemic tetany and nine (1.5 per cent) cases of permanent hypoparathyroidism [were found]." *Id*. Preserving the parathyroids during total thyroidectomies for thyroid malignancy is a difficult technical feat; for this reason some may suggest that compensability be restricted to patients without thyroid malignancy. Others may argue that precisely because of the difficulty of the procedure, the adverse outcome should be made compensable to deter less technically competent surgeons from attempting the operation.

76. Careful observations in the postoperative period will prevent the fatal consequence of uncontrolled hemorrhage. "The most distressing fact is that, though this hazard and possible sequelae are well known on all active surgical services, every 3 or 4 years in most general hospitals some patient loses his life from this cause." *Id*. at 296. Designating "death" as the compensable event rather than "postoperative hemorrhage" serves three goals: (1) Death is obviously not subject to the definitional problems inherent in a term like "hemorrhage." (2) Hemorrhage promptly noticed and controlled will not result in injury significant enough to compensate. (3) While the hemorrhage itself is of questionable avoidability, the surgeon can affect the consequences of hemorrhage by careful postoperative monitoring.

77. Careless dissection and blind clamping of bleeding vessels can produce an injury to the common bile duct. "Perhaps less than half of those who sustain a stricture due to operative injury survive for 10 years." Glenn, *Complications Following Operations Upon the Biliary Tract*, in MANAGEMENT OF SURGICAL COMPLICATIONS, *supra* note 71, at 501, 521.

78. This technical error can be avoided by careful identification of anatomical structures. Its occurrence necessitates reoperation.

79. Duodenal stump leakage is the most serious common complication and the main source of mortality in gastric resections. Surgical judgment, technical skill, and postoperative management are *among* the variables affecting its incidence.

80. As the use of instrumentation in the treatment of GI conditions has increased, instrumental perforation of the esophagus has emerged as a serious complication. This outcome is relatively avoidable.

Gynecology[81]

18. Perforation of uterus during dilatation and curettage
19. Vesicovaginal, ureterovaginal, rectovaginal, or enterovaginal fistula following gynecological procedure on noncarcinomatous patient
20. Permanent damage to ureter

Prostatectomy

21. Rectal injury
22. Permanent urinary incontinence

Treatment of fracture

23. Nerve paralysis following treatment with straps, splits, or casts[82]
24. Function-impairing deformity from malunion of fracture[83]

Blood transfusion

25. Hemolytic reaction[84]
26. Bacterial sepsis
27. Serum hepatitis[85]

Nephrectomy

28. Nephrectomy in the absence of a normally functioning contralateral kidney

It is stressed that the various items on the foregoing list are subject to further specification, which might rule out compensation for patients with a special predisposition toward the result if that predisposition could be clearly identified in practice. Clinicians' assistance is clearly necessary in refining the list in this and other ways.[86] It should be noted that postoperative wound infections are omitted from the list, although they were nominated for inclusion in the original proposal.[87]

---

81. These complications are highly avoidable.
82. "Delayed nerve paralysis is practically always secondary to faulty treatment." Hampton, *Complications of Common Fractures*, in MANAGEMENT OF SURGICAL COMPLICATIONS, *supra* note 71, at 699, 708.
83. "The term 'malunion' really implies union of a fracture in a function-impairing deformity which could have been prevented by more skillful management of the fracture." *Id.* at 709-10.
84. Havighurst & Tancredi 144, 83.
85. *Id.* at 144-50, 83-88.
86. See note 104 *infra* and accompanying text.
87. *Id.* at 134, 76. An explanation of the reasoning behind the decision not to in-

2. *Anesthesiology*

In anesthesiology, highly detailed specification of events compensable under MAI, such as has been attempted for general surgery, is appropriate for dental and peripheral nerve injuries occurring under anesthesia, and such injuries should be included on the list covered by the anesthesiologist's MAI policy. This piecemeal approach seems inadequate, however, to manage the most serious adverse consequences of anesthesia, namely death or irreversible central nervous system damage occurring in a wide variety of surgical circumstances. Although a more sweeping approach is indicated to cover such outcomes, undertaking to compensate all such injuries and deaths occurring during or shortly after the operation seems likely to encompass many occurrences which are essentially unavoidable, being attributable to the patient's deteriorated condition and the inherent risks of surgery. For example, the operative death of an elderly patient with numerous physiological disturbances or of a victim of a gunshot wound to the chest does not raise the same presumption of avoidability which attends the death of a young adult undergoing a gall bladder operation.

Because establishing "operative death" as a compensable event is too nonspecific to assure that the goal of fairness is being realized, it is desirable to separate, in at least a rudimentary way, those fatal cardiac arrests and central nervous system injuries under anesthesia which are likely to be avoidable from those which are not. One possible approach is to inquire deeply into the patient's condition and the particular practices (dosage, type of ventilation, and so forth) employed, but this approach would necessitate costly case-by-case inquiries. A simpler and more outcome-oriented approach is to adopt a broad classification which excludes some patients on the basis of age and the urgency

---

clude this particular adverse outcome as a compensable event may help illustrate the application of the relevant criteria for selection. Postoperative wound infection is unquestionably an adverse outcome of sizable significance; some studies have indicated that a serious postoperative infection results in an average cost of approximately $7,000 per patient to the national economy. Hardy, *Surgical Complications*, in TEXTBOOK OF SURGERY 398, 404 (10th ed. D. Sabiston 1972). Nevertheless, reluctance to designate "postoperative wound infection" as a compensable event is justified for the following reasons: (1) It is not a clinically distinct entity. Some infections are trivial; others are life-threatening. Serious definitional difficulties could be anticipated. (2) Variables other than those within the surgeon's control are primarily determinative of its incidence. "The incidence of wound infection varies from less than 1 per cent in clean primarily closed wounds to 25 per cent or more in wounds created by emergency operations on the injured colon or perforated appendix." Hunt, *supra* note 73, at 28. The type and location of the wound, the type of micro-organisms invading, and the time lag between contamination and the institution of care are as important as surgical technique in determining whether or not an infection develops.

of the procedure. Thus, it is tentatively proposed to make compensable under MAI any death or irreversible central nervous system injury under anesthesia occurring in a patient between six months and sixty years of age undergoing any of the following procedures: tonsillectomy, cholecystectomy, hysterectomy, dilatation and curettage, repair of inguinal or hiatal hernia, abortion, sterilization, uterine suspension, venous stripping, thyroidectomy, mastectomy, and gastrectomy.

The foregoing list encompasses most of the common surgical procedures, but excludes many, such as obstetrical procedures and appendectomies, which must frequently be done on an emergency basis. It thus reflects a judgment that, since the listed procedures are almost always scheduled in advance, the anesthesiologist will seldom be faced with the necessity for anesthetizing a rapidly deteriorating patient who cannot be adequately prepared for surgery.[88] The list of covered procedures could be readily expanded if it were possible to distinguish emergency from nonemergency procedures after the fact and if an undue temptation to treat patients on an emergency basis would not be created. Clinicians' judgments would be necessary to clarify such matters and to identify additional procedures which could be safely included on the list.

One additional variable affecting the likelihood of a cardiac arrest, the competence of the surgeon, needs to be isolated in defining MAI liability of the anesthesiologist, since relieving the surgeon of all responsibility for intraoperative arrest would ignore his critical role.[89] In order to preserve the surgeon's incentives and to meet the fairness criterion in the treatment of anesthesiologists, liability might be divided

---

88. A recent review of 286 anesthesia-related deaths found that the inadequate preparation which complicates emergency surgery was responsible for more than half the fatal outcomes. *Report of Special Committee Investigating Deaths Under Anesthesia*, 12 MED. J. AUSTL. 579 (1970).

89. The law of medical malpractice has found it difficult to draw lines of demarcation between the surgeon's area of responsibility and the anesthesiologist's sphere. Traditionally, the surgeon in an operating room has been held responsible, as "captain of the ship," for all acts or omissions of attendant medical personnel, even of hospital employees, who are deemed to serve the surgeon as "borrowed servants." A. HOLDER, *supra* note 16, at 207-09; 1. D. LOUISELL & H. WILLIAMS, *supra* note 16, ¶¶ 16.01 n.21, 16.05 nn.60 & 67. With advances in the technical demands of anesthesia, the field has become specialized, and the anesthesiologist has become an important figure, medically responsible for the patient's well-being during an operation. Some jurisdictions' malpractice decisions have recognized this bifurcation of responsibility, *e.g.*, Thompson v. Lillehei, 273 F.2d 376 (8th Cir. 1959), while others have not, *e.g.*, Mazer v. Lipschutz, 327 F.2d 42 (3d Cir. 1963), *cert. denied*, 385 U.S. 833 (1966) (noting there can be only one "captain of the ship"). *See also* 1 D. LOUISELL & H. WILLIAMS, *supra* note 16, ¶ 16.06 & nn.87-88; Note, *Pennsylvania's Captain-of-the-Ship Doctrine: A Mid-Twentieth Century Anachronism*, 71 DICK. L. REV. 432 (1967).

between the anesthesiologist and the surgeon as follows: During induction and again during the immediate postoperative period, the anesthesiologist would be liable for fatal or debilitating arrests among patients in the age range and procedure categories specified; from the time of the initial incision until removal of the patient from the operating room, the anesthesiologist and the surgeon would each be liable for half the patient's damages cognizable under MAI.[90] If liability could not be coordinated because the surgeon was not covered by MAI, the usual rules of joint and several liability would presumably govern, leaving the surgeon with the entire residual burden if his negligence should be proved.

Compensability based on patient age and procedure is justified in part by the expectation shared by laymen and physicians alike that death or serious injury should not occur when the anesthesiologist and surgeon are dealing with a basically sound, young organ system and have discretion as to the timing of the procedure. Even though some young patients undergoing elective procedures present difficult problems for the anesthesiologist and surgeon and may suffer an arrest despite the best care, the seeming arbitrariness of providing compensation in such a case is not automatically a ground for rejecting the scheme but should rather be viewed as a price of achieving administrative feasibility. Selection of this method of categorization does not imply fault or avoidability but merely suggests that the quality of care is potentially improvable, and the malpractice problem reducible, by adopting this technique of making physicians responsible for the outcomes they in fact achieve without regard to how or why they occurred.[91] This is

---

90. It is understood that the operating room ritual is such that the relevant points in time are easily marked.

91. This general approach to problems in anesthesiology and surgery appears to be wholly consistent with the interests of the best elements in the medical profession in improving results, as illustrated by the SOSSUS undertakings in quality assessment. SOSSUS REPORT, *supra* note 42, at 191-93. The findings of the National Halothane Study, NAT'L ACADEMY OF SCIENCES, THE NATIONAL HALOTHANE STUDY ch. IV-2 (1969), of substantial divergence among thirty-four hospitals in the outcomes of anesthesia no doubt reflects even wider variations in experience among individual surgeons and anesthesiologists, and reveals the potential for MAI-induced improvement in the quality of outcomes. *See also* SOSSUS REPORT, *supra* note 42, at 190-91. The SOSSUS effort, as well as an ongoing study by the National Academy of Sciences, *see id.* at 189, may shed further light on the existing range of quality. Such studies may also yield useful findings on how to improve surgical results, but there is good reason to anticipate that implementation of such findings would be quicker and more universal with MAI than without it. For a preliminary report on the SOSSUS quality study, see *Study on Quality of Surgery is Unveiled*, MED. WORLD NEWS, Jan. 26, 1976, at 24 (forty-seven percent of adverse events and thirty-five percent of deaths were deemed preventable by surgeons reviewing the case).

not to say, however, that additional refinements could not be made in the definition of the compensable event.[92]

IV. MAI's Problems and Prospects

A. *Will Deterrence Really Work?*

The arguments offered for MAI's deterrence feature and the criteria recommended for designing a selective list of compensable events both assume that medical injuries are in fact deterrable by employing financial incentives. Nevertheless, some observers undoubtedly believe that this assumption would prove to be unwarranted or at least that the quality gains to be expected are so minimal as not to be worth the trouble.[93] Though the question is one which could only be an-

---

92. One further possibility would be to exclude from compensation patients who have undergone other major surgery within the previous year, a circumstance highly suggestive of a fragile or deteriorating physical condition. Also, certain surgical procedures, such as operations on the heart itself, present severe risks and might readily be excluded from MAI coverage.

93. Brook, Brutoco & Williams, *supra* note 6, might take this position judging from their stance on more general issues. Although proof of the effectiveness of MAI-type deterrence in medical care is impossible, but see note 94 *infra*, the field of industrial accidents and workmen's compensation might be consulted for clues. The analogy is a distant one, but there is some doubt that deterrence features in workmen's compensation have reduced accidents. Thus, James Chelius found injury rates *higher* in states with higher benefits. Chelius, *The Control of Industrial Accidents: Economic Theory and Empirical Evidence*, 38 LAW & CONTEMP. PROB. 700, 714-15 (1974). His results have been questioned, however. Oi, *On the Economics of Industrial Safety*, 38 LAW & CONTEMP. PROB. 669, 693-94 (1974). Moreover, it is not clear that the level of benefits correlates with the actual strength of incentives since insurer premium-setting practices may vary. More important, if wage rates adjust to changes in benefit (risk) levels, the expected incentive effect from higher benefits might be cancelled out. *Id.* at 692-93. Thus, the expectation of improved safety may be misplaced. Another study produced results

> consistent with the hypothesis that, across industries, work injury rates are inversely correlated with the cost to employers of injuries. In other words, employers do seem to be responsive in their safety efforts to the cost of injuries. It would therefore appear that, other things being equal, an injury tax would result in a reduction of the injury rate. Smith, *The Feasibility of an "Injury Tax" Approach to Occupational Safety*, 38 LAW & CONTEMP. PROB. 730, 741 (1974).

A further conclusion was that the injury tax "required to reduce these rates by even moderate amounts would have to be very large." *Id.* at 742.

These observations are very far from shedding light on MAI's likely deterrent effect. For one thing, employers face trade-offs between the cost of injuries and the costs of avoiding them and will respond to incentives only if there is a net benefit to them in doing so. Providers under MAI (other than HMOs) would usually have no such cost constraint operating on them, and would be free to respond to the incentive imposed. See notes 24 & 48 *supra*. Of course, incentives might have to be stronger if effective cost constraints existed, as they do in HMOs. *See* Havighurst & Tancredi 156-59, 91-94.

Another reason why industrial injury experience is a poor guide is the relatively

swered empirically with respect to each particular class of injuries, some further explication of MAI's deterrence feature should establish that it is worth serious attention.[94]

Although many untoward medical events are in fact unavoidable because of the limits of scientific knowledge, many other outcomes are not always the result of chance alone but might be avoided at least part of the time by the exercise of greater skill or precaution.[95] If the instances of unavoidable harm could not be readily excluded from compensation by application of a predetermined definition, classification of the suspect outcome as automatically compensable would still be appropriate, since some deterrence could be expected even though flawless provider performance would not eliminate all bad results. Moreover, even if a certain kind of event was technically unavoidable in every instance, its compensability by providers under MAI might still achieve several very useful objectives. First, it might generate more research to obtain the knowledge necessary to avert the unwanted outcome. Second, it might encourage greater circumspection about using the procedure which exposes the patient to the risk. And, third, it might stimulate greater efforts to minimize the adverse consequences once the unavoidable event occurs. It is not obvious, of course, whether the potential gains in these areas would be great enough to warrant incurring

---

minor importance of the matter to employers. Workmen's compensation insurance premiums average around one percent of wages, and safety is not central to the employer's overall business. On the other hand, a health care provider is likely to be highly conscious of MAI premiums and costs and of the outcomes which his patients experience.

94. The original MAI proposal developed a strong case for paying compensation in all cases of adverse reactions following blood transfusions, estimating that $133 million in damages for post-transfusion hepatitis was potentially avoidable under appropriate incentives. Havighurst & Tancredi 144-50, 154-55; 83-88, 90-91. *See generally* Calabresi & Bass, *Right Approach, Wrong Implications: A Critique of McKean on Products Liability*, 38 U. CHI. L. REV. 74, 83-86 (1970); Franklin, *Tort Liability and Hepatitis: An Analysis and a Proposal*, 24 STAN. L. REV. 439 (1972); Kessel, *Transfused Blood, Serum Hepatitis, and The Coase Theorem*, 17 J. LAW & ECON. 265 (1974). The argument for deterrence in this case is very strong, and clinicians should be able to think of other areas (or particular providers) where the potential quality gains are great enough to give MAI intuitive appeal. See also note 91 *supra* for further suggestive evidence.

95. On the distinction between avoidable and unavoidable events, see Gorovitz & MacIntyre, *Toward a Theory of Medical Fallibility*, HASTINGS CENTER REP. 13 (Dec. 1975). These authors, in their highly abstract but interesting article, do not address the difficulty of distinguishing avoidable and unavoidable injuries, the probable ineffectiveness and high costs associated with professional controls, or the possible value of incentives based on something more certain than the possibility of an authoritative finding of culpability or negligence. Oi, *supra* note 93, at 679, notes that many industrial accidents are not avoidable by employers; indeed contributory negligence is no defense to a workmen's compensation claim. MAI's categories will go as far as is practical in distinguishing avoidable from unavoidable events.

the administrative costs of shifting the loss. Nevertheless, the possibility of such benefits would have to be considered for a wide range of events. Moreover, the social desirability of spreading the loss from the injured patient to society as a whole might also point toward allowing compensation in a close case,[96] particularly since providers' costs for such unavoidable events would probably be distributed randomly enough that they could be readily passed on in fees.[97]

Accident avoidance induced by MAI's deterrence feature might frequently result from action taken by parties other than the provider primarily responsible for the care giving rise to the compensable event. Thus, where a particular compensable event occurs, peer-review mechanisms might be triggered to make a judgment on avoidability in the individual case for the purpose of determining whether the responsible provider should be advised, controlled, or disciplined in some way. Such peer oversight deterring future such events—and indeed preventive oversight not occasioned by a particular occurrence—could easily occur without any specific legal compulsion if some of the cost of each compensable occurrence were arranged to fall directly on a provider group which was equipped to take such action, such as a hospital medical staff.[98] Thus, even if an individual physician were too obtuse to

---

96. Havighurst & Tancredi 137-38, 78 (discussion of MAI's "social insurance" aspect, which is regarded as a by-product, not an affirmative goal).

97. But see note 106 *infra*.

98. Several recent proposals have suggested shifting more of the malpractice risk to the hospital as a means of providing (1) a broader base to support the compensation obligation through premiums, which are becoming a very large expense for physicians to bear individually, and (2) a focal point for quality assurance. Roddis & Stewart, *supra* note 52, at 1303; Steves, *supra* note 4, at 1324; VIRGINIA CORPORATION COMM'N—BUREAU OF INSURANCE, MEDICAL MALPRACTICE INSURANCE IN VIRGINIA: THE SCOPE AND SEVERITY OF THE PROBLEM AND ALTERNATIVE SOLUTIONS 79-93 (Nov. 1975). Unfortunately, such a shift might also benefit providers by improving opportunities for concealing and smoothing over situations which would otherwise generate valid claims and for presenting potential plaintiffs with a united front. Physician independence would be threatened by an increase in hospital responsibility. *See, e.g.*, Southwick, *The Hospital as an Institution—Expanding Responsibilities Change Its Relationship With the Staff Physician*, 9 CAL. W.L. REV. 429 (1973). An approach more in line with traditional hospital-doctor relations, which hospitals, insurers, or physicians could initiate with help from state insurance commissioners, would be for the medical staff of the hospital to be treated as an entity for insurance rating purposes.

MAI offers maximum flexibility in allocating responsibility between doctor and hospital. The initial question would be who is the "cheapest cost avoider"—to use Professor Guido Calabresi's phrase, G. CALABRESI, *supra* note 48, at 138—which means in this context only that the party in the best position to take actions to minimize costs should bear them. See notes 48, 63, 93 *supra*. However, the following discussion from the original proposal suggests that roughly the same preventive measures might be taken whichever party is selected to bear a particular risk:

We . . . would expect a risk to be assigned to one [party] or the other in accordance with a judgment about which provider was best able to organize to

respond to the financial incentive, or stood to profit enough to overlook it, other forms of deterrence would also be at work and might be felt in a strengthening of peer review in those institutions where it is now neglected.[99]

A frequently raised concern about introducing deterrence is that it might sometimes work perversely, making matters worse rather than better. This would occur if treatment decisions were biased inappropriately, perhaps leading the physician to choose a treatment mode which, though it was less likely to result in a compensable event, was

---

reduce or eliminate it. Thus, for example, post-operative staph infections would probably be [borne by the hospital] . . . , whereas the surgeon would likely bear the primary responsibility for, say, antibiotic reactions. Although this allocation of burdens will often seem arbitrary because responsibility is shared to a large degree [footnote: For example, staph infections may prove to be more resistant to preventive measures if hospital physicians have used antibiotics indiscreetly over time.], it may prove inconsequential from a quality point of view because the hospital and the medical staff relate in ways which enable them to work together to minimize adverse outcomes. Bargaining between them would surely be initiated whichever way the responsibility was initially assigned, and it is probable that the same preventive actions would be taken whichever party bore the initial loss . . . . It is an important insight that [liability] should create incentives not only for direct action, but also for initiating bargaining with others who are in a position to contribute to obtaining better outcomes. [footnote omitted] Thus, continuing to hold the surgeon responsible for the sponge count would make sense if one wished to see the surgeon remain in control of the operating room and thought that the surgical staff would be effective in persuading the hospital to hire better counters. Havighurst & Tancredi 139-40, 80.

The bargaining referred to is, of course, simply "desirable, quality-oriented interaction between hospitals and their medical staffs. The obstacles to such bargaining are not costs so much as jealousies, which might yield to financial pressures." *Id.* at 140 n.6, 80 n.6.

The foregoing analysis borrows directly from that of Ronald Coase, Coase, *The Problem of Social Cost*, 3 J. LAW & ECON. 1 (1960), and Guido Calabresi, CALABRESI, *supra* note 48, at 150-52, 161-73, to the effect that, *but for "transaction costs,"* assignment of liability to one party or the other would not affect the quality of outcomes. The striking insight is that "transaction costs" with respect to obtaining modifications in hospital-based care are not high and that therefore most of the same injury-preventing measures are likely to be taken whoever is held technically liable. While theoretically sound as far as it goes, this analysis leaves out the possible value of imposing potential risks on more than one actor so as to improve chances that incentives will in fact be acted on. Calabresi escapes this theoretical error by somewhat artificially including information costs in "transaction costs," thus assuming away the limits of any one actor's knowledge of and ability to balance risks and alternatives. *Id.* at 148-49. Particularly where liability insurance limits actual financial exposure and where individual providers might be either ignorant of hazards or willing to take small but unwarranted risks, risk-bearing by institutions as well as individuals, as can be readily arranged under MAI, may make especially good sense.

99. The alternative of mandating and regulating peer review efforts under PSRO or other oversight seems unreliable since going through the motions of peer review is not enough. See text accompanying notes 37-45 *supra*. Wherever it is possible, alignment of financial incentives to coincide more closely with professional obligations offers important advantages. See note 40 *supra*. *Cf.* Havighurst & Bovbjerg, *supra* note 38 (on the need for incentives to stimulate peer efforts at cost control).

not the treatment of choice under the circumstances.[100] The obvious solution to this problem would be to add the undesirable outcome, perhaps even nonrecovery from the condition itself, to the list of compensable events, but this would not always be feasible.[101] It is noteworthy, however, that an event which might be technically unavoidable could be justified as an addition to the list by the need to avoid biasing treatment and by the observation that the technically unavoidable result could be avoided by adopting a better mode of therapy.

Among the factors operating to prevent serious distortion of treatment decisions by MAI's incentives are professional and ethical obligations to provide all needed and appropriate care, traditional peer-review mechanisms, and the availability of malpractice remedies for patients who are given improper treatment.[102] Because the cost to the individual physician of a single compensable event would not be staggering and because the probability of its occurrence in a given case would be quite small, it seems unlikely that judgments would be significantly biased against performing professional obligations. Certainly, the distortions should be less than those introduced by the fault system, which faces the doctor with a personal near-catastrophe if he should ever be caught even slightly off base under the process-oriented rules.[103] While it is clear that incentives cannot be perfectly ordered, it does not seem unrealistic to expect that MAI could bring them more into line with professional responsibilities and quality-assurance goals.[104]

---

100. It is of course possible that in some circumstances the physician would prefer the treatment whose adverse outcome was covered under MAI, fearing the risk of a malpractice suit more.

101. Another way of minimizing the hazard would be to impose the costs on the hospital rather than the physician, relying on the latter to look out for the patients' interests. See note 98 *supra*.

102. Earlier discussion in text accompanying notes 37-45 *supra* does not hold these controls to be useless, only inadequate. MAI simply adds an additional control. Those who would rely totally on professional ethics and controls cannot deny their effectiveness in plugging unavoidable gaps in MAI incentives.

103. An example appeared at a recent seminar: If no other blood is available, should a nurse-anesthetist use twenty-two day old blood, *i.e.* blood which is one day past the expiration date on its label? The answer from the medical-legal experts was "no," but all agreed that under MAI it would be reasonable and good medicine to do so. N.C. Society of Anesthesiologists, Fall Seminar, Charlotte, N.C., Nov. 15, 1975.

104. No adverse outcome of surgery was omitted from the list of compensable events accompanying notes 71-85 *supra* out of fear that needed surgery would be discouraged by inclusion of such an outcome. Neither was any attempt made to guarantee compensation for the adverse consequences of not operating. Nevertheless, it is believed that treatment decisions would not be unduly biased. For one thing, a malpractice lawsuit could be filed for serious neglect of the surgical option. More important, there is strong evidence that surgeons' incentives are at present excessively weighted toward performing

A possibly worrisome example of the bias which MAI might introduce is the possibility that high-risk patients might be actively avoided by providers under an MAI system. Of course, abandonment of a patient is itself a tort[105] and would remain so with MAI. Further, wherever refusals to accept a high-risk patient might occur because the patient's predisposition was apparent prior to the initiation of treatment, it should be possible to define the compensable event in such a way as to exclude those patients who present such obviously increased risks. This course should not be adopted too quickly, however, because MAI could appropriately be designed to encourage the physician to consider the patient's predisposition as a factor in his decision to treat. Moreover, referral to another provider is available as an alternative means of escaping a difficult patient. Such referrals should probably be encouraged by the MAI system, since another provider may be more competent, more specialized, or better equipped to handle the problem. This would presumably be the case with referrals to a major medical center, and presumably the referral physician would be in a position to charge higher fees and therefore to face the greater risks which difficult cases may entail.[106]

Although it is difficult to be totally confident that MAI's deterrence feature would be finely tuned to achieving quality goals, there

---

surgery, without adequate regard for its high costs and attendant risks. *See* Bunker, *Surgical Manpower: A Comparison of Operations and Surgeons in the United States and in England and Wales*, 282 NEW ENG. J. MED. 135 (1970); Lewis, *Variations in the Incidence of Surgery*, 281 NEW ENG. J. MED. 881 (1969). Making surgery's adverse results compensable under MAI might succeed in restoring some balance to surgeons' decisions on the need for radical measures. Again, clinicians' judgments might suggest areas where further attention to these problems would be appropriate.

105. 1 D. LOUISELL & H. WILLIAMS, *supra* note 16, ¶ 8.02, at 192.

106. Irrespective of their competence, some providers are more likely than others to experience particular bad outcomes because of the nature of their practice or their clientele. High-risk physicians would include in particular those in teaching institutions who treat more difficult cases, many on referral from practitioners having less specialized skills and perhaps, under MAI, a justifiable apprehension of a compensable outcome. MAI should not be permitted to cause such high-risk physicians' net incomes to suffer to the point that people would be discouraged from accepting hard cases within their competence or from practicing in such settings.

The best answer to this possible problem is that such skilled physicians can, do, and should charge higher fees, thus not only passing the inherent risks on to the public but also usefully rationing, through higher prices, patients' access to physicians with superior skills. Because such physicians are all similarly situated, none would be at a competitive disadvantage unless he was experiencing a higher-than-normal incidence of claims for the category of patients treated. *See* Havighurst & Tancredi 151-52, 88-89. Although it is important to guard against unfairness in the treatment of providers, there does not appear to be essential unfairness here. Of course, governmental imposition of fee schedules could create unfairness if allowances were not made for differential exposure under MAI.

is nothing inherent in the idea which foredooms it to failure, and the flexibility of the MAI mechanism is such that most objections based on equity and efficiency considerations can seemingly be overcome, at least as a theoretical matter. What is needed for a preliminary assessment of MAI's practical effect is, first, active participation by willing clinicians in the specification of compensable events, and, second, a trial of their list in the real world. Although an experiment of reasonable scope and duration could probably not reliably reveal the effectiveness of MAI in improving the quality of care, it could probably be established that MAI would not do affirmative harm. If so, MAI might appropriately be established even though there was no final assurance of its capacity to improve the quality of care significantly. Since MAI is almost certain to be an improvement over the present system in other respects, any quality gains it might achieve in addition could be regarded as a bonus. The added costs of financing MAI in such a way as to preserve incentives would not be great enough to warrant sacrificing the deterrence element unless it had been conclusively shown to be ineffective.

B. *MAI's Ultimate Scope*

The value of MAI as a replacement for the fault system depends in large part on its coverage. Thus, it would probably have appeal for providers and policy makers only if a substantial proportion of the malpractice claims currently being filed against providers would be obviated or if the dollar costs of the fault system would be dramatically reduced. A judgment on this matter can be made only after a definitive list of compensable events is established and compared to a sample of claims.[107]

---

107. In an effort to appraise the extent to which an MAI scheme covering the events listed above would obviate malpractice claims, the claims file sampled in Rudov, Myers & Mirabella, *Medical Malpractice Insurance Claims Files Closed in 1970*, in MEDICAL MALPRACTICE REPORT Appendix 1, was consulted with the assistance of the Urban Research Center, University of Wisconsin (Milwaukee). Although the data available proved too unspecific as to injury and diagnosis to allow reliable matching of specific claims files against the list, it was estimated that sixty-one percent of the dollars paid out in 1970 on account of claims against anesthesiologists were paid in cases involving death or irreversible central nervous system damage to patients between one and fifty-nine years of age undergoing nonemergency surgery and therefore seemingly falling within one of the compensable categories established. Although these payouts disposed of only about twenty percent of the claims against anesthesiologists which actually resulted in some payment, many of the remaining claims and payments would undoubtedly be obviated by the additional category of compensable events encompassing dental and peripheral nerve injuries. Unfortunately, the lack of detailed information on diagnosis, treatment, and injury made it impossible to identify new categories of events whose addition to the list would obviate additional claims.

It is obvious that MAI development requires highly detailed and readily disaggre-

The appraisal of MAI's prospects must be done on a specialty-by-specialty basis since its feasibility is likely to be greater in some areas than in others. Thus, because of their definitive character and apparent avoidability, hospital accidents, surgical mishaps, adverse consequences of anesthesia, and poor results of orthopedic care lend themselves to delineation as compensable events; much the same reasons account for the heavy incidence of malpractice claims for these same injuries, which suggests in turn a reasonable prospect that MAI can alleviate the malpractice crisis in these hard-hit areas. On the other hand, the diagnostic errors in internal medicine are hard to assess without a full inquiry of the kind provided in the fault system. Thus, internal medicine, fraught with uncertainty and "judgment calls," would be less likely to benefit from MAI; for similar reasons, internists have been less beset by malpractice suits than have the other specialties.[108] It thus appears that MAI will work best in precisely those areas where it is most needed as a remedy for the malpractice situation.

Another question concerning MAI's scope and ability to solve the malpractice-suit problem is whether the list of compensable outcomes, in focusing on definitive, relatively avoidable events, will in fact avoid major administrative costs. To the extent that only the "easy" malpractice claims are eliminated, the cases involving high administrative costs may still remain in the fault system, and attempts to expand the list to cover more equivocal cases may generate litigation over the fuzzier boundary lines.

Until sophisticated clinicians turn an open mind to these issues, firm answers will not be forthcoming. Without careful evaluation of MAI on its own terms, clinicians' and others' opinions on MAI's feasibility may reflect only their uninformed reactions to the idea of deterrence and increased provider accountability.

C. Costs

Probably the main constraint on the growth of MAI to encompass nearly all malpractice claims is the potential overall cost of the system.

---

gatable data on malpractice claims, including fairly precise information on (1) diagnosis, including complications; (2) treatment; (3) injury, with specificity as to nature, seriousness, and damages paid, if any; (4) alleged negligence, so that claims which are not specific to the particular procedure (*e.g.*, failure to diagnose, failure to obtain informed consent, foreign bodies, abandonment, and falls) can be broken out; and (5) physician and patient characteristics. None of the data collection efforts to date has sought detailed medical information of the type needed to appraise, refine, and extend MAI's impact.

108. *Id.* at 15-16.

Any research effort would quickly focus on the incidence of each compensable event and on the total cost which MAI coverage of that event would entail. If the greater number of payments would more than absorb the savings from lower administrative costs and from smaller awards, MAI would appear to threaten to increase the cost of medical care, perhaps substantially. Of course, this is deceptive, since the costs are not new ones but are already being incurred under the present system even though they are to a large extent left where they fall—frequently on the injured patient. Also, the current incidence of the outcomes to be made compensable under MAI is a poor indicator of potential costs, since any strengthening of incentives for improved outcomes should reduce the incidence of bad results and improve the system's overall performance. Thus, acceptance of costs under MAI may avoid greater costs elsewhere and produce a true social saving.[109]

The original MAI proposal discussed the possibility of providing a limited subsidy to the MAI fund in order to keep the insurance premiums manageable, perhaps near zero for providers with good experience. Indeed, the desired incentive for good provider performance could, with a sufficient subsidy, just as appropriately take the form of a bonus for good results as a levy for bad experience. Subsidy possibilities should certainly be considered as a means of assuring that the premium cost would not force providers to bear collectively, even as a conduit, the entire financial burden of the many ills which MAI might cover.

The original MAI proposal also contemplated reimbursements by the MAI fund to collateral sources of payments for medical expenses and wage losses. This recommendation contrasts sharply with other proposals, which would reduce awards by the amount of such payments received, thus effecting major dollar savings.[110] From a social standpoint, of course, such savings are only apparent and not real, since costs

---

109. On the prospective dollar costs and health benefits of classifying hepatitis following blood transfusions as compensable, see Havighurst & Tancredi 154-55, 90-91.

110. *E.g.*, Moceri & Messina, *The Collateral Source Rule in Personal Injury Litigation*, 7 GONZAGA L. REV. 310 (1972); O'Connell, *No-Fault Insurance for Injuries Arising from Medical Treatment: A Proposal for Elective Coverage*, 24 EMORY L.J. 21, 35-36 (1975); Schwartz, *The Collateral-Source Rule*, 41 BOSTON U.L. REV. 348 (1961); Note, *Unreason in the Law of Damages: The Collateral Source Rule*, 77 HARV. L. REV. 741 (1964). Some observers have suggested that adoption of a national health insurance plan would go a long way toward solving the malpractice problem. *E.g.*, Annas, *Medical Malpractice Litigation Under National Health Insurance: Essential or Expendable?*, 1975 DUKE L.J. 1335. This would indeed obviate many suits and permit reduction of awards by the amount of covered expenses, but would simply hide the cost of poor medical results.

to the MAI system would be exactly offset by savings to health insurers and other collateral sources. This fact may well be lost sight of, however, in formulating both governmental policy and policies of private insurance.[111] Nevertheless, the principles of MAI almost certainly require that all the costs of covered injuries pass through its accounting mechanism in order that incentives reflecting the system's costs will not be distorted by the fortuitous presence or absence of collateral sources.

One way of offsetting the seemingly higher dollar costs of MAI would be by drawing some of the suggested subsidies for the MAI fund from the various collateral sources. These third-party payers for health care and reimbursers of lost wages would stand to benefit from MAI reimbursements to them as collateral sources, from the reduced incidence of defensive medicine under MAI,[112] and from the improvements induced by MAI in the quality of care generally. It would seem easy enough to offer MAI reimbursements only to those collateral sources which paid "dues" equal to, say, eighty percent of expected reimbursements. Larger subsidies could also be justified.

D. *Prospects*

The prospects for MAI are problematical. It is possible, though the facts are still not clear, that the scope of MAI would have to be quite broad in order for it to make a major contribution to solving the malpractice problem.[113] Such broad scope would in turn entail the substantial dollar costs of socializing the consequences of many injuries which are now borne privately, and it is quite possible that, to decision-makers in government and the health industry, these costs will not seem worth incurring as an added overt cost of health care even if they represent a much better bargain for the public.[114] Moreover, such deci-

---

111. *See* O'Connell, *No-Fault Liability by Contract for Doctors, Manufacturers, Retailers and Others*, 632 INS. L.J. 531, 532-33 (1975); O'Connell, *An Elective No-Fault Liability Statute*, 628 INS. L.J. 261, 264, 278 (1975).

112. MAI would encourage expenditures to improve outcomes but would obviate unproductive expenditures now allegedly incurred by physicians concerned about malpractice suits. See note 24 *supra* and text accompanying note 5 *supra*. PSROs may be able to impose some restraint on expenditures which were not cost-justified. See notes 14, 48, 93 *supra*.

113. For an opinion that MAI would be too narrowly conceived to solve much of the problem, see Note, *Comparative Approaches, supra* note 19, at 1153-54.

114. What is involved, of course, is a kind of compulsory insurance which, while far better than the present kind (which devotes most of the premiums to contesting claims on technically complex grounds unrelated to the fact of injury), would be somewhat more expensive because of the greatly expanded coverage. Health care costs are politically visible, and anything raising them is likely to be unpopular. Although MAI would only *appear* to be a new cost of health care, it would face difficulty if added expense were entailed. Courts imposing strict liability in tort face no such constraint but lack

sion-makers may fail to attribute any positive value to MAI's quality-assurance feature as a further benefit which might justify the appearance of higher costs, preferring instead the establishment of controls maintained by governmental or professional overseers or by a partnership thereof, such as the PSRO program. Narrowness of focus, a preference for incremental as opposed to drastic change, and commitment to political solutions are characteristic of the policy-making process, so that even a disaster like the law of medical malpractice is more likely, in the normal course of things, to be smoothed over than to be made the occasion for a new departure.

For the foregoing reasons, the MAI idea would probably have little chance even for serious study were it not for the appearance of another proposal for a no-fault compensation system which bids fair to displace the fault system, at least in part, without any legislative action at all. Because this proposal, for what is called "elective no-fault" insurance,[115] relies heavily on selective specification of compensable events in somewhat the same manner as MAI, it is likely to induce the same kinds of evaluation and research which are required to give MAI content and concreteness. Out of the public and private examination of the no-fault notion which the elective no-fault idea is certain to stimulate may emerge a set of realistic policy options which are different from those now apparent, and, in this new environment, MAI may turn out to have a future. A comparison of "elective no-fault" and MAI will set the stage for a concluding speculation on MAI's prospects.

V. A Comparison of MAI and "Elective No-Fault"

Professor Jeffrey O'Connell has proposed "elective no-fault" insurance as a means whereby providers of medical care can escape some of their current malpractice burdens by voluntarily granting their patients limited "no-fault" rights in exchange for the patients' surrender of their right to sue in tort over an outcome made compensable on a no-fault basis. According to O'Connell, the terms of this exchange might be either dictated by providers and made binding on patients under legislation which he has proposed[116] or accomplished without legislation by contracts entered into by providers with their patients.[117] The purpose, much as with MAI, would be to use funds which are now swallowed up in extravagant awards and the adjudication of fault issues

---

the capability to design an MAI scheme with any limits. *Id.* at 1157. *But cf.* Note, *Continuing the Common Law Response to the New Industrial State: The Extension of Enterprise Liability to Consumer Services,* 22 U.C.L.A.L. Rev. 401, 428 n.121 (1974).

115. See text accompanying notes 123 *et seq. infra.*
116. O'Connell, *An Elective No-Fault Liability Statute, supra* note 111.
117. O'Connell, *No-Fault Liability by Contract, supra* note 111.

to pay more claimants smaller amounts automatically.[118] Professor O'Connell's assumption is that there is enough money to be saved by removing the necessity for fault-finding, by reducing payouts to the extent of payments from collateral sources,[119] and by denying recovery for pain and suffering[120] to make such insurance an attractive alternative for both patients and providers,[121] particularly in view of the additional relief provided from the unpleasantness, uncertainty, and delay of malpractice lawsuits.

The elective no-fault model has great appeal. In inviting private transactions to bypass malpractice mechanisms,[122] it obviates the need for legislative reform and calls attention to the opportunity for achieving more far-reaching change than is likely to be wrought through legislatures responding to organized interest groups. The logic of private action to squeeze out the middlemen, primarily the lawyers, is powerful, and it is reasonable to expect that the potential gains will induce action on this front.

A. *Deterrence Under Elective No-Fault*

Although the O'Connell scheme may represent a modest beginning toward a kind of MAI, it is not explicit on the matter of incen-

---

118. O'Connell, *supra* note 110, at 35. The premise is the same as under automobile no-fault—namely that no more and probably less cost will be experienced than under the fault system.

119. *Id.* See notes 110-11 *supra* and accompanying text.

120. *Id.* at 34-35. *See* Havighurst & Tancredi 128-29, 72 (proposing limited pain and suffering awards).

121. It is possible that O'Connell exaggerates the cost savings which his system would yield: (1) Patients with steady or higher incomes would be more likely to have protection from collateral sources, which would reduce their entitlements under the no-fault plan; they would therefore refuse the option tendered, preserving the hazard of large awards based on wage loss. (2) The no-fault policy is more likely to cover outcomes reflecting obvious and easily provable negligence than to cover more questionable outcomes, see note 130 *infra*, which are precisely the ones which occasion most of the major administrative expenses which O'Connell hopes to save. (3) A trade-off clearly exists between the liberality of the no-fault scheme and prospective claimants' propensity to litigate to escape its coverage and qualify for a tort remedy; O'Connell's scheme, by allowing only actual out-of-pocket losses, would induce many skirmishes at the borderlines, unless compensable events were very sharply defined. Of course, a more liberal plan might increase insurer and provider resistance to payment, but this could be dealt with by requiring the insurer to bear the successful claimant's costs of litigating coverage questions. *See* Havighurst & Tancredi 132, 74.

122. Dean Richard Rosett of the University of Chicago Graduate School of Business supports a variant of the O'Connell plan, suggesting that a physician might offer his patients a choice between the present system and a no-fault alternative at a higher or lower price. Rosett, The Medical Malpractice Insurance Crisis, Medical Malpractice Crisis Conference (U. of Md. Law School, Nov. 21-22, 1975). The implied belief that doctors would actively seek to accommodate their patients seems unduly optimistic for reasons stated in notes 127 & 130 *infra*.

tives,[123] and the insurance contemplated might well not feature the experience rating or cost-sharing arrangements contemplated in the MAI model. Conceivably, insurers would find it in their interest to adopt experience rating or to include provider cost-sharing provisions in their policies, but this cannot be counted upon in a heavily regulated, indifferently competitive market.[124] Although providers with better experience might press for price concessions, the organized medical interests which would be engaged in developing the no-fault policy[125] would strongly prefer that costs be shared in a way facilitating their automatic pass-through to patients. Moreover, it is not likely that patients, in contracting privately, would attach particular value to designing an insurance arrangement which preserves providers' quality-inducing incentives.[126] Finally, if the insurance was designed without specific attention to the avoidability of the covered injuries, incentive pricing of it would seem more unreasonable than under MAI.

For the foregoing reasons, introduction of elective no-fault could easily cost society its only opportunity for designing a deterrence feature into the new system for compensating for medical injuries. This result is not inevitable, however, and insurance regulation could well stimulate attention to the design and pricing of elective no-fault insurance which would achieve many of the goals of MAI.

B. *Compensable Events Under Elective No-Fault*

Although the O'Connell plan involves specifying compensable events in much the same manner as MAI, the list of medical outcomes compensable under it would be shorter than under an MAI scheme developed by administrative means pursuant to a statutory mandate. Providers responding to O'Connell's call would have no reason voluntarily

---

123. Professor O'Connell himself has attached no importance to this aspect, though he would probably not oppose the introduction of an incentive feature. His view of the malpractice problem is similar to his view of automobile no-fault, however, where incentives seemed much less likely to work. For a guide to O'Connell's general orientation, see J. O'CONNELL & R. HENDERSON, TORT LAW, NO-FAULT AND BEYOND (1975), which devotes only limited coverage to deterrence possibilities. *E.g., id.* at 624-28.

124. See text accompanying notes 51-55 *supra*.

125. See note 127 *infra*.

126. Although patients might be well advised to insist that incentive features be preserved, their ignorance and traditional trust of physicians would probably result in their acceptance of the insurance protection offered without regard to how it was financed and what it did to provider incentives. In these circumstances it would not be incorrect to characterize quality assurance as an external benefit potentially flowing from the MAI model—that is, as a public good which the contracting private parties themselves have no incentive or opportunity to realize in structuring a program of no-fault benefits to replace fault-based liability, thereby destroying whatever deterrence value the latter may have.

to purchase coverage for avoidable outcomes which, though unfavorable from the patient's point of view, become the subject of malpractice claims in only a small percentage of cases—possibly because any negligence contributing to them is difficult to discover or to prove.[127] Thus, elective no-fault, having its baseline in the existing system and being designed by providers primarily for their own benefit, would be viable only to the extent that physicians perceived a benefit to themselves, in terms of cost and avoidance of unpleasantness, in establishing compensable categories.

Although Professor O'Connell has yet to be specific about the coverage contemplated, he has observed the necessity for broadening the class of compensable events somewhat beyond those readily covered in the fault system in order that some mutuality of benefit between patients and doctors appear when the inevitable legal questions are raised concerning either the constitutionality of any legislation[128] or the enforceability of the contracts employed.[129] It is indeed probable that patients must appear to receive a reasonable *quid pro quo* if legal challenges to elective no-fault are to be resisted, but provider dictation of the terms of an exchange would still produce a greater reduction in patients' malpractice rights and a smaller expansion of their no-fault rights than would a bargaining process in which consumers participated with equal bargaining power and capacity.[130]

---

127. Professor O'Connell contemplates that providers and insurers will jointly design the insurance coverage. Although at some points, *e.g.*, O'Connell, *No-Fault Liability by Contract, supra* note 111, at 532-33; O'Connell, *An Elective No-Fault Liability Statute, supra* note 111, at 264-66, 270-71, he appears to suggest that individual providers could design the coverage they wished to offer (suggesting that competition among providers to offer consumers the most attractive combinations of rights might ensue), this is manifestly impossible given the exigencies of insurance, which require uniform contracts and large groups for rating purposes. The more likely scenario, which O'Connell probably also visualizes, is the development of uniform insurance contracts by specialty societies, to be offered to patients on a take-it-or-leave-it basis. The probability that such contracts of adhesion will be employed is strengthened by the understandable reluctance of providers to haggle with patients over matters raising the spectre of untoward events which might occur in the process of treatment.

128. J. O'CONNELL, ENDING INSULT TO INJURY 204-31 (1975); O'Connell, *An Elective No-Fault Liability Statute, supra* note 111, at 262-63.

129. O'Connell, *No-Fault Liability by Contract, supra* note 111, at 540-42; O'Connell, *An Elective No-Fault Liability Statute, supra* note 111, at 204-31.

130. Possible additions to the list of compensable events fall into three categories: (1) those additions which would benefit doctors and hurt patients (*e.g.*, an outcome now readily discovered and almost automatically compensable with an allowance for pain and suffering, which under MAI would be compensated at a lower rate without significant administrative savings); (2) those additions which would benefit both doctor and patient (*e.g.*, an outcome now occasioning enough administrative costs that all events could be compensated at a cost hardly greater than the old system entailed); and (3) those additions which would benefit patients only (*e.g.*, an outcome previously com-

Legal doctrines designed to prevent unconscionable contracts, while perhaps effective in preventing provider overreaching which makes consumers worse off than they are at present, are unlikely to help patients receive all of the benefits to which they might be deemed entitled. Two serious issues with "elective no-fault" thus emerge: (1) whether the fault system should be displaced only to the extent that it suits providers to displace it and (2) whether the possibly substantial benefits to be derived from partially displacing the fault system should accrue only to providers or should be allocated more equitably between providers and patients.

C. *How MAI Legislation Could Improve Upon Elective No-Fault*

The problems with elective no-fault could be overcome by legislation doing more than simply authorizing providers to adopt, and either offer to or impose on patients, a no-fault plan of their own devising. Such legislation would be more than a simple enabling act blessing private no-fault arrangements, and would establish many of the plan's details while leaving delineation of compensable events to an administrative mechanism. Of course, this administrative process might yield results no different than those under provider-designed elective no-fault if the mechanism were itself dominated by providers, but specific provision would undoubtedly be made for obtaining knowledgeable representation of consumer interests.[131] An exchange of malpractice and no-fault rights between providers and patients would be more likely to produce an equitable outcome if it took place through a political bargaining process than if its terms were dictated by providers.[132] Also,

---

pensated so rarely that significantly increased costs would result under elective no-fault). Physicians would undoubtedly be glad to accept no-fault liability for items in categories (1) and (2) but would not add items in category (3) unless they were convinced it was necessary to do so to overcome legal challenges. See text accompanying notes 128-29 *supra*. Whether they would actually be harmed by further additions is not clear since patients might willingly pay higher fees for the increased protection. Nevertheless, there are many reasons—fee schedules inhibiting fee increases, the risk of government displeasure, reluctance to enter the business of selling a kind of insurance and explaining the hazards it protects against, and so forth—why providers would seek to avoid incurring increased costs and would offer only no-fault coverage designed for their own benefit. Medical traditions being what they are—seriously anticompetitive—, competition would be unlikely to stimulate a range of choice even if the exigencies of the insurance business did not largely preclude experimentation and product differentiation. Instead, organized professional groups, in designing the coverage, will take account of their members' interests alone.

131. The original MAI proposal seemed to promise more professional influence in delineating compensable events than now seems appropriate. *See* Havighurst & Tancredi 163-64, 97.

132. See note 130 *supra*.

the prospects for subsequently expanding the list to achieve new quality-assurance objectives would be substantially enhanced.

Reliance on the administrative process to develop the MAI option would also allow careful attention to all the problems of introducing appropriate incentive features. A statutory mandate to pursue deterrence would stimulate the needed attention to this aspect of the no-fault concept, but if the agency found, on the basis of controlled studies and other evidence, that the deterrence goal was chimerical, it could lay that aspect to rest and still maintain a no-fault scheme for the sake of its value as a less costly alternative to the fault system. Moreover, with the proper mandate, the agency could also elect to pursue quality objectives by administrative means, perhaps by flagging compensable outcomes for peer investigation to detect specific quality failures warranting remedial action. It thus seems clear that the no-fault model could be established legislatively without positive evidence that MAI's incentive feature would improve the quality of care at a reasonable cost. All that is required is a legislative mandate to an administrative agency to develop and make available a no-fault option, to design into the scheme such incentive features as it found workable, and to adopt other quality-assurance mechanisms where deterrence features proved either wholly unworkable or inadequate in and of themselves to achieve quality goals.

Although MAI should certainly have an elective feature of its own,[133] it should not, in contrast to the O'Connell proposal, be neutral

---

133. Presumably providers would opt in or out, and their decisions would bind their patients. This is the approach of the Kennedy-Inouye bill, S. 215, 94th Cong., 1st Sess. (1975), and it would allow consumers to express their preferences through their choice of provider rather than in negotiations, as Dean Rosett contemplates. See note 122 *supra*.

If an MAI plan with reliable quality-assurance incentives were ultimately adopted, certain special inducements for provider participation, in addition to curtailment of their exposure to fault-based liability, might be deemed appropriate. For example, the following measures beneficial to providers participating under MAI might be helpful not only as a stimulus to MAI participation but also as steps in the direction of a policy of primary reliance on outcomes measures of quality rather than on expensive process controls and restrictive input specifications: (1) A provider electing MAI could be given some relief from licensure restrictions on the use of nonphysician manpower. *See* U.S. DEP'T OF HEALTH, EDUCATION AND WELFARE, DEVELOPMENTS IN HEALTH MANPOWER LICENSURE 47-49 (DHEW Pub. No. (HRA) 74-3101) (June 1973); U.S. DEP'T OF HEALTH, EDUCATION & WELFARE, REPORT ON LICENSURE AND RELATED HEALTH PERSONNEL CREDENTIALING 65-70 (DHEW Pub. No. (HSM) 72-11) (June 1971). (2) Physician relicensure and continuing education requirements might be applied only to nonparticipants in MAI. *But cf.* S. 215, 94th Cong., 1st Sess. (1975) (looks the other way, imposing such requirements only on participants in a no-fault scheme lacking quality-assurance incentive). (3) Physicians and hospitals subscribing to MAI could be ex-on quality issues, and, if at all possible, it should represent, in contrast to the Kennedy-Inouye bill, a new departure in quality assurance away from costly and unproven governmental controls. Its coverage and attractiveness to providers should not be governed solely by the scope and severity of the malpractice threat as perceived by individual providers but should instead be dictated in substantial part by affirmative quality concerns and attention to patients' interests. The fault system's defects should not be allowed to infect MAI—to rule it "from the grave," as it were[134]—or to limit its ability to perform a reasonably comprehensive quality-assurance function in areas entrusted to its care.

Despite the foregoing reservations about elective no-fault, which suggest that it would fall short of achieving all that the original MAI proposal held possible, the O'Connell proposal has great force as well as the great advantages of being non-legislative and somewhat incremental in its impact and of bypassing numerous obstacles to adoption of the no-fault concept. Although its widespread adoption might foreclose later attempts to reintroduce incentive features, for the immediate future the tasks involved in developing the O'Connell plan—namely delineating compensable events and testing their impact on malpractice claims and costs—are very much in keeping with advancing the MAI proposal. There is every reason to believe that elective no-fault will be attractive enough to stimulate prompt investment in such research and that some study of MAI will be included in that effort. The outcome should be a much more solid basis for considering the merits of both proposals.

---

empted in whole or in part from quality regulation by PSROs, and health maintenance organizations under MAI could be relieved of PSRO oversight. *See* Havighurst & Bovbjerg, *supra* note 38; Bovbjerg, *supra* note 16. But see notes 48 & 93 *supra*. (4) Hospitals under MAI could be allowed to qualify automatically (or at least more easily) for state licensure, participation under Medicare, and JCAH accreditation. (5) MAI participation could be made more attractive by not cutting back too arbitrarily on plaintiffs' rights under traditional principles.

MAI might prove popular with providers for other reasons besides the foregoing special inducements. Because MAI might be designed, as in the original model, Havighurst & Tancredi 139-40, 79-80, to shift to the hospital certain risks normally borne by the physician, he would escape these risks altogether by participating; by the same token, his exposure as a joint tort feasor would be increased if other participants' liability was limited under MAI and his was not. Moreover, a subsidy to the MAI fund, see text at 109 *supra*, could improve the comparative cost picture substantially. Finally, if the program was properly designed, patients would probably be attracted to it since it would improve their protection overall, and doctors would therefore have some incentive to offer it as an accommodation to their patients.

134. *See* Blum & Kalven, *Ceilings, Costs, and Compulsion in Auto Compensation Legislation,* 1973 UTAH L. REV. 341, 376.

VI. THE RELEVANCE OF SWEDEN'S PATIENT-INJURY COMPENSATION SYSTEM

The Swedish Federation of County Councils has recently procured private insurance for the benefit of patients injured in the course of receiving medical treatment.[135] It is useful to assess the relevance of the Swedish plan and the experience under it to further development of the MAI concept. Despite apparent differences, an examination of the Swedish experience can indeed contribute to an informal assessment of MAI.

The Swedes' ostensible purpose in adopting patient injury insurance (PII) was to provide another link in Sweden's network of social insurance. Concern had been expressed from time to time that compensation could be obtained by injured patients only if they could establish the equivalent of professional malpractice or negligence, which was difficult to do.[136] For this reason, a need for a no-fault compensation scheme was felt to exist. The origins of PII are thus in striking contrast with current U.S. interest in a comparable scheme, which springs from too many recoveries (of too much money) rather than too few and from a primary concern for physicians', rather than patients', interests.[137]

Because of the different purposes underlying the Swedish PII program and MAI, some differences in coverage would be expected. Nevertheless, PII has stopped short of covering many things which would seem reasonable candidates for compensation if avoidance of patient hardship were the only relevant consideration. Some of the lines drawn appear to reflect a vestigial notion of provider fault or avoidability which is difficult to account for under the policy objective professed. In general, what appears is not a dedication to avoidance of patient hardship so much as a belief that reasonable patient expectations should be given recognition in this way. One example is postoperative infections. These were originally excluded from PII coverage, but now infections following "clean" surgery are compensable. Clearly the decision to make a distinction based on cleanliness reflects a belief that avoidability of the

---

135. *See* Cooper, *Sweden's No-Fault Patient-Injury Insurance*, 294 N. ENG. J. MED. 1268 (1976). The present author, with the benefit of a World Health Organization summer fellowship, conducted interviews on the insurance scheme in Stockholm in June 1976. Information on coverage was supplied by Carl Oldertz of the Skandia insurance group.

136. *See* Jonsson & Neuhauser, *Medical Malpractice in Sweden*, 294 N. ENG. J. MED. 1276 (1976). Courts defer to the judgments of the Medical Responsibility Board operated by the National Board of Health and Welfare. Receiving complaints directly and by referral from the courts in private litigation, this Board finds actionable negligence only rarely. *Id.*

137. This is not to say that provider interests were irrelevant in the Swedish decision, however. Provider support was easily obtained, in part because of the prospect of relief from claims and complaints before the Medical Responsibility Board. *See* note 136 *supra*. It should be noted that PII does not displace the patient's legal right to sue for the equivalent of malpractice, though it is not clear what additional damages he might win.

harm by good practice is a relevant consideration, which clearly it would not be if compensation were the only goal. The explanation must lie in some underlying sense of responsibility for the quality of care felt by the county councils, which have voluntarily provided this insurance and are generally responsible for the provision of all care in the Swedish system. Because it springs from a general obligation to provide quality medical care, the coverage of PII may indeed be a good guide to developing MAI coverage. For example, the line drawn on postoperative infections would appear to be the correct one for MAI purposes, though greater specificity might be warranted.[138]

PII also pays for some misdiagnosis, but employs a negligence standard to limit responsibility. Failure to read symptoms correctly is explicitly made a basis for compensation, but requires a finding not merely of error but of departure from "generally accepted medical practice."[139] Similarly, adverse drug reactions are compensable under PII only if the prescription was unwarranted or the manufacturer's instructions were not followed. Injuries attributable to defects in equipment were not compensable under the original plan, but coverage in this area was recently expanded because of recognition that equipment failures are most often the result of actions taken or not taken in the hospital and that subrogation provides adequate recourse against manufacturers.[140]

In general, it appears that the county councils' perceived responsibility for the quality of care has been the chief influence in determining PII's inclusiveness. The county councils' statement of the general principle by which claims are evaluated under PII[141] indicates that compensation for an injury incurred in treatment is to be allowed whenever, if there had been perfect foreknowledge of the patient's condition, the treatment or procedure would have been different or differently performed. The idea is to distinguish those harms reflecting inherent treatment risk from those harms which are not truly inevitable. This is a high standard; but it is a fault-related standard, implying a responsibility to deliver good results as well as a desire not to disappoint reasonable patient expectations. Consistent with its fundamental principles, MAI could adopt such a standard, but it is not necessary that it go so far. In

---

138. The PII insurers have developed a more detailed statement of the coverage of infections, but it is not yet available in English.

139. Omission of a diagnostic test cannot be the basis for a PII claim, but it is anticipated that malpractice claims can be brought where the omission is unwarranted.

140. For further discussion of the subrogation question, see Havighurst & Tancredi 141, 81.

141. Landstingsförbundet, Patient Insurance (undated mimeo on file at the offices of the Duke Law Journal).

any event, the guidelines which are being developed for claims reviewers under PII would surely prove useful in developing MAI.

As one would expect in a socialized system, PII premiums are paid by the county councils and not by the individual providers. Much American interest in PII has focused on the potential use of claims experience for the purpose of improving the quality of care by investigating indications of substandard performance which might be corrected. Because PII is administered by a private insurance group, the claims data are not automatically available to government agencies. Moreover, the insurer is reluctant to share such information because of an anticipated adverse effect on provider cooperation both in advising patients of their claims and in supplying the information needed to evaluate claims. Nevertheless, the county councils, as the purchasers of the insurance and the ultimate providers of care in the socialized system, have both the means and the incentive to obtain this information from the insurer and use it for quality-assurance purposes. Although any quality-assurance benefits which may flow from PII would be largely incidental, the Swedish PII scheme is impressive as a demonstration of the responsibilities which one well-motivated set of providers—the county councils—were willing to accept for the outcomes of the care delivered.

Conclusion

If present legislative endeavors do not reduce the malpractice-suit problem to manageable proportions, pressure for a no-fault compensation system for medical accidents will continue to grow.[143] The cost of compensating patients for all iatrogenic injuries could well be prohibitive, however, even if it were limited to reimbursing only out-of-pocket costs, if national health insurance absorbed most of the medical expenses, and if the administrative costs about which Professor Keeton has warned were reduced by a substantial deductible. There might therefore be a strong temptation to adopt no-fault insurance on a more selective basis, using the technique, employed under both MAI and Professor O'Connell's elective no-fault scheme, of specifying a limited set of compensable events in advance. Once the principle of selectivity was adopted, it seems probable that emphasis would be placed on providing compensation in those categories of cases which are most likely to generate malpractice claims—that is, those in which the regrettable

---

142. Dr. Cooper's finding was that no such use of claims experience had been made, Cooper, *supra* note 135, at 1270, and government officials seemed to have little expectation that much could be expected in this line in the future.

143. *E.g.*, REPORT OF THE SPECIAL ADVISORY PANEL ON MEDICAL MALPRACTICE, STATE OF NEW YORK 53-63 (1976).

outcome is most frequently avoidable. Because the impetus for the entire effort would be to substitute no-fault rights for common-law rights, the list of compensable events would surely appear to the layman to represent a catalog of the system's failures, and it is at least questionable whether the public would be willing to pick up such an itemized bill. In these circumstances, it seems likely that pressure would emerge for preserving some accountability for these costs on the part of those providers whose patients suffer the compensable adverse results. This scenario of course calls for MAI then to enter in shining armor, to slay the malpractice dragon, and to establish in the land a regime based on reason, provider accountability, and compassion for the victims of medical accidents.

Properly understood, MAI is not a radical measure, and it does indeed hold out a hope for avoiding much contentiousness and cost, which are currently by-products of malpractice litigation and which would also attend an effective regulatory scheme designed to make providers accountable by regulatory means and to alter the behavior of a significant number of them in material respects. In these circumstances, it is reasonable to expect the health care system to devote some resources and thoughtful consideration to converting MAI's promising theory into practical reality.[144] Only a limited amount of study would be necessary to qualify MAI for adoption by a forward-looking state legislature, with a direction to an administrative agency to establish the scheme in such a way as to seek a major reduction of both malpractice claims and, through deterrence, medical injuries.

---

144. The American Bar Association's Commission on Medical Professional Liability has recently declared that the MAI concept "has merit" and is seeking funds to launch a major investigation preparatory to a pilot study. ABA Commission on Medical Professional Liability, Interim Report to the House of Delegates, June 26, 1976, at 29. The Commission gave the following reasons for its interest in MAI:
   (a) It retains, in a modified way, the accountability notions of tort law. The lead criterion for determining compensability is "avoidability" of the particular type of incident.
   (b) The designated compensable event format offers a conceptually sound "middle ground" between retaining negligence as the basis for compensation and compensating all those who are medically injured. It retains a general relationship between culpability and compensation, while not requiring a costly case-by-case determination of negligence.
   (c) Designated compensable event [the Commission's name for an MAI-type program] is a flexible tool. It permits a modest start on the enumeration of compensable incidents and the periodic expansion and updating of any such list. Such an incremental approach permits program costs to be taken into account in deciding whether to expand the number of covered incidents. Furthermore, compensability can be worked out differently for different health care provider-patient groups, thus permitting variations from region to region and institution to institution with differing lists of compensable incidents and differing levels of compensation.
   (d) Designated compensable event offers the possibility of creating links between quality of care efforts, malpractice prevention and compensation. By designating compensable events, and by relating those events to general quality of care efforts (particularly in the hospital setting), a strong impetus can be given to prevention efforts. *Id.* at 30.

THE INSURANCE OF MEDICAL LOSSES

RICHARD S. L. RODDIS* AND RICHARD E. STEWART**

We are educated by the American creed of accomplishment to believe that every problem, however defined, is susceptible to solution through the application of reasoned effort. Difficult problems simply are those which demand greater measures of reasoned effort to achieve solution. As a corollary, it is supposed that difficulty and complexity are the same, so that a difficult problem must be a complex problem.

Resignation to unsatisfying states of affairs is not a prized trait in the American character. Hence, when a difficult problem proves intractable despite the earnest expenditure of enough reasoned effort to overcome complexity, an almost automatic response is to proceed to expose villains, whose dishonesty, stupidity, or greed have subverted reasoned effort.

DEFINING THE PROBLEM

The medical malpractice insurance problem has captured the attention of the body politic.[1] It is analyzed in the daily newspapers. It is the subject of extended conferences and studies by a great array of

---

* Dean and Professor of Law, University of Washington Law School; Insurance Commissioner, State of California, 1966-68; Member of the California Bar; Director, Unigard Mutual Insurance Company.

** Senior Vice President, Director and Chief Financial Officer, Chubb & Son Inc.; Superintendent of Insurance, State of New York, 1967-70; Member of the New York Bar.

The authors are indebted for their able and generous assistance to Warren P. Cooper, Vice President and Actuary of Chubb & Son Inc. at the time this article was written and now Vice President and Actuary of INA Corp., and to John K. Cowperthwaite, Jr., Assistant Vice President of Chubb & Son Inc. in charge of underwriting professional liability insurance.

THE FOLLOWING CITATION WILL BE USED IN THIS ARTICLE:

U.S. DEP'T OF HEALTH, EDUCATION AND WELFARE, REPORT OF THE SECRETARY'S COMMISSION ON MEDICAL MALPRACTICE (1973) [hereinafter cited as MEDICAL MALPRACTICE REPORT].

1. *See* STAFF OF HOUSE COMM. ON INTERSTATE AND FOREIGN COMMERCE, 94TH CONG., 1ST SESS., AN OVERVIEW OF MEDICAL MALPRACTICE (Comm. Print 1975). For a discussion of state legislative efforts to deal with the problem, see Comment, *An Analysis of State Legislative Responses to the Medical Malpractice Crisis*, 1975 DUKE L.J. 1417.

experts.[2] Various legislatures either have held, or are planning, special sessions to deal only with it.[3] In pursuit of a solution, there is no want of reasoned effort. Yet it remains a difficult problem of baffling complexity and the search for villains is intense. The fact of the matter is that the medical malpractice insurance problem is not particularly complex and villainy plays only a minor role in it. That does not mean, however, that it is not an intractable problem—at least if its solution takes the form in which any of the organized, involved groups cast it.

The Medical Loss Question Generally

Although this Article will concentrate on medical malpractice in its insurance aspect, that aspect, unavoidably parochial, is no place to begin. We will understand the insurance aspect better if we look first at the broader subject, of which insurance is a part. The subject is the totality of legal and business arrangements provided by society for allocating the financial burden of the losses occurring in the administration of health care. For our purposes, a medical loss occurs whenever a person submits to diagnosis, advice, or treatment (including nontreatment) from one or more professional or institutional providers of health care and winds up being in worse condition than if measures of diagnosis, advice, or treatment other than the ones pursued had been administered.

This definition of loss is very broad, being cast solely in terms of health care causation. It says nothing about whether the loss was culpably caused or about its economic valuation. Loss, so defined, is not the same as legal liability for damages and is not the loss with which the providers' insurers are concerned. All conceptions of loss which go beyond this rudimentary definition are to a greater or lesser extent a product of decisions made in the processes of the legal and business arrangements created by society for determining how the financial impacts of the original loss shall be allocated.

It is important to think of the loss valuation, allocation, and distribution arrangements prescribed by the society as a total and interrelated system.[4] There is always a loss allocation system, even in a hypothetical society which makes no provision, formal or informal, for shifting or

---

2. *See, e.g.*, HOUSE SUBCOMM. ON HEALTH AND ENVIRONMENT OF THE COMMITTEE ON INTERSTATE AND FOREIGN COMMERCE, NATIONAL CONFERENCE ON MEDICAL MALPRACTICE (Subcomm. Print 1975).

3. N.Y. Times, Aug. 13, 1975, at 53, col. 3; *id.* July 1, 1975, at 32, col. 1.

4. *See generally* G. CALABRESI, THE COSTS OF ACCIDENTS: A LEGAL AND ECONOMIC ANALYSIS (1970).

distributing the burden of loss. In such a society, all loss is allocated by default so as to stay with the person (and his dependents) upon whom it first fell. Any legal system, by substantive and procedural rules and by the actual operation of its processes, merely functions to value and allocate the financial burden of medical loss differently. Similarly, the array of insurance and the other private and governmental financial arrangements merely functions further to reallocate and distribute the financial consequences of loss. All of the components of the system interact in ways which progressively alter the economic meaning of loss, fragmenting, shifting, and dispersing the impact of the loss in a myriad of directions.

This can be illustrated by an example. A patient, whose condition has been worsened in the sense we originally postulated as a medical loss, asserts a claim against his physician contending that the physician performed with less than the appropriate level of competence. Because of his worsened condition, the patient incurred $5,000 of additional medical expenses and lost $5,000 of income which he otherwise would have earned. He also experienced pain and inconvenience which, after consultation with his lawyer, he decided was worth $20,000. In some other cultures, pain and inconvenience would not be treated as economically cognizable loss, but our society adheres to the notion that these psychic detriments are susceptible to economic valuation for compensation purposes.[5]

The additional medical expense has been paid by the patient's experience-rated, employer-provided group medical plan and $2,000 of the lost earnings has been reimbursed under a disability income policy individually purchased by the patient. Eventually, a trial results in a judgment for the plaintiff in the amount of $15,000. Of this amount, $7,500 goes to recompense the plaintiff's lawyer, who handled the case on a contingent fee basis, and to pay other expenses of prosecuting the claim. Another $2,500 goes to the group health plan in agreed satisfaction of its contractual subrogation claim. In addition to paying the judgment, the physician's malpractice insurer has expended $5,000 in defense of the claim.

The amounts expended by the malpractice insurer eventually are reflected as a component of the future rates paid by the physician and others in his rate class. To the extent the insurer's rates are inadequate, the cost is borne indirectly by shareholders or other classes of policyholders. Since the physician considers his insurance costs in determining the appropriate level of his fees, those costs are passed on to his

---

5. *See* C. McCormick, Handbook on the Law of Damages § 88 (1935).

patient population in substantial part, though perhaps subject to some adjustment lag. To the extent that they are not passed on as fee increases, they are borne partly by the physician as a reduction in net income and partly by other income taxpayers generally since the insurance premiums are a deductible business expense.[6] To the extent malpractice insurance premiums are passed on as a component of patient fees, the greater part winds up being paid by the various private and governmental health care expense reimbursement systems covering the patient population.[7] The net amounts paid by the group health plan are absorbed into future rates charged to the employer by the plan and eventually reflected in the prices paid by the public for the employer's products. Viewed as a labor cost, the costs of the plan are borne by employees as a substitute for what might have been negotiated as higher wages.[8] The amount paid by the disability insurance carrier is reflected in its future rates and distributed over its insured population.

There are two points to all of this. First, "loss" appears in several perspectives and forms. The patient thought his loss was $30,000, but if we assume that the jury thought it was compensating him initially for out-of-pocket costs and then for pain and suffering, his loss has been valued at $15,000. Of course, the jury may also have discounted the amount of damages because of uncertainty on the liability issue,[9] just as other juries may magnify the pain and suffering award in cases where they view the physician's conduct as morally, rather than merely technically, culpable.[10] And the jury may have been consciously attempting to shift a portion of the patient's presumed legal expenses.[11] In any

---

6. INT. REV. CODE OF 1954, § 162(a).
7. A study of health care expenditures indicated that government programs contributed 37.6 percent of total personal health care expenditures in 1974, while private health insurers paid 25.6 percent of the national total. Worthington, *National Health Care Expenditures, 1929-74*, 38 SOC. SEC. BULL. 3, 16 (Table 6) (Feb. 1975).
8. *Cf.* Larson, *Sex Discrimination As To Maternity Benefits*, 1975 DUKE L.J. 805, 818.
9. Kalven, *The Jury, The Law, and the Personal Injury Damage Award*, 19 OHIO ST. L.J. 158, 167 (1958). Where the trial judge or an appellate court is able to determine that a jury's damage award represents a compromise on the liability issue, the verdict will be overturned. *See, e.g.*, Simmons v. Fish, 210 Mass. 563, 571-72, 97 N.E. 102, 106 (1912) ($200 award for the loss of an eye by a 21-year-old man overturned as a compromise on the liability issue). *See also* J. MOORE, MOORE'S FEDERAL PRACTICE ¶ 59.08[4], at 59-127 to 59-128 n.13 (2d ed. 1974).
10. Kalven, *supra* note 9, at 165-67; Plant, *Damages for Pain and Suffering*, 19 OHIO ST. L.J. 200, 206 (1958); *see also* Van Gordon v. United States, 91 F. Supp. 834 (W.D. Mo. 1950).
11. Jaffe, *Damages for Personal Injury: The Impact of Insurance*, 18 LAW & CONTEMP. PROB. 219, 234-35 (1953); C. MCCORMICK, *supra* note 5, at 277. For a criti-

event, the patient did not come off badly with a net recovery of $12,000, but of course $4,500 came from sources other than the physician's insurer.[12] Loss (including the expenses of allocating and otherwise administering the loss) from the standpoint of the malpractice insurer was $20,000.[13] Total loss passing through all insurance systems was in excess of $27,000, again including loss administration expense.[14]

Second, the loss ultimately was widely, though perhaps not very efficiently, dispersed over random elements of the whole population. Only in a very narrow perspective can one think of the economic consequences of the situation simply in terms of a loss paid by the malpractice insurer and premiums paid by physicians. The real result accomplished by the total loss allocation and distribution system is much broader.

The Insurance Question Generally

In order to write any specified line of casualty insurance coverages an insurer must make a commitment of capital and possess the specialized organizational capability to deal with the line. The necessity for capital commitment results from the social mandate of solidity in the insurance enterprise,[15] and from the regulatory accounting requirement that the insurer initially establish the full amount of the premium for a policy as a liability ("unearned premium reserve") although it incurs most of the expenses attendant to the underwriting of the policy at the outset.[16]

---

cism of this jury tendency, see Morris, *Liability for Pain and Suffering*, 59 COLUM. L. REV. 476, 477 (1959).

12. From the jury award of $15,000, the patient has received $5,000 ($15,000 less $7,500 for the lawyer and the subrogated $2,500). In addition, he has received $5,000 from the group medical plan and $2,000 in disability income, for a total of $12,000. The $4,500 from other sources consists of the $2,000 disability income and the net $2,500 payment from the group health plan.

13. The figure represents the $15,000 award and the $5,000 litigation expense.

14. Of the total, $20,000 passed through the malpractice insurer, $5,000 through the medical group plan, and $2,000 through the disability income policy.

15. J. HANSON, R. DINEEN & M. JOHNSON, MONITORING COMPETITION: A MEANS OF REGULATING THE PROPERTY AND LIABILITY INSURANCE BUSINESS 92-93 (1974). See Kimball, *The Regulation of Insurance*, in INSURANCE, GOVERNMENT, AND SOCIAL POLICY 3, 5-6 (S. Kimball & H. Denenberg eds. 1969); Kimball, *The Purpose of Insurance Regulation: A Preliminary Inquiry in the Theory of Insurance Law*, 45 MINN. L. REV. 471, 477-78 (1961).

16. *See* E. PATTERSON, ESSENTIALS OF INSURANCE LAW 25 (2d ed. 1957):

The unearned premium reserve at the date of the [financial] statement is the amount that would be needed by the insurer to repay all holders of outstanding insurance contracts if on that date the insurer elected to cancel all such contracts and to refund, as the contracts required, "pro rata," i.e. that proportion of the premium paid that the period then *to be* run bears to the total

The goal of financial stability for the insurance enterprise further dictates that an insurer maintain a reasonably proportionate relationship between premium volume and surplus.[17] Given a stable level of premium writings without net loss,[18] the potential surplus drain of new writings is offset by the recapture from reserve of the prepaid expense on earlier policies.[19] But expansion of the level of premium writings results in a net drain on surplus unless surplus concurrently is augmented either through the commitment of additional capital from external sources or through the realization of net profits from underwriting and investment operations.[20] By the same token, erosion of surplus resulting from net losses in underwriting and investment operations reduces the potential volume of insurance which the insurer can write. Hence, although the relationship between premium volume and surplus is not a rigidly prescribed one and is influenced by a number of other variables, there is a point at which either expansion of writings or surplus erosion from operational losses constrains further writings. Viewed either from the standpoint of an individual insurer or of the industry as a whole, there is an ultimate limit which the total capital committed to the insurance enterprise imposes on the aggregate volume of its insurance

---

period of risk prescribed in the contract. This is usually the largest single liability item in such an insurer's balance sheet.
The laws of all states require companies writing certain kinds of insurance, such as fire and property, to maintain unearned premium reserves. *See* R. MEHR & E. CAMMACK, PRINCIPLES OF INSURANCE 829 (4th ed. 1966). *See also* MICH. COMP. LAWS § 500.808 (Supp. 1975).

17. *See* Hofflander, *Minimum Capital and Surplus Requirements for Multiple Line Insurance Companies: A New Approach*, in INSURANCE, GOVERNMENT AND SOCIAL POLICY, *supra* note 15, at 69; R. KENNEY, FUNDAMENTALS OF FIRE AND CASUALTY STRENGTH (4th ed. 1967). For a criticism of use of the ratio of premium written to surplus as a test of financial solidity, see Beckman & Tremelling, *The Relationship Between Net Premium Written and Policyholders' Surplus*, 59 PROCEEDINGS CASUALTY ACTUARIAL SOC. 203 (1972). For a simplified numerical analysis of the effects of premium volume on surplus, see R. HENSLEY, COMPETITION, REGULATION, AND THE PUBLIC INTEREST IN NONLIFE INSURANCE 160 (1962).

18. Profit and loss in the insurance industry is essentially a product of four factors. Income is derived from underwriting profits (*i.e.*, earned premiums) and return on investments; expenses are incurred through the cost of operations and payment of policyholder losses. Net loss is simply the excess of expenses over income for any period. *See generally* R. HENSLEY, *supra* note 17, at 171 *et seq.*

19. Unearned premium reserves are "recaptured" from their separate liability status with the passage of time. For example, a one-year policy with a $120 premium is wholly a liability on the date the insurance takes effect. Three months later, however, $30 has been recaptured to pay expenses, and $90 remains in the liability (unearned premium reserve) account. *See* R. MEHR & E. CAMMACK, *supra* note 16, at 845.

20. For a recent general discussion of factors which influence this relationship, see Forbes, *Capital and Surplus Formation in the Nonlife Insurance Industry, 1956-70*, 14 Q. REV. ECON. & BUS. 15 (Autumn 1974).

writings, and that ultimate limit is called "capacity" in the insurance lexicon.[21]

But money is both fungible and fluid, and in real life the practical capacity of the insurance markets to supply the demand for particular insurance coverages is not so much a function of the ultimate financial limit described above as it is of a complex of managerial decisions as to the allocation of capital and other corporate resources.

Crass though it may seem, profitability is the critical, though not the exclusive, factor in this decision-making.[22] The insurance enterprise, whether thought of as an individual company or as the aggregate of all insurers, can preserve and expand the surplus necessary to meet the growing appetite of our society for insurance coverages of every type only by profitable operations. Profits both directly contribute to surplus and make it possible to attract additional capital from other sources. Though the proposition is so obvious that we hesitate to risk giving needless offense by openly stating it, the unfortunate historical fact is that large segments of the public, many politicians, and an embarrassingly large number of people intimately connected with the insurance business have behaved as if it were not true.

An insurer can derive profits in two ways—from underwriting operations which result in a combination of losses and expenses less than the amount of premiums received, and from favorable results in the investment of funds under the control of the insurer. Insurers also can lose money on both the underwriting and investment sides of the business.

During the past twenty years, underwriting results in the property and casualty business have been uneven in time, by line, and geographically.[23] There have been long stretches in which many insurers have experienced heavy underwriting losses in lines, such as automobile

---

21. *See* Hershbarger, *Insurance Underwriting Capacity: A Psychometric Approach*, 42 J. RISK & INS. 51, 52-53 (1975); R. HENSLEY, *supra* note 17, at 156 *et seq.*

22. *See* Ehre, *Is There an Insurance Capacity Crisis?*, 33 J. INS. 8, 10 (Mar./Apr. 1972); Johnson, *Seamanship for the 70's*, 35 J. INS. 8, 11 (Sept./Oct. 1974). For the development of one profit-maximizing model for insurers, see Spellman, Witt & Rentz, *Investment Income and Non-Life Insurance Pricing*, 42 J. RISK & INS. 567 (1975).

The profitability factor plays its weightiest role during times of insufficient capacity to meet the demand for insurance, as in the post-World War II period in the United States. *See* R. MEHR & E. CAMMACK, *supra* note 16, at 845.

23. *See* Kinder, *A Look at the Leaders: Was Anyone A Winner in 1974?*, BEST'S REV., PROP./LIABILITY INS. 18 (July 1975). *Cf.* Bateman, *The Prospect Before Us*, 33 J. INS. 2, 3 (July/Aug. 1972); Menist, *The Future Begins Today*, 33 J. INS. 2 (Mar./Apr. 1972). For new data on industry performance, see BEST'S AGGREGATES & AVERAGES (Liability and Property).

insurance,[24] which constitute important segments of the total market. For most of the same period of time, however, underwriting losses have been offset by investment gains.[25] There have been few periods when insurers generally have experienced broad underwriting losses and adverse investment results at the same time.

In the sensible economics of times gone by, there probably was logic to the historical pattern. The technique of insurance ratemaking (with its emphasis on past experience as the chief basis for predicting costs), coupled with competitive euphoria and regulatory lag, causes inflation to have deadly effects on underwriting results. But in the past that same inflation tended to be accompanied by increases in the value of equity securities in which property-casualty insurers invested larger and larger proportions of their portfolios.

The emergence of the perverse economics of the 1970s, with inflation and recession occurring together for an extended period of time and even to some extent causing each other,[26] has destroyed the comfort derived by insurance managements and insurance regulators from the familiar stabilizing effect of the alternating economic swings in underwriting and investment results. The years 1974 and 1975 have been underwriting and investment disasters for the property and casualty insurance business unparalleled since the 1930s, if ever.[27]

The effect of these events on the psychology of insurer managements cannot be overestimated. Gone is the heavy orientation toward volume at all costs which had resulted from over-reliance on the equity investment gains to be derived from cash-flow expansion. In a word, there is present in the insurance business a pervasive "Back to Basics" movement. And the basic principle which the managers have discovered is that those who wish to endure in the business of writing insur-

---

24. Automobile insurers experienced a $1.4 billion underwriting loss during the decade of the 1960s. Johnson, *supra* note 22, at 9.

25. *See* Levey, *Balancing Investment and Underwriting Risks*, 76 BEST'S REV., PROP./LIABILITY INS. 10 (Sept. 1975); *cf.* Forbes, *supra* note 20.

26. COUNCIL OF ECONOMIC ADVISORS, ECONOMIC REPORT OF THE PRESIDENT 19 (Feb. 1975).

27. The property and casualty insurance industry lost more than $2.5 billion in 1974. *1974 Underwriting Results By Line of Business*, BEST'S REV., PROP./LIABILITY INS. 10 (May 1975). *See* Herman, *Damage Insurers Hit by Losses on Stocks, Rise in Claim Amounts*, Wall Street J., Jan. 20, 1975, at 1, col. 6. The industry performance in 1975 was expected to be at least as dismal, with loss estimates ranging as high as $4 billion. Daenzer, *A Look Into the Future*, BEST'S REV., PROP./LIABILITY INS. 26 (Dec. 1975); Walker, *Looking Behind the Property/Liability Bloodbath*, BEST'S REV., PROP./LIABILITY INS. 21 (Nov. 1975); 79 NATIONAL UNDERWRITER, Sept. 19, 1975, at 1.

ance contracts must sell those contracts for prices which are adequate to cover the attendant losses and expenses.[28]

MALPRACTICE INSURANCE

Medical malpractice insurance is simply a specialized form of liability insurance. Although there are specialty carriers writing only this coverage,[29] most of it is written by large multiple-line property and casualty insurers.[30] Those insurers write or have the opportunity to write a wide variety of insurance coverages both in the personal and commercial markets. Insurance lines may be classified not only by reference to the type of peril insured, such as fire, legal liability, interruption of business, theft, or defalcation, but also by reference to the nature of the activities or properties from which the risks of loss arise. The writing of fire insurance, for example, on urban residences, farms, cheese factories, and lumber mills constitutes disparate insuring operations each requiring some degree of specialized organizational competence. The design of policy forms, the development of rates, the evaluation of risks, the orientation of the marketing force, and the adjustment of losses all require functional specialization of an insurer's personnel directed toward the particular circumstances of the subject areas in which writings are concentrated. If one wants to write fire insurance on cheese factories, and wind up with more money than grilled cheese, it is helpful to know a good deal about the cheese business.

The writing of any specialty line of coverage requires the allocation of resources to develop the competence to handle the line. It also requires the willingness to absorb the increments to the general expenses and losses of the insurance operation which the specialization of function imposes until such time as it may be supposed that the line will generate a sufficient volume of premiums at rates adequate to carry those expenses and losses. Given the enormous technical and legal complexities involved, the foregoing principles are preeminently applicable to the writing of insurance against the occupational liabilities of individuals and institutions engaged in providing health care.

---

28. See A.M. Best Co., *Comment on the State of and Prospects for the Property/Liability Insurance Industry*, BEST'S REV., PROP./LIABILITY INS. 10, 90-91 (June 1975); Walker, *supra* note 27, at 24, 78.

29. One such specialty carrier is Medical Protective Company. Hendricks, *What Your Next Malpractice Policy May Look Like*, MED. ECON., Apr. 14, 1975, at 29, 30.

30. See Hastings, *Medical Malpractice Background Paper*, in STAFF OF COMM. ON INTERSTATE AND FOREIGN COMMERCE, *supra* note 1, at 16; Kendall & Haldi, *The Medical Malpractice Insurance Market*, in MEDICAL MALPRACTICE REPORT Appendix 522.

One further observation is appropriate concerning the attitudes of insurer managements or, indeed, of anyone else trying to make profitable choices among competing alternatives for the commitment of limited capital and human resources. The managers are prone to view profitability in relation to an assessment of investment risk, meaning the perceived degree of uncertainty as to the desired outcome.[31] The greater the risk, the higher will be the projected rate of return necessary to induce a decision to commit capital and other limited resources to that venture rather than to some other one seen as promising more certain gain.

In the "Back to Basics" climate of insurer management these days,[32] it is understandable that relative certainty and predictive stability in underwriting results may be much prized as characteristics of any line. This is particularly true because historical experience has tended to make insurer managements skeptical about the feasibility of ever deriving really substantial underwriting profits for very long on any of the major, publicly sensitive classes of property or casualty insurance. A combination of regulatory, competitive, and political pressures effectively stifles the opportunity for sustained yield of high underwriting profits, at least for the industry as a whole. The property and casualty insurance business, whatever it may once have been, is not now to be counted among the industries where one is encouraged to risk disaster by the lure of making a killing.

In this light, it is fair to inquire into the experience which the property and casualty insurers have had with medical malpractice insurance and into the types of problems insurance managers may perceive in it.

Policy Forms

The principal coverage with which we are concerned is Physicians Malpractice Insurance, also known as the Medical Professional Liability Policy. As generally written today, it is a very broad and unexceptional form of insurance against costs of defense and liability for damages arising out of the rendering or failure to render the described professional services during the policy period.[33] In addition to the basic coverage

---

31. *See generally* V. BRUDNEY & M. CHIRELSTEIN, CASES AND MATERIALS ON CORPORATE FINANCE 56-66 (1972); B. GRAHAM, D. DODD & S. COTTLE, SECURITY ANALYSIS 48-52, 664-65 (4th ed. 1962).
32. See note 28 *supra* and accompanying text.
33. A typical insuring clause reads as follows:
Payment on behalf of the insured because of injury arising out of:
(a) malpractice, error, or mistake in rendering or failing to render professional services in the practice of the insured's profession committed during the

for the liabilities arising from the professional conduct of the individual physician insured, the policy also covers the vicarious liability of the physician for the professional acts or omissions of others for whom the physician is legally responsible by reason of a relationship such as that of employer and employee.[34] This is not an "omnibus clause,"[35] and does not extend the insurance protection to the other person but rather is intended only to cover the vicarious liability of the named insured. Finally, the form specifically provides coverage for liabilities arising from the insured's participation in professionally related collective activities such as membership on institutional staff committees and accreditation boards.[36]

In the usual form, there are only two specified exclusions from the coverage. The first is for the vicarious liability of the physician as a member of a partnership, stated as an exception in the insuring clause.[37] The second is a specific exclusion from the policy of the liability of the insured as owner or executive official of a hospital, sanitarium, in-patient clinic, laboratory, or business enterprise. Both of these are intended to avoid duplication of coverages ordinarily provided under other commonly extant policies. However, it is common to extend the coverage of the individual policy, either by endorsement or other policy provision, to the physician's partnership liability,[38] and recently to the liability of his professional corporation.

There are, of course, variations in policy coverage and language and some forms are more restrictive. However, we think the foregoing describes a typical coverage and suggests the breadth of the coverage which has evolved in response to the needs of the physicians.

---

policy period by the insured or any other person for whose acts or omissions the insured is legally liable;
(b) acts or omissions committed by the insured during the policy period as a member of a formal accreditation or similar professional board or committee of a hospital or professional society. Parish, *Professional Liability Insurance*, in PROPERTY AND LIABILITY INSURANCE HANDBOOK 478, 484 (J. Long & D. Gregg eds. 1965).

Other examples of insuring clauses can be found in 1 R. LONG, THE LAW OF LIABILITY INSURANCE § 12.02 (1975); 2 D. LOUISELL & H. WILLIAMS, MEDICAL MALPRACTICE ¶ 20.03, at 589 n.25 (1974); McNeal, *Patients, Litigation and Patience*, 33 INS. COUNSEL J. 408 (1966).

34. See note 33 *supra*.
35. An omnibus clause extends protection to persons other than the named insured, under specified circumstances. It is seen frequently in automobile liability policies. 1 R. LONG, *supra* note 33, § 3.01. *See generally* Ratcliffe, *The Omnibus Clause*, 39 J. RISK & INS. 457 (1972).
36. See note 33 *supra*.
37. For an example of such an exclusion, see Shehee v. Aetna Casualty & Surety Co., 122 F. Supp. 1, 7 (W.D. La. 1954). *See also* 1 R. LONG, *supra* note 33, § 12.03.
38. *See* 1 R. LONG, *supra* note 33.

Premium Rates

An obvious characteristic of insurance is that ordinarily the price is set before the cost is known. In medical malpractice insurance the cost is not known for a very, very long time. For a variety of reasons the discovery, assertion, and eventual disposition of malpractice claims tend to stretch over a period of many years after the close of the period of policy coverage.[39] In addition, the experience of the past ten years has shown that the pattern of frequency and cost of claims as they emerged was not susceptible to prediction by accepted and systematic actuarial techniques.[40]

An understanding of the problems involved in the pricing of malpractice insurance may be aided by a description of the actuarial concepts and methods employed and the difficulties which the actuaries encounter in this line.[41]

The procedures of the actuary are conceptually simple. He starts with a body of past experience sufficient to make him feel comfortable about the "credibility" of the data.[42] He brings the premium component of the experience to "current level," *i.e.* the dollars that the exposures or insured entities would generate at today's rate schedules. He may do this by factoring the historical premiums to account for rate changes imposed between then and now, or he may more accurately deal with the historical exposures and rerate them at today's prices, a process called "extending exposures at current level."[43] Then he turns his attention to the losses. His concern is how these losses would look if they were incurred during the period when the new rates to be produced

---

39. MEDICAL MALPRACTICE REPORT 42; Rudov, Myers & Mirabella, *Medical Malpractice Insurance Claims Files Closed in 1970*, in MEDICAL MALPRACTICE REPORT Appendix 1, 9. A representative of a professional liability insurer covering New York physicians reported that less than half the losses incurred in a given policy year had been finally determined five years later, and that a "substantial number" remained undetermined ten years after occurrence. HOUSE SUBCOMM. ON HEALTH AND THE ENVIRONMENT, *supra* note 2, at 14 (Remarks of John Linster). *See also id.* at 12 (Remarks of Warren Cooper).
40. MEDICAL MALPRACTICE REPORT 41-42; Gibbs, *Medical Malpractice Insurance Crisis*, 80 CASE & COMMENT 8, 11 (1975).
41. For a general discussion of actuarial practice in medical professional liability, see Kendall & Haldi, *supra* note 30, at 529-33.
42. For discussions of the importance of credibility in the insurance context, see Mayerson, *The Uses of Credibility in Property Insurance Ratemaking*, 27 GIORNALE DELL' ISTITUTO ITALIANO DEGLI ATTUARI 197 (1964). *See also* Bailey, *Credibility Procedures*, 37 PROCEEDINGS CASUALTY ACTUARIAL SOC. 7 (1950); Longley-Cook, *An Introduction to Credibility Theory*, 49 PROCEEDINGS CASUALTY ACTUARIAL SOC. 194 (1962); Mayerson, *A Bayesian View of Credibility*, 51 PROCEEDINGS CASUALTY ACTUARIAL SOC. 85 (1964).
43. *Cf.* Kendall & Haldi, *supra* note 30, at 531.

will be in effect. He adjusts the historical losses in two ways. First he "develops" them; that is, he accounts for reserve deficiencies or redundancies and estimates what the historical losses will amount to when they are all paid.[44] He then turns his attention to what will probably happen if these developed losses are paid some years later, as will be the case under future rates. To quantify this consideration he uses a "trend" factor,[45] a very important calculation when inflation, changes in the legal environment, and similar forces produce volatile loss costs, in order to project the historical losses to a point in time when future losses are expected to occur.

From the premiums under current rates, and his estimate of future loss values that these rates are calculated to cover, the actuary next calculates a loss ratio at current rates. By looking at known non-loss costs as a function of past premiums and adjusting for expected or known future changes, he can predict what percentage of future rates will be needed to pay such non-loss expenses. The remainder is what will be available to pay future losses, and is called the "expected loss ratio." For instance, if expenses are estimated at twenty percent, eighty percent of the future rate is available to pay claims.

The actuary next compares the loss ratio at current rates with the expected loss ratio. If the former is the greater, rates must be raised to provide the necessary dollars to pay future losses. Let us return to our example. If the expected ratio is eighty percent and the ratio at current rates is 100 percent, the rates must be raised by twenty-five percent. Consider an average premium of $100 under current rates. In this example it would lead to $100 of future loss, but this leaves the insurer no money to pay non-loss expenses. If the rates are raised to $125, a twenty-five percent increase, then eighty percent is $100, the amount necessary for loss, and the other twenty percent of $25 is available for non-loss expense.[46] In like manner, if the expected ratio is the greater, rates should be decreased.

---

44. *See* Lange, *General Liability Insurance Ratemaking*, 53 PROCEEDINGS CASUALTY ACTUARIAL SOC. 26, 32 (1966). *See also* Cook, *Trend and Loss Development Factors*, 57 PROCEEDINGS CASUALTY ACTUARIAL SOC. 1, 2-3 (1970); Stern, *Ratemaking Procedures for Automobile Liability Insurance*, 52 PROCEEDINGS CASUALTY ACTUARIAL SOC. 137, 162 (1965).
45. *See* Lange, *supra* note 44, at 32. *See generally* Cook, *supra* note 44.
46. Another actuary might prefer a different approach, called the "pure premium" method, which will lead him to the same result. A pure premium (perhaps better called a loss cost) is a technical term to denote the average premium that must be collected to pay for losses only, that is, a value that has no consideration for expense. It is calculated by dividing the loss by the number of exposures. In the present case, this second actuary will arrive at the developed, trended losses and divide by the historical exposure count. The value in our example will be $100. Then he divides this by the expected loss ratio, eighty percent, in order to "load" the expected future premium for

Actuarial calculations thus involve three technical considerations, credibility, development, and trending, which, while conceptually simple, may be quite complex in their derivation and computation. In some lines of insurance this trinity is well-defined, with rather standard procedures being generally accepted. Unfortunately, their definition in malpractice insurance is anything but clear. Let us take a look at why this is true.

First, as to credibility, the situation is alarmingly straightforward. In most cases credibility has not been theoretically defined. The larger state programs have by implication been considered fully credible (though there is little uniformity in the number of years to be used in the experience period), and even the experience of smaller states has been accorded credibility, although companywide (or bureauwide) adjustments are made for development and trend. The last represents an acknowledgment of lack of full credibility, but this nod is not a response to any mathematical theory.

The number of medical exposures and claims, the statistics which determine degrees of credibility, are miniscule in comparison with such lines as automobile or homeowners insurance. For example, consider the situation in a populous urban state, New Jersey. The rating bureau's recent filings for private passenger automobiles displayed an annual count of about 1.1 million cars,[47] while a companion homeowners filing was based on an annual home count of about 700,000 units.[48] In contrast, the company writing the medical society's program based its independently devised rates on an annual census of less than 7,000 doctors,[49] with hospital rates calculated from the experience of no more than 110 hospitals.[50] These comparisons are typical. Hence, the first major uncertainty arises from the fact that the value of past data in predicting future losses is mathematically ill-defined and unclear.

The second consideration is loss development, which can be viewed in two independent aspects. The first is what is known as "incurred but not reported" losses, usually abbreviated IBNR.[51] In any type of

---

expense. The answer, of course, is an average premium of $125, which breaks down to $100 (eighty percent) for loss and $25 (twenty percent) for expense. Houston, *The Equivalence of the Pure Premium and the Loss Ratio Methods of Ratemaking*, 23 J. RISK & INS. 72 (1956).

47. Insurance Services Office, Filing with N.J. Insurance Dep't, effective Dec. 1975.
48. Insurance Services Office, Filing with N.J. Insurance Dep't, effective Aug. 1975.
49. Federal Insurance Co., Filing with N.J. Insurance Dep't, effective May 1975.
50. Insurance Services Office, Filing for N.J. Hospital Professional Liability Rates.
51. *See generally* Bornhuetter & Ferguson, *The Actuary and IBNR*, 59 PROCEEDINGS CASUALTY ACTUARIAL SOC. 181 (1972); Tarbell, *Incurred But Not Reported Claim Re-*

insurance there will be claims presented after a policy has expired, but their frequency is noticeably higher in the liability lines written on an "occurrence" basis.[52] Clearly, there can be many reasons why a claimant may not discover an injury or press an early claim. The reasons for late discovery seem apparent; those for late suits are more difficult to perceive. Experience indicates that there are more reasons for delay in the area of medical malpractice than other forms of insurance. To illustrate the phenomenon of extended claims reporting (one of the main factors contributing to the "long tail"),[53] statistics compiled by a major state insurance department are helpful.[54]

Months from the Beginning of a Policy Year[55]	Percent of Number of Claims Reported
24	38
36	67
48	79
60	86
72	91
84	93
96	95
108	96
120	98
132	99
144	100

When all policies are expired, the table shows that only thirty-eight percent of the claims have been reported; it is not until four years thereafter that ninety percent are reported to the company. There are two consequences to this. First, recent years of experience are all but meaningless since so little of the data is known as fact. The actuary thus loses the responsiveness to change that he cherishes in fresh data when he sets out to price the malpractice policy. Second, even when he deals with older years, the actuary must make substantial guesses as to

---

serves, 20 PROCEEDINGS CASUALTY ACTUARIAL SOC. 275 (1933-34), *reprinted at* 58 PROCEEDINGS CASUALTY ACTUARIAL SOC. 84 (1972).

52. "Occurrence" means, simply, that the insurer providing liability coverage for a specified period of time, usually a year, is liable for any accidents that occurred during the period of time without regard to the date the claims are presented, subject, of course, to the appropriate statute of limitations. *See New Form of Malpractice Liability Coverage to be Offered to Doctors*, in MALPRACTICE DIGEST 1 (St. Paul Fire and Marine Ins. Co., Jan./Feb. 1975).

53. *See, e.g.*, MEDICAL MALPRACTICE REPORT 42. The term "long tail" refers to the length of time between the policy period and the final determination of losses.

54. Data made available to the authors by participating private insurers.

55. The term "policy year" means the year during which a policy was written, regardless of when losses on the policy were incurred, reported, reserved or paid. Since policies, good for one year, are written throughout a policy year, the last one of them can expire as late as two years after the beginning of that policy year.

what is yet to be reported. For instance, working in 1975 looking at policy year 1971, he is aware of only two-thirds of the claims. It is this magnitude of uncertainty that distinguishes the malpractice line.

The second aspect of development is what is called "run-off"[56] in insurance jargon. When a claim is reported to the company, a member of the claims staff, an examiner, sets up a case reserve against its future disposition. The reserve is the examiner's best estimate, based on current knowledge, of what the claim will cost when final payment is made. In many lines of insurance the period between initial report and disposition is relatively short, but in malpractice it can be a matter of several years, averaging in excess of three years.[57] Given the nature of inflation and its effect on trend,[58] it is unrealistic to think that examiners can accurately calculate future liabilities, even in those rare cases where the facts and allegations are known at first report. Generally, the original reserves in bulk are insufficient to cover ultimate payments, a fact which in and of itself does not frighten the actuarial mind—so long as the degree of insufficiency is predictable, *i.e.* the presence of well-defined patterns in the past that can be imputed to the future. Unfortunately such consistency is not a hallmark of malpractice run-off. The reason may be a change in carriers, each of whose claims staff subscribes to a different philosophy of reserving. Or even where a single carrier's experience is used for ratemaking there may be shifts in reserve margins as examiners make corrections in case reserves in the course of their continuing reviews of open claims files. In any event, the actuary, if not frightened, is at least concerned and unsure.

The third area of actuarial uncertainty is trend. Over the last several years, the frequency and size of claims have soared beyond any actuarial expectations entertained during these years.[59] For instance, in Southern California the average size of a claim has jumped from less than $6,000 in 1963 to over $12,000 in 1969, and is now estimated at about $30,000.[60] The frequency of claims has spiraled just as dramati-

---

56. "Run-off" is an estimate of a past reserve, and consists of actual future payments on known claims up to a given date, plus anticipated remaining future payments on known claims as of that given date. Skurnick, *A Survey of Loss Reserving Methods*, 60 PROCEEDINGS CASUALTY ACTUARIAL SOC. 16, 21-22 (1973). After a sufficient time period, the run-off becomes fully accurate in most lines, either because all claims are settled prior to the given date or because the open claims can be accurately reserved. *Id.*

57. *See* Steves, *Medical Malpractice in Perspective*, 28 CPCU ANNALS 209, 212 (Dec. 1975).

58. See note 45 *supra* and accompanying text.

59. *See* Steves, *supra* note 57, at 213-15.

60. Data made available to the authors by private insurers.

cally: nine out of 100 doctors had claims made against them in 1963, twenty out of 100 in 1970, perhaps thirty out of 100 today.[61] Had we been dealing with a consistent economic and legal inflation, our actuary could have predicted claims with some accuracy, but looking so far ahead as he must when pricing (due to the long tail) he cannot be blamed for not foreseeing that the rate of change in inflation was shifting. Indeed, in retrospect the rate of change was linear when the rates were made and became exponential when the claims were received.

These three considerations—credibility, development, and trend —are substantially less defined and predictable in medical malpractice than in any other line, and inability to cope with them has led the actuaries to their greatest failures. So much so, in fact, that the company which is perhaps the largest writer of malpractice in the country has declared the occurrence form unpriceable and has agreed to continue in the business only on a claims-made basis, by which it will cover only claims presented in the year of coverage.[62] Such a form bobs the "tail" by eliminating claims (or at least incidents) incurred but not reported during the policy year and by shortening the time between prediction and payment. Other carriers are simply leaving the business.[63] The crisis in the availability of malpractice insurance is due only in part to past underwriting losses. Just as important is continuing and, perhaps, unmanageable uncertainty about future pricing.

The Medical Insurance "Crisis"

We are told that the past is a prologue to the future. From an actuarial standpoint an unstable and unfortunate past does not portend well for the future. A number of factors have combined to cause malpractice liability costs to increase with unpredictable sharpness in recent years. A consideration of those factors in juxtaposition with the behavioral tendencies of insurers may suggest some helpful observations about the future.

Causes

Why has malpractice liability expanded so dramatically, in both frequency and severity of claims? The first reason has to do with the

---

61. *Id.*
62. *New Form of Malpractice Liability Coverage, supra* note 52; N.Y. Times, Jan. 24, 1975, at 34, col. 1.
63. Business Week, Jan. 12, 1976, at 60, 64; N.Y. Times, June 10, 1975, at 78, col. 1; *id.*, June 3, 1975, at 22, col. 8; *id.*, June 2, 1975, at 1, col. 1.

incidence of underlying loss. We do not doubt the validity of the oft-made claim for the excellence of American medical care, at least for those patients to whom it is financially available. Medical education is as good as money can make it. Hospitals and laboratories are magnificently equipped. New drugs and procedures are extensively tested before their general usage. Extensive research efforts produce an endless array of seemingly miraculous advances in technology. Yet we suspect that the incidence of actual loss, in the sense of the original definition we accorded to that term,[64] is relatively high, probably higher than the volume of asserted malpractice claims indicates.[65] Even if the juridical climate is as favorable to claimants as the provider groups contend,[66] the negligence liability system undoubtedly continues to exert a substantial filtering effect on claims. The technology of modern medical care is incredibly complex. The total physiological effects of much that is done are not always known or understood. Many of the drugs and procedures employed involve narrow margins between efficacy and dangerousness. Very large numbers of professionals of various types are engaged in the treatment process and, for a single condition, the patient may be subjected to numerous professional and institutional contacts and decisions. Many physicians, technologists, and institutions have enormous patient contact loads and work under severe time pressures.[67] And finally, almost by definition the exposed population largely consists of people who either have something wrong with them, or think that they do, and submit to processes which they rarely fully understand and under conditions which render them dependent and even helpless to contribute to their own safety. There is reason to

---

64. See text accompanying note 4 *supra*.

65. *See* O'Connell, *Expanding No-Fault Beyond Auto Insurance: Some Proposals*, 59 VA. L. REV. 749, 757 (1973); Steves, *supra* note 57, at 210-15.

66. For examples of physician attitudes in this context, see Masur, *Malpractice Crisis*, N.Y. STATE J. MED. 1554 (Aug. 1975); Wiseman, *Res Ipsa Loquitur*, W.J. MED. 71 (July 1975). The same attitude is visible in statements by insurers. *See* HOUSE SUBCOMM. ON HEALTH AND ENVIRONMENT OF THE COMM. ON INTERSTATE AND FOREIGN COMMERCE, *supra* note 2, at 17 (Remarks of John Linster).

67. Meeting the nation's health manpower needs is a problem which has not escaped the attention of Congress. *See Hearings on H.R. 2956, H.R. 2957, H.R. 2958, and H.R. 3279 Before the Subcomm. on Health and the Environment of the House Comm. on Interstate and Foreign Commerce*, 94th Cong., 1st Sess. ser. 94-3 (1975); *Hearings on S. 3585 Before the Subcomm. on Health of the Senate Comm. on Labor and Public Welfare*, 93d Cong., 2d Sess., pt. 3 (1974). *See generally* Ruhe, *Recent Events of Special Interest to Medical Education*, 234 J.A.M.A. 1326, 1328 (1975). The implementation of a national health insurance program would likely have some impact on physician workload; however, it is not at all clear whether such a plan would increase or decrease the working hours of the physician. *See* Enterline, McDonald, McDonald, et al., *Physician's Working Hours and Patients Seen Before and After National Health Insurance: "Free" Medical Care and Medical Practice*, 13 MED. CARE 95 (1975).

believe that the incidence of error, much of it undoubtedly harmless and most of it not morally blameworthy, is higher than we would like to believe.[68]

The second important factor is the extent to which the compensation process results in the transmutation of medical injury losses into liability claims costs. This is a function of the combined and interactive effect of legal doctrine and the behavior of claimants and their lawyers in asserting claims, of insurers' representatives in settling or defending them, and of judges and juries in deciding contested cases. At an earlier time, not so long ago, successful recovery on medical malpractice claims was difficult due to the substantial barriers erected by the conventional requirements of tort law doctrine and the obstacles to acquiring knowledge of the technical facts involved and to securing the requisite professional testimony. Moreover, patient expectations were more modest and there was less propensity to assert claims. The total process had the effect of suppressing and filtering the extent to which medical injury losses became translated into compensated liability claims.

Over the past twenty-five years, however, there has been a dramatic and apparently accelerating change in this state of affairs. The various factors are chronicled elsewhere in this Symposium and need not be analyzed here, but the litany has become a familiar one: *res ipsa loquitur*, informed consent, breaches in the locality rule, greater availability of expert witnesses, relaxation in the application of the statutes of limitations, expansion of doctrines facilitating multiple defendant liability, open discovery, more sophisticated claimants' lawyers, enhanced public claims consciousness and a prevalent expectation of in-

---

68. Two recent studies indicate serious deficiencies in the quality of medical care. A 1973-75 study made by the American College of Surgeons and the American Surgical Association indicated that 796 of the 1,696 "untoward incidents" arising out of 1,493 surgical operations were avoidable. Eighty-five deaths were deemed avoidable. Child, *The Critical Incident Study of Surgical Deaths and Complications*, 1973-1975 (10th and final SOSSUS Report in the Study of Surgical Sciences for the United States), *discussed in Quality of Surgery Unveiled*, MED. WORLD NEWS, Jan. 26, 1976, at 24. *See also* Cohn, *Surgical 'Incidents' Held Avoidable*, Washington Post, Jan. 22, 1976, at 1, col. 1.

The results of a "self-assessment test" taken voluntarily by 4,513 physicians indicated serious deficiencies of knowledge and a need for further education in the use of antibiotics. The mean correct score on the National Antibiotic Therapy Test was sixty-eight percent. Neu & Howrey, *Testing the Physician's Knowledge of Antibiotic Use*, 293 NEW ENG. J. MED. 1291 (1975).

These quality-of-care studies are reflective of the results reached in a number of earlier studies. *See* Brook, Brutoco & Williams, *The Relationship Between Medical Malpractice and Quality of Care*, 1975 DUKE L.J. 1197. *See also* Pocincki, Dogger & Schwartz, *The Incidence of Iatrogenic Injuries*, MEDICAL MALPRACTICE REPORT Appendix 50, 55.

fallibility of the professionals and their miraculous technology, etc. The cumulative effect of these changes in legal and cultural attitudes and behavior has been a rapid evolution from suppression and filtration toward encouragement and facilitation in the compensation of medical injury losses through the insured tort system. In contemporary personal injury law "negligence" often has little relation to moral culpability, and many claims are founded on the adverse consequences of routine error and failure in the manipulation of complex devices and processes. Given the volume of underlying losses and the tendency toward a general public expectation of assured results of professional performance, it is not likely that the trend in the volume and severity of claims will be reversed.

In this climate, insurer managements, painfully aware of the extent to which they have repeatedly underestimated the trend of development in the past and pressed by capacity needs to achieve consistent underwriting soundness, may be expected to react to the uncertain future by assuming that the trend will be in the direction of more claims and awards arising from the failures of medical procedures to accomplish desired results and to price the insurance accordingly.

Prescriptions

The purpose and obligation of this Article is to describe the medical malpractice insurance problem in its insurance aspect, not to prescribe solutions for it. Nevertheless, a few observations seem to flow quite naturally from the preceding analysis of the situation.

The most basic and obvious observation is that the subject of handling medical losses is far larger than its liability insurance aspect. While insurance is often the device by which the costs of medical losses are made most vivid to providers and patients, so that (as in the current furor) dislocations in the handling of medical losses can be superficially perceived as solely insurance problems, any systematic approach to the subject must include its medical, legal, moral, and other aspects as well as those of insurance.

Whatever we do now, a goodly amount of modesty and, indeed, resignation is definitely called for. Since there is no longer any question that the frequency and size of malpractice awards will continue to increase so long as the present system remains intact, it follows that a larger part of the cost of health care will have to be devoted to paying medical losses than was the case in the past.

It follows, that is, unless society singles out one or more of the participants in the medical loss system for expropriation. A balanced solution, designed to reduce loss costs by modifying the rights and duties of many or all of the participants in the system, is one approach, and a quite reasonable and not unlikely one. However, for any one of the involved interest groups to seek to save its own interests by trampling on the interests of other participants in the system is quite another matter. Nor is the latter unheard of in the current excitement. With that in mind, one should view with skepticism legal changes which would unfairly force loss costs back onto the patient,[69] insurance capacity changes which would force insurers to subsidize the system,[70] or insurance coverage changes which would unfairly leave the physician unprotected and the patient uncompensated.

Assuming that society is dissatisfied with the present level and allocation of medical loss costs, a balanced approach to the problem might consist of three parts; the first two are beyond the scope of this Article, and the third is the insurance aspect.

The first part would be better control of medical losses themselves. It cannot be questioned that many of today's insured medical losses result from the failure of some health care professionals to meet the standards of professional competence to which society quite justly holds them. Some of these situations would seem to be avoidable by, for example, tighter regulation of health care providers, peer review in questionable cases, and closer surveillance by medical societies and practicing physicians' groups.

The second would be to re-examine the legal rules governing the right to recover for medical losses and the amount of that recovery, as well as the role and compensation of the legal profession in the medical loss cost-allocation system. This re-examination would certainly have to include such questions as limitations on recovery for pain and suffering, limitations on contingent fees for attorneys, and modification of the rule that damages are to be measured without regard to funds received from collateral sources.[71]

---

69. *See* Havighurst, *"Medical Adversity Insurance"—Has Its Time Come?*, 1975 DUKE L.J. 1233. For a discussion of state legislative limitations on provider liability or patient recovery, see Comment, *State Legislative Responses, supra* note 1, at 1418-24.

70. North Carolina has ordered all general liability insurers authorized to write coverage in the state to participate in a reinsurance program for medical professional liability. N.C. GEN. STAT. §§ 58-173.34 to .51 (1975 Supp.). The statute has been challenged by insurers, and a state court has found the plan unconstitutional. State Farm Mutual Ins. Co. v. Ingram, 44 U.S.L.W. 2255 (N.C. Super. Ct., Dec. 9, 1975).

71. For a discussion of recent state legislative developments in these areas, see Comment, *State Legislative Responses, supra* note 1, at 1442-50.

We recognize that all of these possibilities involve troublesome questions of overall

The third part of a balanced solution concerns insurance and, in turn, consists of two aspects. The first is designed to reduce the uncertainty in malpractice liability ratemaking, both in the interest of fairness to insured and insurer and in the interest of reducing the uncertainty as to financial result which has made insurer managements so fearful of this line. It merely involves applying to the malpractice situation the familiar insurance techniques of policyholder dividends or retrospective, experienced-based rating. These techniques are widely used in large commercial property and casualty coverages today,[72] and, indeed, have been used on a small scale in medical malpractice itself. Granted that the "long tail" of medical malpractice losses renders the making of rates most inexact and susceptible to huge errors,[73] this approach would simply involve setting the initial premium rate at the high end of everyone's best guess as to the correct rate, perhaps with a top or seriously disputed layer of premium being held in trust by an independent third party. Then, after a suitable loss development period

---

legal policy. Of paramount concern is the question of the propriety of singling out the area of health care provider liability for extraordinarily favorable legal treatment. If these measures are sound limitations on medical malpractice liability, then why are they not equally appropriate as limitations on claims against product manufacturers, lawyers, plumbers, or automobile drivers? After all, the dispersal of the costs ultimately to the public as a whole is not likely to be demonstrably different.

The related questions of limitation on general, or "pain and suffering" damages, and on contingent fees pointedly pose the issue. Clearly, these features of the legal process in personal harm cases create opportunities for jury awards far in excess of economic loss and strong incentives for lawyers to pursue those opportunities energetically. And the large element of "juridical hazard" with which the liability and damage issues in these cases are infected significantly affects the settlement practices of insurers. A substantial portion of the recoveries through this system goes to lawyers. See Dietz, Baird & Berul, *The Medical Malpractice Legal System*, in MEDICAL MALPRACTICE REPORT Appendix 87, 105-06. We recognize, therefore, that the right to unlimited pain and suffering damages, coupled with the contingent fee system, creates a situation which is susceptible to abuse and in some cases may foster undesirable behavior by lawyers, claimants, and insurers. Yet we should honestly admit that to single out the medical profession as beneficiary of special immunities from pursuit by lawyers does seem to establish a ring of protection around what must be our country's highest paid profession, simply to protect it from the alleged depredations of another of the country's highest paid professions. If we want to solve these problems, as we should, we should do so systematically and not subject by subject. Thus, in "solving" the contingent fee problem, one has to come to grips with the reasons for its existence. Liability cases, particularly in technical and professional fields, require the expenditure of considerable time, effort and money by claimants' attorneys. Until our society is prepared to find other ways of assuring that lawyers who represent claimants will be reasonably compensated in all cases, drastic limitation of contingent fees may lead to effective denial of representation in many cases.

72. *See* R. MEHR & E. CAMMACK, *supra* note 16, at 812-15; J. MAGEE & D. BICKELHAUPT, GENERAL INSURANCE 435-36 (7th ed. 1964).

73. See notes 51-63 *supra* and accompanying text.

and pursuant to prior agreement as to the ultimate profit or loss to the insurer, the insurer or third party would refund to the insured physician, medical society, medical group, or whatever, the amount of premium that was left over after the losses were paid. While mechanically rather complex, this approach is conceptually simple and would seem to have the desired effect of having the insured profession carry its own liability costs, without the capitalization and management problems which beset attempts by physicians to organize a mutual company themselves.[74]

The foregoing insurance rating approach might well be coupled with a liability and coverage change which would offer some hope of controlling losses as well as paying for them. Such a change is somewhat beyond the knowledge of the writers of this Article, but its general outlines would be as follows. A large portion of malpractice claims arise out of procedures performed in hospitals.[75] Hospitals carry malpractice insurance and it would be possible to provide by law that the hospital's insurance must cover any claim arising out of a hospital procedure, that the physician's insurance would not apply, and that the hospital would have no claim against the physician. Hospitals are large institutions which are better able to withstand, protect against and distribute financial shocks than are individual practitioners. They are the best instrumentality we now have for policing the professional conduct of physicians, and the contemplated insurance change would give them every incentive to be more vigilant. Finally, their institutional continuity would suit them better than an individual practitioner to the sort of long-term retrospective rating program described above.[76]

As the reader can see from our own analysis of the insurance aspects of the medical malpractice problem, all that is certain about our three proposals is that they would leave a great many people quite unhappy. Fortunately, however, the problem is today the object of so much raging discontent that those dissatisfied with our, or any other, moderately reasonable program could scarcely be more numerous, more vigorous, or more vocal than they are today. As we noted at the outset, the medical malpractice insurance problem is not complex; it is merely intractable.

---

74. Mutual companies have been formed in San Francisco and Los Angeles, *Survey Shows Gains in Liability Legislation, But Problems Remain*, AM. MED. NEWS, Jan. 12, 1976, at 9, and similar attempts are underway in many other areas. *Id.* at 9-13.

75. Rudov, Myers & Mirabella, *supra* note 39, at 10.

76. *See* Steves, *A Proposal to Improve the Cost to Benefit Relationship in the Medical Professional Liability Insurance System*, 1975 DUKE L.J. 1305, 1325.

A PROPOSAL TO IMPROVE THE COST TO BENEFIT RELATIONSHIPS IN THE MEDICAL PROFESSIONAL LIABILITY INSURANCE SYSTEM

MYRON F. STEVES, JR.*

Prior to the last ten years, the cost of medical malpractice insurance was not a major concern of the health care system. As a percentage of gross revenues, the cost of coverage was not significant,[1] and the premium expense had no marked effect on the way in which practitioners and health care institutions delivered their services.[2] Providers bought a contract where the primary interest was defense.[3] The public benefited

---

* Myron F. Steves, Jr., CPCU, is completing his studies for a Ph.D in Business and Applied Economics with a Specialization in Insurance at the University of Pennsylvania, where he studied under a S.S. Huebner Foundation Fellowship. Mr. Steves worked as a systems analyst/management engineer at the Graduate Hospital of the University of Pennsylvania from 1969 to 1973. He is currently a partner in an excess and surplus lines insurance agency in Houston, Texas, where he specializes in placing medical liability insurance.

THE FOLLOWING CITATIONS WILL BE USED IN THIS ARTICLE:
U.S. DEP'T OF HEALTH, EDUCATION AND WELFARE, REPORT OF THE SECRETARY'S COMMISSION ON MEDICAL MALPRACTICE (1973) [hereinafter cited as MEDICAL MALPRACTICE REPORT];
Questionnaire Re Medical Professional Liability Insurance, Technical Appendix, in *Hearings on S. 482, S. 215, S. 188 Before the Subcomm. on Health of the Senate Comm. on Labor and Public Welfare*, 94th Cong., 1st Sess. 552-601 (1975) [hereinafter cited as Technical Appendix].

1. See Steves, *Medical Malpractice In Perspective*, 28 CPCU ANNALS 209, 215-16 (1975); Steves & McWhorter, *Notes on the Malpractice Insurance Market*, 28 CPCU ANNALS 224, 232-33 Table XI (1975). See also Kendall & Haldi, *The Medical Malpractice Insurance Market*, in MEDICAL MALPRACTICE REPORT Appendix 494.

2. Although premium expense has not been a factor historically, the fear of malpractice litigation is said to result in an overutilization of many diagnostic studies and a possible underutilization of aggressive but hazardous forms of therapy. See Project, *The Medical Malpractice Threat: A Study of Defensive Medicine*, 1971 DUKE L.J. 939. See also Weinberger, *Malpractice—A National View*, 32 ARIZ. MED. 117 (1975). But cf. Bernzweig, *Defensive Medicine*, in MEDICAL MALPRACTICE REPORT Appendix 39-40.

3. The first obligation in medical professional liability policies has always been "to defend"; until recently, few policy contracts allowed insurers to settle a claim without provider approval. See 1 R. LONG, THE LAW OF LIABILITY INSURANCE § 12.08 (1975); 2 D. LOUISELL & H. WILLIAMS, MEDICAL MALPRACTICE ¶ 20.06 (1974). The predecessor organization of the Medical Protective Insurance Company of Fort Wayne, Indiana, was a physician's defense league permitted by an act of the Indiana Legislature in 1889. MEDICAL PROTECTIVE CO., DEFENDING THE DOCTOR 3. The New York group insurance plan was named "The Professional Medical Liability Insurance and Defense Program." The Canadian and English physician organizations, in name and in attitude, are defense leagues.

to the extent that the assets of particular providers were not impaired by successful litigation and that providers were reminded of their legal responsibilities. Occasionally, a victim of a significant injury, alleged to have been negligently caused, received compensation.

In more recent years the price of professional liability insurance has increased to the point where it is no longer an insignificant proportion of provider gross revenue.[4] Furthermore, if the distribution of premium cost among the various types and specialties of providers is considered, the impact of increased premiums is multiplied. The direct cost of insuring the professional liability hazard is approaching the level where it is not unreasonable to assume that the price level and structure of the insurance system affects the quantity and quality of services rendered by health care providers.[5]

Given the escalation of insurance costs, it is in the public interest to evaluate the consumer benefit derived from the provider's malpractice premium. Altering the patterns of liability exposure which insurance must protect in the health care system may increase incentives for quality control and injury prevention as well as provide a more stable foundation for an insurance market in the face of rising premium costs. Although insurance is a follower with respect to legal trends, it may be innovative with respect to exposure base and rating in ways that place emphasis on comprehensive risk management. This Article suggests such an innovation in the form of a shift in liability exposure and premium cost burdens which, while departing radically from the current focus on individual practitioners, will benefit the public through encouragement of improved quality of care while easing the ever-increasing financial burden of providers.

THE DIFFERING FINANCIAL INTERESTS OF PROVIDERS AND PATIENTS

Under the system of civil jurisprudence that exists in the United States, providers may be held liable for damages arising out of the rendering of, or failure to render, professional services when these services depart from an accepted standard of care and result directly in damage to the patient.[6] It is the risk of financial loss resulting from this

---

4. See notes 58-75 *infra* and accompanying text.
5. *But see* Brook, Brutoco & Williams, *The Relationship Between Medical Malpractice and Quality of Care*, 1975 DUKE L.J. 1197, 1209-15.
6. *See* C. WASMUTH, LAW FOR THE PHYSICIAN 20-21 (1966); Purdue, *The Law of Texas Medical Malpractice,* 11 HOUSTON L. REV. 2, 21 (1973). *See also* A. HOLDER, MEDICAL MALPRACTICE LAW 1-61 (1975).

liability that is the immediate concern of providers, a concern which motivates them to purchase insurance and encourages them to establish incident-reporting systems and other risk management techniques to prevent or minimize the impact of liability claims. While professional and ethical considerations, supported by accreditation, licensure and the stimulation of third-party reimbursement programs,[7] do give providers a substantial stake in reducing injuries and monitoring the quality and quantity of patient service, the liability claim and the insurance premium necessary to protect against the claim are explicit and substantial costs that no provider may ignore.

The financial interests of the patient population differ from those of the providers who pay for protection against potential civil liability. Consumers are concerned with injuries per se[8] because, both individually and collectively, injuries reduce wealth. Patients have a direct economic and social cost irrespective of the existence of transfer mechanisms to shift or spread the burden of harm which has occurred. First- or third-party insurance programs may make implicit costs explicit or may reallocate expense, but total costs are not reduced unless the frequency and severity of injuries are reduced. From the patient viewpoint, of course, injuries are primary even if the narrow ground of a provider's civil liability is considered.[9]

The differing financial interests of providers and patients with respect to injuries are highlighted by reference to available information on the relative numbers of injuries, negligent acts, and malpractice claims that occur in the health care system. In a 1972 study conducted at the request of the Department of Health, Education and Welfare

---

7. Licensing requirements for medical practitioners are established at the state level, cf. C. WASMUTH, supra note 6, at 31-32, and represent minimum qualifications. Accreditation is done by a variety of organizations, the most important of which is the Joint Commission for the Accreditation of Hospitals (JCAH). Third-party payors, particularly the Medicare and Medicaid programs administered by the Department of Health, Education and Welfare, impose review standards which emphasize the control of utilized services which the programs are requested to reimburse.

8. Injuries, in this context, are defined as harm caused or aggravated in the course of medical treatment. It is harm that occurs because of a provider's active intervention or failure to intervene where such was required by medical convention. The term, as used herein, does not include all deterioration of human functions that occur because of disease, illness, accident, or aging. Nor does it include discomfort not considered harmful which is a byproduct of accepted diagnostic or therapeutic regimens. See Pocincki, Dogger & Schwartz, *The Incidence of Iatrogenic Injuries*, in MEDICAL MALPRACTICE REPORT Appendix 50, 51.

9. Adverse and untoward results of medical supervision and treatment are, of course, the basis for nearly every medical malpractice claim. See MEDICAL MALPRACTICE REPORT 24-25.

Secretary's Commission on Medical Malpractice,[10] medical records were selected at random from the discharge records of two hospitals. When the 821 records in the sample were analyzed for iatrogenic injuries,[11] the overall injury rate at the two sample hospitals was found to be approximately 7.5 percent.[12] If this percentage is applied to the total number of patients discharged from all health care institutions, it is estimated that over 2.6 million persons are injured annually in the course of medical treatment.[13]

Of the injuries observed in the study, forty-four percent were classified as "minor temporary" and thirty percent as "major temporary." Permanent injuries classified as "significant," "major," "grave," and "death" accounted for eighteen percent of the total.[14]

It was believed that twenty-nine percent of the injuries observed in this retrospective sample were due to negligence. Applying the results of the sample to the total number of discharges that occurred in the two hospitals, the survey indicated that 517 injuries may have been negligently caused.[15] However, the estimated number of malpractice claims to be filed by patients discharged in 1972 against the hospital and its medical staff was only thirty-one.[16]

---

10. Pocincki, Dogger & Schwartz, *supra* note 8.

11. Iatrogenic is derived from the Greek word *iatros*, or physician. It refers to physician-caused injuries. See note 8 *supra*.

12. Pocincki, Dogger & Schwartz, *supra* note 8, at 63. The authors of this study believed that the injury rate observed was the lower bound for the institutions surveyed. Charts classified as not involving injuries at any stage were excluded, while charts classified as involving injuries were included at several stages, with a chance for rejection at each stage. *Id*. at 54.

13. The estimate is based on the 35,506,190 admissions for all types of health care institutions in the United States in 1974. AM. HOSPITAL ASS'N, HOSPITAL STATISTICS 13 Table 1 (1975).

14. Pocincki, Dogger & Schwartz, *supra* note 8, at 56-57. "Minor temporary" includes improperly set fractures and infections induced by operations or lack of antibiotics. "Major temporary" includes burns, broken ankles from falls, significant drug side effects, or severed nerves or tendons. "Permanent major" includes paraplegia, blindness, or brain damage. "Grave" means quadriplegia, severe brain damage, or life-long care. For another classification scheme for severity of injury, see Rudov, Myers & Mirabella, *Medical Malpractice Insurance Claims Files Closed in 1970*, in MEDICAL MALPRACTICE REPORT Appendix 1, 9-11.

The reviewers used a confidence scale of one to six to indicate the strength of their responses from "unsure" to "confident." In ninety-three percent of the cases the reviewers were above four on this confidence scale, with six being the mode response.

15. Pocincki, Dogger & Schwartz, *supra* note 8, at 50. The confidence response averaged 2.3 on the scale explained in note 14 *supra*. However, records involving injuries were reviewed for the standard of care rendered. No attempt was made in this survey to ascertain the quantity of negligent or substandard care that did not result in injury.

16. *See id*. at 62.

In another study cited in the H.E.W. report, "accidents attributable to sanctioned and well-intentioned diagnosis and therapy were noted in about five percent of all patients admitted to medical wards."[17] Finally, a study of over 1,000 patients extending from August 1, 1960, to March 31, 1961, attempted to tabulate noxious responses or "episodes" occurring among patients if they resulted from acceptable diagnostic or therapeutic measures deliberately instituted in the hospital.[18] Reactions arising from inadvertent errors by physicians or nurses were excluded. Nevertheless, twenty percent of all patients suffered some type of accident, and 4.7 percent of the accidents were classified as "major."[19]

THE FREQUENCY AND SEVERITY OF MEDICAL NEGLIGENCE

Information on the quality of health care services is scarce but there are indications that much of the care rendered does not meet minimal standards. Two studies, now somewhat dated, attempted to measure the qualitative level of medical care rendered in this country. In 1956, Osler Peterson, a staff member of the Rockefeller Foundation, and his team of doctors watched North Carolina physicians treat pa-

---

17. Barr, *Hazards of Modern Diagnosis and Therapy—The Price We Pay*, 159 J.A.M.A. 1452, 1456 (1955).

18. Schimmel, *The Hazards of Hospitalization*, 60 ANNALS OF INTERNAL MED. 100 (1964).

19. *Id.* at 108. Information obtained from a hospital association corroborates these findings in a somewhat different way. In the twenty years of that program's existence approximately 700,000 incident reports were filed with the insurer. Incident reports cover an assortment of occurrences, including slips and falls, medication errors, equipment failures, losses of personal belongings, adverse reaction to therapies, hospital-acquired infections, and anesthesia accidents and surgical mishaps. What percentage of these reports involved injuries is not known, but it would be reasonable to assume that a significant portion involved some mishap that either caused or might have caused physical harm. In this same period 15,000 claims were filed. Of these reported claims, a hospital association source estimates that only fifteen percent were associated with previously filed incidents. Personal interview with Douglas Dutton, California Hospital Association, Spring 1975. The figures are rough estimates based on experience from 1955 through 1973. Recently, the computer claim analysis used by the insurer was modified to indicate when a claim was first reported as an incident.

According to one estimate of the incidence of hepatitis related to transfusions, two million people receive blood in the course of a year. Of those receiving blood, 1.5 percent (30,000) develop overt hepatitis which requires hospitalization. Of these, ten percent (3,000) die from an acute episode. Those surviving are hospitalized for a period averaging twenty-eight days, with an additional month required for convalescence. A conservative estimate of the economic loss from this injury alone is $175 million per annum, assuming the incident rates are accurate. *See* Havighurst & Tancredi, *"Medical Adversity Insurance"—A No-Fault Approach to Medical Malpractice and Quality Assurance*, 51 MILBANK MEMORIAL FUND Q. 125, 154 n.10 (1973), *reprinted in* 613 INS. L.J. 69, 90 n.10 (1974).

tients in their offices. Peterson concluded that sixty percent of the therapy was below acceptable standards.[20] Later, from 1962 to 1964, a medical team from the Columbia University School of Public Health studied a random sample of patients in the New York City hospitals. In this study forty-three percent of the care was ruled less than "good" and twenty-three percent was labeled "poor."[21] "Below acceptable standards" and "poor" do not necessarily reflect care which would result in tort liability if the care produced injury, for much depends on the standards chosen as normative and the objectivity and perception of the reviewer. However, the magnitude of these statistics suggests that the negligence may be extensive.[22]

The size of the negligence universe may also be related to patterns of surgery performed in the United States. The fee-for-service system, for whatever advantages it may have, has the unfortunate disadvantage of placing economic incentives on the side of performing more operations.[23] Furthermore, this system encourages more radical operations and procedures which in another environment might more readily be referred to surgeons with special interests in a particular disease. Although this type of "negligence" is difficult to prove in individual cases, there are indications that a significant amount of such surgery is being performed.[24]

---

20. Peterson, Andrews & Spain, *An Analytical Study of North Carolina General Practice 1953-54* (pt. II), 31 J. MED. EDUC. 1 (No. 12, 1956). *See* Cordtz, *Change Begins in the Doctor's Office*, FORTUNE 84, 132 (Jan. 1970).

21. Cordtz, *supra* note 20, at 132.

22. Other more recent studies lend credence to the results of these earlier attempts to assess the quality of medical care. *See* Roddis & Stewart, *The Insurance of Medical Losses*, 1975 DUKE L.J. 1281, 1298-99 & n.68; Brook, Brutoco & Williams, *supra* note 5, at 1201-02. *See also* Rensberger, *Unfit Doctors Create Worry in Profession*, N.Y. Times, Jan. 26, 1976, at 1, col. 1.

23. A study by a House of Representatives subcommittee found that approximately 2.4 million unnecessary surgeries were performed in 1974, at a cost to the American public of $4 billion. Approximately 11,900 deaths were attributed to such unnecessary procedures. SUBCOMM. ON OVERSIGHT & INVESTIGATIONS, HOUSE COMM. ON INTERSTATE & FOREIGN COMMERCE, COST & QUALITY OF HEALTH CARE: UNNECESSARY SURGERY 5-6 (Subcomm. Print, Jan. 1976).

24. Crile, *The Surgeon's Dilemma*, HARPERS 30-38 (May 1975). Excess surgery is significant because of the inherent risks of operations and anesthesia. Dr. Crile indicates that mortality rates from appendicitis, including deaths resulting from the surgery itself, are highest in the areas where more appendectomies occur. Under the fee-for-service system, patients undergo surgery at more than twice the rate of subscribers to prepayment health plans (sixty-nine versus thirty-three per 1,000). *Id.* at 30. The lower rate is comparable to surgery rates in Western European countries. A comparison between fee-for-service and prepayment plans in the District of Columbia revealed that the former group had eighty-six percent more appendectomies, 250 percent more tonsillectomies, and fifty-two percent more hysterectomies than a similar group covered by

The use of such surgical practices raises the question whether economic incentives in the health care system are misplaced. Moreover, the issue of negligence is raised to the extent that injuries are increased when unnecessary surgery is performed or the best resources available are not used.[25] Even though imprudence of this type may not produce a verdict for the plaintiff except in the most flagrant case, such activity should not be excluded from the broad definition of negligence.[26]

Despite a lack of comprehensiveness in the studies and surveys cited, available information does support the proposition that a significant number of patients are injured in the course of medical treatment by medical intervention. Furthermore, there are indications that providers, in more cases than they are likely to admit, offer the public services of less than acceptable quality. Finally, if the study commissioned by H.E.W.[27] is at all representative, a substantial portion of

---

a prepayment plan. Faltermayer, *Better Care at Less Cost Without Miracles,* FORTUNE 80, 126 (Jan. 1970). Obviously, the observation that prepaid plans may underutilize surgery is a relevant, though not a controlling, consideration.

Dr. Crile also cites examples of incentives for the performance of more radical operations where simpler ones would suffice. Crile, *supra,* at 32. It is not uncommon in the United States to remove thyroid nodules by surgery rather than doing a needle biopsy to clarify the diagnosis. Thyroid cancer is one of the rarest causes of death by cancer while five to ten percent of all older women have lumps in their thyroids. *Id.* The delayed conversion of surgeons to simpler forms of breast surgery that avoid radical mastectomies is another example cited. *Id.* This radical procedure fell from favor in Europe and Canada prior to its demise in the United States. Thus, the subtle but substantial influence of fee-for-service systems over medical decisions again appears to indicate deviation from an appropriate standard.

Finally, Dr. Crile discusses examples of difficult and dangerous surgical procedures which, unlike routine operations, require esoteric skills. *Id.* at 35. The mortality rate from one of these operations, radical resection of cancer in the pancreas, varies significantly according to the physician performing the procedure. In the hands of specialists with an interest in the disease, chances of dying from the operation itself are less than seven percent. In the hands of a generalist, the mortality rate averages thirty-two percent and ranges up to forty-six percent. *Id.* If a specialist is available, is it reasonable for the generalist to proceed?

Cardiovascular teams might provide another example. It has been reported that a team must operate at least once or twice a week, with daily frequency preferred, to maintain optimal proficiency. Surgery Study Group, Inter-Society Comm'n for Heart Disease Resources, *Optimal Resources for Cardiac Surgery,* 44 CIRCULATION A-221, A-223 (1971). If studies were to show that operation times were reduced and patient survival rates improved the more frequently a surgical team was employed, what would the prudent person conclude as to the appropriateness of using the under-employed team in non-emergency cases?

25. *See* SUBCOMM. ON OVERSIGHT & INVESTIGATIONS, *supra* note 23.

26. For a general historical treatment of the development of the negligence action as a narrowing of the basis for imposing civil liability, see James, *Analysis of the Origin and Development of the Negligence Action,* in DEPARTMENT OF TRANSPORTATION, AUTOMOBILE INSURANCE AND COMPENSATION STUDY 35 (1970).

27. See text accompanying notes 10-19 *supra.*

medical injuries can be related to deviations from accepted standards of care.

If the H.E.W. percentages are used to calculate size estimates for the various categories, the results are staggering.[28] Of the 2.6 million estimated annual iatrogenic injuries, eighteen percent,[29] or 468,000, would be classified as serious permanent injuries and another thirty percent,[30] or 780,000, would be major temporary. If the twenty-nine percent possible negligent causation[31] is applied in turn to these results, there would be a basis for 135,700 malpractice claims requesting compensation for serious permanent injuries or deaths and 226,200 seeking damages for major temporary ailments against health care providers. Moreover, these projections assume that patients with minor injuries do not sue.

Claim Frequency

Information available on reported malpractice claims indicates that the number of claims pursued is far less than the above estimate of potential claims. The H.E.W. survey estimated that 13,000 files were closed in 1970. Of these, 7,900, or sixty percent, were based on formal claim allegations and 5,100 on incident reports from insureds. These 13,000 files were generated by 11,739 occurrences, eighty-two percent of which resulted in a claim against only one insured.[32]

Of the 5,100 files based on incident reports, only 1,400, or twenty-eight percent, were closed with payment. Of the 7,900 files based on formal claim allegations, 4,000, or slightly over fifty percent, resulted in

---

28. Extrapolation of the H.E.W. study results, which are based on a small sample of files from two hospitals, admittedly does not produce highly reliable statistical estimates. However, given the corroboration from other studies on the magnitude of the injury universe, see notes 17-18 *supra*, the resulting figures become reasonable. The internal distribution as to negligent causation or severity of injury is not as creditable, yet even here it must not be assumed that the estimates are invalid. If the negligence estimate were correct, it would mean that at least ninety-eight percent of discharged patients received adequate care by legal standards. The principal conclusion is that the number of possible claims is very likely much greater than the number of suits filed by attorneys, a conclusion supporting the assertion that frequency could continue to increase at a steady pace.
29. See text accompanying note 14 *supra*.
30. See text accompanying note 14 *supra*.
31. See text accompanying note 15 *supra*.
32. S. Dietz, Final Report: The Study of Medical Malpractice Claims Closed in 1970, at 80 Table IV-1, 82 Table IV-2 (1973). (An interim report of this study is in the Medical Malpractice Report Appendix 1-25.) The number of insureds per claim file was strongly correlated with payment patterns. Only twenty-three percent of files closed with payment of $100,000 or more involved one insured.

payment. The paid-to-closed figure for both categories combined was 41.5 percent.[33] The claim study estimated that 10.6 percent more claim files were opened in 1970 than were closed.[34] Applying this percentage, 14,375 claim files were believed to have been opened in 1970. Through the use of linear extrapolation, which assumes a constant rate of increase from one year to the next, the number of files opened from 1971 to 1975 may be calculated at 15,900, 17,600, 19,500, 21,500, and 23,800, respectively.

The Insurance Services Office (ISO) data on physicians and surgeons for recent policy years indicates that there has been an escalation in the rate by which the frequency of incurred claims is increasing (Appendix I). The annual increases between the latest three years of available data for physicians and surgeons have run sixteen, thirty, and twenty-eight percent respectively between policy years 1970-71, 1971-72, and 1972-73.[35] Based on a curve of best fit,[36] the ISO calculated

---

33. *Id.* The percentage of claims closed with payment is affected by the insurers' guidelines for establishing a claim file. For instance, insurers underwriting medical associations, where efforts are made to encourage reporting of incidents and where every incident report results in the opening of a claim file, may close only twenty to twenty-five percent of all claim files with payment. However, if incidents which do not become formal claims are omitted from the denominator, the payment percentages reach the forty- to fifty-percent range. Likewise, carriers that establish claims only when they expect an actual payment to be made, regardless of the source of the report, may close sixty percent of their files with payment. Using H.E.W. data, the author calculated that 1.40 claims were paid per 100 physicians in 1970. Calculations on other data bases produce an estimated paid claim frequency of 1.34, 1.55, and 2.20 per insured physician for equivalent time periods. Author's Survey of Professional Liability Insurance Companies (unpublished research done by Myron F. Steves, Jr., in preparation for his Ph.D. dissertation being completed at the University of Pennnsylvania). The data was gathered and updated between 1972 and 1975. The individual carrier is not identified by name due to an agreeement made at the time of data collection.

34. MEDICAL MALPRACTICE REPORT 7 Figure 1.

35. Data for 1974 will not be available until the spring of 1976 because of the bureau's policy year reporting system.

36. The best known method of fitting a line to a set of data points is that of least squares. It is the line where the sum of the differences between the observed data points, in this case the frequency of claims per 100 physicians per year, and the estimated points is minimized. Linear lines of best fit assume a constant increase in slope. When it is not believed that a straight line will fit a set of points satisfactorily because of the nonlinearity of the relationship, a simple curve or exponential line may yield a more satisfactory fit. The frequency of malpractice claim reports is such that a curvilinear line appears to provide a better basis for estimation than a linear one. Linear trends, however, provide conservative estimates as well as calculations that are more easily understood by the regulators who must approve rate filings. *See* P. HOEL, INTRODUCTION TO MATHEMATICAL STATISTICS 169-75 (1966). *See also* N. DOWNIE & R. HEATH, BASIC STATISTICAL METHODS 172-73 (2d ed. 1965); B. LINDGREN, STATISTICAL THEORY 294-300 (1962).

The Insurance Services Office is a statistical agent and rating bureau for the large

a trend factor on claim frequency of +12.1 percent per annum for use in its 1975 rate filings.[37]

ISO data for hospitals indicated a trend factor of +12.2 percent also based on a curve of best fit.[38] The increases between the last four available policy years were 13.7, 14.6, and 27.4 percent, respectively (Appendix II). A hospital insurer, not reporting to the bureau, experienced stable frequencies from 1966 to 1970 with an upsurge in the range of fifteen to eighteen percent in the next three calendar years, and a jump of thirty percent in the first part of 1974.[39]

Another carrier with a significant volume of doctors reported increases from eight to ten percent in the late sixties and early seventies. However, 1974 showed an increase of twenty-five percent.[40] One insurer with a book dominated by Class I and II physicians[41] experienced frequency increases of 15.7 percent, 28.4 percent, and 68.3 percent between policy years 1971-72, 1972-73, and 1973-74, respectively.[42] A specialty carrier with a stable book of business writing in an area outside the nation's trouble spots reported a seventy percent increase in the first part of 1974 over 1973. Final results lowered the initial estimate but the increase in frequency still exceeded forty percent.[43]

A county medical society survey showed an increase in doctors named in claims of over sixty percent per annum from 1969 to 1974.[44] The latest yearly increases were less than the average but still in the thirty percent range.[45] In Cook County, Illinois, malpractice suit filings

---

multiple-line stock insurance companies as well as for a number of other carriers. ISO reporting companies write a large percentage of the professional liability coverage in the country. The data in the review is based on approximately forty percent of the physician exposure in the United States.

37. INSURANCE SERVICES OFFICE, 1975 REVIEW OF PHYSICIANS AND SURGEONS PROFESSIONAL LIABILITY INSURANCE, Exhibit 2, Sheet 2, *reprinted in* Technical Appendix 568, and Exhibit 5, Sheet 5 (Apr. 18, 1975).

38. INSURANCE SERVICES OFFICE, 1975 REVIEW OF HOSPITAL PROFESSIONAL LIABILITY INSURANCE, Exhibit 2, Sheet 2, and Exhibit 4, Sheet 5 (June 12, 1975).

39. Author's Survey, *supra* note 33.

40. *Id.*

41. Class I and Class II are general practitioners or internists who perform little or no surgery, and who thus have minimal exposure to extremely large malpractice claims. For a discussion of the ISO classification scheme for medical professionals, see Kendall & Haldi, *supra* note 1. *See also Hearings on S.482, S.215, and S.188 Before the Subcomm. on Health of the Senate Comm. on Labor and Public Welfare*, 94th Cong., 1st Sess. 537-39 (1975).

42. Author's Survey, *supra* note 33.

43. *Id.*

44. *Id.*

45. *Id.*

were up twenty percent in the first half of 1975. Between 1973 and 1974, filings had increased 56.7 percent.[46] In a court docket survey conducted by a physicians committee from several counties in Michigan, malpractice suits filed increased 193 percent from 1970 to 1974, and the year 1974 showed an increase of 61 percent over 1973.[47]

Claim Severity

The concern of both providers and insurers over the increased frequency of claims has been heightened by an increase in claim severity. According to the H.E.W. report, the average paid claim cost was $10,600 in 1970 for all providers combined.[48] However, this average increases by fourteen to fifteen percent per annum on a total limits basis if ISO data are used to calculate a trend. If paid losses are broken down by layer, total payments below $5,000 per claim have increased from five to eight percent in recent years. Payments below $25,000 have increased in the ten- to twelve-percent range, while payments in excess of $25,000 have posted increases exceeding twenty percent.[49]

The latest trend factors employed for purposes of calculating the ISO rate revisions for 1975 were 10.2 percent for limits of $25,000/75,000 and 14.7 percent for total limits based on lines of best fit.[50] Another program had a long-term linear trend of 10.2 percent, moving to 11.8 percent if years corresponding to the ISO calculations are used. The latest years available, which do not include 1973 or 1974, indicated increases of twenty-four percent. A third carrier reported se-

---

46. *Relevant Ramblings*, COOK COUNTY JURY VERDICT REP., Apr. 11, 1975, at 1.
47. PHYSICIANS' CRISIS COMMITTEE, COURT DOCKET SURVEY 8 (1975). *See* Altman, *Study Finds Malpractice System No Service to Public*, N.Y. Times, Aug. 3, 1975, § 1, at 41, col. 5.
48. S. DIETZ, *supra* note 32, at 80. A paid claim average excludes from the denominator all claims closed without payment of indemnity and includes only indemnity payments in the numerator. The $10,600 is an average for all providers. In general, physicians and surgeons have higher average and median amounts paid on their behalf than other providers. Hospitals follow this trend, partly because many cases arise out of their hotel functions, which do not involve the same risk of serious injury as does the specialized care rendered by physicians. Nurses and pharmacists have the lowest amount paid on their behalf; the H.E.W. study found no payment in excess of $4,000 for this category of provider. *Id.* at 108.
49. Author's calculations based on ISO rate reviews issued from 1967 to 1975.
50. Technical Appendix 567. Corroborating the ISO trends, one insurer incurred an average yearly increase in paid losses of 12.7 percent from 1964 to 1973, with years corresponding to the ISO figures indicating an increase of 13.7 percent per annum. The years 1971 to 1973 showed an increase of 25.3 percent. The jump between 1973 and 1974, not included in these trend calculations, exceeded forty percent. Author's Survey, *supra* note 33.

verity increases on an annual basis ranging from ten to sixteen percent in recent years.[51]

The mean value of dollar awards escalated from $65,000 in 1965 to the $300,000 range in 1973 and 1974,[52] and there have been at least twenty-five settlements or awards in excess of $1 million from 1968 to the end of 1974, most of these in the last two years. Eighteen of these were in California, only five of which were recorded prior to March, 1973. If settlements and awards in excess of $300,000 are tabulated in California, excluding million-dollar awards, three were made in 1969, five in 1970, nine in 1971, thirteen in 1972, twenty-four in 1973, and twenty-nine in 1974. Prior to 1973, seventy-five percent of these payments were the result of verdicts. With the pattern of recovery established, however, sixty percent of the high payments in 1973 and 1974 were out-of-court settlements.[53]

The expected annual increase in premium costs for medical professional liability insurance can be estimated by combining the frequency and severity trends observed. The combined trend of the ISO on this basis is 23.6 percent per annum for losses at or below the $25,000/75,000 level,[54] while the total limits trend factor would be 26.4 percent.[55] This figure is similar to the estimate made in a recent report to the Auditor General in California indicating an expected claim cost trend of 27 percent.[56] At this rate of increase, premiums would double every three years.[57]

---

51. Author's Survey, *supra* note 33.

52. *The Doctor's New Dilemma*, NEWSWEEK, Feb. 10, 1975, at 41. The article stated that the quoted figures excluded awards over $1 million, but a conversation with Jury Verdict Research, Inc., revealed that these large awards actually were included. The basis for these figures is not a total sampling of all verdicts but only a tabulation of those reported or discovered by Jury Verdict Research.

53. The figures in text were obtained through the author's tabulations over the last several years from data published in PROFESSIONAL LIABILITY NEWSLETTER (D. Rubsamen ed.). These trends are not confined to California. One company writing nationwide, excluding New York and California, estimates that thirteen claims in excess of $100,000 arising from 1972 occurrences will be settled. Estimates for 1974 and 1975 are sixty and 190, respectively. *Excess Claims Rising Rapidly*, MALPRACTICE DIGEST 6 (Mar./Apr. 1975, St. Paul Fire & Marine Ins. Co.).

54. Technical Appendix 567. With respect to professional liability insurance limits, the dollar value before the slash is the amount for which the insurer is liable per claim; the value after the slash is the aggregate of the carrier's liability for any one policy year.

55. *Id.* at 568 (Total limits trend calculated by author).

56. INTERIM REPORT TO THE AUDITOR GENERAL: STATE OF CALIFORNIA, CONCERNING MEDICAL MALPRACTICE INSURANCE STUDY 3 (Sept. 1975).

57. In INTERIM REPORT, *supra* note 56, the investigators concluded that the "current malpractice crisis has been caused in part by poor pricing by the insurance industry, for premiums have increased erratically while claim cost increases have been relatively steady." *Id.* at 1. With respect to the ISO filings, the price level for basic limits has

Premiums as a Percentage of Expenditures on Health Care

Escalating malpractice premiums, attributable in large part to the increased frequency and severity of claims, have always been vital to providers concerned with their professional liability exposure. However, broader social interest in the resolution of medical malpractice insurance problems has developed only recently, for until the last two years insurance costs were not significant in terms of total national expenditures on health care. In 1970, the H.E.W. Commission estimated that $300 million in premiums were paid by health care providers. This figure represented less than one half of one percent of the $75 billion expended on health care during that year.[58] According to this author's estimates, the same statistic for 1974 was only a little over one half of one percent. Since then the situation has changed rapidly. Malpractice cost will represent one percent of the health care costs in 1975 and 1.5 percent in 1976. By 1980, this percentage could exceed 2.5 percent.[59]

While premium costs are increasing significantly over historical levels, medical liability exposure still does not appear significant when compared with total health care expenditures.[60] These figures, how-

---

increased 6.8, 14.1, 11.8, and 8.3 percent for the calendar years 1970 to 1973 for physicians. Hospital premiums increased 15.2, 9.9, 8.4, and 0.4 percent during the same four year period. In 1974, physician premiums jumped 52.5 percent and hospital premiums 49.6 percent. The 1975 indicated increase for physicians was 142.9 percent, with hospital premiums requiring a similar adjustment. Changes in the increased limit factors have exhibited the same trend. Limits of $100,000/300,000 could be purchased for a factor of twenty percent of the basic $25,000/75,000 premium up until 1968. Steves & McWhorter, *supra* note 1, at 227 Table IV. In 1969, twenty-five percent was required. From 1970 to 1974, twenty-eight and thirty-two percent were required for physicians and surgeons respectively. In the fall of 1974, the percentages were forty-nine and fifty-two. The 1975 filings require seventy-four percent for physicians and seventy-seven percent for surgeons. *Id.*

The current price level changes are catch-up increases for previous years. However, given the magnitude of these increases, 1976 rate revisions may very well be nominal, regardless of the long range trends in frequency and severity. Providers, regulators, and insurers alike are only beginning to realize the necessity of increasing premiums to reflect statistical trends before the data on recent losses matures.

58. MEDICAL MALPRACTICE REPORT 12n.5.

59. Steves, *supra* note 1, at 215. The 1974 figure is based on a premium estimate of $500 million and expenditures of $94 billion. The 1975 figure is based on premiums between $1 billion and $1.2 billion and expenditures of $115 billion; the year 1976 is based on figures of $2 billion and $129 billion. The 1980 figure assumes that medical costs increase ten percent per annum while malpractice premiums go up twenty-five percent per year from 1976 to 1980.

60. In 1974, $14 billion was paid to carriers for insurance to cover automobile accident liability. *See* INSURANCE INFORMATION INSTITUTE, INSURANCE FACTS 12 (1975).

ever, ignore the distribution of premium and income within the health care sector of the economy. Because of differences in exposure to losses from liability claims, seventy percent of the premium dollars paid are contributed by physicians and surgeons,[61] while only twenty percent of total expenditures on health care are made in payment of physician services.[62]

Similarly, the percentage of gross income expended by physicians for professional liability insurance, when viewed on an overall basis, is relatively small. In 1970, 1.34 percent of physicians' gross income was spent for professional liability insurance.[63] By 1974, this percentage had risen to 1.89 percent, and the estimates for 1975 and 1976 are 3.68 and 6.68 percent, respectively.[64] If malpractice premiums were spread evenly over all medical specialties, even the projected figures would not disrupt the health care delivery system. However, premiums are not spread uniformly over all practitioners.[65] The forty percent classified as surgeons pay seventy-five percent of the insurance premiums, and if Class III general practice surgeons, ophthalmologists, and proctologists are excluded, fifty-five percent of the premium is paid by twenty-five percent of the physicians.[66]

Depending on the estimate of the aggregate personal expenditures for automobiles, this means that from ten to fifteen percent of the direct costs of the private passenger transportation system are related to automobile accidents. Sixty percent of these premiums were for third-party liability. *Id.* The total economic cost of auto accidents in 1973, of course, was much higher than those losses covered by insurance. The Insurance Information Institute estimates the latter figures at $30.4 billion. *Id.* at 50. Although provider liability insurance payments have increased dramatically when expressed as a percentage, the direct cost of insuring the medical malpractice exposure is substantially under the cost of insuring the hazard of automobile accidents.

61. The Author's Survey resulted in an estimate of slightly more than seventy percent. The H.E.W. study by Kendall and Haldi derived an estimate of slightly less than seventy percent for 1970. Kendall & Haldi, *supra* note 1, at 509 Table III-6.

62. In fiscal 1973, physician services accounted for 18.4 percent of total national health expenditures. OFFICE OF RESEARCH & STATISTICS, SOCIAL SECURITY ADMIN., RESEARCH AND STATISTICS NOTE 1, at 3 Table 2 (Feb. 19, 1975). In 1970, the figure was 19.6 percent, and in 1960 it was 21.1 percent. *Id.* at 7, Table 4. *See* BUREAU OF THE CENSUS, U.S. DEP'T OF COMMERCE, STATISTICAL ABSTRACT OF THE UNITED STATES 70 Table 101 (96th ed. 1975). *See also* Worthington, *National Health Expenditures 1929-74*, 38 SOCIAL SECURITY BULL. 3 (1975).

63. Steves & McWhorter, *supra* note 1, at 232 Table XI. The calculations were based on fiscal year figures obtained from the SOCIAL SECURITY BULLETIN, 1955 to 1974.

64. Steves & McWhorter, *supra* note 1, at 232 Table XI.

65. Current ISO class differentials have a spread of eight to one. *Id.* at 226 Table III. Sixty percent of all physicians are in Classes I or II, with most of these in Class I. Many surgical specialists are charged five times the basic rate, while obstetrician/gynecologists and plastic surgeons are assigned a factor of six. Neurosurgeons, orthopedists, and thoracic and vascular surgeons are assigned the highest multiple, eight.

The effect of this skewed premium distribution is related to the gross incomes of the individual medical specialties. According to the American Medical Association's seventh periodic survey of physicians, the average malpractice expense was less than two percent of gross income and less than five percent of total professional expense. The general surgeons' liability premiums equaled 2.4 percent of gross income and 7.4 percent of professional expense. For obstetrician/gynecologists the percentages were 3.0 and 7.9. Anesthesiologists, however, paid 4.5 and 18.9 percent of income and expenses, respectively, for their insurance protection. At the other end of the scale, internists paid 1.0 and 2.4 percent while pediatricians paid 0.9 and 2.1 percent.[67]

Variations in geographical ratings compound the skewed distribution based on specialization. While location affects physician income, its impact on premium levels is most significant. The AMA survey indicates that the mean burden of premiums related to gross income varies considerably by state. In 1970, statewide average premiums for malpractice insurance were 3.53 percent of gross income in New York, 3.25 percent in California and 2.06 percent in Florida.[68] Pennsylvania, Ohio, and Connecticut averaged 1.28 percent, while Mississippi, South Carolina, and New Hampshire were at the low end of the range with 0.86, 0.78, and 0.69 percent respectively.[69]

The latest ISO rate level recommendations corroborate the pattern observed in the AMA survey. The countrywide average premium for $25,000/75,000 limits indicated in the 1975 rate review was $984. The range, however, stretches from $273 for New Hampshire to $3,348 for California, or from .27 to 3.40 times the average.[70] The median premium of approximately $745 is lower than the average. Based on this median base premium, standard ISO class differentials, and excess limits factors, Class I physicians would pay $2,026 for $1 million/3 million in coverage while Class VII surgeons would pay $16,569 per

---

66. Author's calculations, based on figures in INSURANCE SERVICES OFFICE, PHYSICIANS AND SURGEONS—DIFFERENTIAL STUDY 1975 (Apr. 28, 1975).
67. The percentage calculations in the text are based on data in the AMA's 1973 Profiles of Medical Practice, AM. MED. ASS'N, PROFILES OF MEDICAL PRACTICE (1973), and corroborated by data abstracted from the AMA Seventh Annual Survey, prepared by the Department of Social and Economic Research of the AMA's Center for Health Services Research and Development and provided to the author on special request.
68. AMA Seventh Annual Survey, *supra* note 67.
69. *Id.*
70. The figures in text are the author's calculations, based on data from INSURANCE SERVICES OFFICE, *supra* note 37. The median premium is the median state Class I premium for basic limits (Wisconsin $739 and Minnesota $752).

annum. The range for the top-rated surgeons based on ISO filings would be from $6,334 in New Hampshire to $77,674 in California.[71]

The uneven distribution of the premium burden by specialty is aggravated by other characteristics of the physician and type of practice. Physicians practicing alone earn less than average incomes while partnerships and informal associations earn greater than average incomes.[72] Furthermore, physicians in the earlier and later years of practice earn less than practitioners in their middle years, a phenomenon not unrelated to the volume of services rendered.[73] Since premiums tend to be uniform within rating classes, the older physician in solo practice may well be paying an even larger percentage of his gross income for premiums than the averages indicate. If gross income is low and premium expense high because of specialty, as in the case of anesthesiologists,[74] the collateral effects of practice organization and age, as related to the volume of services rendered, may place the physician in an extremely vulnerable position. At this point, premium levels may result directly in physicians' decisions to change, modify, or abandon their practice.[75]

---

71. Author's calculations. The premium for the Class VII surgeon in California is several times that which is suggested as an adequate rate by the carriers active in that state. However, the ISO premium level assumes a .667 permissible loss ratio and .333 for other expenses and profit. The net rate for losses would be $51,808. Further, the differentials between classes has not been as wide in parts of California as it has been in other parts of the country, a factor which would further reduce this figure. Also, the fact that the exposure reported to ISO is not a large percentage of the writings in California and may be weighted with physician, in contrast to surgical, exposure might also have an impact. Finally, if a twenty-five percent factor were applied to account for investment income, the ISO premium approaches the upper limit of what has been suggested with respect to prices in the California market. Since the premiums charged in the state have been understated historically, it is hard to dismiss the "modified" ISO figure as having no basis. Even if it is assumed that the 1976 price for the highest-rated specialist should be $25,000, it will be in the range indicated as required by the ISO between 1978 and 1980, depending on what modification is made to the $77,674 figure.

72. The average gross income of solo practitioners in 1973 was estimated at $78,789, while two-person groups averaged $99,135 per physician. The average for all practitioners was $83,969. CENTER FOR HEALTH SERVICES RESEARCH AND DEVELOPMENT, AM. MED. ASS'N, PROFILE OF MEDICAL PRACTICE 1974, at 195, 204.

73. CENTER FOR HEALTH SERVICES RESEARCH AND DEVELOPMENT, *supra* note 72, at 197-200. Income, age of practitioner, and average number of office visits are strongly correlated.

74. See text accompanying note 67 *supra*.

75. Although there is relatively little formal documentation of the phenomenon, there is evidence that premium levels do affect practice decisions. As an insurance broker dealing in this area, the author would estimate that at least a dozen such cases have come to his attention in the past year. The most frequent example is the Class III General Practice Surgeon who derives approximately ten percent of his income from

Concentration on Malpractice Claims

The ways in which price, quantity, and quality of health care services are affected by concerns over legal liability or the conventional methods of insuring this liability are not well documented. However, there is little doubt that providers, particularly physicians, perceive themselves to be in a disadvantageous position and are seeking to improve their present situation. Individual proposals, designed either to affect the pricing and availability of malpractice insurance or to alter or narrow the civil liability of providers, are continually being advanced.[76] Unfortunately, most of the propositions concentrate on malpractice *claims*. While claims have a direct cost chargeable to physicians and other health care providers, they represent the smallest percentage of medical accidents.[77] Iatrogenic injuries and substandard care which do not result in claims should be of more immediate concern to provider and consumer alike. Nevertheless, economic incentives are such that a disproportionate share of the attention of those best able to control the quality of medical care is directed toward claim reduction.

This phenomenon is tied directly to the reliance of our economic and social structure on the legal concept of negligence, which holds the actor personally responsible when deviation from an acceptable standard causes harm. The actor is responsible for his actions only if they result in a finding of wrongdoing.[78] As a practical matter, the actor is not liable for all negligent acts, for the evidentiary burden is on the injured party, and the actor is legally responsible only when the person damaged can prove by a fair preponderance of the evidence that the actor owed him a duty of care, departed from that duty, and damaged his interests as a direct result of that departure.[79] Application of negligence principles to the delivery of health care services means that providers are financially liable for only a small portion of the medical accidents which in fact occur.

A continued focus on claims may result in dilution of the quality

---

surgery. The effect of this activity on his insurance premiums is such that his surgical practice generates little or no net income. *Cf.* Brook, *supra* note 5, at 1212-13. The author is aware of another situation where a surgeon specialist shifted to a medical practice five years prior to the normal retirement age. Part of the reason was the difficulty of paying a full surgical premium while gradually restricting surgical activity.

76. For a discussion of recent state legislative attempts to meet the immediate problems created by the current malpractice insurance crisis, see Comment, *An Analysis of State Legislative Responses to the Medical Malpractice Crisis*, 1975 DUKE L.J. 1417.

77. See notes 20-47 *supra* and accompanying text.

78. *See* James, *supra* note 26, at 51-56. *See generally* W. PROSSER, HANDBOOK OF THE LAW OF TORTS 143-179 (4th ed. 1971).

79. *See generally* C. WASMUTH, *supra* note 6.

control function of the present liability system, since only those injuries with a high likelihood of producing malpractice claims of significant value become of direct economic importance to the provider. Furthermore, since the frequency of claims is low compared to the total volume of services rendered, the cost of focusing on a known hazard may not be financially justified. Because of the exposure base used for rating professional liability insurance, even individual practitioners and health care providers who follow exacting quality control procedures are not likely to receive any direct financial benefit for their efforts.

Concentration on the claim universe to determine both the medical and nonmedical aspects of insured malpractice losses is not without reward, however. Studies of the types of claims alleged, the severity of injuries incurred, the characteristics of claimants and defendants, and the effect of attorney representation supply useful information to providers of health care.[80] For example, inspection of claim files may reveal the hazards of failing to establish rapport with patients, of practitioners commenting on work done or results obtained by colleagues, and of the risks involved in using certain collection procedures. Improvement in these areas could result in the filing of fewer claims when injuries occur. Indeed, fewer injuries might occur if provider-patient relationships were warmer and medical personnel were more aware of the complaints of their clients. Nevertheless, if from the standpoint of the general economy, as well as that of individual patients, injuries are by far the larger and more costly occurrences when compared to claims, it would appear proper to concentrate on the former in designing a system to monitor the quality and quantity of services rendered, even though some benefit may be gleaned from attention to the latter. Furthermore, claims by definition involve the possibility of litigation, a factor not conducive to frank and open discussion of injury prevention.

Emphasis on Injuries

One alternative to concentration on claims is to place the direct cost of a much larger subset, that of injuries occurring in the course of medical treatment, on the shoulders of health care providers. Under one such proposed system, termed Medical Adversity Insurance,[81] the relative avoidability of an injury, not negligence, is the criterion for

---

80. *See, e.g.*, MEDICAL MALPRACTICE REPORT; MEDICAL MALPRACTICE REPORT Appendix; Mills, *Medical Lessons from Malpractice Cases*, 183 J.A.M.A. 1073 (Mar. 1963).

81. *See generally* Havighurst & Tancredi, *supra* note 18. *See also* Havighurst, "*Medical Adversity Insurance*"—*Has Its Time Come?*, 1975 DUKE L.J. 1233.

designating an adverse medical event as compensable. The cost burden is placed on the provider best able to effect an improvement in quality control and a concomitant reduction in the frequency and severity of injuries. The example of hepatitis incident to transfusion illustrates the type of event that this system would compensate as well as the magnitude of the financial incentives that would be involved.[82]

Despite the conceptual appeal of a system that employs financial incentives and market mechanisms to encourage injury prevention, the likelihood that such a scheme would be accepted by government and the special interests involved is remote. The program makes significant implicit costs explicit, a violation of the laws of practical politics.

The alternative means of achieving control of the quality and quantity of medical services is through regulation. The principal source of this type of control is the self-regulation imposed by the providers themselves, since the good intentions and moral character of those engaged in the healing arts are primary. The values of the providers find formal expression in the bylaws of medical societies, requirements of organizations like the Joint Commission for the Accreditation of Hospitals (JCAH), and laws governing licensing and medical practice.[83]

Third-party payors, originally Blue Cross and Blue Shield and private health insurers, and now the government-sponsored Medicare and Medicaid plans, have reinforced incentives to comply with acceptable medical standards by insisting upon functioning utilization review, medical audit, and tissue committees in the hospitals they reimburse.[84]

---

82. See note 19 *supra*. The state of the art does not allow detection of the hepatitis virus in whole blood in most circumstances. However, the contamination rate of paid donor blood is known to run higher than that of voluntary donor blood, perhaps ten times as high. See Franklin, *Tort Liability for Hepatitis: An Analysis and a Proposal*, 24 STAN. L. REV. 439, 444-45 (1972). Despite this statistic, twenty-five percent of all transfusions in this country employ the more hazardous product. *Id.* at 441. Although the good will and moral integrity of providers is on the side of reducing reliance on paid donor blood, substantial economic incentives are not. Even though no court has accepted the doctrine that use of paid donor blood is negligence, emphasis on injury reduction suggests that it might be appropriate to apply a concept of enterprise liability if harm is caused when hepatitis is transmitted by this category of blood.

83. *See* D. HARNEY, MEDICAL MALPRACTICE 122-30 (1973) (use of accreditation criteria as medical standards). See note 7 *supra* and accompanying text.

84. Utilization review usually requires that the need for continued patient care be certified at regular intervals once a patient's length of stay exceeds some normative criterion. Medical audits are random reviews of physician services rendered in hospitals to verify that they are of appropriate quality. Tissue committees monitor the results of surgery, and pathology reports indicate whether removed tissues are normal or abnormal. If a surgeon's percentage of either falls outside an acceptable range, a more comprehensive review of his surgical practices is undertaken by the tissue committee.

The 1972 amendments to the Social Security Act,[85] requiring the creation of Professional Standards Review Organizations (PSROs),[86] have expanded the concepts of community- and hospital-based peer review. Concerned with review of care financed by federal funds, the PSRO system will provide decentralized control of the quality and quantity of the services rendered by institutional as well as individual providers. The initial concentration will be on utilization of hospital facilities and, to the extent possible, the PSROs will defer to hospital review committees where the activities of these committees are judged satisfactory by the new standards. The PSROs will have the power to withhold authorization for payment of health claims as an incentive for providers to render only necessary services of acceptable quality. The organizations will also have the duty to disclose adverse decisions relating to providers, at least in the event of recurrent and flagrant violation of standards. Of equal, if not greater, importance, however, will be the dissemination of comparative information on the normal practices and standards of other providers both within and without the local organization. Combined with evaluative studies of the efficacy of particular procedures and the etiology of specific diseases, these methods of monitoring utilization should promote a better health care system.[87]

Focusing Liability on the Hospital

The existing regulatory system of controlling quality of health care services and the general acceptance of negligence law limit the approaches one may take to resolve the current problems of malpractice litigation and medical malpractice insurance. However, it is possible to construct a system that ameliorates the problem of increasing premium costs and, at the same time, strengthens incentives to prevent injuries. While liability insurance would not be the primary mechanism for providing quality control as in the medical adversity insurance program, it would be supportive of the regulatory structure.

The proposed concept would shift the legal liability exposure and the cost of insuring it from individual practitioners to institutional

---

85. Pub. L. No. 92-603, § 249F, 86 Stat. 1429 (codified at 42 U.S.C. §§ 1320c-1 to c-19 (1973)).

86. The constitutionality of this PSRO program was upheld by the Supreme Court in Association of Am. Physicians & Surgeons v. Mathews, 96 S. Ct. 388 (1975).

87. *See generally* Staff of Senate Comm. On Finance, Background Material Relating to Professional Standards Review Organizations (Comm. Print. 1974); Comment, *PSRO: Malpractice Liability and the Impact of the Civil Immunity Clause*, 62 Geo. L.J. 1499, 1500-02 (1974); Note, *Federally Imposed Self-Regulation of Medical Practice: A Critique of the Professional Standards Review Organization*, 42 Geo. Wash. L. Rev. 822 (1974).

providers for incidents occurring within institutional settings.[88] Thus, the liability and liability insurance premium resulting from acts of physicians and surgeons would be transferred to hospitals, where seventy-five percent of all claims arise.[89] The remainder of the exposure would be a non-hospital risk that could be insured by practitioners on an individual basis.

Although the concept is simple, the values of such a premium shift are numerous:

Distribution of Premiums. The premium burden of the professional liability exposure would match more evenly the expenditure patterns for health services in the economy. Hospital care expenditures are twice those for physician services.[90] Assuming adjustment in charges by both providers, it is likely that malpractice insurance premiums would approach a proportional distribution with respect to gross revenue from services.

Continuity. The bulk of the premium expense would fall on hospital corporations, which have a much broader capital base and a more reliable cash flow than the economic unit of physicians in solo or small group practice common in this country's health care delivery system. Institutional providers, both legally and structurally, can be expected to continue in existence indefinitely, for their operation and ability to pay premiums is not predicated on the good health or survival of any one individual.

Among other considerations, the continuity of a corporate enterprise means that the insurance industry can approach coverage problems with a broader range of techniques. For example, a "claims made" policy form could be used without adversely affecting the interests or increasing the uncertainty that a particular injury to a patient by a practitioner would be an uninsured loss.[91]

---

88. The Virginia Bureau of Insurance has proposed such a plan. BUREAU OF INS., STATE CORP. COMM'N (Virginia), MEDICAL MALPRACTICE INSURANCE IN VIRGINIA: THE SCOPE AND SEVERITY OF THE PROBLEM AND ALTERNATIVE SOLUTIONS 81-93 (1975).

89. Rudov, Myers, & Mirabella, *supra* note 14, at 1, 10. Figures in the seventy to seventy-five percent range are reported in other surveys; one *early* survey indicated that seventy-one percent of physician cases examined were related to occurrences in hospitals. Sadusk & Waterson, *Professional Liability*, 87 CAL. MED. 192, 198 (1957).

90. Of total health expenditures in 1973, 18.4 percent were for physician services and 38.6 percent were for hospital care. Office of Research and Statistics, *supra* note 62, at 3, Table 2; *see also* Bureau of the Census, *supra* note 62, at 70, Table 101.

91. A "claims made" policy provides coverage based on the year in which a claim is first reported. An "occurrence contract" provides coverage based on the time of occurrence of the act giving rise to the allegation of negligence. *See New Form of Malpractice Liability Coverage to be Offered to Doctors*, MALPRACTICE DIGEST 1 (Jan./Feb. 1975, St. Paul Fire and Marine Ins. Co.). One problem in the shift from an occurrence

Premium Volume. The premium volume generated per risk by the proposed system, taken in conjunction with the consideration of continuity, would make experience and retrospective premium agreements more feasible.[92] Use of very high deductibles, self-insured retentions, and aggregate excess insurance plans would become more practical.[93] The expertise in risk management employed successfully in other industries would become more applicable to the corporate entities providing health services.

From the marketing standpoint, increased premiums per risk, with less uncertainty in pricing, should encourage innovative thinking, if not outright competition, among insurers for this type of business. The great opportunities for monitoring and controlling the exposure insured would be an additional encouragement.

Exposure Basis. Insurers could experiment with exposure bases other than the individual doctor or the occupied hospital bed. Exposure might be tied more appropriately to the types of patients treated, the kinds of surgery performed, the number of anesthetics given, or any combination of these measures.[94] Another possibility would be to tie the initial premium to gross receipts.[95]

Among its other advantages, a hospital-based exposure system would mean that new practitioners, or practitioners who desire to restrict the quantity of services they render, could make a decision without

---

to a claims made form is how to insure against claims arising out of occurrences during the final year of a physician's practice.

92. *See* Roddis & Stewart, *supra* note 22, at 1302-03.

93. A larger hospital paying a premium of $1 million under the existing system might pay as much as $4 million under the proposal suggested. At this level, retaining a significant deductible amount or a proportional share of all losses would provide incentive for risk control. *Cf.* Havighurst, *supra* note 81, at 1251. One basis for this arrangement would be for the risk to retain the first $100,000, or some other appropriate amount, of each loss as well as the excess over that figure up to a maximum amount. An insuring arrangement would be triggered when the aggregate of the losses in excess of $100,000 was greater than a predetermined amount. The size of the retention would depend on the premium volume that would be generated on a straight insurance basis.

94. The California Hospital Association program currently charges a rate per occupied bed, per outpatient visit, per emergency service visit (higher than outpatient rate), and a rate for each surgery (defined as one in which a general anesthetic is used), as well as charging a premium for the employed physicians. The concept proposed in text is designed to make such a system as refined as is practicable, assuming there is a relationship between the types of services rendered and exposure.

95. A gross receipts premium basis for rating physicians has been evaluated by insurers and regulators and rejected because of the fact that there is no direct correlation between income and exposure in the malpractice situation. 2 NAT. ASS'N INS. COMMISSIONERS PROC. 607 (1971). However, as a point of departure for general hospitals, the concept may be more appropriate.

regard to the financial considerations posed by existing classification and rating procedures of insurers.

Effect of Premium Increases. Assuming premiums continue to increase, hospital providers would be in a better position to pass the costs through the system than would the individual practitioner. Hospitals, with their detailed charge structures, could build in the additional expense with little disruption. With overhead already high, the relative increase in room rates or facility and procedure charges required would be less than the increase most physicians would be forced to charge. The increment per patient discharged, although readily identifiable, would not represent a significant portion of total charges to the patient.[96] In addition, patients tend to be better insured for care rendered in a hospital setting.[97]

Furthermore, hospitals are generally reimbursed on a cost basis for Medicare and Medicaid patients,[98] as well as for service benefits provided under Blue Cross coverages in some jurisdictions.[99] Such retrospective cost reimbursement contracts would automatically absorb premium increases, in sharp contrast with the practice prescribed for physicians which dictates billing on a fee-for-service basis only within the bounds of "usual and customary" rates.[100] In the case of the various medical aid programs administered by state governments, payment schedules rather than customary fees are the norm. Such schedules are unlikely to respond to rapid increases in insurance costs as they affect particular specialties rendering particular types of services.

Incentive for Quality Control. The hospital and its medical staff would have increased incentive to control the quality of services. This incentive would result from several factors. First, the magnitude of

---

96. In Virginia, for example, it has been estimated that shifting the malpractice burden to hospitals would increase the daily per bed rate by only $1.20. BUREAU OF INS., *supra* note 88, at 83-84. *But see Hearings on S. 482, S. 215 and S. 188, supra* note 41, at 333 (testimony of HEW Secretary Weinberger); *id.* at 380 (statement by Alexander McMahon, President of American Hospital Ass'n).

97. In 1973, only 11.4 percent of national expenditures on hospital care were handled through direct payments. OFFICE OF RESEARCH AND STATISTICS, *supra* note 62, at 9, Table 5. In contrast, 36.4 percent of expenditures on physician services in the same year were in the form of direct payments. *Id.* at 8, Table 5.

98. For a discussion of the impact of cost reimbursement, see Falk, *Financing for the Reorganization of Medical Care Services and Delivery*, 50 MILBANK MEMORIAL FUND Q. 191 (1972).

99. In areas where Blue Cross plans provide health insurance for a large segment of the population, cost reimbursement is used rather than payment of charges. The five-county area around Philadelphia is one example.

100. *See generally* BLUE CROSS-BLUE SHIELD OF NORTH CAROLINA, USUAL, CUSTOMARY, AND REASONABLE: AN EXPLANATION FOR M.D.s (1974).

premium volume would draw the attention of the medical staff, as well as the board of directors and administrative staff of the hospital, to the problems of claims and injury prevention.

Second, hospitals provide an independent basis for control and review of medical practice. Although the professional ethics of the providers and the requirements of third-party payors are obviously the primary impetus for effective control, the addition of a monetary incentive in the form of substantial malpractice premiums would encourage these review boards to give additional attention to problem areas. If the premium were based on a per surgery or a per anesthetic charge, subject to modification for experience, incentive to review both quantity and quality of services would be enhanced.

Third, the hospital would have an expanded opportunity to prepare a more sophisticated data base for medical injuries as well as for claims. The premium dollars paid by a single institution would justify research and development of a more elaborate quality control system that would integrate information either as yet uncollected or maintained separately by hospitals, physician committees, and insurance companies.

Finally, the premium volume, combined with better information on the efficacy of various quality control procedures, might make it possible to provide direct economic benefits for alterations and improvements in standards, procedures, or methods of monitoring the quality and quantity of services rendered. Experience might indicate that, like fire insurance, debits and credits could be assigned for specific features of the health care system operation.

Professional Standards Review Organizations. Taken together, the advantages of the proposed system of centralizing liability exposure with respect to acts occurring within institutional settings support the goals and concepts proposed in the legislation establishing the Professional Standards Review Organizations.[101] The proposed liability system provides additional incentive for an evaluation of health care which has quality improvement as an objective, but, for very practical reasons, gives priority to control of the utilization of services.[102]

Alternative Compensation Plans. The hospital provides a better forum for experimentation with alternative methods of compensating

---

101. See text accompanying notes 85-87 *supra*.
102. The methods of evaluating quality of care are not as sophisticated as those for regulating the quantity of services rendered. Utilization review and tissue committee controls, for example, focus on the quantity of services. Utilization review, however, is a function of quality control because of the correlation between length of stays and complications of medical treatment.

injured parties. For instance, if arbitration of claims is desired, patients, prior to entering the hospital, could be requested to agree to this method for resolving disputes. A provision for rescission of the arbitration agreement within thirty days of discharge would alleviate the problems of adhesion.[103] The hospital has advantages in the implementation of this arrangement that do not exist in a physician's office practice unless a large clinic is involved. Alternate methods for resolving patient dissatisfaction or of compensating some injuries without regard to fault could find a suitable testing ground under the proposed system.

Advantages in Litigation. If a case goes to trial, there is an advantage to health care providers in presenting a common defense. The surgeons, anesthesiologists and all the employees of the institution need not buy out of litigation by way of settlement for fear of being caught in a crossfire of accusations. Cases could be evaluated on their merits and arbitrary damage allocations according to availability of liability limits avoided. This unifying of defendant interests might work to the advantage of plaintiffs as well. Meritorious claims could be settled under circumstances that might delay settlement if the interests of the defendants were separate. An example would be the situation where it is difficult to determine which act, in a series of mishaps, actually caused the injury[104] or when settlement is not made promptly because of the reluctance of one of several defendants to settle.

Practitioners' Liability. The remaining office liability of practitioners could be handled in many ways. One proposal would be to encourage the local societies or, perhaps, the national specialty associations to organize insurance programs.[105] This structure might promote a flow of information within specialties that would result in injury reduction for both hospital and nonhospital exposure. Nominal surcharges to premiums for tabulation and communication of information about injuries might be one way to encourage prevention. A single nationwide defense league might be feasible as well, with the hospital

---

103. The California Hospital Association, in cooperation with its legal counsel and the Farmers Insurance Group, applied such a procedure on a demonstration basis in California.

104. *See, e.g.,* Starr v. Fregosi, 370 F.2d 15 (5th Cir. 1966); Ybarra v. Spangard, 25 Cal. 2d 486, 154 P.2d 687 (1944).

105. Based on expected 1976 premium levels, a level rated premium on the range of $1,000 to $1,500 would provide high limit protection for the physician's office exposure. A level rated concept becomes feasible because forty-eight percent of all claims filed against Class I physicians arise from events outside the hospital. For Class II doctors the same percentage is forty-six and for Class III it is thirty-two. For the surgical specialists the rates are in the ten- to fourteen-percent range. *See* S. Dietz, *supra* note 32, at 103, Table VI-3.

exposure eliminated from the base. In this way the national association could concentrate on a manageable subset of malpractice problems.

While physicians may welcome a shift of liability exposure and premiums to the institutional providers, they may well be concerned with the corresponding shift from practitioner independence to more centralized institutional control. However, under the proposed system, the bulk of the actual supervision would continue to be exercised by the physicians themselves through the medical staffs. The governing boards of the hospitals would have an increased interest in seeing that the medical staff in fact performed its function. In light of the current judicial trends interpreting corporate liability,[106] as well as the regulatory pressures exerted by PSROs,[107] physicians will continue to be supervised more carefully and will lose some measure of independence regardless of the insurance system employed. Thus, the proposed system does not break entirely new ground, and its overarching policy of quality patient service is one which all physicians should weigh against their concerns over medical independence.

Institutional concern would center on the substantial financial burden placed on hospitals until charge structures and operating procedures could be appropriately modified. In contrast to this burden, individual providers would be seen as the beneficiaries of at least a short-term windfall. However, normal market pressures and negotiations between the two providers should resolve any significant initial economic disturbances caused by the proposed plan.[108] For example, in the initial year physicians could contribute to a hospital premium fund an amount based on the proportion of hospital-based services rendered during the year to all services. This part of the total premium could then be allocated to the specific institutions with which the practitioner was affiliated.[109] In subsequent years, the contribution could be scaled down until the physician paid only for his office exposure.

---

106. *See* Mitchell County Hosp. Authority v. Joiner, 229 Ga. 140, 189 S.E.2d 412 (1972); Moore v. Board of Trustees of Carson-Tahoe Hosp., 88 Nev. 207, 495 P.2d 605 (1972), *cert. denied*, 409 U.S. 879 (1972); Darling v. Charleston Community Memorial Hosp., 33 Ill. 2d 326, 211 N.E.2d 253 (1965), *cert. denied*, 383 U.S. 946 (1966). See also D. RUBSAMEN, HOSPITAL CORPORATE RESPONSIBILITY 11 (to be published).

107. See notes 85-87 *supra* and accompanying text.

108. It is possible that a premium sharing arrangement might be implemented as a permanent device for some of the smaller hospitals in rural communities.

109. The medical record abstracting systems employed by most hospitals routinely tabulate information on the number of surgeries by type for each physician. Medical services could be similarly tabulated on the number of admissions per physician. These data would be the basis for proration of a physician's premium in the first year or years of transition.

Another possibility would be to shift the hospital exposure from an "occurrence" to a "claims made" form.[110] This pattern of claim reporting would give the hospital several years to adjust to the new situation before the full impact of the shift in exposure was realized.[111] Meanwhile, physicians could contribute the difference in their premiums, which resulted from exclusion of hospital exposure, to the surplus of one or more broadly based physician-owned or -controlled insurance companies suggested to handle the office exposure.

For the first few years after the transition, patients could expect fees for physician services to remain relatively constant. Gains from the changeover in liability exposure would offset the routine increases attributable to inflation. Interim price controls or procedures designed to monitor provider income and expense could also be implemented on a short-term basis to stabilize profit margins during the transition period.

CONCLUSION

As the total cost of malpractice has become an increasingly significant portion of health care expenditures, public interest in maximizing the benefits derived from premiums paid has grown. Unfortunately, the existing pattern of insuring against medical malpractice does not meet these growing expectations of proper premium utilization. The premium burden falls on physicians organized in small economic units that cannot support proper quality control with information feedback. The individual practitioner's exposure unit allows for little pricing flexibility, resulting in almost no economic incentive to prevent injuries. While premiums tend to be uniform within medical specialties in a particular territory, irrespective of quality or quantity of service, the distribution of losses by specialty skews premiums in such a way that a growing number of practitioners are finding the increased costs an unbearable financial burden. Thus, the liability system has often become counterproductive and has affected delivery of service without proper regard for the broader requirements of an optimal health care system.

What is needed is a system which supports the broader concept of control of injuries while readjusting the cost burden of malpractice claims. Shifting premium expense to the hospitals satisfies both these criteria. Premium burdens would be placed where they could best be

---

110. See note 91 *supra*.
111. Data collected in the Author's Survey, *supra* note 33, indicate that claims might be expected on the following basis for physicians: first year, thirty percent; second year, thirty percent; third year, twenty-five percent; fourth year, ten percent; and fifth year, five percent. Patterns of claim reports vary by state; further, the dollar value of reports is not necessarily constant over all periods.

borne and where mechanisms for quality control already exist. Making the hospital liable for services provided within its walls would shift a large amount of premium to one location where traditional insurance techniques are more easily applied and risk management more feasible. Finally, the residual office exposure would be such that any number of innovative methods could be implemented to insure the non-hospital risk as well as promote injury prevention.

While certain transitional problems cannot be wholly avoided, proper planning and cooperation between individual and institutional health care providers can minimize any problems that do arise. Indeed, any short-term difficulties pale beside the problems attendant to the current system of insuring medical malpractice, a system neither the public nor the provider can afford to retain.

APPENDIX I

ISO POLICY YEAR, CLAIM FREQUENCY PER 100 INSURED PHYSICIANS, 1966-1973

(Developed to 123 months of maturity)

Policy Year Ending December 31	Actual	Exponential Line of Best Fit
1966	1.741	1.573
1967	1.925	1.763
1968	1.835	1.976
1969	2.105	2.214
1970	2.125	2.481
1971	2.469	2.780
1972	3.299	3.115
1973	4.149	3.491

Source: Questionnaire Re Medical Professional Liability Insurance, Technical Appendix, in *Hearings on S.482, S.215, S.188 Before the Subcomm. on Health of the Senate Comm. on Labor and Public Welfare*, 94th Cong., 1st Sess. 568 (1975).

APPENDIX II

ISO POLICY YEAR, CLAIM FREQUENCY PER $100,000 OF PREMIUM, FOR HOSPITAL PROFESSIONAL LIABILITY, 1967-1973

(Developed to 123 months of maturity)

Policy Year Ending December 31	Actual	Exponential Line of Best Fit
1967	2.613	2.363
1968	2.567	2.651
1969	2.875	2.975
1970	3.139	3.337
1971	3.570	3.744
1972	4.092	4.200
1973	5.211	4.712

Source: Insurance Services Office, 1975 Review of Hospital Professional Liability Insurance, Exhibit 2, Sheet 2 (June 12, 1975).

MEDICAL MALPRACTICE LITIGATION UNDER NATIONAL HEALTH INSURANCE: ESSENTIAL OR EXPENDABLE?[†]

GEORGE J. ANNAS,[*] BARBARA F. KATZ,[**]
ROBERT G. TRAKIMAS[***]

"Medical malpractice" denotes the basis for a civil action brought by a patient against a physician for injuries resulting from negligence. The current method for compensating victims of these occurrences is primarily a fault-and-liability insurance system.[1] The first principle of tort liability is that the party at fault pays for the damage inflicted upon an innocent victim. Whether a doctor is at fault is determined in an adversary proceeding, with both the doctor and the patient represented by counsel. The triers of fact have the task of ascertaining whether

---

[†] Copyright © 1976 by George J. Annas.
[*] B.A. 1967, Harvard College; J.D. 1970, Harvard Law School; M.P.H. 1972, Harvard School of Public Health. Director, Center for Law and Health Sciences, Boston University; Assistant Professor, Boston University School of Medicine.
[**] B.A. 1972, Boston University; J.D. 1974, Boston University School of Law. Staff Attorney, Center for Law and Health Sciences, Boston University.
[***] A.B. 1972, University of Michigan; J.D. 1976, Boston University School of Law.
THE FOLLOWING CITATION WILL BE USED IN THIS ARTICLE:
U.S. DEP'T OF HEALTH, EDUCATION AND WELFARE, REPORT OF THE SECRETARY'S COMMISSION ON MEDICAL MALPRACTICE (1973) [hereinafter cited as MEDICAL MALPRACTICE REPORT].
1. See generally Keeton, *Compensation for Medical Accidents*, 121 U. PA. L. REV. 590 (1973). This system has been severely criticized by advocates of the "no-fault" insurance concept. See J. O'CONNELL, ENDING INSULT TO INJURY (1975); Dornette, *Medical Injury Insurance—A Possible Remedy for the Malpractice Problem*, 78 CASE & COMMENT 25 (Sept.-Oct. 1973); Dornette, *Medical Injury Insurance—Proposed Model Legislation*, J. LEGAL MED. 24 (Mar. 1975); Havighurst & Tancredi, *"Medical Adversity Insurance"—A No-Fault Approach to Medical Malpractice and Quality Assurance*, 613 INS. L.J. 69 (1974); O'Connell, *Elective No-Fault Liability Insurance for All Kinds of Accidents: A Proposal*, 608 INS. L.J. 495 (1973); O'Connell, *The Best Way to Adapt No Fault Insurance to Malpractice*, MED. ECON., June 23, 1975, at 106; O'Connell, *Proposed: "No-Fault" Insurance to Stem Malpractice Suits*, PRISM 12 (July 1974); O'Connell, *Elective No-Fault Liability By Contract—With or Without an Enabling Statute*, 1975 U. ILL. L.F. 59. See also Calabresi, *Optimal Deterrence and Accidents*, 84 YALE L.J. 656 (1975).
However, many influential groups, such as the American Hospital Association and the Massachusetts Bar Association, oppose the concept of no-fault malpractice insurance. 11 HOSP. WEEK, Apr. 11, 1975, at 1; Kickham, *President's Message*, 15 MASS. B. ASS'N NEWS LETTER 2 (Apr. 1975).

the defendant was at fault, and if so, what compensation he must pay for the injury. The formula for determining whether the physician is liable to the patient is commonly phrased in terms of his failure either to "possess the degree of professional learning, skill and ability which others similarly situated ordinarily possess," or to "exercise reasonable care and diligence in the application of his knowledge and skill to the patient's case."[2]

Medical malpractice litigation is not new. The first recorded case occurred in England in the thirteenth century, and one of the earliest suits in the United States took place in 1794.[3] By 1845, physicians had indicated their alarm at the increase in such claims.[4] Alternatives to the jury trial were recommended, mainly by doctors. The Massachusetts Medical Society suggested having a disinterested physician adjudicate malpractice claims by patients.[5] In 1872, the American Medical Association recommended that in medical malpractice cases which required expert testimony, physicians be appointed independent arbiters by the judge.[6]

Yet, in spite of this traditional concern over the tort liability system by the medical profession, there was no medical malpractice "crisis" as we know it until well into the 1970s.[7] Sickness was accepted by most people as a common occurrence. Medicine was a limited science and adverse results were often regarded as the expected outcome.

Since World War II the number of malpractice suits, in absolute numbers, has increased steadily.[8] Even today, however, though the

---

2. *Medical Malpractice: A Consideration of the Problem*, 27 HEALTH L. BULL. 1 (Nov. 1971).

3. Cross v. Guthrey, 2 Root 90 (Conn. 1794). *See* Gussow, *Answers Can and Must Be Found To the Malpractice Situation*, J. LEGAL MED. 20 (Mar. 1975).

4. Burns, *Malpractice Suits in American Medicine Before the Civil War*, 43 BULL. HIST. MED. 41, 52 (1969). There are no reliable statistics for the total number of medical malpractice actions initiated before the Civil War. Yet an early commentator stated that "legal prosecutions for malpractice in surgery occur so often that even a respectable surgeon may well fear for the results of his surgical practice." J. ELWELL, A MEDICO-LEGAL TREATISE ON MALPRACTICE AND MEDICAL EVIDENCE, COMPRISING THE ELEMENTS OF MEDICAL JURISPRUDENCE 82 (1866). Indeed, it was believed that some practitioners were stopping their surgical practices because of the threat of malpractice. *Id.*

5. D. KONOLD, A HISTORY OF AMERICAN MEDICAL ETHICS: 1847-1912, at 50-51 (1962).

6. *Id.*

7. By "crisis" we mean the inability of physicians to purchase malpractice insurance at reasonable premiums, and, in rare cases, the inability to purchase such insurance at any price. In the past, many doctors did not even bother to buy malpractice insurance, even though rates were low. Gussow, *supra* note 3.

8. For recent figures, see Malpractice in Focus: The Problem . . . And Some Solutions 11, 12-13 (AMA source document prepared by editors of *Prism*, Aug. 1975).

medical malpractice situation in the United States is generally considered to be a critical problem, most physicians still go through their entire professional lives without being sued, and those who are sued, are rarely sued more than once.[9] The majority of hospitals, regardless of

---

Many factors led to this increase. More people could afford to receive medical care and, therefore, the number of opportunities for something to happen which would lead to a malpractice claim increased. See *Malpractice Insurance Plagues Numerous Physicians, Hospitals*, 4 WASHINGTON DEVELOPMENTS 1, 4 (Jan. 31, 1975). Most other factors directly involve the rise of the hospital as the center of complex health care delivery. Medical technology became increasingly complex and sophisticated. Porter, *Consumer Is Making Demands As Malpractice Crisis Grows*, Boston Herald American, May 28, 1975, at 14, col. 4. William Curran, professor of legal medicine at Harvard University, feels that most malpractice cases are the result of the inherent risks of modern medicine with its rapidly developing techniques. *Malpractice: MD's Revolt*, NEWSWEEK, June 9, 1975, at 63. The general practitioner was replaced by the specialist, teams of physicians, and medical institutions. Auerbach, *Specializing Intensifies Malpractice Rate Issue*, Washington Post, May 12, 1975, at A2, col. 3. The center of much medical practice moved from the office and home to the clinic and hospital. Altman, *The Complexities of Medical Practice and Malpractice*, N.Y. Times, June 5, 1975, at 28, col. 4. This resulted in more impersonal care and a deterioration of the intimate doctor-patient relationship, thereby creating further misunderstanding and disharmony. *Malpractice Cooperation Urged*, 3 HEALTH LAWYERS NEWS REP. 1 (Apr. 1975). See also Neeson, *Mysticism Lost*, 232 J.A.M.A. 374 (1975); Ribicoff, *Medical Malpractice: The Patient vs. The Physician*, TRIAL 11 (Feb./Mar. 1970):

> When the patient-physician "rapport" remains on a high level of competence and trust, most patients will ride out a bad result through much pain and suffering and expense without resort to a malpractice lawsuit. But when that "rapport" is inadequate in the beginning, and is permitted to deteriorate en route, a malpractice suit is likely to follow.

Most of the larger awards made in medical malpractice cases have been against hospitals. *See, e.g.*, Niles v. San Rafael, Civil No. 624,337 (San Francisco Super. Ct., Feb. 5, 1973); Miadema v. Glendora Hosp., Civil No. — (Los Angeles Super. Ct., June 4, 1973); Stearns v. Park Ave. Hosp., Inc., Civil No. — (Pomona Super. Ct., May 1, 1973).

Simultaneously with these changes in the practice of medicine came a growing consumer movement in society. Fellers, *When Lawyers and Doctors Clash*, 2 BARRISTER 8 (Summer 1975). The trend was for the public to seek compensation for all injuries, resulting in an increase in personal injury litigation. More lawyers entered the malpractice litigation field, making the retention of competent plaintiff's counsel easier. Waxman, *Spiraling Costs: A Health Care Slide*, TRIAL 23, 24 (May/June 1975). Finally, the interest of the media in medicine and its advances not only added to the public's knowledge, but often led to unrealistic expectations of a physician's ability. This has often been referred to as the "Marcus Welby syndrome." Altman, *Doctors Told Unrealistic Hopes Add to the Malpractice Crisis*, N.Y. Times, June 16, 1975, at 12, col. 4.

While currently available statistics are inadequate to determine for certain, it is entirely possible that the actual *incidence* of medical malpractice cases, in terms of doctor-patient and hospital-patient contacts, has remained relatively constant over the past two decades.

9. In 1970, medical malpractice claims were made for only one out of every 226,000 patient visits to doctors. MEDICAL MALPRACTICE REPORT 12. Although exact figures for 1975 are not presently available, even making the unlikely assumption that the incidence of claims has more than doubled, it would still be only one out of every

size, go through an entire year without having a single claim filed against them.[10] Jury trials of these claims are also unusual, with fewer than one trial held for every ten claims resolved,[11] and eighty percent of all jury verdicts are in favor of the physician-defendant.[12]

Nevertheless, the fear of being sued permeates the medical community, and has an impact on almost every facet of the system. It affects health care practices and forms of medical treatment, the distribution of health manpower, the modes of processing claims through the legal system, and the attitudes of the public toward the delivery of health care and toward the doctor-patient relationship in particular.[13] The main component is an insurance crisis in which, as in the automobile insurance controversy, the availability and cost of medical malpractice insurance is in a state of turmoil.[14]

100,000 patient visits. In 1974, malpractice actions were pending against one out of every ten physicians. Malpractice In Focus, *supra* note 8, at 13.

10. MEDICAL MALPRACTICE REPORT 9, 12.

11. Rudov, Myers & Mirabella, *Medical Malpractice Insurance Claims Files Closed in 1970*, in MEDICAL MALPRACTICE REPORT Appendix 1, 13.

12. *See* Auerbach, *Malpractice: The Doctor's Dilemma*, Washington Post, May 18, 1975, at C3, col. 6. Most patients who are injured by malpractice never receive any compensation for their injury. Cerra, *Malpractice Claims: Many Are Filed, But Few Are Paid*, N.Y. Times, June 1, 1975, § 1, at 46, col. 4. There are many times more medical injuries than there are claims. Auerbach, *supra*, at C3, col. 2. Some estimates put the number of significant injuries from medical malpractice at 750,000 annually. *Medical Self-Regulation and Malpractice*, 293 NEW ENG. J. MED. 562 (1975). The patient is more likely to sue if his injury is severe and he has no other sources of financial assistance. MEDICAL MALPRACTICE REPORT 25. Because of the complex medical issues involved and court backlog, lawsuits last between two and six years, or two to three times longer than other personal injury cases. *Id.* at 10-11. During this extended period the injured party receives no money and yet is least able to bear the cost of his medical and rehabilitation bills.

13. *See* Bird, *Three Views on Malpractice: Doctor, Lawyer, Patient*, N.Y. Times, Apr. 23, 1975, at 47, col. 7.

14. Estimates of the rise in the cost of malpractice insurance premiums in recent years have varied between 50 and 1,000 percent. MEDICAL MALPRACTICE REPORT 8-14. In 1960, the Secretary's Medical Malpractice Commission estimated the cost of professional liability coverage at $60 million. Insurance industry estimates, which are usually conservative, suggest a total premium paid in 1975 of well over $1 billion. Between 1960 and 1970, malpractice insurance premium volume for dentists rose 115.7 percent; for hospitals, 262 percent; for physicians other than surgeons, 540.8 percent; and for surgeons, 949.2 percent. Malpractice in Focus, *supra* note 8, at 20.

Other figures are equally revealing. A New York obstetrician had to pay $9,433 in 1974 to keep himself adequately covered against lawsuits. A specialist in a high-risk field like neurosurgery had to pay $14,329. *Suing the Doctor*, TIME, July 15, 1974, at 78. Some physicians have at times found it difficult to purchase any insurance, with a number of insurance companies leaving the medical malpractice business altogether. *Malpractice Carrier Sails Away*, MED. WORLD NEWS, Mar. 24, 1975, at 23; Hendricks, *What Your Next Malpractice Policy May Look Like*, MED. ECON., Apr. 14, 1975, at 29; *A.M.A. Moves to Enter the Insurance Field in the Malpractice Battle*, N.Y. Times,

Numerous critics place much of the blame for this situation on the tort liability system and recommend its abolition.[15] Because of the tort system's current unpopularity, the impending passage of some form of national health insurance may be used as an excuse to eliminate it in medical cases. In an attempt to determine the effects of such a policy, this Article will examine the workability of the traditional tort liability system to demonstrate that the aforementioned problems are not inherent to the system, but merely are the result of its current mode of application. Accordingly, the use or discontinuance of the tort system under national health insurance should rest not on hollow slogans, but on a careful examination of the system's coverage, cost, quality control, and consumer responsiveness.

I. THE TORT LIABILITY SYSTEM

Many aspects of the tort liability system have been attacked as contributing to the malpractice crisis. *Res ipsa loquitur*, informed consent, statutes of limitations, *ad damnum* clauses, damages for pain and suffering, unlimited damages, and the contingent fee system have been the primary targets. It will be demonstrated in this section that *none* of these characteristics accounts for the current malpractice "crisis"— they are only lightning rods in the storm of controversy surrounding this issue.

June 20, 1975, at 33, col. 4; *Teledyne Says It Erred in Letting Unit Cover Medical Malpractice*, Wall Street J., Feb. 19, 1975, at 19, col. 1-2.

Hospitals have experienced a similar increase. For example, annual malpractice premiums for Long Branch Memorial Hospital in California rose from $12,000 in 1965 to $820,000 in 1975. *Malpractice Insurance Plagues Numerous Physicians, Hospitals, supra* note 8, at 4. In 1969, Massachusetts General Hospital paid $120,000 for malpractice coverage. In the past year alone, the cost has risen from $300,000 to $1,200,000 for the same coverage. Comments of Dr. Thomas S. Durant, Assistant Director, Massachusetts General Hospital, at Conference, The Great Medical Malpractice Crisis of 1975, Harvard School of Public Health, May 1, 1975. According to the Department of Health, Education, and Welfare, hospitals pay about two-thirds of the $1 billion annual cost of malpractice insurance premiums. The cost of this insurance is necessarily passed on through fees and charges and is ultimately paid by the patient. Approximately fifty cents of the daily cost for every patient in the average hospital is for the hospital's malpractice insurance. But in California, premiums paid represent a $4.65 additional charge per hospital bed every day. *Malpractice Insurance Plagues Numerous Physicians, Hospitals, supra* note 8, at 1. Hospitals in Massachusetts may be forced to increase their room rates by eight to ten dollars per day in order to pay for increased cost of malpractice insurance. *Malpractice Crisis Stirs Concern*, Boston Herald American, Apr. 7, 1975, at 3, col. 2.

15. A complete examination of the concept of "fault" in civil litigation is beyond the scope of this work and has been dealt with in detail in numerous other articles. See note 1 *supra*.

Res ipsa is invoked under special circumstances to shift the burden of persuasion in a case from the plaintiff to the defendant. Three conditions must exist for the application of *res ipsa*. First, an injury of the kind which usually does not occur in the absence of negligence must have taken place. Second, the conduct or mechanism causing the injury must have been under the exclusive control of the defendant(s). Lastly, the plaintiff must have been free of any contributory negligence.[16] A typical case is a sponge left inside the patient after surgery. With the growing availability of discovery methods, however, *res ipsa* loses much of its importance and can be viewed merely as a general rule of circumstantial evidence. Indeed, recent statistics show that it plays a part in fewer than fifteen percent of all medical malpractice cases that reach the appellate level.[17]

The doctrine of informed consent has also received much criticism from the medical community.[18] This concept, which has its roots in late nineteenth and early twentieth century battery cases, simply states that before a patient is asked to consent to a treatment, procedure, or operation, the physician should be required to make certain disclosures. These disclosures include risks of death or serious disability, alternative treatments, consequences of not undergoing any treatment, problems of recuperation, and success rates. The medical arguments against this doctrine are essentially three: (1) this information will unduly frighten patients; (2) patients will not understand this information or it will take too long to explain in a way they can understand; and (3) this doctrine permits patients to sue physicians in the absence of any negligence in the performance of the treatment, procedure, or operation. Physicians have reacted vehemently to recent cases basing the amount of information that must be disclosed on a legal rather than a medical community practice standard, and have urged in a number of states, such as New York, the enactment of legislation specifically designed to radically curtail the use of this doctrine in a malpractice action.[19]

All of the evidence, however, seems to point to the fact that a well-informed patient is the *least* likely to sue his physician, and that curtailment of information disclosure is likely to lead to unrealistic ex-

---

16. W. PROSSER, HANDBOOK OF THE LAW OF TORTS 214 (4th ed. 1971).

17. Dietz, Baird & Berul, *The Medical Malpractice Legal System*, in MEDICAL MALPRACTICE REPORT Appendix 87, 128.

18. The concept was roundly condemned by former A.M.A. President Charles Hoffman in his dissent in the Secretary's Malpractice Report. MEDICAL MALPRACTICE REPORT 122.

19. N.Y. PUB. HEALTH LAW § 2805-d (McKinney Supp. 1975). *See* Trout, *New York State Malpractice Legislation*, J. LEGAL MED. 26 (July/Aug. 1975).

pectations followed by suits alleging malpractice in the presence of a less than expected result.[20] Thus, the elimination or weakening of this doctrine, while it will remove the few suits founded primarily on this cause of action,[21] is likely to increase significantly patient distrust of physicians and therefore malpractice actions in general. Moreover, the doctrine that patients, not physicians, should have the ultimate decision regarding specific therapies is so important to both self-autonomy and rational decision making that no erosion of it should be permitted. Exceptions relating to emergencies and cases where the physician can document serious adverse patient effects resulting from full disclosure should be strictly limited to prevent them from engulfing the rule of routine full disclosure.

Although each state establishes its own statute of limitations, the usual maximum permissible interval for initiating tort suits is within two years of the date of the tortious act.[22] An extension is sometimes granted for medical malpractice actions when the act of negligence is not apparent or is concealed by the negligent doctor, the most common exception being for foreign objects left within the patient's body after an operation.[23] In such cases the statute of limitations begins to run when the patient knew or had reason to know of the injury or negligent act.[24] For minors the statute of limitations for medical negligence is usually tolled until the individual attains the age of twenty-one, or eighteen in appropriate states.[25] This extended capacity for minors has been the central target of attacks on the statutes,[26] although a shortening of the two-year limit has been proposed as well.[27]

---

20. Annas, *Avoiding Malpractice Suits Through the Use of Informed Consent*, CURRENT PROBLEMS IN PEDIATRICS (to be published Mar. 1976).

21. Probably less than ten percent of the suits fall within this category. Dietz, Baird & Berul, *supra* note 17.

22. *See, e.g.*, N.Y. CIV. PRAC. LAW & RULES § 203(f) (McKinney 1972).

23. *See* Flanagan v. Mount Eden Gen. Hosp., 24 N.Y.2d 427, 248 N.E.2d 871, 301 N.Y.S.2d 23 (1969); N.Y. CIV. PRAC. LAW & RULES § 214-a (McKinney Supp. 1975).

24. "[W]here a foreign object is left in a patient's body during the course of a surgical operation, the period of limitations begins to run when the patient knows or had reason to know about the foreign object and the existence of the cause of action based upon its presence." Tramutola v. Bortone, 118 N.J. Super. 503, 513, 288 A.2d 863, 868 (1972), *rev'd in part on other grounds and modified in part on other grounds*, 63 N.J. 9, 304 A.2d 197 (1973). In medical malpractice cases, the statute of limitations commences to run "from the time of discovery of a right of action," that is "when the patient knows or should know that he has suffered injury or damage." Waldman v. Rohrbaugh, 241 Md. 137, 145, 215 A.2d 825, 830 (1969).

25. *See, e.g.*, N.J. STAT. ANN. ch. 2A, § 14-21 (1952). *Cf.* IND. ANN. STAT. § 16-9.5-3-1 (Burns 1975), which limits infancy disability to age six, at which time the two-year statute of limitations for tort actions begins to run.

26. *See* Welch, *Medical Malpractice*, 292 NEW ENG. J. MED. 1372, 1376 (1975).

27. A number of states have already altered the law to begin the statute of limita-

The reasons for placing a time limit on the period during which suit may be filed are twofold: first, to prevent victims from suing alleged wrongdoers long after memories and details have become obscured, or medical records lost, and second, to allow persons to reconstitute their lives and escape the ever-impending threat of a lawsuit.[28] In addition, statutes of limitations aid insurance companies in predicting the extent of their losses for any period so that they can adjust premiums to cover payouts.[29] The application of statutes of limitations in malpractice cases, and particularly the tolled statute for minors, is often blamed for the high insurance rates which must be charged to cover the contingency of delayed losses.[30]

---

tions with occurrence of the incident. Several, including Indiana, Texas, and Michigan, have fixed the deadline at two years after the act for most claims. See note 25 *supra*. California is considering a change to three years after occurrence, Florida has established the deadline at four years, and Maryland and Illinois, among others, have set the cutoff at five years. Hendricks, *Your Malpractice Protection*, MED. ECON., Sept. 29, 1975, at 105, 110. The American Medical Association has suggested the following:

> Insofar as they are suspended during minority or until the injury is actually discovered the statutes should be rectified to the extent necessary to reduce the "long-tail" problem. Therefore, no action for damages for personal injury whether based on tort or breach of contract, should be brought against any provider of medical care, *unless*
> (1) The action is commenced within two years after the date on which the act or omission occurred (exposure) which is alleged to have caused the injury, or
> (2) Thereafter within six months of the date on which the person injured or the claimant knew or reasonably should have known (discovery) of the existence of such personal injury, but
> (3) In no event shall any such action for damages be commenced more than five years from the date on which occurred the act or omission which is alleged to have been the cause of the injury. Fellers, *supra* note 8, at 71-72.

28. Riddlesbarger v. Hartford Ins. Co., 74 U.S. (7 Wall.) 386, 390 (1868); W. PROSSER, *supra* note 16, at 144.

29. Golladay & Smith, *Who Shall Pay? An Analysis of the Malpractice Crisis*, 6 RESEARCH & ANALYTIC RESEARCH SERIES 3 (Center for Medical Sociology and Health Services Research, Health Economics Research Center, University of Wisconsin 1975). As one insurance official stated, "If you can't determine rates based on your losses—and its nearly impossible in malpractice insurance—then you don't belong in the business." Ribicoff, *supra* note 8, at 13.

30. A limitation of twenty-three years of age for minors may seem arbitrary. Such a lengthy time span during which a suit can be brought inevitably invites the chance that the medical treatment of a child will be judged by the more advanced standards existing when suit is brought, regardless of the judicial cognizance and admonition to the jury of the time factor. Yet before a shorter period is selected, inquiry should be made as to whether there are any circumstances which would cause the negligent treatment of a child to be less likely to manifest itself than negligent care of an adult. For example, limitations on a child's ability to communicate effectively might suggest that a two year statute of limitations should not begin to run until children are old enough to understand their bodies and communicate a problem. However, ability to communicate appears too subjective a standard for establishment of a uniform age. A more relevant difference between children and adults is physical development. Using this criterion, a two year limitation period would not begin to run for children until the child's skeletal growth stopped (*e.g.*, age thirteen in girls, age fifteen in boys, or age fourteen

A statute of limitations of two years does not appear to produce unwarranted claims and does not seem unduly lengthy in light of the above policies. In fact, a shorter limitations period might induce many claims to be made—which would not have been substantiated after a lengthier lapse of time and investigation—in order to protect against the contingency that later pain or slow recovery was discovered to be due to negligent care.

Elimination of *ad damnum* clauses, the estimate made by the plaintiff in his complaint as to the amount of damages he has suffered, has been proposed in many "malpractice alleviation" statutes.[31] These damage requests often substantially overstate the probable range of recovery in order to emphasize both the severity of the plaintiff's injury and to set a bargaining position. Therefore, since they may not reasonably be related to actual damages, their abolition should probably be encouraged.[32] Placing some limitations on damages for pain and suffering, a subjective injury which requires some speculation by the jury, might also be warranted.[33]

A ceiling on the amount of total damages which can be awarded in a particular case has also been proposed in numerous malpractice alleviation statutes. For example, an Indiana statute has limited personal liability for each individual physician to $100,000, and total damages for the entire suit to $500,000, with any damages exceeding $100,000 to be paid from a reinsurance pool funded by premiums from all insurance carriers in the state.[34] Such a ceiling might help to contain costs, but only at the expense of seriously injured patients.[35] Of course, with national health insurance paying all or at least the most

---

as a compromise). A skeletal growth limitation would be objective and it appears to correlate well with full manifestation of any negligent treatment upon minors.

31. Welch, *supra* note 26, at 1374. *E.g.*, IND. ANN. STAT. § 16-9.5-1-6 (Burns 1975) (eliminates the requirement of *ad damnum* clauses).

32. Dornette, *Indiana Adopts Malpractice Legislation*, 3 J. LEGAL MED. 26, 27 (June 1975); Welch, *supra* note 26, at 1347. Abolition was also recommended by the Secretary's Commission on Medical Malpractice. MEDICAL MALPRACTICE REPORT 38.

33. It should be noted that this criticism of damage awards for pain and suffering is applicable to the entire tort liability system, and is not limited to medical malpractice cases.

34. IND. ANN. STAT. § 16-9.5-2-2 (Burns 1975). *See New Indiana Law Will Cut Negligence Suits, Improve Care*, 17 PHYSICIAN'S LEGAL BRIEF 1 (Fall 1975).

35. Another suggested way for relieving the financial burden on defendants of damage awards is to permit collateral sources of compensation to be used to mitigate the amount of the damages awarded. These include continuing sources of income, health and accident insurance, social security benefits, workmen's compensation, disability insurance, and the income tax treatment given the monetary award. *See* Hirsch, *Malpractice Crisis: Fact or Fiction*, 80 CASE & COMMENT 3, 4 (July/Aug. 1975).

expensive medical bills, as will be discussed later,[36] the problem of suing in order to meet large medical bills will be eliminated.

Few lawyers handle medical malpractice cases on anything other than a contingent fee basis.[37] This payment system is often cited as contributing to the rise in malpractice claims.[38] Such a belief is contrary to both the theoretical and actual operation of the system. Patients bring malpractice suits, not lawyers. Blaming the legal profession for such suits is akin to blaming the fire department for arson.[39] Contrary to encouraging the filing of malpractice suits, the contingent fee structure actually compels lawyers to screen out claims which are spurious or for which recovery appears less than probable, as well as to refuse claims for which damages would not amount to a sum sufficient to reimburse their expenses.[40] Since the attorney, rather than the patient, bears the financial risk of losing the suit, he has no incentive to invest any time or money in a claim for which recovery appears doubtful.[41] In addition, with the average fee rate approximately one third of recovery, many lawyers decline malpractice cases which will probably achieve settlements or awards of less than $10,000 because the expected compensation for the amount of time expended is not seen as worthwhile.[42] The threshold value for the acceptance of cases for which recovery is less than probable would, on the average, be higher. Thus, although the vast majority of malpractice claims have been found to have some merit, most are rejected by the lawyers to whom they are brought.[43] This also means that only a small percent-

---

36. See notes 56-82 *infra* and accompanying text.
37. Under this system, a lawyer does not get paid for anything other than his expenses unless the suit is won, in which case he takes thirty to fifty percent of the award. Porter, *Consumer Is Making Demands as Malpractice Crisis Grows*, Boston Herald American, May 28, 1975, at 14, col. 3.
38. See Bloom, *Malpractice—The Mess That Must Be Ended*, 106 READER'S DIGEST 79 (Apr. 1975); Hirsch, *supra* note 35, at 3.
39. Annas, *Don't Blame Lawyers for the Malpractice Mess!*, AM. MED. NEWS, Mar. 3, 1975, at 8.
40. *See* Sharpe, *Contingent Fee—Physician Protection*, TRIAL 21 (Feb./Mar. 1970).
41. *Id.*
42. Contrary to encouraging the filing of malpractice suits, the contingent fee structure actually compels lawyers to screen out claims which are spurious or for which recovery appears less than probable, as well as to refuse claims for which damages would not amount to a sum sufficient to reimburse their expenses. See Dietz, Baird & Berul, *supra* note 17, at 113-20.
43. A recent study showed that lawyers reject twenty-three percent of malpractice cases for economic reasons. *Malpractice Cooperation Urged*, *supra* note 8, at 2. However, another study found that a large segment of defendant and plaintiff lawyers believed the contingent fee system had little impact on an attorney's decision not to take a malpractice case. Dietz, Baird & Berul, *supra* note 17, at 119.

age of injured patients who seek legal help actually obtain it.[44]

Of course, when two malpractice claims with similar prospects of recovery compete for an attorney's time, the contingent fee structure, with its flat rate of reimbursement, may encourage acceptance of the more shocking and sensational case, since it has the greater likelihood of eliciting jury sympathy and, accordingly, a larger recovery. The sliding scale fee structure, in which the percentage fee decreases as the plaintiff's award increases, would eliminate the purely financial inducement to accept claims with potentially large awards and would eliminate the potential which the contingent fee system has for wiping out a substantial portion of the injured person's recovery.[45] However, it should be noted that this redistribution of the recovery between the patient-plaintiff and the attorney would affect neither the size of the award,[46] nor the volume of suits.

Considering the patient's choice of possible schemes for payment of counsel fees, patients with large potential recoveries might prefer a per diem rate if they were certain of recovery, but most persons would prefer the lawyer to bear the financial risk of losing a case. In this sense, the contingent fee system encourages the filing of more cases by permitting the poor and lower middle class patient to seek legal aid which he would never have been able to afford under a per diem payment scheme. Yet, as noted above, the contingent fee probably encourages only the filing of meritorious claims by these lower income patients. In addition, the rise in the cost of malpractice suits here is comparable to that in Great Britain, although the contingent fee for attorneys is not employed there.[47] The contingent fee, therefore, is not a major factor in the development of the medical malpractice problem, and its elimination would do little to solve the dilemma.

The present tort system is also blamed for "defensive medicine," the alteration of modes of medical practice for the sole purpose of avoiding legal liability.[48] The annual costs of such practices have been

---

44. See note 12 *supra*.
45. New Jersey was an early leader in this area. In 1971 it scaled contingency fees so that a lawyer could collect only about $27,000 on a $100,000 award or settlement, and no more than ten percent of amounts exceeding $100,000. *See* Hendricks, *supra* note 27, at 113-14 (suggests limit on contingent attorney fees to fifteen percent on malpractice awards exceeding $100,000).
46. This would only be true if the jury were not instructed as to the application of the sliding scale fee structure to the damage award.
47. Curran, *The British Experience in Medical Malpractice: An Upward Trend*, 288 NEW ENG. J. MED. 249 (1973).
48. *Tort Law Criticized and Defended*, in MEDICAL MALPRACTICE, A DISCUSSION OF ALTERNATIVE COMPENSATION AND QUALITY CONTROL SYSTEMS 2, 3 (D. McDonald ed.

estimated at from $1 to $7 billion[49]—estimates that alone call the entire notion of defensive medicine into serious question. Moreover, those studies which have been done, although all in the emergency ward setting, indicate that based on professional standards too few, rather than too many, diagnostic tests are being performed.[50] At the present time all that can be said is that we do not know the extent to which "defensive medicine" is practiced,[51] but we do know that much that poses as "defensive medicine," such as appropriate expert consultations and the keeping of better medical records, is in fact improved health care.[52] The fact that it has been imposed by the tort system is an advantage rather than a disadvantage of the present system. Moreover, its existence demonstrates the ability of the present tort system to change physician behavior, something no other measure, such as continuing education or licensing examinations, has been able to accomplish.[53]

The present tort system may leave much to be desired, but the major arguments against it from the physician's perspective are unimpressive.[54] Any modifications contemplated under national health insurance should aim at improving one or more of the following four measures of success without impinging on the others: effective qual-

---

1971); Graham, *Malpractice Suits Rise, Lead Doctors to Treat Patients With Caution,* Wall Street J., Jan. 8, 1971, at 1, col. 6. Under this definition all defensive medicine is, of course, bad medical practice since it deviates from standard medical practice for non-medical considerations. Its impact may also be the opposite of what is hoped for, *i.e.* a physician may get sued for the adverse reactions from an *unnecessary* test or procedure he performed for "defensive" purposes.

49. Golladay & Smith, *supra* note 29, at 4; Regier, *The View From HEW on Federal Involvement in the Malpractice Situation,* J. LEGAL MED. 19 (June 1975); Wolfe, *The Real Victim,* TRIAL 26, 30 (May/June 1975). *See also* Hassard, *Change Tort System?: Pro,* MED. WORLD NEWS, Sept. 8, 1975, at 60, 62.

50. Brook & Appel, *Quality-of-Care Assessment: Choosing a Method for Peer Review,* 288 NEW ENG. J. MED. 1323 (1973); Brook & Stevenson, *Effectiveness of Patient Care in an Emergency Room,* 283 NEW. ENG. J. MED. 904 (1970). These studies may also indicate, however, that *all* physicians are doing too many tests in the sense that most of the patients in these studies felt better no matter what the physicians did or did not do to them.

51. Bernzweig, *Defensive Medicine,* in MEDICAL MALPRACTICE REPORT Appendix 38, 38-40. *But see Defensive Medicine? Doctors Say Yes!,* TRIAL 65 (Mar./Apr. 1973).

52. Project, *The Medical Malpractice Threat: A Study of Defensive Medicine,* 1971 DUKE L.J. 939.

53. Even the imposition of national standards under national health insurance holds little promise for increased use of licensing as a means of quality control, since this method rarely ferrets out gross incompetence.

54. The general opinion among lawyers seems to be that the tort system is preferable to any of the proposed alternatives. *See* Goldstein, *Malpractice Claims,* N.Y. Times, June 6, 1975, at 18, col. 1; Goldstein, *Doctors Called Opposed to Rights,* N.Y. Times, June 3, 1975, at 22, col. 1.

ity control, complete patient coverage, cost effectiveness, and responsiveness to the consumer-patient.[55]

II. NATIONAL HEALTH INSURANCE

Assuming that some form of national health insurance will be implemented in the near future,[56] the impact of such a new fiscal and delivery system of health services upon the health care system must be determined before assessing the role malpractice litigation should play. Although national health insurance is primarily aimed at financing medical care, with reduction of medical negligence only a secondary target, changes in the finance system will produce side-effects which will definitely influence the current medical negligence problem.[57] Cost, quality, and extent and duration of service are among the factors which will probably be affected by a national health insurance program.[58]

The numerous national health insurance proposals, which run the gamut from merely increasing the funding of present programs to rede-

---

55. *See* Annas, *Medical Malpractice: Are the Doctors Right?*, TRIAL 59-63 (July 1974). For an overview of what the states are doing to solve the medical malpractice problem, see Malpractice in Focus, *supra* note 8, at 30. One or more malpractice bills have been enacted into law this year in twenty-eight states, a total of seventy laws. 3 STATE HEALTH LEGISLATION REPORT (Oct. 1975); Comment, *An Analysis of State Legislative Responses to the Medical Malpractice Crisis*, 1975 DUKE L.J. 1417.

56. It has been estimated that a national health insurance program could become law in 1977 or 1978, but that a two-and-a-half year "tooling-up" period would be required after the law is enacted and before benefits actually begin. *National Health Insurance: Reassurance From the Left*, MED. ECON., June 9, 1975, at 133. At the present time, there is a feeling among Congressional leaders that NHI must take a back seat to anti-recession measures. *NHI Prospects Recede*, 3 HEALTH LAWYERS NEWS REP. 1 (Feb. 1975). Yet Leonard Woodcock, President of the United Auto Workers, has predicted that NHI will become a key issue during the 1976 presidential election. *The AHA Reaffirmed Its Support for H.R. 1*, 11 HOSP. WEEK, Apr. 18. 1975. at 1.

57. For example, encouragement of group practice rather than individual practitioner provision of health services may further depersonalize the physician-patient relationship, resulting in less communication, less understanding and a greater willingness to blame the provider for adversities.

58. All national health insurance bills attempt to extend health service coverage, in terms of both population and benefits, at a tolerable cost to the consumer. The unpredictable occurrence of serious illness or injury, coupled with the prohibitively high cost of medical treatment and care, have compelled focus on potential means for distributing the uneven and uncertain costs of health care to make it a manageable burden for consumers.
    Subsumed under the cost and extended coverage objectives in many proposed plans are the goals of controlling the quality of medical care; increasing the supply of medical personnel, including the development of new levels of medical personnel; improving facilities, such as the implementation of new delivery systems; and distributing resources to underserved areas to rectify supply-demand imbalances.

signing the fiscal and delivery mechanisms, reveal the lack of a political and medical consensus on how best to provide universal comprehensive health care. While it is a definite oversimplification, for our purposes[59] the three basic approaches to national health insurance can be defined as follows: catastrophic coverage, subsidy-credit, and uniform-comprehensive. We will argue that only some form of the comprehensive approach is likely to have any impact on the way medical care is currently delivered in this country, and consequently on any method of reimbursement for negligently-induced injuries within the health care system.

A. *Catastrophic Coverage.* The basic model for this type of coverage[60] provides that the entire amount of a family's medical bills will be paid after a certain level has been reached (*e.g.*, $1,500 annually). The purpose is simply to prevent people from having to sell their homes and completely rearrange their lives because of a serious illness in the family. A modification of this approach would base the amount of the annual direct expense limit or "deductible" on the family's income. If low enough, the deductible would be zero; if high, the deductible would be correspondingly large.[61] The advantages of such a proposal would accrue to the poor in that the welfare-non-welfare distinction would be removed, and even low income families who currently do not qualify for Medicaid would be covered after only a minimal deductible expenditure. While this form of insurance would probably have the effect of increasing demand, especially for out-patient services, it is unlikely that it would have any other major impact on the current health care system since it will in no way change the manner in which health services are delivered, and thus the current tort system would continue to serve the same function it presently does.

B. *Subsidy-Credit Alternatives.* These proposals currently out of favor, would give either subsidies or tax credits to individuals in order to purchase commercial health insurance. Their main purpose

---

59. Since the objective of this Article is to determine what role malpractice litigation should play under national health insurance, many important aspects of the insurance question which are irrelevant to this discussion, such as whether revenues for the various proposals derive from payroll taxes or general revenues, will not be treated.

60. All 1975 national health insurance bills protect against catastrophic illness or injury. However, the National Catastrophic Illness Act of 1975, H.R. 1373, 94th Cong., 1st Sess. (sponsored by Rep. Roe) and the Medical Expenses Tax Credit Act, H.R. 3328, 94th Cong., 1st Sess. (1975) (sponsored by Rep. Martin), S. 600, 94th Cong., 1st Sess. (1975) (sponsored by Sen. Brock) are confined to such protection.

61. For example, the deductible under the National Catastrophic Illness Act of 1975 is an amount $1,500 less than adjusted gross income except for individuals or families with adjusted gross incomes less than $2,000. The deductible diminishes from $500 at $2,000 of adjusted gross income to zero at $1,000 or less of income. H.R. 1373, 94th Cong., 1st Sess. § 2015(b).

is to replace Medicare and Medicaid and encourage all individuals to purchase their own insurance programs. Politically the plan is unattractive since Medicaid currently provides more benefits than do commercial carriers, and the poor and middle class might not be persuaded to purchase commercial insurance. Moreover, because these proposals rely on current forms of health insurance, they include all of the weaknesses in the present system. They are essentially instruments to redistribute income, and should be judged as attempts at welfare reform rather than improvements in health care insurance. In the unlikely event that such a program is adopted, however, the present tort system would have to be maintained since a plan of this type would merely change the financing mechanism while leaving essentially the same system for delivering health care.

C. *Uniform Comprehensive Health Insurance.* The final major category of health insurance, and the one most likely to prevail in the future, is comprehensive coverage for the entire population.[62] The major differences between proposals of this type involve the amount of direct federal intervention in quality control, modes of health care delivery, the utilization of deductibles, coinsurance premiums, and finally, the types of services which are not covered (*e.g.*, dental, psychiatric, home health care).

Perhaps the most ambitious plan is Senator Kennedy's Health Security Act,[63] which would require no deductibles or coinsurance payments by the patient and would cover all medically necessary health services if rendered by a qualified provider.[64] Such providers would have to abide by certain quality control regulations, such as PSRO monitoring of services.[65] Institutions would have to maintain utilization review procedures, as well as other standards, to assure the medical necessity of operations, a medically adequate level of treatment and care, and the efficient use of health care facilities.[66] Individual practition-

---

62. Four "comprehensive benefits" bills were introduced in 1975: (1) The Health Security Act, S. 3, 94th Cong., 1st Sess. (sponsored by Sen. Kennedy and AFL-CIO Committee on National Health Insurance), H.R. 21, 94th Cong., 1st Sess. (sponsored by Rep. Corman); (2) National Comprehensive Health Benefits Act of 1975, H.R. 2050, 94th Cong., 1st Sess. (sponsored by Rep. Staggers); (3) National Health Care Services Reorganization and Financing Act, H.R. 1, 94th Cong., 1st Sess. (sponsored by Rep. Ullman and The American Hospital Association); (4) National Health Care Act of 1975, S. 1438, 94th Cong., 1st Sess. (sponsored by Sen. McIntyre and the Health Insurance Association of America), H.R. 5990, 94th Cong., 1st Sess. (sponsored by Rep. Burleson).
63. S. 3, 94th Cong., 1st Sess. (1975), H.R. 21, 94th Cong., 1st Sess. (1975).
64. *Id.* § 21.
65. *Id.* §§ 41, 141, 145.
66. *Id.* §§ 43, 51.

ers would be subject to continuing education requirements.[67] Treatment by a qualified specialist and, except in an emergency, referral from a general practitioner would be prerequisites of reimbursement for major surgery and other special operations.[68]

Financial inducements, either educational loan forgiveness or income supplements, would be used to redistribute health personnel to the underserved rural and inner city areas.[69] Development of more efficacious delivery systems would be concentrated in attempts to stimulate the growth of Health Maintenance Organizations (HMOs).[70]

Less radical than the Health Security Act are national health insurance proposals which share the cost of benefits with the patient and gradually adopt comprehensive coverage over a period of years.[71] Cost-sharing and graduated coverage are attempts to limit the demand expected from national health insurance.[72]

---

67. *Id.* § 142.
68. *Id.* § 143.
69. *Id.* §§ 103, 105.
70. *Id.* §§ 103(a), 104(a). HMOs are prepaid group practice organizations which offer comprehensive health services either through their own facilities and staff or by referral of their enrolled members to outside sub-contracted facilities and personnel on a continuous 24-hour basis. HMOs have been able to provide comprehensive services to their members at a fraction of the cost spent in the non-organized delivery sector. The reasons postulated include: (1) better health status (fewer acute problems) among their members due to emphasis upon primary or preventive care, and health education of their members; (2) economies of scale, especially in administrative and record-keeping; (3) lower hospitalization rates because of (a) primary care and (b) a built-in fiscal incentive to utilize the best, yet most efficient, treatments and resources. Quality care is maintained by competition among HMOs and the threat of malpractice litigation. The fiscal incentive has two facets: (1) governmental reimbursement for services on the basis of a prospectively-approved budget, and (2) compensation from members on a prepaid per capita basis rather than fees for services rendered. The only two factors that counterbalance the interest of the HMO staff in cost-efficiency are malpractice suits and competition between HMOs which is non-existent today. *See generally* Bovbjerg, *The Medical Malpractice Standard of Care Required of HMO Practitioners*, 1975 DUKE L.J. 1375.

Under the Health Security Act, HMOs can receive grants or loans for planning and construction costs, or expansion costs, and can be subsidized in toto for operating deficits incurred during the first five years, S. 3, 94th Cong., 1st Sess. §§ 103, 104, especially helpful since HMOs do not reach economies of scale until their enrollments approach 30,000, which may not be accessible within the initial years of growth. Other competitive advantages for HMOs would be broader drug coverage and broader psychiatric coverage for HMO enrollees than for patients of solo practitioners. *Id.* §§ 22, 25. Supplementing HMOs with seventy-five percent of the differential between their actual institutional (hospital and nursing home only) care costs and the average institutional care costs for non-HMO-enrolled persons would be a special incentive to operate efficiently. *Id.* § 87.

71. H.R. 2050, 94th Cong., 1st Sess. (1975); H.R. 1, 94th Cong., 1st Sess. (1975); H.R. 5990, 94th Cong., 1st Sess. (1975); S. 1438, 94th Cong., 1st Sess. (1975).

72. For example, under the National Health Care Act of 1975, S. 1438, 94th Cong.,

The implementation of utilization review procedures at health care institutions is the primary quality control under all of these types of proposals.[73] The Health Care Act, for example, makes utilization review a condition of reimbursement for comprehensive ambulatory care centers and of approval of rates by the state, which is necessary in order to obtain federal cost-sharing.[74] In addition to utilization review procedures, HMOs and Health Care Corporations (HCCs)[75] must implement in-service training programs and must provide for the continued professional education of their staff.[76] The Health Care Services Act explicitly orders each HCC to review annually the qualifications and on-the-job performance of every individual practitioner who has contracted with the HCC in order to determine the range of treatment and procedures he is competent to perform.[77]

The expansion of preventive and ambulatory health care is also stressed throughout all of the bills.[78] Health maintenance measures, such as periodic checkups and immunizations, are fully covered without copayments under the Health Care Services and Comprehensive Benefits Acts.[79] Each bill also encourages, through technical and financial supports, the development of comprehensive ambulatory care centers or prepaid group practice organizations (HCCs and HMOs), which are designed to provide medical services and preventive care

---

1st Sess., H.R. 5990, 94th Cong., 1st Sess., a broad spectrum of benefits, similar to the comprehensive benefits of the Health Security Act, S. 3, 94th Cong., 1st Sess., H.R. 21, 94th Cong., 1st Sess. (1975), is to be established in two installments encompassing ten years. A flat deductible of $100 would have to be satisfied before the insurance plan would reimburse providers for eighty percent of a patient's medical bill (*i.e.,* twenty percent coinsurance rate). S. 1438, 94th Cong., 1st Sess. § 501. Total coverage, suspension of copayments, day limits, and consultation limits, is attained when medical expenses reach ten times the applicable deductible amount, or $1,000 for all persons except those over sixty-five or with low incomes who enjoy subsidized deductibles. *Id.* §§ 501, 531.

73. S. 3, 94th Cong., 1st Sess. § 51 (1975); H.R. 5990, 94th Cong., 1st Sess. § 308 (1975); H.R. 1, 94th Cong., 1st Sess. § 244(a) (1975); H.R. 2050, 94th Cong., 1st Sess. § 1701 (1975).

74. H.R. 5990, 94th Cong., 1st Sess. §§ 308, 531 (1975).

75. HCCs, established under the National Health Care Services Reorganization and Financing Act, operate and function similarly to HMOs. See note 70 *supra.*

76. H.R. 2050, 94th Cong., 1st Sess. §§ 1701, 1758 (1975); H.R. 1, 94th Cong., 1st Sess. §§ 244(a), 245 (1975); S. 3, 94th Cong., 1st Sess. §§ 131, 142 (1975).

77. H.R. 1, 94th Cong., 1st Sess. § 245 (1975).

78. S. 3, 94th Cong., 1st Sess. §§ 103(a), 47(a)(6) (1975); H.R. 1, 94th Cong., 1st Sess. § 2(C) (1975); H.R. 2050, 94th Cong., 1st Sess. §§ 2(b)(1), 1701 (1975); H.R. 5990, 94th Cong., 1st Sess. §§ 301, 308 (1975).

79. H.R. 2050, 94th Cong., 1st Sess. § 1712 (1975); H.R. 1, 94th Cong., 1st Sess. § 122 (1975).

programs more efficaciously than the traditional health care delivery system.[80]

Comprehensive coverage of all essential health services would place great demand and stress upon the present health care delivery system. One study has estimated that comprehensive coverage, as under the Health Security Act, would increase demand for ambulatory care thirty to seventy-five percent, while requests for other, formerly uninsured services, *e.g.*, prescription drugs and dental care, might be expected to increase at an even steeper rate.[81] Utilization of hospital services under full coverage has been predicted to grow a "modest" ten percent since most persons are already covered by insurance that includes hospitalization benefits.[82]

---

80. S. 3, 94th Cong., 1st Sess. §§ 103 *et seq.* (1975); H.R. 1, 94th Cong., 1st Sess. §§ 218 *et seq.* (1975); H.R. 2050, 94th Cong., 1st Sess. § 1745 (1975); H.R. 5990, 94th Cong., 1st Sess. §§ 301 *et seq.* (1975). To insure a competitive edge for the development of HMOs and HCCs, the federal government would subsidize ten percent of the premiums of persons who enroll with HMOs or register with HCCs. H.R. 2050, 94th Cong., 1st Sess. § 1722(c) (1975); H.R. 1, 94th Cong., 1st Sess. § 102(C) (1975).

81. Newhouse, Phelps & Schwartz, *Policy Options and the Impact of National Health Insurance*, 290 NEW ENG. J. MED. 1345, 1346 (1974). This estimate is, however, seen by some critics as a slight exaggeration, since persons in poor health, with low incomes and low time values, would constitute a disproportionate share of those who currently lack coverage of outpatient services prior to national health insurance. Low income persons spend less on medical care than others, but this factor is negated when third parties pay all or most of the medical expenses. Low time value (*i.e.*, waiting or travel time would not deter visits by the unemployed or salaried, as it would the "time-poor professional, executive or self-employed") and poor health would result in greater usage of ambulatory care facilities among the newly-covered than among others. *Id.* at 1347; Sparer & Anderson, *Utilization and Cost Experience of Low-Income Families in Four Prepaid Group Practice Plans*, 289 NEW ENG. J. MED. 67, 69, 72 (1973). *But see* Greenlick, *Comparing the Use of Medical Care Services By a Medically Indigent and a General Membership Population in a Comprehensive Prepaid Group Practice Program*, 10 MED. CARE 187 (1972). Adding a deductible or coinsurance feature would only serve to deny treatment to those who might need it most.

82. Newhouse, Phelps & Schwartz, *supra* note 81, at 1345. The HMO prepayment scheme, whereby a member prepays an annual fee and in return receives a comprehensive range of health care services (with nominal charges for certain visits and treatments), encourages the HMO staff to keep hospitalization at a minimum. *See* MacLeod & Prussin, *Continuing Evolution of Health Maintenance Organizations*, 288 NEW ENG. J. MED. 439 (1973); Note, *The Role of Prepaid Group Practice in Relieving the Medical Care Crisis*, 84 HARV. L. REV. 887, 921-27 (1971). One study found significant increases in inpatient service demand as well as ambulatory care demand. Broida, Lerner, Lohrenz, *et al., Impact of Membership in an Enrolled, Prepaid Population on Utilization of Health Services in Group Practices*, 292 NEW ENG. J. MED. 780, 782-83 (1975). The conclusions of this study are suspect, however, due to the fact that participating physicians were salaried before joining the HMO, rather than operating on fees for service. In addition, any initial study is suspect because increased checkups and ambulatory care will reveal acute problems ignored at first.

III. Impact of National Health Insurance Upon Medical Negligence

While they may be viewed only as negotiating positions, provisions directed specifically at the medical malpractice problem are contained in each of the national health insurance comprehensive coverage proposals. The Health Care Act and the Health Security Act would preclude recovery in malpractice awards for expenses of treatment and rehabilitative care covered under a qualified health insurance policy or under the Act, respectively.[83] Neither the Comprehensive Benefits Act nor the Health Care Services Act explicitly excludes such excessive recovery. The latter, however, does provide for internal grievance procedures and hearings concerning monetary claims of patients against providers.[84]

National health insurance may also be able to play a preventive role in medical negligence. Analysis of the incidence of malpractice claims reveals discrimination among geographical regions and between medical specialties. Health care practitioners in urban areas, especially surgeons, incur more malpractice claims,[85] and consequently pay higher insurance premiums, than their rural counterparts. Concomitantly, urban areas are relatively overserved by health care practitioners, especially dentists and surgeons, although not by hospitals, as compared with less populated areas of the United States.[86] A more plaintiff-oriented legal climate and more alert consumerism among urban populations may account for the difference. The general tendency of rural populations to be treated by the local general practitioner with whom the family has had experience and developed trust over the years may also account for fewer malpractice claims in less populated areas, as does the fact that many residents of rural communities go to specialists in urban areas for the type of sophisticated medical care which often forms the basis for possible malpractice actions.

Whether overrepresentation of practitioners, the presence of more

---

83. H.R. 5990, 94th Cong., 1st Sess. § 501(a) (1975); S. 3, 94th Cong., 1st Sess. § 54 (1975).

84. H.R. 2050, 94th Cong., 1st Sess. §§ 1745(a)(9), 1757(b) (1975); H.R. 1, 94th Cong., 1st Sess. § 236 (1975).

85. Specialists are sued most often. Almost sixty percent of the malpractice suits filed in 1970 involved surgeons. Averbach, *Specializing Intensifies Malpractice Rate Issue*, Washington Post, May 12, 1975, at A2, col. 1. Indeed, a recent study involving forty-four states reported that one out of every seven general surgeons is facing a malpractice complaint. *Malpractice: Rx for a Crisis*, TIME, June 16, 1975, at 49.

86. Kendall & Haldi, *The Medical Malpractice Insurance Market*, in MEDICAL MALPRACTICE REPORT Appendix 494, 524-29.

specialists as opposed to general practitioners,[87] or the performance of more surgery is responsible for the greater incidence of malpractice claims in the urban sector, most national health insurance proposals will help to alleviate the situation. All of the "comprehensive benefits" bills provide financial incentives to help redistribute health care personnel to the underserved areas of the United States.[88] The bills also promote the development of ambulatory care centers or HMOs.[89] Emphasis upon ambulatory and periodic preventive care will serve to alleviate the gap in patient-doctor rapport. Development of new levels of health care personnel, such as ambulatory care practitioners, may restore a type of health care provider with whom the patient can maintain a continuing relationship. In addition, association with an HMO for all health services may facilitate rapport between the patient and practitioner when specialty treatments or operations must be undergone. Receiving specialist care through an HMO with whom one has had regular contact will foster more understanding, if only because of familiarity with administrative routines, than if the patient had been referred to an "outside" specialist. At the same time, however, group practice delivery of health care, with its centralized administration of services, could increase the bureaucratization and assembly-line approach to providing health care.[90] Alienation of patient trust and rapport might continue, calling for a new level of health care personnel devoted primarily to communicating with the patient, informing him of his rights, and restoring confidence in the health care provider.

National health insurance does not specifically address itself to malpractice premium rates, although it does suggest the possibility of governmental regulation. Under all of the "comprehensive benefits" bills, private health insurers must maintain an "acceptable" ratio of premiums collected to benefits paid out. Such regulation of malpractice rates appears likely if private insurers are not excluded altogether

---

87. Overall, there are twice as many surgeons in proportion to the United States population as there are in England and Wales; Americans also undergo twice as many operations as Britons do. *How Good Is Your Doctor?*, NEWSWEEK, Dec. 23, 1974, at 46, 48. *See also* Bunker, *Surgical Manpower: A Comparison of Operations and Surgeons in the United States and in England and Wales*, 282 NEW ENG. J. MED. 135 (1970).

88. S. 3, 94th Cong., 1st Sess. §§ 103, 105 (1975); H.R. 5990, 94th Cong., 1st Sess. §§ 201, 202, 204 (1975).

89. See note 70 *supra*. According to recent government statistics, there are 173 HMO plans serving over 5,700,000 people. Owens, *Where You Fit in With HMOs*, MED. ECON., Sept. 28, 1975, at 48.

90. *See* Mechanic, *The Organization of Medical Practice and Practice Orientations Among Physicians in Prepaid and Nonprepaid Primary Care Settings*, 13 MED. CARE 189 (1975).

from the health insurance field. Equalization of insurance rates on a national or regional basis, or governmental subsidization of malpractice premiums, would destroy much of the financial inducement for a doctor to improve his own standard of practice. It would also decrease the incentive among the medical profession to police its own ranks. On the other hand, physician-owned insurance companies might provide strong financial incentives for peer review within the policy holder group.

Large-scale organization of the medical profession into local prepaid group practices, as promoted by most national health insurance "comprehensive benefits" bills, could likewise provide a solution. Medical negligence could be insured against either by the group practice or by private insurers, with the group practice as the unit of adjustment. Within the group practice, premiums could be prorated as a percentage of salary, or paid as an operating expense of the group practice. This arrangement could create an incentive on the part of the group practice to discipline its members and minimize malpractice.[91]

---

91. Individual staff members could be induced to improve their standard of practice by profit-sharing plans among the group members, and in the group practice through compulsory education, restriction of privileges and income, or expulsion. Strong peer review with effective sanctions would be essential, because group insurance will blunt the financial incentive to practice with care which is generated when the individual is wholly responsible for the cost of malpractice insurance.

Making the group practice the unit of adjustment for insurance rates, rather than the individual practitioner, rectifies two unwarranted disparities in current malpractice premium rates. First, rate differentials between medical specialties would be largely eliminated, and second, relief would become available for those practitioners who do not practice full time yet presently pay rates comparable to those who do, e.g., teachers and "the retiring." While it may be argued that those practitioners who practice less than full time are more likely to commit mistakes, the necessity of training practitioners and the "phasing out" of practitioners' careers probably warrants granting pro rata concessions in rates. Premium differentials between general practitioners and specialists, e.g., between orthopedic and general surgeons, are not warranted by questions of competency. Many factors other than general competency account for the disparities. Foremost among such factors is the lack of past acquaintance, present communication and general rapport between specialists and patients. Unlike the family doctor with whom the patient periodically discusses his problems, the specialist is an unknown who often treats the patient in the impersonal confines of an operating room and who often only briefly communicates with the patient. *New York's Special Problems*, MED. WORLD NEWS, Feb. 24, 1975, at 25. The rapport and trust which a general practitioner enjoys with his patients are seldom experienced by the specialist. Another factor is the type of treatment administered. The general practitioner usually indulges in minor treatments for minor ailments. The specialist, on the other hand, engages in more radical treatments involving complex procedures and sophisticated technology. The risk of some adversity, either an accident, negligent behavior, or unexpected complication, increases as the procedure becomes more complex and sophisticated. Kendall & Haldi, *supra* note 86, at 588-90.

As long as all group practices provide a comprehensive range of services, including high-risk specialties, group practice rates most likely will be fair, will relieve high insur-

While preventing some forms of negligence, national health insurance may simultaneously encourage defensive medicine in its worst form—unnecessary and potentially harmful tests and procedures.[92] Although malpractice paranoia is blamed for overutilization of ancillary services and facilities, a want of cost controls and fiscal responsibility among health care providers is probably at the root of the problem.[93] Under the traditional fee-for-service system, the physician, who ordinarily makes the decision whether and by what mode to treat, passes his costs to the patient, and usually, beyond that, to the insurer. There is no financial incentive for the doctor to treat only when necessary and to utilize the most efficient method available. In fact, since the doctor's income increases proportionately to his expenses, cost-saving is discouraged. To the extent that third parties, either governments or private insurers, cover the patient's bills, the patient also lacks incentives to save costs. National health insurance, by extending full coverage to the indigent and chronically ill, will exacerbate the lack of patient cost-consciousness.

Without financial incentives controlling the utilization of facilities and ancillary services,[94] other factors influence volume and choice. For instance, the possibility of malpractice litigation compels the doctor to optimize chances for an acceptable outcome regardless of cost. The incentive to practice defensively is extremely strong because the costs of a malpractice suit to the provider, manifested in insurance premiums, reflect not only the value of the injury in terms of patient compensation, but also the costs of defining and measuring the injury, and the costs of shifting financial responsibility to the provider, *i.e.* legal fees and insurance administration costs. The ideal balancing of costs for optimum allocation of health care resources and optimum patient care would counterpose the benefits of utilizing additional services to gain more complete knowledge (in order to reduce the calculated risks of a procedure) against the costs of adverse outcomes. But the costs of adverse outcomes are grossly inflated under the present system because legal and insurance costs constitute a substantial portion of tort liability

---

ance costs for certain specialties, and will induce high levels of quality care through competition. If all or most services are not provided by group practices, federal subsidies will probably be necessary to sustain the independent provision of high-risk services.

92. See notes 48-53 *supra* and accompanying text.

93. *See* Project, *supra* note 52; Bernzweig, *supra* note 51, at 38-40; Freeborn, *Determinants of Medical Care Utilization: Physicians' Use of Laboratory Services*, 62 AM. J. PUB. HEALTH 846, 852 (1972).

94. An extensive discussion of defensive medicine concluded that lack of cost constraints is the primary cause of overutilization of medical resources. *See* Project, *supra* note 52.

costs. Consequently, providers are economically compelled to practice defensively without efficient optimization of patient care.[95] The stress which advances in medical research and education place upon the panoply of new diagnostic and therapeutic tools available to the physician also ignores costs.[96] To redress this imbalance in cost consideration, health care practitioners must bear the financial risk of overuse of services. Prepaid group practices and utilization review procedures impose cost-consciousness upon their staffs as to choice of diagnostic and therapeutic approaches. Moreover, not only costs, but also deleterious effects, as from excessive radiations, must be considered. The malpractice suit rather than peer review would be more responsive to this latter concern. Conservative medicine, the avoidance of complex or specialty procedures because of the high incidence of complications, injuries, and consequently, malpractice suits, is not wholly detrimental either. Limiting the practice of specialty procedures to specialty-certified practitioners, such as anaesthesiologists, who perform the particular procedures more frequently than general practitioners, and who have more of an incentive to keep informed on the latest discoveries concerning these procedures, will serve to improve the quality of care delivered and will also reduce the need for confirmatory consultations.[97] Yet, to the extent that malpractice concerns induce practioners to remain with the traditional, commonly-practiced methods of treatment, rather than try the latest, perhaps more effective, yet not commonly accepted approaches, conservative medicine may retard improvement in the quality of health care.[98]

IV. The Efficacy of the Tort Liability System Under National Health Insurance

In general, full health care coverage under one of the "comprehensive benefits" acts should reduce the number of malpractice suits, although without necessarily a corresponding reduction in the occurrence of medical negligence. Those persons who suffer minor injuries

---

95. Golladay & Smith, *supra* note 29, at 8.
96. Childs & Hunter, *Non-Medical Factors Influencing Use of Diagnostic X-ray by Physicians*, 10 MED. CARE 323 (1972).
97. The Health Security Act, S. 3, 94th Cong., 1st Sess. (1975), restricts coverage of specialty procedures to those operations performed by certified practitioners.
98. Witness the legal problems incurred by the innovator of the spinal jack operation, now commonly employed under the name of Harrington Rod, to correct scoliosis, referred to in the informed consent suit in Fiorentino v. Wenger, 26 App. Div. 2d 693, 272 N.Y.S.2d 557 (2d Dep't 1966); an appeal was taken by the hospital alone in Fiorentino v. Wenger, 19 N.Y.2d 407, 227 N.E.2d 296, 280 N.Y.S.2d 373 (1967). As will be argued later, PSROs may have the same effect.

allegedly due to negligence and therefore require a small amount of additional medical care, such as a subsequent operation to remove a forgotten sponge, will probably not sue their health care provider since their insurance will cover the cost of the original and any additional medical care. None of the "comprehensive benefits" bills discusses this correctional care, but it would most likely be covered where medically necessary. When cosmetic surgery and other elective procedures would be appropriate to rectify any harm caused by medical negligence, the patient would have to recover against the medical personnel or institution at fault, since such nonessential care is not covered by national health insurance. Even though all "comprehensive benefits" bills, except the Health Security Act, demand twenty percent copayments for many charges, it is doubtful that this cost to the patient will have great impact in most cases. If the twenty percent charge becomes a significant cost to the patient, catastrophic coverage would be triggered, thereby eliminating any charge to the patient. Recovery for lost wages would still be received through a tort suit. The "catastrophic benefits" bills would reduce the number of malpractice suits by a lesser degree, since only extensive or very expensive correctional treatment would be covered by insurance. However, eliminating some of the "police" function that private malpractice suits perform will put additional strain on either internal or administrative regulatory procedures to check the occurrence of medical negligence.

However, to the extent that national health insurance coverage will eliminate direct payment of expensive medical bills, some small impact upon the overall malpractice problem should be expected,[99] since the patient will only be likely to pursue the malpractice claim if a true injury has occurred, rather than because his total expenses appear oppressive.

The medical negligence problem must be handled by implementing procedures to improve the quality of medical care, designing a more efficient compensation system, and installing procedures to make the health care system more responsive to the consumer. Moreover, all this must be accomplished at a socially-acceptable cost.

A. *Quality Control.* Recognition that the medical malpractice insurance crisis has arisen because most suits are the result of actual medical injuries often caused by negligence, leads to the conclusion

---

99. It should be noted, however, that Britain, which has a nationalized health service in which medical costs are fully paid by the government, is experiencing a rise in malpractice suits comparable to that in the United States. Curran, *supra* note 47, at 252.

that more effective quality control mechanisms are needed. The viability of the medical malpractice suit as one mechanism for regulating the quality of health care depends upon the ability of alternative procedures to perform the function with comparable efficacy. The essence of quality control is control by the person receiving services, so that in this sense the term is used to mean "accountability." In addition to private policing by patient-victims through malpractice suits,[100] possible vehicles for quality monitoring include internal policing by health-care providers, and external policing by administrative agencies.

Regulation by an outside administrative body has never been attempted, and judging from analogous regulatory failures this method seems unattractive.[101] Compared to the privately-initiated malpractice suit, peer review is also a poor substitute. Established peer review programs, such as utilization review committees and PSROs, lack the degree of adversity present in privately-initiated malpractice actions.[102] Doctors and other health care providers are not motivated to discipline their peers by the monetary incentives that encourage patients to press malpractice claims. Professional pride is a limited incentive; while the desire to keep the stature of doctors and other medical practitioners at a high level may sometimes compel the elimination

---

100. *See* Roemer, *Controlling and Promoting Quality in Medical Care*, 35 LAW & CONTEMP. PROB. 284, 297 (1970):
> As a sort of last resort for quality control, one may consider the rights of the patient to sue the doctor or hospital or both for harm suffered from improper medical care. The exercise of this right has obviously been increasing in recent years, as patients—with the aid of lawyers—have become more aware of it, as the sanctity of the medical profession in the public eye has diminished, and as the courts have become more demanding of what may be expected of the average provider of medical service.

The Waxman Report of the California Assembly Select Committee on Medical Malpractice (June 1974) considered alternatives to the medical malpractice suit and found that
> [w]hile there do exist quality control mechanisms within the government and medical establishment, these mechanisms are not sufficiently effective. At the present time, malpractice litigation is clearly the most significant external pressure prompting physicians to practice quality medicine. Cartwright, *Change Tort System?: Con*, MED. WORLD NEWS, Sept. 8, 1975, at 60, 64.

101. Administrative agencies also lack sufficient flexibility to monitor the rapidly changing standards of health care.

102. A preliminary inquiry is needed to determine what degree of adversity is optimal for ferreting out and preventing medical negligence. Since estimates show that the number of malpractice claims actually filed represents only a fraction of the potential claims possible for injuries due to participation in the health care system, Rudov, Myers & Mirabella, *supra* note 11, at 13, 20-21, the level of adversity manifested in malpractice claims appears less than optimal. The discontinuity of personal medical care needs supports the notion that patient adversity alone is insufficient for inducing improvement of health care services. The desire among discharged patients not to return to an institution for treatment, or undergo treatment for the same illness again, counters the incentive to sue in order to alter the procedures of a doctor or health care institution.

of gross incompetency, the incentive is likely to wane when the deterrence of technical incompetency, such as not having kept abreast of the most recent and most effective medical procedures, is the objective.

Thus, in order to evaluate the adequacy of peer review programs, it is necessary to determine whether health care providers alone can attain at least the level of adversity generated through private medical malpractice suits. Group practices which operate on a profit-sharing basis offer a financial incentive for more extensive peer review coupled with more severe sanctions.[103] All of the "comprehensive benefits" bills stress the expansion of the group practice mode of delivery. To the extent that the staff of an HMO is concerned with the financial viability of the organization or receives supplemental income according to a profit-sharing scheme, a financial incentive exists to scrutinize and discipline peers. However, group practice organizations usually compensate their staffs with an adequate base salary. This guarantee of a comfortable financial position mutes the incentive to discipline peers.[104] Money supplements for continued professional education, expanding areas of expertise, or keeping the incidence of medical injuries below a targeted level might raise the competency level of individual and institutional health care providers, but would not create the financial incentive to "beef up" peer review programs. Since the medical profession already enjoys the highest esteem among vocational roles, an appeal to professional pride will not necessarily produce intensified peer review and discipline. To date the strongest generators of peer review within health care institutions have been laws which condition funding or reimbursement upon effective utilization review programs,[105] and malpractice suits holding hospitals liable for inadequate monitoring of staff performance.[106] Since it is doubtful that doctors will be provided with an incentive sufficient to lead them to discipline their peers, and since malpractice awards provide a strong stimulus for health care institutions to scrutinize their staffs, it appears the private malpractice suit will still be necessary for monitoring the quality of patient care.

In addition to these practical and historical considerations, it currently appears that the PSRO program is being implemented in such a way as to encourage the use of additional medical tests and proce-

---

103. See note 91 *supra* and accompanying text.
104. *See* Note, *The Role of Prepaid Group Practice, supra* note 82.
105. *See, e.g.*, Pub. L. No. 92-603 (1972) (PSRO legislation).
106. *See* Darling v. Charlestown Community Mem. Hosp., 33 Ill. 2d 326, 211 N.E.2d 253 (1965), *cert. denied*, 383 U.S. 946 (1966) (case result caused changes in hospital procedure).

dures with little or no regard for cost,[107] and with no record of the effectiveness of the tests and procedures encouraged.[108] As Professor Clark Havighurst has concluded, "PSRO legislation alone does not supply the incentive needed to make PSROs achieve more than minor improvements over 'business as usual'."[109]

This leaves us with the private malpractice action. Not only does the system present a pervasive method of accountability for individual action, it also gives the patient a status more equal to that of the health care provider. The ability of the patient to bring a malpractice suit if he feels it warranted has a potentially great psychological value, as does the knowledge that a lay jury from the community, rather than a panel of "defendant-sympathetic experts," will determine the outcome of the suit. Limiting quality monitoring to internal peer review control would increase suspicion about the best efforts of health care providers.[110] Moreover, while malpractice litigation cannot substitute for more comprehensive systems of review (such as PSRO, PEP, or utilization review),[111] it can serve to weed out the extremely incompetent and often dangerous practitioner that these systems either miss or permit to continue to practice.[112] Malpractice findings should also be routinely made available to licensing authorities so that removal or suspension of licenses can be undertaken where appropriate. To date only a few states have made attempts to "feed back" malpractice case

---

107. Havighurst & Blumstein, *Coping With Quality/Cost Trade-Offs in Medical Care: The Role of PSROs*, 70 Nw. U.L. REV. 6 (1975).

108. *See* R. CARLSON, THE END OF MEDICINE (1975); I. ILLICH, MEDICAL NEMESIS (1975).

109. Havighurst & Blumstein, *supra* note 107, at 68.

110. This psychological need could be satisfied by allowing patients to instigate disciplinary proceedings against providers within peer review groups, although the feeling of impartiality emanating from a judicial determination would be compromised.

111. *See* Degenshein & Ceccarelli, *The End Result System*, 292 NEW ENG. J. MED. 704 (1975); Gonnella & Zeleznik, *Factors Involved in Comprehensive Patient Care Evaluation*, 12 MED. CARE 928 (1974); Grimm, *Evaluation of Patient Care Protocol Use by Various Providers*, 292 NEW ENG. J. MED. 507 (1975); Nelson, *Relation Between Quality Assessment and Utilization Review in a Functioning PSRO*, 292 NEW ENG. J. MED. 671 (1975); Williamson, *Evaluating Quality of Patient Care*, 218 J.A.M.A. 564 (1971). Complications are usually monitored as well as outcomes. Deviation from a selected tolerable range triggers a process review to determine whether certain procedures were carried out whenever a particular condition or complication was indicated. If the process analysis reveals that staff procedures were deficient, either new guidelines are promulgated or special education is imposed upon selected personnel. Process checklists, such as PEP, are utilized regularly by institutional staffs as guides for care.

112. One situation involved Dr. John Nork, a California surgeon, who over the course of a decade allegedly performed more than thirty unnecessary laminectomies that left many of his patients crippled for life. Gonzales v. Nork, Civil No. 228566 (Sacramento Super. Ct., Nov. 19, 1973).

findings for quality control purposes.[113] Wasting this source of extensive review of health care providers' performance seems deplorable.[114]

Finally, the ultimate effect of a properly functioning tort system would be to minimize the total number of injuries by giving those responsible for them a financial (or other) incentive to reduce such injuries. This function is accomplished by at least two methods in medical malpractice litigation: through insurance premiums and through a public trial. The premium impact can be minimized severely if physicians are permitted to pass on easily the increases in their rates to their patients, either directly or through third-party reimbursement. Under a system of national health insurance, it may also be appropriate for a federal agency to take over the malpractice insurance business altogether, and for the federal government under proper circumstances to pay a physician's entire malpractice premium. In these circumstances there would be little, if any, financial incentive to avoid sloppi-

---

113. *See, e.g.*, CAL. HEALTH & SAFETY CODE § 1305(a) (West Supp. 1975):
   Every insurer providing professional liability insurance to a health facility . . . shall report . . . to the state department any final judgment over three thousand dollars ($3,000) rendered against such health facility . . . in, or any settlement over three thousand dollars ($3,000) . . . of, a claim or action for damages for personal injuries caused by an error, omission, or negligence in the performance of its professional services, or by the performance of its professional services without consent.
See also IND. ANN. STAT. § 16-9.5-6-2 (Burns 1975) (The "appropriate board of professional registration and examination" shall be apprised of the name of "every" health care provider (except hospitals) against whom a judgment is rendered or settlement made so that the board may review the "fitness of the health care provider to practice his profession.").

114. Stimeling, *Information Feedback Might Avert Medical Mishaps*, J. LEGAL MED. 29 (June 1975). It should be noted, however, that there are definite drawbacks to this method. Malpractice awards and settlements are poor indices of the need for disciplinary sanctions or education improvements. Most malpractice cases are tried by juries whose non-expert findings cannot be readily or reliably interpreted to determine when to restrict privileges or impose educational requirements. Jury, and judicial, confusion of negligent or incompetent practice with unusual medical results, in particular, makes their findings an inappropriate basis for imposing followup remedies. Malpractice settlements reflect considerations of time, cost, adverse publicity, and the possibility of losing before what are conceived to be plaintiff-sympathizing juries, as well as strict issues of fault. Moreover, the size of jury awards and out-of-court settlements sometimes relate to the severity of the injury or the rarity of the result, rather than to the seriousness of the incompetent behavior. However, malpractice claims (after a medico-legal lay screening panel has eliminated the non-meritorious cases), settlements and awards could be used to trigger peer group investigations and the imposition of sanctions, although the time lag between the negligent act and the malpractice finding would diminish the effectiveness of such procedures. Remedial education or disciplinary measures would then be recommended by health care providers reviewing the performance of their peers, depending upon whether negligence, gross incompetence, technical incompetence or lack of scientific understanding was responsible for the adverse result. Thus, malpractice findings alone are not effective data for these quality control purposes, but rather could be used to supplement the peer review requirements of national health insurance plans.

ness. One way to retain such incentive, however, would be to include a deductible in all malpractice insurance policies that is sufficiently large to provide a financial incentive to avoid negligence. Such a deductible could, for example, range from five to twenty-five thousand dollars, and could vary on the basis of income. It would not be recoupable through either increased fees or third party reimbursements. While deductibles have often been proposed as a way of preventing patients from abusing the health-care delivery system through overuse, it is ironic that they are almost never mentioned as a way to prevent system abuse by providers.[115] In addition, since the vast majority of medical malpractice suits are settled for much less than five thousand dollars,[116] such a system could also drastically reduce insurance premiums.

Insofar as a public trial is seen as distasteful to physicians and psychologically important to patients it should be retained to fulfill a deterrent role—both in encouraging physicians to avoid the necessity of experiencing it, and in assuring patients that it is available to them if they are negligently injured.

B. *Compensation for Injury.* In addition to promoting quality health care, the tort liability system also compensates victims of medical negligence. While coverage under national health insurance will relieve part of this problem by removing most medical expenses from the computation of damages, tort litigation would still seem to be necessary in order to allow the plaintiff-patient to recover the remaining elements which presently form the basis for compensation, such as lost wages, pain and suffering, and punitive damages. Nevertheless, the medical malpractice liability system is a somewhat deficient compensating mechanism. First, not all negligently caused injuries are compensated. To receive compensation, the patient-victim must at least be able and

---

115. The only example we have been able to find of the use of deductibles in medical malpractice is not entirely encouraging, however. In that instance an insurance executive noted that one of his insured physicians was paying an annual premium of about $18,000 a year, with a $2,500 deductible per claim. He went on to note that he was "a superb doctor. His problem is that he handles an enormous patient load, makes at least $400,000 a year and to do it successfully, he cuts corners. By doing this he has small malpractice claims which normally his deductible takes care of. He doesn't really damage people—he never cuts off the wrong leg or any of the other dreadful things you often read about. But he does have four to five claims a year." Barnett, *Medical Malpractice Suits Vex*, 318 J. COMMERCE, Nov. 27, 1973, at 2 (quoting K.C. Eberhard, executive vice-president, Signal-Imperial Insurance Group of Los Angeles). As this example illustrates, payment of a deductible may only encourage physicians to spread themselves even thinner, taking more patients than they may be able to adequately deal with in order to increase their gross income.

116. *See* Rudov, Myers & Mirabella, *supra* note 11, at 13.

willing to sue the health care provider in a medical malpractice action. Legal counsel must be hired, medical testimony in some form (either textbook evidence or expert witnesses) must be available, and the patient-victim must be willing to expend time and commitment on a lengthy trial if an initial settlement is not forthcoming. Thus, only the most sensational and severe injuries are consistently pursued.[117] Plaintiff lawyers estimate that they accept only one in eight clients who attempt to engage their services.[118] While spurious claims may represent a substantial portion of those cases refused, many claims are rejected because the potential recovery is too low or it is too difficult to obtain sufficient evidence of medical negligence.[119] Add to that figure the meritorious claims which the patient-victim does not pursue because he considers the cost and energy expenditure of litigation prohibitive, and the conclusion is that the medical malpractice liability system only compensates a small percentage of the victims of medical negligence.

Second, only a small percentage of the malpractice insurance premiums paid by health care providers is received by patient-victims as compensation for their injuries. Ideally, health care providers should bear the financial burden of negligent medical treatment, *i.e.* providers should directly reimburse patient-victims for the value of their losses due to negligently-caused injuries. Of course, in the final analysis, society as a whole always bears the financial burden of medical negligence through increases in health care prices. However, under the present compensation system, almost eighty percent of health care provider premiums are allocated for legal and insurance costs.[120] Such a large overhead seems grossly inefficient.

Third, the medical malpractice liability system sometimes confuses actual medical malpractice with injuries caused by presently unavoidable risks inherent to certain procedures, or not preventable because of imprecise medical knowledge.[121] Patient-victims who have incurred rare or unexpected injuries are often presumed by courts, and especially by juries, to have received negligent treatment. Unreasonable

---

117. See notes 37-43 *supra* and accompanying text.
118. Dietz, Baird & Berul, *supra* note 17, at 97.
119. *See id.* at 97-100.
120. See note 14 *supra*.
121. W. PROSSER, *supra* note 16, at 228. *See generally* Wolfsmith v. Marsh, 51 Cal. 2d 832, 337 P.2d 70 (1959); Seneris v. Haas, 45 Cal. 2d 811, 827, 291 P.2d 915, 924 (1955); Rubsamen, Res Ipsa Loquitur *in California Medical Malpractice Law—Expansion of a Doctrine to the Bursting Point*, 14 STAN. L. REV. 251, 270-80 (1962).

public expectations that medicine can supply cures for all ailments have helped to foster such confusion.[122]

When it forces health care providers to insure patients against the calculated risk of an adverse outcome, malpractice liability imposes an unwarranted burden upon these providers and misallocates our limited health care resources. Yet, more troublesome than the financial burden, which the providers can pass on through higher fees, is the stigmatization of practitioners as negligent or incompetent because their patients incurred an unexpected complication or outcome. Compensation for rare adverse results should not be sought through the tort liability system unless the stigma of negligence and incompetence is carefully reserved for a true negligence finding, and is not associated solely with a compensation award for the plaintiff. However, divorcing these two concepts appears unlikely within the present tort liability system. For the reasons elaborated above,[123] the tort liability system should be restricted to resolving allegations of medical negligence, with arbitration[124] and medico-legal screening panels[125] supplementing the adjudi-

---

122. *See* Altman, *Doctors Told, supra* note 8.
123. See notes 100-22 *supra* and accompanying text.
124. Arbitration is a nongovernmental procedure for settlement of disputes between private parties. Parties to a dispute submit their differences to the judgment of an impartial party appointed either by mutual consent or statutory provision. Thus, the decision to arbitrate may be initiated by agreement of the parties or be imposed upon them. Both approaches are currently being used to a small extent for settlement of malpractice disputes. Arbitration imposed by statute or by court decision is generally applied to disputes under a certain maximum amount, with the jury trial system preserved for the larger cases. *See* Bergen, *Arbitration of Medical Liability*, 211 J.A.M.A. 175, 176 (1970).

Proponents of arbitration maintain that it lowers legal fees, allowing small claims and claims involving difficult evidentiary problems to be compensated. Legal costs are lowered because only a short time is permitted for case preparation, cross-examination is not allowed, and strict evidentiary rules are suspended, thereby allowing hearsay and other excludable evidence to be produced in order to establish a cause of action. In addition, the need for expert witnesses is diminished since the arbitration panel is usually composed of health care experts who are acceptable to both sides. *See* Averbach, *A Plaintiff's Attorney Says: Malpractice Cases Don't Belong in the Courts!*, HOSP. PHYSICIAN 56 (Jan. 1969); Coulson, *The Malpractice Mess: Is Arbitration the Answer?*, 99 MED. TIMES 131 (Oct. 1971); Ludlam & Hassard, *Arbitration*, 114 CAL. MED. 102 (May 1971); *Arbitration of Malpractice Claims*, 28 ARIZ. MED. 391 (May 1971).

Where arbitration is final and binding, the same saving of costs holds true. Where appeal for a trial *de novo* is allowed, limitations can be placed upon the appeal procedure to restrain appeals and thereby effectuate a cost saving. The appellant, under appropriate circumstances, can be charged the costs of appeal and the appellee's legal fees, as well as be required to post a security bond guaranteeing the payment of appellate costs. Another possible restraint is the admission at trial of the arbitration panel's findings, either as presumptions or merely as evidence. Even when such cost and evidentiary restraints are not imposed upon the appeal process, arbitration should lessen the judicial

cation process. Imposing arbitration for claims which probably would not result in profitable recoveries if fully litigated (*e.g.*, below a

---

burden by discouraging those claims which cannot be proved even before the more permissive arbitration panel, with its relaxed evidentiary standards.

The availability of a prompt decision by arbitration may encourage early settlement of claims. For the health care provider there is the benefit of comparative privacy and an absence of public cross-examination. No transcript is required unless by party request, and the arbitrator's decisions are not published. Arbitration awards would probably attract less attention than jury awards, especially if the amounts were in accord with predetermined schedules. *Arbitration of Malpractice Claims, supra,* at 392.

Of course, the lack of publicity has negative consequences for quality control, especially if transcripts and records are not made of the arbitration hearing. The feedback from malpractice cases that could be potentially harnessed for quality control purposes would be eliminated if arbitration panel hearings were not recorded. In general, the more subdued level of publicity would put greater pressure upon peer review and disciplinary measures to sustain the quality level of health care. Therefore, it should be recommended that arbitration findings be fully reported for quality control purposes. Reporting of arbitration findings could be accomplished in two forms. One system could report findings *sans nomina*. Such reporting would locate problem areas or institutions needing intensified preventive programs against injuries and negligence, yet at the same time not damage the reputations of individual practitioners. The alternative to this method, full disclosure of the names of practitioners found negligent, would exert pressure directly upon the individual practitioners to improve their health care practices.

Those who are critical of the use of arbitration to resolve malpractice claims contend that the major motivation behind establishing arbitration is to benefit hospitals, doctors, and the insurance industry, with little benefit for the patient. *See The Case for Arbitration,* in MEDICAL MALPRACTICE, *supra* note 48, at 8, 12. They argue that the proposed advantages of speed and economy apply only to the hearing phase, since it neither reduces the overall time required for claim resolution nor economizes greatly the preparation phase.

It must be conceded that to the extent that arbitration attempts to resolve claims with finality, the costs of operation to the parties may well approach those of a judicial proceeding. Moreover, if the arbitration system employed is not binding on the parties, it may add yet another expensive stage to the current jury trial process. *Cf.* Baird, Munsterman & Stevens, *Alternatives to Litigation, I: Technical Analysis,* in MEDICAL MALPRACTICE REPORT Appendix 214, 215 (present arbitration plans reduce court dockets by only 0.7% of the total volume of malpractice claims).

125. *See* Karcher, *Malpractice Claims Against Doctors: New Jersey's Screening Procedure,* 53 A.B.A.J. 328 (1967); Matte, *A Neutral Screen,* TRIAL 34 (Mar./Apr. 1973); Williams, *Joint Medico-Legal Plan for Screening Medical Malpractice Cases,* 96 VA. MED. MONTHLY 297 (1969); *Are Malpractice Screening Panels the Answer?,* MED. ECON., Mar. 1, 1971, at 106; *Documentary Supplement, Medical-Legal Screening Panels as an Alternative Approach to Medical Malpractice Claims,* 13 WM. & MARY L. REV. 695 (1972). Indiana's scheme places three physicians and one non-voting lawyer-chairperson on the panel. Conspicuously absent is any consumer or patient-advocate representative. IND. ANN. STAT. § 16-9.5-9 (Burns 1975). *See New Indiana Law Will Cut Negligence Suits, supra* note 34.

Mandatory mediation panels have been employed recently in New York with positive results in decreasing the number of cases proceeding to trial and in reducing the amounts of compensation. The three-member mediation panels consist of a state supreme court justice, a lawyer, and a physician. Parties may be represented by counsel, the hearings are informal, and no stenographic record is kept. If the case proceeds to

$10,000 potential recovery threshold) would result in more equitable resolution of malpractice claims. Injured patients for whom the costs of malpractice litigation are prohibitive could receive a less costly, expedited decision as to whether malpractice was the cause, thereby making less seriously, yet negligently, injured persons eligible for relief. Mandatory screening panels, through a preliminary opinion on the merits, could encourage settlements or abandonment of claims.

Following a determination of negligence by the appropriate adjudicative procedure, *i.e.* litigation, arbitration, and/or screening panel, a simplified hearing before a regional panel of compensation experts could decide a value for the injury, perhaps based in part on a compensation schedule. The panel could be composed of physicians, lawyers, insurance experts, and consumers, who would sit on the board for a staggered tenure of about three years, thereby allowing each member to become experienced in the field of compensation, yet without allowing any particular individual to become entrenched in an extremely powerful position. A sitting panel would probably reduce the arbitrariness of awards, be less susceptible to emotional pleas, and be more responsive to the actual damage value of the injury. Employment of a schedule of benefits as a base would also stabilize awards. The compensation schedule would originally be based on present medical malpractice awards and insurance industry figures, but would be continually revised and updated based on actual panel experience in the area and changes in the community. It should be noted that the crucial factor which differentiates this scheme from a "no fault" system is that no compensation will be awarded by this panel unless a finding of negligence has been previously made through adjudicative means.

C. *Responsiveness to Consumers.* A major problem with large hospitals and HMOs is their increasing depersonalization. Health care administrators often overlook the fact that while medical personnel may be familiar with their institution's routine, most outsiders are not, and that this unfamiliarity can cause irritation and anxiety. Even under the best circumstances, being a patient in a hospital or in an HMO can make a person uncomfortable and can magnify his dissatisfaction with his medical treatment.[126]

---

trial, statements made in the course of the hearings are not admissible. Ragan, *A Malpractice Experiment in New York*, 100 MED. TIMES 23 (Feb. 1972). *See AMA Malpractice Liability Plan Accents Risk Control of Doctors*, TRIAL 5 (Sept./Oct. 1971); Lee, *New Court Directions: The Medical Malpractice Mediation Program*, 9 TRIAL LAWYERS Q. 86 (1973); Owens, *Compulsory Malpractice Mediation: Don't Sell It Short*, MED. ECON., June 9, 1975, at 94, 99.

126. *See* Annas, *supra* note 20.

The quality of the relationship between the patient and the health care provider, whether doctor, hospital, or HMO, may of course influence the patient's decision whether to file a malpractice suit.[127] The health care provider's failure to recognize this fact often creates an atmosphere for future problems and complications to develop into a malpractice action. The claim itself is often merely the tangible evidence of the final breakdown of the patient-provider relationship.[128]

Numerous factors lead to this breakdown. Interpersonal problems between the provider and the patient may cause a dissolution of the necessary rapport during the course of therapy. Some physicians charge that lawyers and legal rules are at the base of the deterioration of the doctor-patient relationship.[129] However, physicians are aware that they may be the cause of this problem. In one recent survey, forty percent of doctors responding named "poor communication between physicians and patient" as the single most common cause of malpractice suits.[130] In many instances a genuine misunderstanding exists on one or both sides. The physician may believe that he has explained everything, but the patient may not have understood and may be fearful of asking questions. This problem is particularly acute with those patients who belong to low-status classes in society. Physicians occupy a high status position, and status differentials in general are maintained and acknowledged by various forms of deference. Generally, the greater the social distance between the doctor and patient, the more reluctant the patient will be about questioning or confronting the physician.

There is a general need for more effective communication between physician and patient, particularly as to diagnosis, proposed course of treatment, and possible complications, since these items have the most potential for malpractice litigation. In addition, changes in the type of care physicians render have aggravated the communications problem. Doctors have begun to spend more of their time with the acutely ill, performing such tasks as reading laboratory and x-ray reports, while devoting very little time to the "routinely" ill and their health care questions. Although this shift sharpens the physicians' technical skills, it diminishes their reliance on physical examinations

---

127. See Kupers, *It Takes More Than Insurance to Protect Against Malpractice Suits*, J. LEGAL MED. 33 (Mar. 1975).

128. Bachman, *Doctors: Move Closer to Your Patient!*, TRIAL 25 (May/June 1975).

129. See Ferber & Martin, *New Prey for Ambulance Chasers?*, MED. ECON., Apr. 28, 1975, at 126; *Quicksilver—Emotion and Fear*, TRIAL 15 (May/June 1975).

130. Pabst, *A Medical Opinion Survey of Physicians' Attitudes on Medical Malpractice*, in MEDICAL MALPRACTICE REPORT Appendix 83, 84.

and history-taking—two important situations in which the patient has direct contact with a credible and responsible individual provider.[131]

Intimate rapport with patients is not only good medical practice, but is also a prime malpractice prophylactic.[132] The interpersonal relationship between doctor and patient, rather than any technical or scientific achievement, often prevents a patient from suing his physician. It is interesting to note that in many states with a low incidence of malpractice litigation, such as Montana, New Hampshire, and Vermont, there are large numbers of rural communities in which close, personal relationships develop over the years between physician and patient.[133] This pattern differs dramatically from the overall trend of an increasing percentage of health care being provided through neighborhood health clinics, HMOs, and outpatient departments of hospitals. Institutionalized medicine tends to be far more impersonal than care provided by a trusted family doctor, and many patients feel unable to make their needs and complaints effectively known in these settings. The shift toward institutionalized medicine accounts for the findings of a recent survey which demonstrated that most people felt that the doctor-patient relationship today is not as good as it was twenty years ago.[134]

Patients often have unrealistic expectations regarding the outcome of medical treatment, based in part on misinformation. These patients will likely be disappointed, but some patient dissatisfaction might have been avoided had the doctors involved discovered the patient's expectations and, where necessary, attempted to redirect those expectations in more realistic directions. Perhaps all patients have come to have expectations which are far out of proportion with reality.[135] And pro-

---

131. Childs & Hunter, *Non-Medical Factors Influencing Use of Diagnostic X-Ray by Physicians*, 10 MED. CARE 323 (1972); Donaldson & London, *Time Study of Doctors and Nurses at Two Swedish Health Care Centers*, 9 MED. CARE 457 (1971); Freeborn, *Determinants of Medical Care Utilization: Physicians' Use of Laboratory Services*, 62 AM. J. PUB. HEALTH 846 (1972); Hardwick, *Clinical Styles and Motivation: A Study of Laboratory Test Use*, 13 MED. CARE 397 (1975); Mechanic, *General Medical Practice: Some Comparisons Between the Work of Primary Care Physicians in the United States and England and Wales*, 10 MED. CARE 402 (1972).

132. See *How to Avoid Malpractice Suits*, MED. WORLD NEWS, Sept. 22, 1975, at 61, 62.

133. Giddings, *Why the Malpractice Plague Is Passing Some States By*, MED. ECON., May 26, 1975, at 37. See also Thurlow, *Yes, There Is a Malpractice Paradise*, MED. ECON., Jan. 18, 1971, at 142.

134. Peterson, *Consumers' Knowledge of and Attitudes Toward Medical Malpractice*, in MEDICAL MALPRACTICE REPORT Appendix 658.

135. Wilson, *Doc Welby Wows Public, Gives Med Biz Shot in Head*, Boston Sun. Globe, June 29, 1975, at A7, col. 2; *Malpractice, Rx for a Crisis, supra* note 85, at 49-50.

viders, on their part, have done little or nothing to limit those expectations, preferring instead to enjoy the esteem and economic and social status of their position.[136]

The medical malpractice crisis may, in fact, be due in large measure to the failure to recognize the human needs of patients, the professional limitations of providers, and the shared responsibilities of members of the community for the health of their fellow citizens. With rare exceptions, the tort liability system provides the only mechanism by which patients who have, or think they have, suffered an injury as a result of negligent medical treatment can obtain redress.

A number of hospitals have recognized this problem, and have developed a system of "patient representatives" to help "humanize" the hospital atmosphere. This innovation followed a recommendation by the Report of the Secretary's Commission on Medical Malpractice that every hospital establish a patient grievance mechanism.[137] However, few of the approximately 350 systems presently functioning in hospitals as patient grievance mechanisms have adequate authority to deal with those problems which often lead to malpractice claims.[138] The job description of the patient service representatives instructs them to deal with non-medical, non-fiscal, minor complaints of a public relations nature, thereby limiting these representatives to a cosmetic role in the patient care continuum.[139] Although many of these efforts are to be applauded, none operate on the major complaints which induce malpractice suits, and therefore can provide only a marginal reduction in the incidence of such suits against health care institutions.[140]

This problem becomes more acute under a system of national health insurance, since the provision of health care services could well become increasingly institutionalized and impersonal. A recent survey of HMO officials revealed that many viewed the large organizational character of their facility as likely to make their patients more willing to sue the HMO than they would be to sue a private practitioner.[141]

While the elimination of direct payments by the patient under a system of national health insurance will make care more available to

---

136. Altman, *Doctors Told, supra* note 8.
137. MEDICAL MALPRACTICE REPORT 84.
138. *Profile of Patients' Rights and Hospital Patient Representatives*, HEALTH PERSPECTIVES 3 (Feb./Mar. 1974).
139. According to the American Hospital Association, patient service representatives exist in 462 hospitals. Thompson, Lupton, Renck, *et al., Patient Grievance Mechanisms in Health Care Institutions*, in MEDICAL MALPRACTICE REPORT Appendix 758, 760.
140. *See, e.g.*, Cote, *The Patient's Link*, TRIAL 28, 29 (Mar./Apr. 1973).
141. Curran & Moseley, *The Malpractice Experience of Health Maintenance Organizations*, 70 Nw. U.L. REV. 69, 81 (1975).

many, it also may make the provider less concerned about patient acceptance and attitudes than in a system in which the patient directly compensates the provider. It will therefore be necessary to build into the system some mechanism, at least at the hospital and HMO level, to help the patient exercise his legal rights and obtain all the information he needs about his medical condition, the health care facilities, the proposed treatment and its risks and benefits, alternative treatments, problems of recuperation, and staff qualifications.[142] To perform this function, and simultaneously to decrease the number of malpractice suits prompted by impersonal attention, inadequate preparation for an adverse reaction or result, unnecessary surgery, and poor physician-patient and staff-patient relationships, we propose the development of a national medico-legal office with representatives in every major hospital and HMO.

These representatives would work for the national health insurance system. This separation of the representatives from the health care institution is essential for the proper functioning of the mechanism. Each representative must know that his primary obligation is to provide assistance for the patient, and that his relationship with the hospital or other medical facility is not one of employer to employee. In this way the representative could feel free, when necessary, to oppose those decisions which the institution might think in its own best interest, without fear of financial repercussions.

Every member of the medico-legal office would be legally empowered to help patients exercise their legal rights to such things as full and complete medical information, consultations, treatment refusals, discharge delays, and transfer requests.[143] In order to have an adequate awareness of these rights and knowledge of the manner in which they function in the health care continuum, it seems essential to have the personnel of the office composed of individuals from diverse disciplines, including, but not limited to, representatives of law, medicine, social work, and psychology.

On the individual hospital or HMO level, there would be a separate medico-legal office, again staffed with similar personnel who are in the employ of the national health insurance system and not of the particular health care institution in which the specific office is located.

---

142. *See* Annas & Healey, *The Patient Rights Advocate: Redefining the Doctor-Patient Relationship in the Hospital Context*, 27 VAND. L. REV. 243 (1974).

143. *See generally* G. ANNAS, THE RIGHTS OF HOSPITAL PATIENTS (1975); JOINT COMM. ON ACCREDITATION OF HOSPITALS, ACCREDITATION MANUAL FOR HOSPITALS 1-2 (1973).

These representatives would be available to help resolve patient-staff disputes at the facility level without resort to litigation. This function would include settlement attempts following the occurrence of a medico-legal problem,[144] as well as efforts to prevent problems through early interaction with patients,[145] and provider-patient education concerning applicable health law issues, particularly patients' rights.[146] In addition, the representatives would collect data on the types of patient complaints that most often lead to malpractice actions, using this information as a basis for devising methods for preventing these problems in the future. Thus, the ultimate goal of a properly functioning medi-

---

144. This function would include categorization of common patient complaints, with notation of appropriate measures called for, and accompaniment of the patient by the representative throughout the in-hospital attempt at resolution. It could also include, assuming authority was received from the health facility's insurance carrier, settlement negotiations.

145. This could be accomplished in the following manner. Upon completion of registration for each patient, the clerk would page the patient representative to inform him of the patient's arrival. As soon as it is medically permissible, the representative would explain to the patient that if at any time during his visit, or a subsequent visit concerning a related complaint, he desires assistance in resolving any problems—such as billing, communications with the provider, or medical care—he should ask to speak with the patient representative. It should be noted as well that the entire staff of the facility should be informed of the services of the medico-legal office and its personnel. In addition, they should be encouraged to call the office if any situation arises in which the patient desires assistance from the representative.

146. Provider-patient education programs might be developed in numerous ways. For example, there could be a mini-course, consisting of two sessions of two hours' duration, which would be required of the entire staff of the institution. These courses would include instruction in problems of communication (e.g., importance of clear communication, ways of documenting what has been communicated, common pitfalls in communication); recognition of medico-legal problems; the role and function of the medico-legal office personnel; the type of patient complaints received or anticipated; the procedures for handling specific problem situations; and several important legal principles, such as informed consent and access to medical records. A broader, nine-month seminar program could then be offered to the staff. Participation in this would be optional, but highly encouraged. Each session would meet for two hours a month. The material to be covered would include medical decision-making; recognizing legal problems; clarifying communications with patients; compensation for personal injuries; professional liability; patient rights; rights and duties concerning emergency medical care; regulation of the medical profession; cooperation with law enforcement agencies; rights of the dying patient; and confidentiality and privacy. Special medico-legal sessions could be designed and added for specialty groups, such as transplant surgeons and ancillary laboratory staff. In addition, office personnel could offer periodic seminars on medico-legal issues, as well as initiate the publication of a bi-weekly newsletter outlining significant developments in the law and demonstrating specific problems and solutions encountered by the medico-legal office. A patient education program could be accomplished by having representatives of the medico-legal office attend meetings of community groups, offering seminars to the community which would familiarize it with the existence and functions of the office, as well as providing information concerning patients' rights and responsibilities under the law.

co-legal office is to make the system both more responsive to patients and to simultaneously decrease the number of malpractice suits.

V. Conclusion

Catastrophic health insurance or credit-subsidy proposals will not have much impact on the manner in which health care is currently delivered. However, a system of comprehensive health insurance, available to all, will. Under such a plan the current tort system should be retained as the primary method for quality control, and deductibles added to the insurance policies both to increase incentives for care and to decrease premiums. Alternative methods might, however, be devised to provide more universal coverage at a more reasonable cost. It might also be advisable to limit the role of malpractice litigation to questions of incompetence and negligence, and assign the compensation function to another mechanism.

In addition, even though the tort system aids in making the health care system more responsive to patient demands, hospitalized patients are unlikely to be able to exercise the legal rights necessary to fully participate in medical decisions regarding their health care. In such cases patient satisfaction can be enhanced, and the incidence of medical malpractice reduced, by the introduction of an effective patient grievance mechanism in every major health care institution. It would be most appropriate for such an office to be independent of the health care institution, and inclusion of it in a program of national health insurance seems best.

While there are major problems with the present tort liability system, they are not those commonly ascribed to it by the medical profession. The system should be judged strictly on the basis of cost-effectiveness, quality control, medical coverage, and responsiveness to consumer desires. When evaluated under these criteria, the tort system, with the modifications suggested in this Article, retains an important function in any system of national health insurance. We thus conclude that it is more essential than expendable.

THE MEDICAL MALPRACTICE STANDARD OF CARE: HMOs AND CUSTOMARY PRACTICE*

RANDALL BOVBJERG**

OUTLINE

INTRODUCTION

THE APPLICATION OF MALPRACTICE LAW TO HMO CARE
A. *HMOs' Structure, Incentives, and Contribution to Health Care Delivery*
B. *HMOs' Approach to Medical Risk Evaluation*
C. *Malpractice Standards and HMOs*

PROBLEMS WITH THE CURRENT MALPRACTICE APPROACH TO HMOS
A. *Inadequate Valuation of the Costs and Results of Reducing Risks*
B. *Overemphasis on Methods of Care*
C. *Potentially Excessive Penalties for Noncustomary Care*
D. *Unduly Narrow Focus on the Risks of Individual Procedures*

A PROVISIONAL SOLUTION WITHIN THE CUSTOMARY APPROACH: HMO CUSTOM AS THE STANDARD OF CARE

CONCLUSION

INTRODUCTION

Medical care is a risky business. Health care providers risk their reputations and malpractice suits, but patients run the principal risks, namely that medical care may fail to achieve the expected improvement or may cause some new harm. Some risk is of course inescapable because it is inherent in the very nature of the medical enterprise—

---

* Work on this Article was supported by grant number HS 01539 from the National Center for Health Services Research, United States Department of Health, Education and Welfare.
** Research Attorney, Program on Legal Issues in Health Care, Duke University. A.B. 1968, University of Chicago; J.D. 1971, Harvard Law School.
THE FOLLOWING CITATIONS WILL BE USED IN THIS ARTICLE:
    A. HOLDER, MEDICAL MALPRACTICE LAW (1975) [hereinafter cited as HOLDER];
    D. LOUISELL & H. WILLIAMS, MEDICAL MALPRACTICE (1973) [hereinafter cited as LOUISELL & WILLIAMS];
    W. PROSSER, HANDBOOK OF THE LAW OF TORTS (4th ed. 1971) [hereinafter cited as PROSSER];
    U.S. DEP'T OF HEALTH, EDUCATION AND WELFARE, REPORT OF THE SECRETARY'S COMMISSION ON MEDICAL MALPRACTICE (1973) [hereinafter cited as MEDICAL MALPRACTICE REPORT];
    McCoid, *The Care Required of Medical Practitioners*, 12 VAND. L. REV. 549 (1959) [hereinafter cited as McCoid].

that enterprise being the attempt to alter already present hazards of undesirable outcomes by sometimes drastic means whose effectiveness and safety are often uncertain. But health care providers, by providing additional services or by taking further precautions, can frequently avoid or reduce many, perhaps most, medical hazards—although at some cost in resources and in new risks created.

Not all avoidable risks should be avoided, however, since many are very unlikely either to occur or to cause significant harm, and the resources that would be consumed to avoid them always have valuable applications elsewhere. Individuals and society must somehow decide how much medical risk reduction is appropriate, given the alternatives, their costs, and the relative values of the expected outcomes. The law of medical malpractice exerts a large and apparently growing influence on the risk reduction actually undertaken by medical care providers.

One kind of provider, the Health Maintenance Organization, or HMO,[1] is especially well suited to weigh all relevant factors in deciding how, and how much, to reduce the medical risks faced by its enrollee-patients. HMOs' distinguishing characteristic is that they undertake to provide all the medical care their enrollees need in exchange for fixed, advance capitation payments. Precisely because they must provide comprehensive care from an inelastic pool of resources, HMOs are well motivated to scrutinize the effectiveness of every risk-reducing measure they might take. Moreover, because their responsibility for care is comprehensive and because their organization usually allows them to provide more integrated services than most other providers, HMOs are well situated to compare each possible risk reduction with other uses of the available resources and to choose the most productive course of action.

In these respects, HMOs stand in distinct contrast with the dominant mode of American medical practice, fee-for-service, wherein patients (or governmental or private financing mechanisms) pay for each service rendered by a variety of independent providers (doctors,

---

1. The term "HMO" was coined by Dr. Paul Ellwood, Jr., and his colleagues at the Institute for Interdisciplinary Studies (InterStudy) in Minneapolis and adopted by the Nixon Administration for several policy proposals. *See, e.g.*, Ellwood, Anderson, Billings, *et al., Health Maintenance Strategy*, 9 MED. CARE 291 (1971). InterStudy's definition ensures that HMOs will have the risk-evaluation incentives discussed here.

> An HMO is an organization in which the HMO itself and/or participating physicians accept contractual responsibility to assure the delivery of a stated range of health services, including at least ambulatory and in-hospital care to a voluntarily enrolled population in exchange for an advance capitation payment (and assumes at least part of the financial risk and/or shares in the surplus for the delivery of ambulatory and hospital services). HEALTH SERVICES INFORMATION, Oct. 20, 1975, at 2.

hospitals, and so on). Unlike HMOs, fee-for-service providers have only weak financial incentives to weigh costs in evaluating possible risk-reducing measures, since neither they nor their patients are able to apply insurance money saved in one area to other, more productive uses. Nor does the fee-for-service providers' organization usually enable them to compare directly the value of a wide range of different health-promoting services and to implement their evaluations in practice.

How medical care providers approach risk-reduction decisions is very important in understanding the law of medical malpractice. Malpractice law does not purport independently to assess the reasonableness of risky behavior in order to determine the optimal levels of risk avoidance and risk acceptance, but instead enforces a standard of care derived almost entirely from the customary practice of providers themselves. In drawing its standard of care from the usages of the medical services market, the law may inadvertently perpetuate or exacerbate the deficiencies of that market in assessing the appropriate level of expenditures on risk reduction.

Although in a perfect world such customary practice might acceptably approximate the social optimum by aggregating the risk-assessing wisdom of informed individuals, in reality malfunctions of the marketplace for medical services may make this standard socially inappropriate as a guide to proper practice. Whereas the legal standard made sense when providers or their paying patients regularly had to assess risk-reducing measures in terms of their costs and the value of results achieved in establishing patterns of conduct, the customary practice standard of care has become increasingly inappropriate as third-party payment has subtly changed medical practice by gradually eroding the system's cost-consciousness. The apparent result has been a contemporary standard of care that exposes to substantial legal risks any provider who fails to imitate existing patterns of care, thus aggravating an already serious tendency of medical care providers to adopt ever more procedures without careful consideration of the expense and results involved. Many providers, indeed, are said to practice "defensive" medicine in response to this perceived legal threat, performing extra tests and taking additional precautions prompted more by legal fears than by medical expectations.

This Article deals with the specific problem that legal enforcement of customary practice standards derived from fee-for-service norms may discourage innovative HMO practice based upon a different and possibly more accurate evaluation of the costs or risks involved or employing a different method of achieving similar risk reduction. Such a push to HMO conformity may in turn eliminate the healthy economic and philosophic competition between different medical approaches which might otherwise develop between HMO and fee-for-service providers. Related problems of the medical custom standard include undue judicial concentration on determining what medical methods are customary, to the exclusion of judging the risk reduction and results actually achieved; excessive penalties for noncomformity alone, without regard to comparative costs and results; and inappropriate consideration of medical risk reduction problems in isolation from one another. These shortcomings not only pose malpractice problems for HMOs but also show how difficult it is—especially within the confines of the current legal approach to medical injuries—to weigh all relevant considerations in attempting to determine the socially optimal level of medical risk reduction.

THE APPLICATION OF MALPRACTICE LAW TO HMO CARE

A. *HMOs' Structure, Incentives, and Contribution to Health Care Delivery*

Because HMOs must finance all needed care from the limited budget supplied by enrollee capitation payments,[2] they are highly motivated to count costs, as well as risks and results, in deciding what care to provide.[3] The financial exigencies of prepayment engender strong

---

2. Though all HMOs meeting the InterStudy definition, see note 1 *supra*, provide very comprehensive care for the basic prepaid premium, HMOs do not provide literally one hundred percent of medical needs without further charge. There are often coverage limitations, though fewer than are common in conventional insurance policies; for example, many HMOs do not provide free drugs. *E.g.*, U.S. DEP'T OF HEALTH, EDUCATION, AND WELFARE, BUREAU OF COMMUNITY HEALTH SERVICES, INCLUSION OF PHARMACEUTICAL SERVICES IN HEALTH MAINTENANCE AND RELATED ORGANIZATIONS: A REVIEW OF SUPPLEMENTAL BENEFITS (DHEW Pub. No. (HSA)74-13017, 1974). Moreover, HMOs' subscribers may have to make nominal additional payments for some services. Note, *The Role of Prepaid Group Practice in Relieving the Medical Care Crisis*, 84 HARV. L. REV. 887, 902-03 & n.4 (1971).

3. There are many variations on the basic HMO theme, with considerable diversity in comprehensiveness of coverage, integration of services, and organization of affiliated provider groups. *See, e.g.*, Prussin, *HMOs: Organizational and Financial Models* (pts. 1-3), 55 HOSP. PROGRESS 33 (Apr. 1974); *id.* at 56 (May 1974); *id.* at 60 (June 1974). The character and strength of HMO economizing and risk-evaluating activities may vary accordingly.

Organizationally, HMOs may be either prepaid group practices (PGPs), of which the best known example is probably the Kaiser-Permanente plan, or foundations for medical care (FMCs), of which the archetype is the San Joaquin, California, FMC. *See, e.g.*, Egdahl, *Foundations for Medical Care*, 288 NEW ENG. J. MED. 491 (1973); Phelan, Erickson & Fleming, *Group Practice Prepayment: An Approach to Delivering*

incentives for HMOs continually to weigh the medical effectiveness and value of their expenditures and to curb, for example, superfluous x-rays and other tests.[4] Their resource constraint and duty to serve an entire population also encourage HMOs both to maintain enrollees' health, through education and preventive medicine wherever cost-effective, and to find and treat health problems before they become acute and require still more expensive measures, for which HMOs cannot be reimbursed. The comprehensiveness and integration of their services give HMOs numerous occasions to evaluate alternatives in seeking to achieve maximum health benefits for given expenditures[5]—for ex-

---

Organized Health Services, 35 LAW & CONTEMP. PROB. 796 (1970).

The merits of PGPs versus FMCs in their various incarnations have been debated elsewhere, and the respective virtues of the two forms of medical organization are not relevant here. At issue here are the extent to which HMOs' efficiency incentives lead them to create patterns of resource use and styles of care different from those of the fee-for-service system and the implications of these differences for medical malpractice. Either PGP or FMC organization may raise these issues; the remainder of this Article does not generally distinguish between the two, except where the implications of the differences are major.

4. The degree of risk to which the HMO is subjected for financial losses from overutilization of health care services may vary among HMOs. The way in which HMOs translate their institutional economizing incentives into decision-making rules for the doctors actually providing and ordering the services also varies. PGP doctors are usually salaried; they have no incentive to provide extra services of only marginal risk-reducing value, because their income is not increased by doing so. Roemer, *On Paying the Doctor and the Implications of Different Methods*, 3 J. HEALTH & SOCIAL BEHAVIOR 4, 11 (Spring, 1962). Their positive incentive to economize comes from the identification of their future prosperity with that of the PGP, the ability to use savings from reduction in utilization for other services, and review of their care. FMC doctors are paid a fee for each service rendered and thus retain the usual fee-for-service incentive to increase their income by providing ever more services. However, FMC peer review must pass on the value of many services provided and, if charges exceed revenues, some FMCs' doctors' fees may be retroactively reduced. These factors motivate FMC physicians to weigh costs. Egdahl, *supra* note 3, at 492, 495. FMC doctors' cost-controlling incentives are probably weaker than those of PGP providers because they are imposed by outside review rather than by the nature of the financing and because FMC doctors typically retain a considerable outside practice, from which habits for serving insured fee-for-service patients probably carry over into their FMC practice. These different FMC and PGP arrangements may nevertheless have similar practical effects, and it is acceptable to speak generally of HMO cost-counting incentives regardless of their exact strength or their method of implementation.

5. Prepayment might instead motivate HMOs to maximize, for example, their own profits or their personnel's salaries rather than enrollees' health. See note 9 *infra*. Having to pay for all needed care, including that necessitated by their own neglect or ineffective treatment, provides some protection against tendencies toward underservice. Other protections include subscribers' ability to detect underservice, professional ethics, some government regulations, and, of course, malpractice liability. The point is to create malpractice incentives to deal with underservice without, in the process, inappropriately interfering with HMOs' desirable ability to count costs in evaluating what care to provide.

ample, by replacing physicians' services with nonphysician care when appropriate, or by substituting outpatient for expensive inpatient care.[6] HMOs' scope and integration also enable them to maintain unified medical records, which can save time and resources as well as avoid needless exposure to the hazards of inaccuracy and of duplicative or incompatible diagnostic or therapeutic procedures. HMOs' multiprovider organization also facilitates quality control through consultation, referral, peer review, and other mechanisms,[7] while the lack of charges for each service saves administrative costs, eases access to medical care, and encourages subscribers to make full and early use of their HMO's services.[8]

HMOs are not perfect, however. Their budget constraint and lack of fee-for-service inducement to provide care can lead to overeconomizing and neglect of valuable opportunities to reduce patients' risks.[9] Moreover, HMOs may feature some disadvantages of large-scale organization, including reduced responsiveness to individual needs.[10] Finally, HMOs do not appeal to all health care consumers; despite much attention from health policy analysts, many HMOs have had difficulty attracting enrollees and surviving in the medical services marketplace.[11]

Nonetheless, there is substantial evidence that most prepayment plans in fact provide comprehensive care which is of low risk and high

---

6. This factor is stronger among the more tightly integrated HMOs. FMCs do not typically build their own outpatient clinics, for example, but depend instead on existing facilities. FMC providers may thus not be able to perform certain procedures outside rather than inside hospitals. Similarly, small PGPs may rely more heavily on inpatient services than those which are larger and more comprehensive. HMOs may still be said generally to offer wide opportunity for different allocations of medical resources, though the exact situation varies from HMO to HMO.

7. See, e.g., P. ELLWOOD, P. O'DONOGHUE, W. MCCLURE, R. HOLLEY, et al., ASSURING THE QUALITY OF HEALTH CARE 21-22 (1973); Greenlick, *The Impact of Prepaid Group Practice on American Medical Care: A Critical Evaluation*, 399 ANNALS 100 (1972); Institute of Medicine, Nat'l Academy of Science, HMOs: Toward a Fair Market Test 52 (policy statement, May, 1974).

8. The impact of these factors may be reduced by increased waiting time for medical attention in some HMOs. H. SCHWARTZ, THE CASE FOR AMERICAN MEDICINE 180-81 (1972).

9. The extreme example would be allowing a patient to die rather than to undertake an expensive and perhaps uncertain treatment. See, e.g., H. SCHWARTZ, supra note 8, at 177. The worst HMO abuses are likely to occur in plans serving the least-informed consumers, especially under conditions of government financing. See, e.g., Schneider & Stern, *Health Maintenance Organizations and the Poor: Problems and Prospects*, 70 Nw. U.L. REV. 90 (1975). See note 5 supra.

10. E.g., Phelan, Erickson, & Fleming, supra note 3, at 797-98.

11. It is not clear to what extent HMOs' difficulties in this regard are due to dissatisfaction of potential enrollees. Legal and professional restraints against HMOs

quality—and at a lower cost than fee-for-service care—by deviating from many standard practices of fee-for-service providers.[12] HMOs have therefore been seen by many observers as an important and salutary development in organizing health care services.[13] HMOs' promise of improved access to and quality of care is important when many have come to speak of a "right" to health care,[14] and HMOs' economizing abilities are important virtues at a time when health care consumes about one twelfth of the country's gross national product.[15] In fact, HMOs may help economize on two levels: first, HMOs are motivated to strive for an efficient internal allocation of health-care resources, to maximize the productivity of the resources they control; second, HMOs may facilitate consumer valuation of health care as a whole in a way that even insured fee-for-service care cannot. By offering a very comprehensive health care package, HMOs enable subscribers to budget for medical care, to express their evaluation of the total worth to them of all medical services—compared with their other expenditures. To the extent that they are informed, subscribers' choice of an HMO may also indicate what customary level of risk-reducing measures they desire.[16]

Some HMO proponents emphasize HMOs' potential to improve access and to provide high-quality care at reasonable costs,[17] whereas

---

and their physicians are also responsible. *Compare* Institute of Medicine, *supra* note 7, at 19-49, *with* H. SCHWARTZ, *supra* note 8, at 154-58.

12. NATIONAL ADVISORY COMMISSION ON HEALTH MANPOWER, REPORT 197-229 (1967); Donabedian, *An Evaluation of Prepaid Group Practice*, 6 INQUIRY 3 (Sept. 1969); Roemer & Shonick, *HMO Performance: The Recent Evidence*, 51 MILBANK MEMORIAL FUND Q. 271 (1973).

13. *See, e.g., Health Maintenance Strategy, supra* note 1; MacLeod & Prussin, *The Continuing Evolution of Health Maintenance Organizations*, 288 NEW ENG. J. MED. 439 (1973); Saward & Greenlick, *Health Policy and the HMO*, 50 MILBANK MEM. FUND Q. 147 (1972); Note, *The Role of Prepaid Group Practice in Relieving the Medical Care Crisis*, 84 HARV. L. REV. 887 (1971). See also sources cited in notes 17-18 *infra*. HMOs have also achieved federal recognition as a desirable innovation. *See* Health Maintenance Organization Act of 1973, 42 U.S.C. §§ 300e *et seq.* (Supp. III, 1973); *The President's Message to the Congress Proposing a Comprehensive Health Policy for the Seventies, February 18, 1971,* 7 WEEKLY COMPILATION OF PRESIDENTIAL DOCUMENTS 244 (1971).

14. For example, Leonard Woodcock, President of the International Union, United Automobile Workers, has maintained that "every American has a right to quality health care services . . . ." *Hearings on National Health Insurance Before the Senate Comm. on Finance,* 93d Cong., 2d Sess., at 145 (1974).

15. Mueller & Gibson, *National Health Expenditures, Fiscal Year 1975,* 39 SOCIAL SECURITY BULL. 3, 5, Chart 1 (Feb. 1976).

16. See note 119 *infra*. While a person's joining an HMO does indicate that the level of care it offers is satisfactory at that time, insofar as the subscriber can judge it, membership does not preclude a subscriber's purchasing outside medical services should the actual onset of illness or other circumstances change the subscriber's evaluation of HMO coverage or services.

17. These are typified by the supporters of the HMO Act of 1973, which mandates

others attach more importance to HMOs' cost savings—achieved at little or no sacrifice in quality—which may lead other providers to balance cost and quality more effectively, thus reducing total health care expenditures.[18] In any case, HMOs' ability and incentives to evaluate and choose appropriately among different medical procedures are essential to their social value, and undue interference with these HMO attributes by malpractice law or otherwise[19] would be unfortunate.

B. *HMOs' Approach to Medical Risk Evaluation*

If HMOs were unfettered by outside requirements, they could be expected to expend resources on risk reduction only until their expenditures could be used to achieve greater benefits in alternative uses, such as reducing other risks, expanding coverage, lengthening clinic hours, lowering premiums, and extending medical services in other ways.[20] Neither HMOs nor other providers, of course, have special expertise in valuing the increments of illness and health, injury and cure, pain and relief, disability and recovery, or death and life that are at stake in the risks they assess. Such valuations can come only from patients themselves or from courts or other governmental authorities acting on patients' behalf. Nonetheless, because they provide an entire population with comprehensive care, HMOs are uniquely qualified to choose the proper mix of medical inputs and processes[21] for each

---

very comprehensive services for federally recognized HMOs. *See, e.g.*, W. Roy, THE PROPOSED HEALTH MAINTENANCE ORGANIZATION ACT OF 1972 (1972); American Public Health Ass'n, *Health Maintenance Organizations: A Policy Paper*, 61 AM. J. PUB. HEALTH 2528 (1971).

18. *See, e.g.*, Havighurst, *Health Maintenance Organizations and the Market for Health Services*, 35 LAW & CONTEMP. PROB. 716 (1970); McNeil & Schlenker, *HMOs, Competition, and Government*, 53 MILBANK MEMORIAL FUND Q. 195 (1975); Institute of Medicine, *supra* note 7.

19. One article, Havighurst & Bovbjerg, *Professional Standards Review Organizations and Health Maintenance Organizations—Are They Compatible?*, 1975 UTAH L. REV. 381, considers the likely impact on HMOs of a nonmalpractice set of standards—those of the federally mandated PSROs under the Medicare and Medicaid programs.

20. This behavior would characterize a rational HMO dedicated to maintaining the health of enrollees. But see notes 5 & 9 *supra*.

21. "Inputs" refers to the providers and facilities used in health care. "Processes" are the methods or specific procedures used by health care providers. An important reason why HMOs are uniquely qualified to determine the value of inputs and processes is that, as providers of comprehensive care to entire populations, they have the ability to gather the requisite data to determine medical effectiveness of different care, as individual providers do not. *See, e.g.*, Brook, *Critical Issues in the Assessment of Quality of Care and Their Relationship to HMOs*, 48 J. MED. EDUC. 114, 132-33 (Apr. 1973).

type of case; that is, HMOs can equalize, within the limits of the state of the art, the marginal risks that subscribers face from all hazards and maximize the health benefits to subscribers for the amount of money they are willing to devote to health care services.[22]

It may be argued that the level of care embodied in malpractice standards is not susceptible to such analytic trading off of risks because the incidence and severity of bad outcomes associated with any given risk-reducing measure are unpredictable at best and unavoidable at worst. Malpractice law indeed often purports to deal with slippery and seemingly nonquantifiable matters of risk reduction, such as whether a provider's skill is sufficient for a particular procedure or whether an apparent slip of a scalpel in a particular case was culpable carelessness or an unavoidable side effect of a difficult procedure. Nonetheless, much of malpractice law involves quite discrete and manageable concerns, such as whether particular diagnostic procedures should be undertaken or whether particular safety precautions are appropriate. Such matters clearly may be analyzed for medical and cost effectiveness, which HMOs are well equipped to undertake.

In reality, moreover, even risks seeming to involve simple personal carelessness are often not entirely of a different and unmanageable type, but can instead profitably be treated as the far end of the same continuum. Numerous measures might be taken to reduce the risk of virtually any untoward result, if only marginally, and these are subject to rational scrutiny as to their risk-reducing effectiveness, their cost, and their other consequences. Except in emergency cases, for example, consultation or supervision could be required, stricter diagnostic or therapeutic protocols might be established, and so forth. In any case, an HMO could hire additional personnel, or fee-for-service providers could accept fewer patients, so as to allow more time to be devoted

---

22. This is not meant to imply that HMOs always make optimal decisions, judging only cost and value to patients; factors other than the incentives engendered by a fixed budget and the necessity to please enrollees are also involved. For example, the common training and continued association of HMO and fee-for-service physicians are likely to influence the HMO approach to medical decision-making in the direction of majority practice. An HMO management's close ties with labor unions or dependence on them for enrollees may lead to exclusive use of union-made products or services, almost regardless of cost and quality concerns. Legal restrictions may play a part, as where licensing laws prevent doctors from delegating certain tasks to trained and efficient assistants who are not state-certified. Malpractice fears may also deter an HMO from instituting cost-justified innovations. Finally, and perhaps most importantly, limited knowledge (or the expense of learning more) may impede the optimizing of risk reduction. The important point is that HMOs, unlike almost any other providers, are well motivated and constituted to seek efficiency. It is not argued that they always succeed.

to individual cases, thus reducing the probability of inadvertent error. Similarly, more highly trained (or more experienced or more careful) personnel would presumably lower risks. All such measures—obviously accompanied by some monetary or other cost—would somewhat lessen the incidence of bad results and negligence. Admittedly, because of lack of knowledge, human imperfection, patient idiosyncrasies, or pure chance, some risk is irreducible regardless of the effort and resources expended. Such truly unavoidable risk, however, may be more appropriately considered within the domain of the doctrine of informed consent[23] than as a matter of the proper level of risk avoidance under the malpractice standard of care considered here, since by hypothesis no amount of care can reduce the risk. In any event, despite the irreducibility of some risks, there remains wide scope for HMOs, freed of pressure to conform to fee-for-service practices, to consider the value of particular risk-reducing actions.

C. *Malpractice Standards and HMOs*

Malpractice law has traditionally judged the behavior of medical care providers almost exclusively by the customary practice of their peers,[24] rather than by the usual standard of socially appropriate care— the behavior of a hypothetical "reasonable and prudent" man under the same or similar circumstances. Thus, only in rare cases (predominantly those where risk evaluations can arguably be made by laymen) do courts independently evaluate medical conduct.[25]

The paradigm of the standard of care required of any medical care provider is that required of physicians, classically formulated as a duty to

---

23. Where economic or practical reasons make serious risks of medical intervention irreducible, doctors must so apprise their patients and obtain their consent to proceed before undertaking the intervention. *See* Note, *Informed Consent in Medical Malpractice*, 55 CALIF. L. REV. 1396 (1967); Note, *Informed Consent as a Theory of Medical Liability*, 1970 WIS. L. REV. 879. Where medical intervention cannot completely eliminate the bad result expected from the underlying condition, providers are also protected from liability by the rule that due care does not guarantee a cure. *See, e.g.,* Carl v. Matzko, 213 Pa. Super. 446, 249 A.2d 808 (1968).

24. *See, e.g.,* HOLDER 40-43, 53-55; 1 LOUISELL & WILLIAMS ¶ 8.04; McCoid 558-60; Note, *An Evaluation of Changes in the Medical Standard of Care*, 23 VAND. L. REV. 729 (1970).

25. Such cases include leaving a sponge inside a patient after an operation, surgically removing the wrong organ or part of the body, very incompetently setting a fracture, burning a patient with hot water bottles, and failing to sterilize instruments. *See generally* PROSSER 227-28; McCoid 621-31. In such cases, expert testimony showing deviation from customary practice is not required. Note, *Medical Specialist May Be Found Negligent as a Matter of Law Despite Compliance with the Customary Practice of the Specialty*, 28 VAND. L. REV. 441 (1975).

possess the learning and skill and to use the care and diligence of the ordinary practitioner in similar circumstances and to apply their best judgment on behalf of patients.[26] The standard does vary for different providers, regions, and circumstances. Practitioners have traditionally been held only to that level of care customary in their own or similar localities.[27] Where doctors differ as to what procedure is appropriate, physicians may depart from the majority's customary practice to follow that of a "reputable" or "respectable" minority of practitioners.[28] Further, those holding themselves out as specialists are held to the customary level of skill and care of their fellow specialists, presumed to be a higher standard than that of a general practitioner.[29]

Malpractice law's enforcement of customary practice standards of care has gone beyond simple requirements that doctors perform their chosen treatments carefully, so as to avoid iatrogenic injury,[30] and now appears to govern the most basic decisions in medicine. Thus, a provider may be liable for failing to follow customary practice in making a diagnosis or in choosing a treatment,[31] although proof of causal con-

---

26. *See, e.g.,* Pike v. Honsinger, 155 N.Y. 201, 210, 49 N.E. 760, 762 (1898); 1 LOUISELL & WILLIAMS ¶ 8.04; McCoid 558-60. Successful suits are almost always founded on breach of the duty of care; it is extremely difficult to show lack of skill or knowledge or failure to use best judgment. 1 LOUISELL & WILLIAMS ¶ 11.05 & nn. 19-20.

27. *E.g.,* 1 LOUISELL & WILLIAMS ¶ 8.06; Comment, *Standard of Care for Medical Practitioners—Abandonment of the Locality Rule*, 60 KY. L.J. 209 (1971); Comment, *A Review of the Locality Rule*, 1969 U. ILL. L.F. 96. Specialists are frequently held to a national rather than a local standard. *See, e.g.,* Naccarato v. Grob, 384 Mich. 248, 180 N.W.2d 788 (1970); Note, *Torts—Medical Malpractice—Michigan Abandons "Locality Rule" with Regard to Specialists*, 40 FORDHAM L. REV. 435 (1971).

28. Bruce v. United States, 167 F. Supp. 579 (S.D. Cal. 1958); HOLDER 44-45; 1 LOUISELL & WILLIAMS, ¶ 8.04; PROSSER 163; McCoid 565.

29. HOLDER 55-57; 1 LOUISELL & WILLIAMS ¶ 8.04; McCoid 566.

30. For example, when a patient with a broken arm comes to a doctor, the physician is enjoined to set the fracture carefully, and to avoid making the cast too tight. *See* 2 LOUISELL & WILLIAMS 614. Such safety standards govern the risks of medical intervention itself, and—while important in themselves—do not directly affect the central medical decisions on what care would best reduce the hazards of the underlying illness or condition. HMOs and other innovative providers are probably least affected by this aspect of malpractice law. (Standards of carefulness may have an indirect impact on basic medical decisions; if a particular procedure must be carried out with extreme care, the resulting increase in difficulty or cost may well cause the choice of an alternative method.)

31. The doctor confronted with a probable fracture, to continue the prosaic example of note 30 *supra,* is expected to conform to the standard practice of taking diagnostic x-rays before setting the arm. *See* 1 LOUISELL & WILLIAMS ¶ 2.10 n.40; 2 LOUISELL & WILLIAMS 719. Moreover, malpractice standards may dictate the form of treatment itself. For instance, a broken arm should be set in a cast rather than given some other therapy. *E.g.,* Walkenhorst v. Kesler, 92 Utah 312, 67 P.2d 654 (1937) (chiropractor

nection with subsequent injury is more difficult where the complaint involves failure to alter satisfactorily the natural course of a disease or condition rather than introduction of new harm.[32] Such malpractice regulation of providers' decision-making is a powerful and threatening influence, going as it does to very fundamental matters of medical judgment. Though cases alleging negligent diagnostic and treatment decisions have in the past been relatively infrequent,[33] their importance seems to be growing,[34] with the result that the standard of care is more and more seen as addressing not only the carefulness to be exercised but also the medical care to be rendered. Providers' perception that omission of available procedures can be an important determinant of liability may well prompt providers to adopt elaborate diagnostic and therapeutic regimes without clear consideration of their cost and value.[35] This aspect of malpractice law may be the most troublesome for innovative and cost-conscious providers.

The malpractice standard of care applied to HMO health care services is the same as that governing medical services generally. In practice, however, HMO exposure to liability may differ from that of other providers. For one thing, an HMO itself, as well as its constituent hospitals, physicians, nurses, and other personnel, may be liable for malpractice, under either contract[36] or negligence[37] theories of respon-

---

found negligent for treating fractured hip with manipulation); Tell v. Taylor, 191 Cal. App. 2d 266, 12 Cal. Rptr. 648 (1961) (osteopathic manipulation of fractured hip negligent).

32. See notes 84-86 *infra* and accompanying text.

33. Diagnostic errors (and the consequent failure to treat a condition) have not traditionally been an important basis for malpractice claims. Among malpractice insurance claims settled in 1970, only one in seven allegedly negligent incidents involved diagnostic failures. Rudov, Myers & Mirabella, *Medical Malpractice Insurance Claims Files Closed in 1970*, in MEDICAL MALPRACTICE REPORT Appendix 1, 9.

34. *See, e.g.*, Curran & Moseley, *The Malpractice Experience of Health Maintenance Organizations*, 70 Nw. U.L. REV. 69, 85 n.72 (1975); Note, *Negligence—Medical Malpractice—Should Lack of Diligence in Diagnosis Resulting in Loss of Chance to Live Be a Compensable Injury?*, 3 SETON HALL L. REV. 505 (1972).

35. The lack of consideration given to cost and value in setting customary practice is a major theme of this Article. See notes 46-76 *infra* and accompanying text.

36. *See generally* Curran & Moseley, *supra* note 34, at 70-77. HMOs' contractual liability for enrollee injuries is somewhat problematic. HMO contracts are thoroughgoing, typically promising to provide all needed medical services within certain rather comprehensive limits. See generally sources cited in note 3 *supra*. A sample subscriber-HMO contract is printed in J. KRESS & J. SINGER, HMO HANDBOOK 54-62 (1975). A disgruntled subscriber-patient might sue in contract if an HMO simply failed to offer particular services or facilities it had promised to provide. A more radical complaint might be that the HMO contract entitled a subscriber to particular procedures that were

sibility, thus allowing plaintiffs an additional potential defendant, though not altering the standard of care applied.[38] Other differences

---

inappropriately withheld. This is essentially a claim of negligent failure to treat, which courts might or might not choose to hear in contract. In any such inquiry, the exact wording of the HMO contract and the definition of medical "need" would be crucial; this inquiry would greatly resemble one for negligence, and what services are "needed" under an HMO's contract would probably have to be determined by reference to medical custom generally. Ironically, while this Article contends that customary practice may often be a poor malpractice standard for HMOs, some customary standards would be essential to limit HMOs' contractual obligations.

Alternatively, a warranty of due care might be legally implied from an HMO's undertaking to treat patients, as one often was in early malpractice cases. *See, e.g.,* Adkins v. Ropp, 105 Ind. App. 331, 334, 14 N.E.2d 727, 728 (1938), *quoting* Adolay v. Miller, 60 Ind. App. 656, 659-60, 111 N.E. 313, 314 (1916) ("a physician . . . is held in law to have impliedly contracted [to] exercise at least reasonable skill, diligence and care"). *See generally* HOLDER 1-7. However, few jurisdictions today still allow malpractice complaints to be framed in contract, rather than in tort; most hold that malpractice actually sounds in tort. *E.g.,* Gauteri v. New Rochelle Hosp., 4 App. Div. 2d 874, 166 N.Y.S.2d 934 (1957), *aff'd,* 5 N.Y.2d 952, 157 N.E.2d 172, 183 N.Y.S.2d 803 (1959). *See generally* 1 LOUISELL & WILLIAMS ¶ 8.03; McCoid 550-53; Miller, *The Contractual Liability of Physicians and Surgeons,* 1953 WASH. U.L.Q. 413; Note, *Contractual Liability in Medical Malpractice,* 24 DEPAUL L. REV. 212 (1974).

37. Like all employers, HMOs are responsible for the negligence of their employees or agents under the doctrine of *respondeat superior.* Bernardi v. Community Hosp. Ass'n, 166 Colo. 280, 443 P.2d 708 (1968); PROSSER § 70; RESTATEMENT (SECOND) OF AGENCY § 219 (1957); Southwick, *The Hospital's New Responsiblity,* 17 CLEV.-MAR. L. REV. 146 (1968).

HMOs may also be responsible for the provision of care by non-employees under what seems to be an emerging doctrine of institutional negligence: where patients justifiably look to a health care institution to select, supervise, or vouch for the actual provider of care, the institution must take appropriate steps to protect patients from unwarranted risks. This principle seems to be the common thread of several developments in hospital liability. Thus, hospitals may be held liable for the negligence of non-employee doctors under a theory of apparent agency, especially where a doctor's principal practice is in the hospital. *See* Beeck v. Tucson Gen. Hosp., 18 Ariz. App. 165, 500 P.2d 1153 (1972) (radiologist); *Principles of Hospital Liability,* 2a HOSP. L. MANUAL ¶ 2-1 nn.46 & 51 (1972). Hospitals may also be liable for insufficiently weighing the potential risk of harm to patients from non-employee doctors with hospital "staff privileges." *See* Purcell v. Zimbelman, 18 Ariz. App. 75, 500 P.2d 335 (1972); Mitchell County Hosp. Authority v. Joiner, 229 Ga. 140, 189 S.E.2d 412 (1972); *Principles of Hospital Liability, supra,* ¶ 1-4 n.35 (1972). Another source of hospital liability may be emerging—a duty to supervise ongoing institutional care and, where appropriate, to require consultation in the interest of preventing unduly risky care. *See* Darling v. Charleston Community Memorial Hosp., 33 Ill. 2d 326, 211 N.E.2d 253 (1965), *cert. denied,* 383 U.S. 946 (1966); Southwick, *The Hospital as an Institution—Expanding Responsibilities Change Its Relationship With the Staff Physician,* 9 CALIF. W.L. REV. 429, 443-53 (1973).

Such precedents from hospital law could easily be applied to HMOs, since HMOs' promises to provide their enrollees with health care services are much more direct than are those of hospitals. Moreover, HMOs' control over services may also be greater,

in HMO and fee-for-service malpractice experience, such as patients' increased willingness to sue engendered by impersonal HMO care, are sometimes cited,[39] but these are largely behavioral rather than legal and are unrelated to this Article's main concern, the impact on HMOs of the customary practice standard itself. This impact is strong not only because of the fundamental influence of the standards themselves but also because of the generally increasing frequency and cost of malpractice claims and all medical care providers' concern about them.[40] Malpractice standards are thus coming to constitute an ever more considerable incentive toward customary practice.[41]

---

since HMOs periodically negotiate, on behalf of their subscribers, specific terms of service with their associated doctor groups which actually provide the services. *See, e.g.,* Curran & Moseley, *supra* note 34, at 74-75. A sample medical service agreement and hospital contract are presented in J. KRESS & J. SINGER, *supra* note 36, at 63-80.

38. HMO liability founded on Darling v. Charleston Community Memorial Hosp., 33 Ill. 2d 326, 211 N.E.2d 253 (1965), *cert. denied*, 383 U.S. 946 (1966), might conceivably result in a somewhat different standard of care than would HMO liability grounded in *respondeat superior*. Whereas the latter vicarious liability would typically result from HMO providers' deviance from standard practice, *Darling* found negligence in part in the defendant institution's deviance from its own regulations—not necessarily the same as those of other providers. *Id.* at 331, 211 N.E.2d at 257.

39. *E.g.*, Curran & Moseley, *supra* note 34, at 81. *See also The Malpractice Crisis: How It Affects HMOs* (pt. 2), HEALTH SERVICES INFORMATION, Sept. 22, 1975, at 5.

40. Until the 1960s, the probability of a provider's being sued for malpractice in connection with any single service was extremely low. A 1957 American Medical Association survey found that only one doctor in seven (*i.e.* about fourteen percent) was a malpractice defendant at any time during his entire career. *Opinion Survey on Medical Professional Liability*, 164 J.A.M.A. 1583 (1957). An extreme, non-representative contrast is the 1972 experience in northern California, where twenty-one claims were filed for every 100 physicians. CAL. ASSEMBLY SELECT COMM. ON MEDICAL MALPRACTICE, PRELIMINARY REPORT 15 (June 1974).

The much-discussed current malpractice "crisis," however, is less a problem of physicians actually being sued than it is one of liability insurance—its decreasing availability and increasing cost. *See, e.g.*, Malpractice in Focus (Aug. 1975) (an AMA Source Document prepared by the editors of *Prism*). How much legal standards have contributed to these problems (as opposed to patients' litigiousness, larger jury awards, and other factors) is quite uncertain, but it is clear that great publicity has made doctors more aware than ever of the importance of malpractice standards and legal doctrines for their practice. *See, e.g.*, Welch, *Medical Malpractice*, 292 NEW ENG. J. MED. 1372 (1975).

41. Six years ago, a leading authority commented, "[T]he most effective mechanism for coercing compliance with customary standards of care is the threat of malpractice litigation . . . ." Bernzweig, *HEW Response to the Subcommittee*, in SUBCOMM. ON EXECUTIVE REORGANIZATION, SENATE COMM. ON GOVERNMENTAL OPERATIONS, 91ST CONG., 1ST SESS., MEDICAL MALPRACTICE: THE PATIENT VERSUS THE PHYSICIAN 18 (Comm. Print 1969). Since then, the latest "crisis" has further exacerbated malpractice fears—probably even beyond the actual increased impact of malpractice suits and awards. Despite the financial protection of malpractice insurance, providers generally dislike any brush with the legal process. See also notes 48 & 88 *infra*.

Problems with the Current Malpractice Approach to HMO Care

HMO practice, like all medical care, should be subject to judicial scrutiny. But the best means of implementing such legal oversight are debatable. The current use of customary medical practice as the malpractice standard of care poses a number of troubling problems, particularly for innovative providers like HMOs. The following discussion of four such problems is predicated on the realistic postulate that much is uncertain about the provision and value of health care services, so that there is a considerable legitimate leeway for HMOs to diverge from majority custom, on either medical or economic grounds.

Medical practitioners generally—regardless of the form of their payment—often disagree about the medical effectiveness of particular procedures.[42] Such divergent medical views may involve not only the obvious difficulty of choosing between types of medical intervention (is one drug, operation, or treatment as good as another—in result and risk?), but also less obvious cases of selecting the proper provider (are paramedicals as competent as doctors in certain fields?) or style of care (is outpatient treatment preferable to inpatient care in some instances?). A cost-conscious HMO, for example, might choose to treat heart attack victims in their homes rather than in hospital coronary care units. There is substantial medical research evidence, largely from Britain, that at-home treatment achieves the same results as hospital care,[43] but American custom is decidedly contrary, and thus outpatient

---

42. *See generally* A. COCHRANE, EFFECTIVENESS AND EFFICIENCY: RANDOM REFLECTIONS ON HEALTH SERVICES (1972). Because of their immediate resource constraints, however, HMOs might be expected to question more readily a procedure's medical effectiveness than might fee-for-service practitioners. But see note 89 *infra*.

43. Mather, Pearson, Read, *et al.*, *Acute Myocardial Infarction: Home and Hospital Treatment*, 3 BRIT. MED. J. 334, 336-37 (1971). *See also* A. COCHRANE, supra note 42, at 50-54; Hofvendahl, *Influence of Treatment in a Coronary Care Unit on Prognosis in Acute Myocardial Infarction*, ACTA MED. SCANDINAVIA 519 (Supp. 1971); Hutter, Sidel, Shine, *et al.*, *Early Hospital Discharge After Myocardial Infarction*, 288 NEW ENG. J. MED. 1141, 1143-44 (1973) (heart patients receive no additional benefit from three weeks' hospitalization over two weeks' stay).

There is growing recognition that in much of modern medicine, as in coronary care, the benefits of customary practices are either not well established or not worth their costs in resources and new risks. For excellent short summaries of this line of thought, see A. COCHRANE, *supra;* Neuhauser, *The Future of Proprietaries in American Health Services*, in REGULATING HEALTH FACILITIES CONSTRUCTION 233, 233-37 (C. Havighurst ed., 1974); and U.S. DEP'T OF HEALTH, EDUCATION, AND WELFARE, PUBLIC HEALTH SERVICE, FORWARD PLAN FOR HEALTH, FY 1977-81, at 144-61 (DHEW Pub. No. (OS)76-50024, 1975).

treatment might create considerable malpractice problems where patients suffer reverses or die.[44]

An HMO's practice might also diverge from fee-for-service custom because of a different valuation of the benefits undeniably achieved by customary action or nonactions. Thus, there might be universal agreement that a certain test improves the accuracy of a diagnosis from ninety to ninety-five percent in some moderately serious and generally treatable condition; a fee-for-service doctor would almost certainly perform such a test if it were readily available and covered by insurance, since no obvious benefit for his patient or himself could be achieved by foregoing the potential insurance payment.[45] On the other hand, an HMO might decide that its subscribers' resources were better spent, for example, on upgrading the staff of its emergency room than on the test. Such valuation problems are at the heart of tort law's establishing appropriate levels of risk and, in various forms, cause the most intractable difficulties in the application to HMOs of standards derived from customary insured fee-for-service practice.

A. *Inadequate Valuation of the Costs and Results of Reducing Risks*

Whereas the law of negligence generally evaluates risky behavior through an independent judicial assessment of its reasonableness, medical malpractice cases judge health care providers almost exclusively by their compliance with customary medical practice.[46] Whether this substitution of medical custom for judicial evaluation is desirable depends upon how well customary practice standards achieve the goals of negligence law.

A major goal of tort standards is to achieve the socially optimal level of risk in the various activities society undertakes, including providing medical care.[47] Negligence rules accomplish this by holding non-optimal behavior substandard and by requiring compensation of

---

44. For example, Armstrong v. Svoboda, 240 Cal. App. 2d 502, 49 Cal. Rptr. 701 (1966), held that a doctor was negligent in not immediately hospitalizing a patient whose electrocardiogram indicated possibly serious cardiac abnormalities. Hospitalization for known heart attack would seem to be *a fortiori* required.

45. *See* Brook, Brutoco, & Williams, *The Relationship Between Medical Malpractice and Quality of Care*, 1975 DUKE L.J. 1197. Diagnostic "accuracy" is used here to mean overall correctness of diagnosis. Such lay terminology glosses over the technical difference between a test's sensitivity and its s̩pecificity; more properly, one might hypothesize that a test increases true positive or true negative diagnoses and decreases false positives or false negatives. *See* McNeil, Keeler & Adelstein, *Primer on Certain Elements of Medical Decision Making*, 293 NEW ENG. J. MED. 211 (1975).

46. See notes 24-29 *supra* and accompanying text.

47. Deterrence and compensation are often cited as twin goals of tort law. *E.g.*, W. SEAVEY, P. KEETON, & R. KEETON, CASES AND MATERIALS ON THE LAW OF TORTS 1 (1964). Deciding what behavior should be deterred and which injuries should be

victims injured by failure to take appropriate safety measures.[48] The relevant considerations here are the degree of risk of the activity, the risk-reducing capacity of various precautionary steps, and the costs and benefits of running and reducing the risks; the law should encourage taking all risk-reducing steps the cost of which is smaller than the cost of running the unreduced risk.[49]

The customary practice of parties engaged in a given enterprise is quite relevant to judicial evaluation of whether particular safety measures are appropriate, and evidence of customary practice is generally admissible for the factfinder to weigh in deciding whether the standard of due care was met.[50] The probative value of such evidence is somewhat limited, though many virtues are sometimes ascribed to

---

compensated, however, requires deciding upon the optimal level of risk for each activity. See Mechanic, *Some Social Aspects of the Medical Malpractice Dilemma*, 1975 DUKE L.J. 1179, 1190-91. See also sources cited in note 49 *infra*.

48. This simplified formulation ignores negligence law's concern that a duty to act be established before the cost of risk-running versus risk-reduction calculus is applied. In the case of medical malpractice, the duty to avoid negligence to a patient is clear, and deciding when the provider-patient relationship is established is seldom difficult. Malpractice insurance lessens the direct impact of negligence rules on medical providers, but the related threat of cancellation of premium rises transmits some financial incentive, and more subtle motivations are also at work.

49. Requiring measures to reduce risk where the marginal cost of each reduction of risk is less than its value (the cost of running the risks and allowing injuries to occur) will achieve the optimum amount of risk reduction, that is, the minimum injury and injury prevention costs. R. POSNER, ECONOMIC ANALYSIS OF LAW 69-70 (1973); Brown, *Toward an Economic Theory of Liability*, 2 J. LEGAL STUDIES 323 (1973); Calabresi & Hirschoff, *Toward a Test for Strict Liability*, 81 YALE L.J. 1055, 1057 (1972).

> Judge Learned Hand's famous statement formulated just such a test:
> The degree of care demanded of a person by an occasion is the resultant of three factors: the likelihood that his conduct will injure others, taken with the seriousness of the injury if it happens, and balanced against the interest which he must sacrifice to avoid the risk. Conway v. O'Brien, 111 F.2d 611, 612 (2d Cir. 1940), *rev'd on other grounds*, 312 U.S. 492 (1941).

See Posner, *A Theory of Negligence*, 1 J. LEGAL STUDIES 29 (1972); Note, *Comparative Approaches to Liability for Medical Maloccurences*, 84 YALE L.J. 1141 (1975).

Theoretically, other legal rules which incorporated the correct social valuations of costs, risks, and results could achieve the same optimal result. A strict liability test, for example, could induce exactly the same level of risk-reducing precautions; a major difference would be that the cost of injuries not worth avoiding would fall on medical care providers rather than on injured patients as under the fault system. See Calabresi, *Optimal Deterrence and Accidents*, 84 YALE L.J. 656, 666-70 (1975). (This might also mean that different amounts of medical care would be undertaken.) At the theoretical extreme, under idealized circumstances of perfect information and no transaction costs, market economic theory holds that any (or no) liability rule would achieve optimal risk reduction, since the parties involved would bargain with each other (by hypothesis, at no cost) until optimality was attained. Coase, *The Problem of Social Cost*, 3 J. LAW & ECON. 1 (1960); Calabresi, *Transaction Costs, Resource Allocation and Liability Rules—A Comment*, 11 J. LAW & ECON. 67 (1968). Malpractice rules, however, are negligence rules, and only the negligence approach is considered here.

50. PROSSER 162, 227; Morris, *Custom and Negligence*, 42 COLUM. L. REV. 1147, 1153-54 (1942).

it.[51] At a minimum, however, evidence of custom shows the practical and economic feasibility of undertaking certain safety precautions (and customary omission, in contrast, may indicate the inappropriateness of undertaking them) and establishes that a defendant had the opportunity to learn what untaken precautions were feasible.[52] Evidence of medical custom, of course, plays a much larger role.

There seem to be two principal justifications for judicial reliance on medical custom to set malpractice standards. The first is intensely practical: most medical decision-making is beyond the ken of laymen—patients, judges, and juries alike—so that decisions and evaluations of them are thought better left to experts, with the judicial role largely limited to weighing credibility.[53] This rationale is apparent in the major exception to the requirement for expert testimony of medical negligence, namely, that laymen may testify to, and lay factfinders may independently evaluate, alleged negligence involving circumstances clearly comprehensible to non-experts, such as failure to x-ray a suspected fracture. The rationale is partly persuasive: clearly, only medical experts can be expected to assess medical probabilities—the normal and usual hazards of certain conditions, the likely success of particular risk-reducing interventions, and so on.[54] In this, medicine, like other

---

51. Among these rather nebulous attributes are the stability that custom brings to society; the desirability of limited autonomy for certain groups, *e.g.*, professionals; custom's internal moral quality of rightness; and the harshness of requiring more than customary safeguards. See Linde, *Custom in Negligence Law*, 11 CAN. B.J. 151, 152-54 (1968).

52. Morris, *supra* note 50, at 1147-53.

53. This judicial deference to medical expertise parallels the typical patient's deference to his doctor's opinion. See notes 63-66 *infra* and accompanying text. Clarence Morris clearly states this rationale: "[N]o other standard [than medical custom] is practical. Our judges and juries are usually not competent to judge whether or not a doctor has acted reasonably. The conformity test is probably the only workable test available." *Id.* at 1164.

54. The pervasive impact of uncertainty in medical care may well be the decisive factor here, as in many aspects of the health care enterprise. See Arrow, *Uncertainty and the Welfare Economics of Medical Care*, 53 AM. ECON. REV. 941 (1963). Despite a physician's possession of acceptable skill and use of accepted procedures, one can never be sure that the desired outcomes will be achieved. At its most basic level, this is the familiar problem of causality. Doctors accept a diagnosis or therapeutic procedure as effective based upon statistical evidence of its efficacy in a certain proportion of cases; absolute certainty that a method will be followed by a certain result is elusive and rare. Moreover, clear and undisputed proof of effectiveness by the accepted methods of statistically standardized or randomized controlled trials is surprisingly uncommon. The clinical judgment of each doctor thus has a very large role to play. Under these circumstances, it is easy to understand the law's reluctance to set its own independent standards, which would require judging whether particular procedures actually cause the risk reduction (achieve the results) they are meant to. The question of causal connection of medical procedure and particular result, of course, arises not only in deciding on

technical areas, is not susceptible to unaided judicial inquiry. However, doctors and other medical providers are not experts in *valuing* in social terms the expected results or costs inherent in particular standards; in fact, they may quite inappropriately weigh the social costs of taking a risk-reducing precaution, even where they very accurately assess its medical effectiveness. Nonetheless, by accepting medical custom as the legal standard of care, malpractice law has implicitly left both the assessment of risk and the valuation of cost and results to the judgment of medical practitioners. It should be recognized that the standards thus established can only be as good as the circumstances and incentives which give rise to medical custom.

The second rationale for customary practice standards in fact recognizes this, but asserts that custom—representing the aggregate of individual judgments as to what medical care is appropriate—can best set the social norm. This reasoning starts with an ideal type of customary standards of care and safety—those established in the course of perfectly free market transactions between parties who are fully informed, equal in bargaining position, and capable of extensive and inexpensive bargaining. Custom developed under such circumstances should indeed indicate the socially optimum level of risk avoidance— at least as between the bargaining parties, since they should know better than any court how much they want to reduce their own risks. Parties to hazardous activities can bargain with each other to reduce risks as much as they feel worthwhile, and to have irreducible risk fall on the party better able to bear bad results. Medical risks seem particularly well covered by this reasoning, since they are almost exclusively limited to the individual patients involved,[55] who theoretically participate in valuing them and agree to undergo them.[56] Since third

---

the appropriate standard of care, but also in assessing whether failure to meet the established standard actually caused a given injury. Here, though expert testimony is again needed, it is not determinative; the final decision is the legal factfinder's. 1 LOUISELL & WILLIAMS ¶ 11.20; B. SHARTEL & M. PLANT, THE LAW OF MEDICAL PRACTICE 147-52 (1959). See also notes 84-88 *infra* and accompanying text.

55. There are some exceptions to this—for example, a surgeon may operate on the wrong person. Interestingly, in this case of harm to an outsider, malpractice liability follows almost automatically upon proof of the facts, and the law does not look to medical practice as a guide. *E.g.*, O'Grady v. Wickman, 213 So. 2d 321 (Fla. Dist. Ct. App. 1968). (Such cases may be treated as batteries rather than as negligence.) In the main, however, a decision on one patient's standard of care directly affects only that patient.

56. In theory, if fully informed patients knowingly chose the level of care they actually received, no legal intervention would be necessary. See note 49 *supra*. In reality, of course, patients largely put themselves in their doctors' hands; what they seek from medical providers is their medical expertise, including knowledge of what risk-

parties not privy to provider-patient agreements on care are not at risk, their exclusion from standard-setting is immaterial. Provider-patient agreements as to what risk reduction is appropriate may thus be taken to establish the socially optimal standard of care for all.[57] The medical custom rule has been cogently defended on this market-theory ground.[58]

These theoretical underpinnings of medical custom standards are unfortunately not very persuasive in practice, at least not to the extent that the standards draw upon the customs of insured fee-for-service practitioners, who dominate the medical care market.[59] Most attacks on the rule emphasize that it may perniciously allow an entire industry—or subset thereof—to legitimize its own corner-cutting as the standard of due care, validating through its own practice what independent assessment would label negligence.[60] Neither the theory nor the law of customary practice standards gives much attention to the possibility that an entire industry may set standards too high, or perhaps too high in some areas and too low in others. In the usual market case, of course, a rational decision-maker will not behave uneconomically with respect to safety precautions (and thus systematically lose money) by undertaking procedures which add less value to a marketable product or service than they cost[61] or by foregoing procedures which would reduce risk more than they cost.[62] The peculiar organization and economics of contemporary insured fee-for-service medical care, however, do not fit these classic optimizing economic assumptions. In particular, fee-for-service practice is apt systematically to give insufficient weight to the cost of providing services, as opposed to the reduction of risk they achieve. Since malpractice law adopts medical custom as

---

reducing steps are appropriate. *See, e.g.*, Arrow, *supra* note 54, at 964-66. See also notes 63-66 *infra* and accompanying text.

57. Because individuals cannot appropriately judge their own standards of care, see note 56 *supra*, malpractice law undertakes to protect them from aberrant physicians' judgments through the custom rule.

58. R. POSNER, *supra* note 49, at 72.

59. About 6.5 million people are now enrolled in HMOs, according to InterStudy, HEALTH SERVICES INFORMATION, Aug. 11, 1975, at 1, so that some 200 million others are served—if at all—by fee-for-service providers.

60. *See, e.g.*, The T.J. Hooper, 60 F.2d 737 (2d Cir. 1932); Favalora v. Aetna Cas. & Sur. Co., 144 So. 2d 544 (La. App. 1962).

61. Morris, for example, succinctly dismisses this consideration: "Super-cautious industrial usages are conceivable, but the self-interest of businessmen checks milquetoastish fears." Morris, *supra* note 50, at 1161.

62. Of course, the relevant risks here are those to the parties in the transaction or to others whom the liability rule internalizes into the transaction. Risks to outsiders will be ignored, except as a matter of charity or public relations.

its standard, its requirements of due care are also often apt to be too high.

The theoretical assumption that customary medical practice reflects provider-patient agreements on risk reduction is also highly suspect. Providers and patients do not usually negotiate over the provision of health care services.[63] Providers have a near-monopoly on medical expertise; once patients make the initial decisions to seek care, they generally delegate most decision-making to medical professionals. Of necessity, patients rely on their doctors and others to evaluate the medical risks they face, both from disease and from medical intervention. Indeed, a doctor's principal products are his knowledge, skill, and expertise. Physicians make almost all medical decisions, including what standard of care is appropriate, and most patients—especially very sick ones—simply accept the services their doctors decide are needed.[64] This physician dominance underlies the common observation that doctors can "create demand" for their own and other medical services.[65] Given this delegation of decision-making, patients' purchases of medical services are hardly arm's-length transactions between well-informed equals agreeing on the provision of a certain standard of care for a certain price according to their interests and evaluations. Rather, doctors are relatively free to consider many other factors besides the benefit and cost to the patient and the probable reduction of risk in deciding whether to provide or order a given service.[66]

Nonetheless, the dominance of physicians in decision-making would not by itself necessarily result in standards of uneconomical risk reduction; most doctors doubtless take quite seriously their fiduciary

---

63. In contrast, an HMO's subscribers, at least as a group, may well be able to bargain over the general style of their medical care, including, for example, what facilities are to be provided and whether physician assistants are acceptable. But sick HMO patients are no more apt to bargain over the actual provision of their care than are fee-for-service patients—perhaps less so, since they do not pay extra for the services received.

64. *See, e.g.*, Lave & Lave, *Medical Care and Its Delivery: An Economic Appraisal*, 35 LAW & CONTEMP. PROB. 252, 258-59 (1970).

65. This is supported by the finding that spending on physicians' services is best predicted by technology and the number of physicians and not by patient demand factors. V. FUCHS & M. KRAMER, DETERMINANTS OF EXPENDITURES FOR PHYSICIANS' SERVICES IN THE U.S., 1948-1968, at 2 (1973).

66. Such factors could include the effect on provider income, professional or institutional prestige, humanitarianism, desire to experiment, desire to maintain high technical expertise, and even the desire to avoid any chance of a malpractice suit, however nonmeritorious. None of these has any bearing on what standard of risk reduction is appropriate, yet they clearly may influence medical custom.

duty to patients and would not bankrupt them in an uncertain quest for small reductions in risk. Doctors owe no fiduciary duty, however, to the insurers and government agencies that pay for the lion's share of medical care, including almost all hospital care, where most malpractice claims arise.[67] In the insured fee-for-service sector, sick patients perceive nearly "free" care, providers see open-ended financing, and third-party payors (largely governmental and private insurers) are removed from the provision of services and have only weak capabilities for injecting cost considerations into the balance.[68] Providers of insured medical services can be expected to consider not whether their patients or society can afford a particular risk-reducing measure, but rather only whether their patients will receive any medical benefit. Freed of cost concerns, physicians often feel an ethical obligation to do everything possible for their patients.[69] As a moral principle under the circumstances this may be unimpeachable, but it is clearly a poor decision rule for the social valuations of malpractice law.[70]

---

67. Between eighty and ninety percent of Americans are estimated to have some form of health insurance, with half of them carrying quite comprehensive coverage. Mueller, *Private Health Insurance in 1973: A Review of Coverage, Enrollment, and Financial Experience*, 38 SOCIAL SECURITY BULL. 21 (Feb. 1975). Private insurers and governmental programs now pay about sixty-six percent of personal health care expenditures, while individuals pay only about thirty-three percent themselves, Mueller and Gibson, *supra* note 15, at 14, Table 5, but just how much malpractice occurs in the course of uninsured and insured care is not clear. One would expect most malpractice to arise from serious cases, the expense of which is likely to be covered by insurance. For example, ninety-two percent of personal health care expenditures for hospital care is now paid for by third parties, *id.* at 15, Chart 2, and about seventy-five percent of malpractice claims filed concern hospital occurrences, Rudov, Myers, & Mirabella, *supra* note 33, at 10.

68. This analysis of the workings of insured fee-for-service medical care is not original. An extremely clear and complete presentation is given in McClure, *The Medical Care System Under National Health Insurance: Four Models that Might Work and Their Prospects* 1 J. HEALTH CARE POL., POLICY. L. 22, 31-39 (1976).

69. Thus, a doctor notes, "as a physician, I have been taught throughout my professional career that I had an absolute obligation to my patients to provide them with the highest quality medical care within my reach, almost without regard to cost." Caper, *The Meaning of Quality in Medical Care*, 291 NEW ENG. J. MED. 1136 (1974). *See also* V. FUCHS, WHO SHALL LIVE? 60 (1974) (physicians guided in part by "technological imperative" to do everything they can, "regardless of the benefit-cost ratio").

70. This analysis is not meant to condemn insurance, which is a salutary means for policyholders to reduce the uncertainties of their otherwise unpredictable financial outlays for illness. Further, people doubtless also buy insurance because it enables them to buy more risk reduction collectively than they could individually; not all insurance-financed safety measures are worth less to policyholders than their cost. Nonetheless, because of the structural separation of the roles of policyholder, insurer, doctor, and patient, medical decisions on insured care are made with little regard for cost. Unlike HMOs, third-party insurers have not developed effective claims-reviewing capabilities. Testimony of C. Havighurst, *Hearings on Competition in the Health Services Market*

That many insured fee-for-service providers do in fact often provide too much care and take too many precautions[71] is most obviously illustrated by the prevalence of "unnecessary" surgical or other procedures,[72] including "defensive" medicine.[73] The existence of these phenomena—which are of no use to patients—is widely conceded, though their extent is much debated.[74] (Some commentators claim to detect a more subtle phenomenon: a pervasive tendency in customary practice to seek to eliminate all risks to patients, regardless of cost.[75]) Significantly, many such assessments that the fee-for-service sector over-treats its patients are made by comparing usual practice with that of HMOs.[76]

The main deficiency of the medical custom rule is that it derives the malpractice standard of care from medical practice dominated by insured fee-for-service care, the providers of which can make decisions with little regard for actual social cost. Applying such standards to HMO practice pressures HMOs to conform to this non-optimizing behavior and reduces the likelihood that HMOs will evolve different styles of practice offering valuable insights to other providers and to legal standard-setters alike.

Before the Subcomm. on Antitrust and Monopoly of the Senate Comm. on the Judiciary, 93d Cong., 2d Sess., pt. 2, at 1076-77 (1974).

71. However, just as availability of insurance may cause over-reduction of risks in some areas, lack of insurance coverage may somewhat inhibit taking justifiable precautions in others.

72. *See, e.g.,* Blackstone, *Misallocation of Medical Resources: The Problem of Excessive Surgery,* 22 PUB. POLICY 329 (1974); McCarthy & Widmer, *Effects of Screening by Consultants on Recommended Elective Surgical Procedures,* 291 NEW ENG. J. MED. 1331 (1974).

73. "Defensive medicine" is the pejorative term used to describe complete dominance of legal over medical considerations, either undertaking an unneeded medical procedure to protect a provider against lawsuit rather than to benefit a patient or not undertaking a useful procedure out of fear of suit.

74. For example, *compare* Welch, *supra* note 40, at 1375 (defensive medicine costs at least $3 billion annually), *with* Project, *The Medical Malpractice Threat: A Study of Defensive Medicine,* 1971 DUKE L.J. 939, 957 (phenomenon exists, but is overrated).

75. Havighurst & Blumstein, *Coping with Quality/Cost Trade-Offs in Medical Care: The Role of PSROs,* 70 Nw. U.L. REV. 6 (1975). The authors call the phenomenon "the quality imperative." *Id.* at 20-30.

76. Blackstone, *supra* note 72, at 343-44. Some other studies of unnecessary procedures compare rates in the United States with those of Great Britain, where the health of the population is comparable to that of the United States and where the National Health Service, which provides comprehensive care from limited resources, closely resembles a nationwide HMO. Bunker, *Surgical Manpower: A Comparison of Operations and Surgeons in the United States and England and Wales,* 282 NEW ENG. J. MED. 135 (1970).

B. Overemphasis on Methods of Care

Not only is the theoretical and practical desirability of deriving malpractice standards from practice in the contemporary medical services market quite uncertain, but there is also a danger that the nature of the customary standards themselves may tend to inhibit medical practice from best evaluating medical risks. Medical custom standards, like other negligence standards, necessarily address the manner in which people ought to act and the precautions they ought to take, not the level of risk or pattern of results they ought to achieve.[77] But, lacking an independent assessment of reasonableness, this concentration on methods of care—potentially including nearly everything health care providers do—makes malpractice standards a very thoroughgoing regulation[78] and may well inappropriately increase costs and inhibit

---

77. Since the relation between a particular medical procedure and the final result is seldom totally clear, the perfect system for judging optimal risk reduction would look almost exclusively at the pattern of outcomes achieved, the actual effects on patients' health. Improved results, after all, are the goal of the presumably risk-reducing inputs and processes used, and the use of statistical results would obviate the need for case-by-case analysis of causation. *See generally* ASSURING THE QUALITY OF HEALTH CARE, *supra* note 7, at 25-49. James W. Bush, M.D., has suggested using a "coefficient of causality" he has developed to supersede the traditional notion of proximate cause. MEDICAL MALPRACTICE: A DISCUSSION OF ALTERNATIVE COMPENSATION AND QUALITY CONTROL SYSTEMS 22-24 (D. McDonald ed., Center for the Study of Dem. Inst., 1971). Although malpractice law commendably intervenes only after a demonstrably bad result, in practice the law must concern itself with methods used rather than with results achieved. Particularized standards of conduct help achieve compliance with legal requirements of the optimum level of risk reduction; it would be difficult for providers to obey an injunction to achieve a certain level of risk and no more. One book, 1 LOUISELL & WILLIAMS ¶¶8.04-.05, for example, praises the legal adoption of particularized standards of practice as "objective," unlike the "subjective" reasonable man test. Moreover, since every malpractice case involves only one outcome, a bad one, some standards must be adopted to distinguish acceptable from unacceptable bad outcomes. The formulation of legal standards guiding the use of inputs and processes serves this function. The essential determination to be made is whether the adopted standards actually achieve the desired outcome. This determination is left to medical custom.

78. Malpractice considerations may constrain medical decision making at almost every point. See notes 30-31 *supra* and accompanying text. The application of negligence principles to nonmedical activity usually involves less thoroughgoing specification of behavior. Car manufacturers, for example, may be enjoined to produce safe vehicles, but need not mimic their competitors' construction of bumpers or brakes. Moreover, product liability does not typically spell out all the attributes a car should have, whereas almost every aspect of a medical provider's business—his knowledge, skill, judgment, and choice of particular procedures—may be heavily influenced by malpractice considerations.

Malpractice law seems to have undertaken to govern what would in other contexts be contractual concerns of purchasers, perhaps because patients, as very poorly informed consumers, must rely on their doctors and therefore need more legal protection. It is also true that decisions on the appropriate level of risk to personal safety are less central to

beneficial development of alternative methods to achieve similar results.

In the case of medical malpractice, the standards are those for selecting the medical inputs and processes to be used (whose contribution to risk reduction is not always clear), and their appropriateness, unlike that of other negligence standards, is not usually subject to independent judicial scrutiny. Many medical practices, of course, are of established efficacy, achieving undoubtedly valuable reductions in risk at reasonable cost.[79] In fact, the effectiveness and value of some customary methods may be so obvious as to take them out of the customary practice rule altogether and place them in the province of normal negligence judgment by a factfinder unaided by expert testimony. Most often, however, causation and the valuation of risk and results are unclear; these are major reasons for adopting legal standards from medical custom in the first place.

There is thus a real danger that customary methods and procedures may assume a validity independent of their actual worth and may be followed (or enforced) for their own sake. At its worst, such a situation is what all doctors despise as "cookbook" medicine,[80] but its effects are probably most pernicious for prepaid providers, who may have to forego a more valuable procedure for every less valuable one they feel obligated by malpractice law to provide. Concentration on what procedures should be given is, of course, an important part of medicine; and "cookbook" medicine differs only in emphasis and degree from what might be called "textbook" medicine. The medical custom malpractice regime, however, by focusing attention almost

---

the principal transaction in nonmedical cases than in the medical sphere. Thus, for example, automobiles' capacity, style, comfort, and the like are the principal concerns of car buyers, and the passengers' safety and appropriate level of risk are only two among many concerns. In the provision of health care services, however, the central goal and overriding concern is the patients' personal health and safety, so that standards of care are of the essence.

79. This is true both of measures to reduce the basic risk of bad outcome from an existing illness or condition and of measures to reduce the risks of the medical intervention itself. For example, few would question the law's wisdom in calling for doctors to treat a major infectious disease with a widely known, cheap, and effective drug having only minor side effects. Similarly, the law may confidently require a meticulous sponge count at the close of all surgical operations (with an exception for emergency cases where speed is more important than avoiding post-operative complications from a neglected sponge).

80. "Cookbook" medicine, following required procedures by rote without exercising independent clinical judgment, has of late been most vehemently denounced in connection with PSRO standards, see note 88 *infra*, rather than malpractice standards, but the two phenomena are similar.

exclusively on what practices are customary, instead of on what practices are desirable, contributes to the basic problem: all concerned may lose sight of the standards' actual impacts on end results (except perhaps the bad one in the particular lawsuit under consideration), and innovative providers, including HMOs, may be inhibited from developing less expensive methods to achieve similar results.

Moreover, malpractice enforcement of customary practices may act as a kind of crude ratcheting mechanism, allowing more and more elaborate procedures to become standard, but not—or only slowly— allowing an established procedure to fall into disuse. Without independent judicial assessment of the effectiveness and value of the criteria, malpractice standards can change only as customary practice changes—and providers' customs will follow standard practice because of malpractice fears. It is possible, in fact, that the legal imprimatur given particular methods through malpractice litigation may encourage providers to play "catch-up" or "keep up with the Joneses" by routinely offering ever more ways of reducing ever smaller risks.[81] Whether such behavior should be condemned for putting providers on a treadmill of inflationary and unneeded procedures or praised for inducing a beneficial upward spiral of quality depends upon whether or not the methods adopted reduce risk commensurately with the costs and other risks they engender—and neither the medical services market nor the judicial malpractice approach is now structured to answer that question.

The situation is not entirely bleak. Medical practice is not monolithic, and the adoption by malpractice law of customary practice standards does not always lock HMOs and other providers into a "one right way" approach to care. There are often several standard styles of diagnosis or treatment, and the "reputable minority" exception to the medical custom rule may legitimize them,[82] allowing HMOs and others to choose a method on their own medical and cost-effectiveness grounds. Moreover, malpractice law does not actually compel the provision of standard services, but merely penalizes the failure to provide them when injury is the proximate result. If a particular customary

---

81. Many observers think that hospitals, in particular, show a marked tendency to acquire ever-increasing capabilities to perform medical procedures, presumably for enhancing institutional prestige and attracting staff physicians. Feldstein, *Hospital Cost Inflation: A Study of Nonprofit Price Dynamics*, 61 AM. ECON. REV. 853 (1971); Newhouse, *Toward a Theory of Nonprofit Institutions: An Economic Model of a Hospital*, 60 AM. ECON. REV. 64 (1970). Such tendencies could only be powerfully reinforced by potential malpractice liability for failure to perform customary procedures.

82. See note 28 *supra* and accompanying text. It is not clear, however, that the law will recognize a reputable minority's rejecting customary practice when the rejection depends upon doubts of economic efficiency rather than of medical efficacy.

practice is truly ineffective,[83] not following it will cause no harm,[84] and an HMO might safely dispense with it.

The requirement of causal connection between nonconformity and injury is thus theoretically a major protection against the forced adoption of relatively ineffective medical procedures by HMOs and others. In practice, however, though adoption of customary practices as the legal norm may not directly require their use, their mere existence, which enables plaintiffs to characterize nonconformity as negligence, probably has a considerable *in terrorem* cautionary effect, for several reasons. First, as a legal matter, some decisions seem to reflect a weakening of the causation requirement, at least in serious cases.[85] Second, as a practical matter, the very existence of a customary standard of practice carries a strong implication that the approved method works. It is probably very difficult to convince a factfinder confronted with an injury that standard treatment would not have been any more

---

83. Where an HMO can easily demonstrate that standard practices are useless, it may be sure of avoiding liability for omitting them. This situation is probably rare. More often, customary practice will have some utility, but not enough, in the HMO's estimation, to warrant its costs. Here, an HMO might nonetheless decide not to conform, if the price of potential liability is less than that of conformity. Such liability may constitute an excessive penalty for nonconformity. See notes 91-98 *infra* and accompanying text.

84. However, harm may nonetheless ensue from the underlying illness and be difficult to distinguish from that allegedly due to substandard care. *See generally* 1 LOUISELL & WILLIAMS ¶ 8.07. Even where customary practice is completely or nearly ineffective in reducing risks, medical providers may still comply out of fear that legal factfinders will not be able to distinguish the bad results due to the underlying illness from those due to omission of the customary practice. The availability of evidence of failure to conform as a "sword" for the plaintiff may thus have a considerable impact on providers even where causation is not clear.

85. These cases involve a failure to provide the particular procedure required by malpractice standards or providing it too late, allegedly "causing" the injury by failing to prevent it. For example, the court in Hicks v. United States, 368 F.2d 626 (4th Cir. 1966), stated:
> When a defendant's negligent action or inaction has effectively terminated a person's chance of survival, it does not lie in the defendant's mouth to raise conjectures as to the measure of the chances that he has put beyond the possibility of realization. If there was any substantial possibility of survival and the defendant has destroyed it, he is answerable . . . . *Id.* at 632.

See also Note, *Medical Malpractice—Rejection of "But For" Test*, 45 N.C.L. REV. 799 (1967); Note, *Negligence—Malpractice, supra* note 34. Thus, where failure to give standard treatment was followed by death, plaintiff need not show that decedent would probably have lived if given the treatment, but merely that he would have had a substantial chance of living. If extended to less serious cases, such an approach to causation would surely motivate health care providers to do everything possible for patients out of fear of malpractice liability. *See also* Clark v. United States, 402 F.2d 950 (4th Cir. 1968) (failure to perform diagnostic test to distinguish between kidney infection and blocked ureter in a timely manner).

effective than the noncustomary treatment,[86] especially because in medical cases causation is often not clear-cut. By definition, moreover, customary practice will have numerous adherents, some doubtless ready to testify to its utility, even if it is only marginal: otherwise, they would not use it. Third, so long as following customary practice is an almost certain defense to malpractice suits,[87] providers' strong desire to avoid any brush with litigation will lead them to conform, regardless of their own evaluations of the practice's merits.[88] Certainly, where fee-for-

---

86. As Curran notes, "It is axiomatic that a bad result is not in itself proof of negligence, yet it comes close to it at times." Curran, *Professional Negligence—Some General Comments*, 12 VAND. L. REV. 535, 541 (1959). Further, if a plaintiff can succeed in categorizing departure from customary practice as "experimentation," recovery will be almost automatic because of the old rule that "a doctor experiments at his peril" (unless informed consent is obtained). *See, e.g.*, Slater v. Baker, 95 Eng. Rep. 860 (K.B. 1767); Carpenter v. Blake, 60 Barb. 488, 514 (N.Y. Sup. Ct. 1871), *rev'd on other grounds*, 50 N.Y. 696 (1872). Of course, a defendant will simultaneously seek to show that the noncustomary practice was a proven technique of a reputable minority.

87. See notes 24-26 *supra*. In a few cases, courts have looked beyond customary practice, making an independent negligence determination. *See, e.g.*, Helling v. Carey, 83 Wash. 2d 514, 519 P.2d 981 (1974). This may or may not evidence a trend. *See* Note, *Comparative Approaches, supra* note 49, at 1149 n.44.

88. The availability of the customary practice defense as a shield may be a more important incentive for conformity than the threat of the standard as a sword. This incentive is particularly strong because avoiding litigation, with its attendant bad publicity, personal trauma, and great inconvenience, may be even more important to physicians than the successful defense of a lawsuit once begun, since almost all damages are typically paid by malpractice insurance. The strength of the "shield" effect is apparent from the controversy surrounding the "civil immunity" clause of the PSRO legislation, 42 U.S.C. § 1320c-16(c) (Supp. II, 1972), which purports to protect doctors acting in conformity with PSRO norms from malpractice liability. Comment, *PSRO: Malpractice Liability and the Impact of the Civil Immunity Clause*, 62 GEO. L.J. 1499, 1505-07 (1974); Note, *Professional Standards Review and the Limitation of Health Services: An Interpretation of the Effect of Statutory Immunity on Medical Malpractice Liability*, 54 BOSTON U.L. REV. 931 (1974); Note, *Federally Imposed Self-Regulation of Medical Practice: A Critique of the Professional Standards Review Organization*, 42 GEO. WASH. L. REV. 822, 837-42 (1974).

The AMA opposes the civil immunity provision because it "could have the unintended and undesirable effect of pressuring practitioners to adhere to the [PSRO] norms." AMA Council on Legislation, PSRO Amendments 2 (May 1, 1974). The controversy heated up in January, 1975, when Caspar Weinberger, then Secretary of Health, Education and Welfare, whose department is the home of the PSRO program, called for compliance with PSRO norms to be accepted "as a real defense to a malpractice suit . . . ." *Malpractice Insurance Denials Spark Weinberger's Concern*, PSRO LETTER, Jan. 15, 1975, at 3-4. AMA President Malcolm Todd, M.D., vehemently opposed even such use of PSRO norms, ostensibly because it would "reduce medicine and medical practice to a 'cookbook' approach . . . ." Am. Med. News, Jan. 13, 1975, at 1, col. 2. *See also id.* at 4, col. 3. (The AMA supports amendments to eliminate the offending provision. *See, e.g.*, Statement of the AMA, *Hearings on H.R. 5515 & 5528 Before the Subcomm. on Health, House Comm. on Ways and Means*, 94th Cong., 1st Sess. (Sept. 19, 1975).) The "cookbook" problem, however, is inherent in the PSRO concept, regard-

service insurance will pay for services or precautions of questionable risk-reducing utility, they are likely to be provided in order to comply with customary practice standards, becoming in the process more thoroughly established than ever and creating even larger pressures for conformity. HMOs, having no such outside insurer to pay for customary services, might be expected to resist more strongly the malpractice pressure to provide them,[89] but enforcement of customary practice as the legal standard nonetheless probably exerts a profound influence on every phase of the health care enterprise of HMOs[90] and other innovative providers.

C. *Potentially Excessive Penalties for Noncustomary Care*

Malpractice law, after adopting standards to reflect the optimal level of risk, must correctly motivate potential tortfeasors to meet those standards by penalizing those whose conduct would otherwise unacceptably increase risk. Tort law seeks to achieve this by requiring those whose conduct is deemed unduly risky to pay for all injuries caused that could reasonably have been avoided, requiring no compensation for injuries resulting from acceptably risky behavior. In the malpractice sphere the strong emphasis on compliance with customary practice and the difficulty of the causation issues may easily combine to create an excessive penalty for noncustomary behavior, like that of HMOs. The danger is that nonstandard practice may be assessed for damages that would not have been averted by adherence to custom.

---

less of PSRO norms' impact on malpractice. Since the AMA grudgingly accepts the PSRO program itself, *see, e.g.*, AMA, A Summary of AMA's Policy on PSRO, in PSRO Information Kit (Oct. 1974), the real objection seems to be that clearly making PSRO norms a malpractice shield would more effectively motivate conformity than the PSROs' own sanctions could. Malpractice law would also apply the norms more broadly than would PSROs' own supervision of medicare and medicaid care.

89. One study's HMO interviews, however, found that HMOs are just as likely as other providers to practice "defensive" medicine. Curran & Moseley, *supra* note 34, at 85. This finding tends to support the proposition that customary practice malpractice standards considerably disrupt HMO incentives to devote their limited resources to the medically most effective uses, but it may also reflect, to some extent, other professional influences. These influences are difficult to distinguish from the impact of malpractice law, since the legal standard itself is largely derived from medical custom.

90. It would seem, however, that FMC HMOs—almost by definition—could not be shown to deviate from customary practice, since FMCs typically utilize most or all physicians in a county medical society. (PGP HMOs, in contrast, use small physician panels.) See note 3 *supra*. Nonetheless, FMCs may prescribe methods somewhat different from the same doctors' customary fee-for-service practice. The first malpractice case to consider the application of the medical custom rule to such circumstances should make interesting reading.

The all-or-nothing rule of compensation works well where legal factfinders are capable of assessing an activity's level of risk and can easily judge whether unreasonable behavior caused the particular injury at issue. In most cases, we feel comfortably able to distinguish harm caused by failure to take justified safety measures from harm which would have occurred despite all reasonable precautions. Questions of medical causation, however, may often be a matter of probabilities and not clear-cut, making it difficult to distinguish injury caused by noncustomary practice from that which would have occurred anyway.[91]

If a noncustomary practice at issue in a malpractice suit can be shown by expert testimony to reduce risk below customary levels, ensuing injuries should not be compensated; this result could be achieved either by finding a lack of proximate cause or by holding the noncustomary practice non-negligent as a "reputable minority" practice.[92] The classic dilemma of noncustomary behavior, however, is posed by an increased risk of bad results knowingly undertaken in exchange for other benefits—for example, further improving the results in successful cases, increasing comfort, or saving money to spend on reducing other risks or to return to patients. This is exactly the sort of behavior likely to be engendered by HMOs' efficiency incentives.[93]

Unfortunately, malpractice law does not now and probably cannot structure appropriate financial incentives to deal solely with *increased* risk accompanying noncustomary behavior. For example, even the most highly trained, board-certified anesthesiologist can expect a certain mortality rate in connection with a particular operation—perhaps

---

91. *See, e.g.*, 1 LOUISELL & WILLIAMS ¶ 8.07. Clearly, cases involving alleged failure to provide certain care—the cases with which this Article is primarily concerned—are more difficult in this respect than are cases involving alleged injury from the medical care provided.

92. A showing that a noncustomary procedure is just as effective in reducing risks to patients as is customary procedure would satisfy the essence of the requirement that a minority practice be "reputable" to be accepted. Such objective evidence is certainly preferable to subjective consideration of whether practitioners using non-standard procedure have good reputations, but may be difficult and expensive to develop.

93. How characteristic of HMOs this behavior actually is depends upon how resistant HMO subscribers are to price increases and upon how much other factors, including malpractice concerns, counterbalance HMOs' natural cost-counting incentives. See note 89 *supra*. HMOs would wish to alter the pattern of care established by malpractice standards only if their valuations of the costs, risks, and results were different from those implicit in the standards. By hypothesis, negligence standards that accurately reflect social valuations could not be improved upon, though this Article has argued that customary practice does not in fact make such correct valuations. See notes 67-76 *supra* and accompanying text. Whether an HMO and its subscribers nonetheless ought to be able knowingly to choose a different level of care from the hypothetical social optimum is discussed at note 119 *infra* and accompanying text.

one tenth of one percent. If such personnel are generally available and surgeons utilize their services for most of those operations in the relevant locality, their level of training may well set the standard of care, and those deaths will be uncompensated. Personnel with less training might well experience a higher rate, perhaps two tenths of one percent. Using the less-trained personnel might constitute negligence,[94] but not all those thereby injured should be compensated. Noncustomary practice in this case by hypothesis causes one extra death per thousand procedures, but may cause two lawsuits. The problem cannot be approached as one of the negligence standard itself, since by definition breach of custom is malpractice. It must be seen as a problem of causation and damages, which is unfortunate because of the all-or-nothing rule of damages and the lack of an acceptable means of determining which of the two potential plaintiffs was injured by deviation from accepted practice. No middle ground is now available to reflect such uncertainty as to causation, since compromise verdicts are unlawful.

As a practical matter, it is quite likely that the hypothetical nonstandard practice would be condemned by a jury in both cases, if there were undisputed breach of the customary practice, testimony as to the general efficacy of the customary practice, and clear injury.[95] As a matter of law, the problem of the uncertain plaintiff injured by increased risk might seem to be covered by the rule denying recovery where it could be predicated only on the factfinder's speculation as to which of two causes was responsible for an injury.[96] Neither result is satisfactory; what is needed is a financial incentive related to incremental risk, which cannot be provided through the case-by-case approach of malpractice law under normal tort procedures.

One analogy does suggest itself, though it is doubtful that it could be applied, namely, tailoring compensation to degree of culpability, as in apportionment of damages among defendants according to degree of fault[97] or in reduction of damages according to the comparative negligence of the plaintiff.[98] Legislation along these lines would provide

---

94. In Pederson v. Dumouchel, 72 Wash. 2d 73, 431 P.2d 973 (1967), for example, the Supreme Court of Washington found a hospital liable for allowing an unsupervised dentist, rather than a doctor, to administer general anesthesia.
95. See note 86 *supra* and accompanying text.
96. *See, e.g.*, Schulz v. Feigal, 273 Minn. 470, 476, 142 N.W.2d 84, 89 (1966).
97. UNIFORM CONTRIBUTION AMONG TORTFEASORS ACT § 1; PROSSER § 50; Note, *Adjusting Losses Among Joint Tortfeasors in Vehicular Collision Cases*, 68 YALE L.J. 964, 981-84 (1959).
98. *See* WIS. STAT. ANN. § 895.045 (Supp. 1975); Abraham & Riddle, *Comparative Negligence—A New Horizon*, 25 BAYLOR L. REV. 411 (1973).

a theoretically valid solution, but the same problems of accurate judicial assessment of risk which underlie the medical custom rule would probably make such an approach impractical.

D. *Unduly Narrow Focus on the Risks of Individual Procedures*

A major virtue of the HMO concept is the great control each HMO has over the allocation of all health care resources for a given population.[99] That control theoretically enables an HMO to undertake the optimum amount of risk reduction in each and every medical area, thus maximizing the aggregate health of the HMO population by equalizing the marginal value of risk averted in each area.[100] In particular, an HMO can theoretically fund the proper amounts of preventive and acute care, pre-operative and post-operative treatment, diagnostic and therapeutic procedures, care for one type of condition or illness and care for another, and so on, throughout the entire medical spectrum. Perhaps the most fundamental objection to application of the current malpractice approach to HMO care is that its case-by-case setting of standards—largely reflecting fee-for-service practice—interferes with this great potential of HMOs to adjust the standards of care in one area to accommodate those in another. Malpractice law's enforcement of customary practice does not recognize the relevance of risks in any area other than the one being litigated.

In the course of one treatment a single patient may undergo diagnosis, surgery, post-operative hospital care, and follow-up treatment. In the fee-for-service sector each phase of this care may well be undertaken by a separate provider (or combination of providers), and each phase will be governed by a standard of care set independently of the others. The practices of anesthesiologists set the anesthesia standard, those of surgeons the surgery standard, and those of other specialists the standards in their respective fields—but there is no incentive to determine whether some of the resources devoted to

---

99. Highly integrated and comprehensive PGPs obviously have more control over resource allocation than do FMCs, whose providers use independently owned and operated facilities. See also note 3 *supra*.

100. Theoretically, HMO subscribers would be best served if the last dollar spent on each action achieved the same value of health; otherwise, adjusting expenditures from less to more productive areas could improve subscriber health at no additional cost. Some health-promoting expenditures are directly or indirectly governed by malpractice standards; others are not. Within the medical areas affected by malpractice law, there is also room for adjusting expenditures according to which are most cost-effective in reducing risks. It is this type of adjustment which HMOs may be impeded from making by malpractice norms set in the fee-for-service sector, where such reallocations of resources are usually far more difficult, if not impossible, to make.

careful surgery might be better spent, for instance, on more nurses. Malpractice law will set and enforce each of these standards separately.[101] This means that very different levels of care can and do prevail in different areas.[102] An HMO, responsible for all care, has the capability to gather adequate data, evaluate the findings, and take appropriate precautions at each stage of care, according to the costs, values, and risks throughout diagnosis and treatment, and also has the incentive and ability to shift resources from one area to another if similar overall risks can be achieved at less cost. This ideal resource-allocation process may be extraordinarily difficult to achieve in practice because of limited knowledge and high costs of data-gathering, implementation, and the like. But the potential is there, and HMOs' unique capabilities and incentives in this regard could be nullified by requiring them to follow the patterns of risk-reducing measures established by very different fee-for-service practice.

An even more basic task than harmonizing the standards for different phases of one type of care is balancing the risk-reducing worth of care for different illnesses and of preventive versus acute care. Which is more important: very highly qualified surgeons or more residents in the emergency room; screening for birth defects or treating middle-aged hypertension? Fee-for-service medicine cannot effectively address such questions, since these issues are not encompassed within the jurisdiction of any decision-maker who controls, provides, or finances care. Nor can malpractice litigation, concentrating on a particular kind of bad result in an individual case, offer much guidance in this important social area; the judicial process is inadequate for consideration of such broad resource-allocation issues. It may not be too much to ask of malpractice law, however, that it refrain from enforcing standards which effectively deter HMOs from achieving whatever progress in this area is feasible within the state of the medical art.

---

101. This is not meant to imply that the law of malpractice will actually govern all medical actions. Malpractice standards can best deal with the most straightforward medical cases; where particular services are not clearly and directly related to individual bad results, malpractice is a poor enforcement tool. Many risk-reducing measures may be seen statistically to improve results without their omission's being demonstrably related to particular bad results. For example, clean hospital corridors might be very important for quick recovery of patients, but the problems of proving that filthy ones caused harm would normally be insuperable.

102. In fact, some authorities think that simple measures to coordinate the fragmented approach to health care within large hospitals may be the most valuable contribution to overall risk reduction that can now be easily made—at very little cost compared with using much more highly qualified practitioners or expensive diagnostic or treatment procedures to reduce risks. ASSURING QUALITY OF HEALTH CARE, *supra* note 7, at 63.

A Provisional Solution within the Customary Approach: HMO Custom as the Standard of Care

Both fairness and socially appropriate risk reduction would be served by independent assessments of fee-for-service and HMO care by the same standards of reasonableness, with full judicial cognizance of the importance of costs.[103] Instead, the law must rely upon medical custom to set standards: despite numerous theoretical and practical objections, no workable replacement for this approach seems likely to emerge in the foreseeable future. Under these circumstances, it seems desirable to insulate HMOs from having to follow the custom of a very differently organized system of medical care. There is one way to recognize the legitimacy of HMO practices in the absence of independent judicial assessment of each noncustomary practice. The law could

---

103. Judicial evenhandedness and full social consideration of costs in standard-setting could be achieved by well-informed judicial evaluation of negligence, and there is some indication that courts may be turning away from a strict customary practice approach to malpractice. Note, *Evaluation of Change, supra* note 24, at 745-47; Note, *Comparative Approaches, supra* note 49, at 1149 n.44. In Helling v. Carey, 83 Wash. 2d 514, 519 P.2d 981 (1974), for example, the Supreme Court of Washington held the failure to administer a particular diagnostic test negligent as a matter of law, in spite of undisputed evidence of customary practice to the contrary. The court seemed to reason that a pressure test for glaucoma should be routinely given to all ophthalmological patients because of the seriousness of glaucoma-induced loss of sight and the small expense and low risk of the test itself. *Id.* at 519, 519 P.2d at 983.

In this case, however, custom may well have correctly assessed the costs and risks in not administering the test to people under forty because of the rarity of glaucoma before that age. *See* Note, *Comparative Approaches, supra* note 49, at 1149 n.38. The *Helling* court, however, took no account of the magnitude of the risk sought to be reduced, which, for the plaintiff in her late twenties, was less than one in 25,000. The plaintiff had a history of repeated vision problems, however, 83 Wash. 2d at 515-16, 519 P.2d at 981, and the court might have limited its holding by placing her in a higher-risk category to which different customary standards might have applied, *id.* at 517-18, 519 P.2d at 982. Instead, the holding effectively requires ophthalmologists to omit the test at their peril, and 25,000 patients will have to pay for the diagnosis of a single illness. The concurring opinion, *id.* at 520, 519 P.2d at 984, correctly noted that this result in fact closely resembles a strict or absolute liability approach—but following the new customary practice set out by the court will immunize providers and prevent compensation to the injured (in the likely event that the test is not 100 percent foolproof), so that neither optimal deterrence nor full compensation is achieved. If *Helling* is typical of independent judicial assessment of negligence, HMOs and other providers would be better off without it.

A more rigorous negligence assessment should be possible, and the growing literature of medical cost-benefit analysis, especially of diagnostic tests, may facilitate this in the future. *See, e.g.,* Mass. Dep't of Public Health, *Cost-Benefit Analysis of Newborn Screening for Metabolic Disorders,* 291 NEW ENG. J. MED. 1414 (1974) (finds screening cost-justified; but note failure to discount future savings to present value); Neuhauser & Lewicki, *What Do We Gain from the Sixth Stool Guaiac?,* 293 NEW ENG. J. MED. 226 (1975).

accept HMO custom as determinative of due care, to the same extent that insured fee-for-service custom is now accepted, in effect allowing this subgroup of medical practitioners to set its own malpractice standards. Whether or not a particular HMO practice was negligent would thus be judged by the practice of other HMO providers under comparable circumstances.[104]

Such a solution may at first blush seem radical, since it would in some cases accept as appropriate two different standards of care—HMO and fee-for-service—for a single treatment or diagnosis. In many cases, however, the standards would probably be nearly identical because of widespread agreement on the worth of particular practices. Moreover, the differences in standards would not necessarily reflect different levels of risk reduction, but often only variations in the style of achieving a similar risk of bad outcomes.[105]

Actually, it is not so surprising that different medical standards should be accepted as appropriate, given the uncertainties inherent in much medical care and the inability of malpractice law to evaluate most medical risks and the risk-reducing or -enhancing effects of different standards. After all, it is these factors which have led to reliance on market-oriented standards in place of judicial judgment. Malpractice law formerly accepted the coexistence of a great variety of health care practices in the medical marketplace—each "school of practice" had its own practitioners, standards, and prices—and judged each case by the custom of the school of treatment of the health care provider elected by the patient.[106] Malpractice law today, while it holds all providers to certain minimum requirements,[107] accepts multiple standards where noncustomary practice is supported by a "reputable minority" of practi-

---

104. Courts should, nevertheless, continue to examine HMO customary practice for reasonableness whenever judicial assessment is feasible, see note 103 *supra*, to the same extent that fee-for-service custom is also scrutinized.

105. HMOs offer good quality care, comparing favorably with that of providers in general. See note 12 *supra*.

106. *E.g.*, Klimkiewicz v. Karnick, 150 Colo. 267, 372 P.2d 736 (1962) (chiropractor); Force v. Gregory, 63 Conn. 167, 27 A. 1116 (1893) (homeopath). The "school of practice" doctrine has faded somewhat as modern allopathic medicine has come to be accepted as the only scientifically valid school, and both licensure and malpractice law reflect this. Other "schools" have adopted medical tenets, like osteopathy, or accepted limited scopes of practice, like chiropractic. A nonmedical doctor or health care practitioner will be judged by the standards of medical doctors if the care given constitutes medical practice. *E.g.*, HOLDER 44. The "school" approach has merged into the similar "reputable minority" approach, but now usually covers minority opinion among medical doctors. Spiritualists, magnetic healers, and the like do not constitute reputable minorities. PROSSER 163.

107. PROSSER 163.

tioners on the ground that it is just as effective medically as majority practice.[108] Furthermore, there is precedent for dual standards of care, on economic as well as medical grounds, in the different standards applied to specialists and general practitioners[109] and in the rationale underlying the locality rule.[110]

An HMO custom rule would be broader than the current "repu-

---

108. See authorities cited at note 28 *supra*. This doctrine is not well suited for examining the legitimacy of all noncustomary HMO practice, however. It is normally applied where there is a medical disagreement on the risk-reducing effectiveness of different procedures, as where one group of surgeons favors on medical grounds one operation and another a different operation. The difficult HMO case, in contrast, arises from a noncustomary HMO valuation of agreed-upon medical facts. The doctrine is also applied on a procedure-by-procedure basis, which would complicate consideration of the likely HMO rationale—that a given procedure is not provided because another is more valuable.

109. Medical specialists and general practitioners coexist, providing services which frequently overlap, but under markedly different malpractice standards of care. The performance of specialists is measured by the standards of fellow specialists. Those standards are higher than those of doctors generally, and may be national rather than local. See note 27 *supra*. Malpractice law thus accepts at least two different standards, with different economic antecedents and consequences, for identical procedures. The patient's choice of provider will determine the standard of care he receives. The ostensible rationale for a higher specialist standard is that specialists hold themselves out as more than ordinarily qualified. Belk v. Schweizer, 268 N.C. 50, 56, 149 S.E.2d 565, 569 (1966); 1 LOUISELL & WILLIAMS ¶ 8.04 n.60. Lurking in the background, though not seen as crucial, is the fact that specialists typically are paid considerably higher fees, a factor which surely has some bearing on their ability to maintain a higher standard. That patients may choose a GP's lower standard of care, perhaps for reasons of lower cost, lends some support to the notion that separate HMO standards, resulting largely from cost considerations, are appropriate.

110. The locality rule, as traditionally applied, reflects a very real concern for the costs of achieving particular standards of care, though the rule is not usually discussed in those terms. Normally, the application of different standards in different localities is explained by the great variation among regions in the availability of facilities, personnel, and continuing education. Isolated practitioners, for example, have been thought unable to keep abreast of developments in medicine elsewhere. HOLDER 53-54; McCoid 569-70. Such differences are not due to an absolute impossibility of meeting higher standards, but rather in large measure can be explained as a matter of cost. The most backward area could, after all, allow its doctors six months of the year to train at some advanced medical center, or achieve a very high standard of care, except perhaps in cases of the utmost emergency, by simply providing helicopter service to the Mayo Clinic. Nonetheless, the locality rule retains, and it is important that it does, an implied recognition that different costs may dictate different medical malpractice standards.

So analyzed, the locality rule supports the legitimacy of weighing costs in setting standards for HMOs, but a separate HMO standard is not strictly analogous to separate rural standards. HMOs, like rural areas, are apt to balk at the cost of meeting some customary malpractice standards, but, unlike rural areas, not because of the practical impossibility of raising the cash. The reason, instead, is a different valuation of the worth of the standard. Moreover, people are more apt to have considered what standard of care they will receive when joining an HMO than when moving to a rural area.

table minority" doctrine,[111] but narrower than a "school of practice" rule accepting completely different philosophies of medical care.[112] Allowing HMO custom to set negligence standards would be a recognition that, theoretically, HMO risk-reducing incentives are just as appropriate as those of fee-for-service providers for judging the social value of particular care, and that, empirically, the quality record of HMOs is excellent.[113] In taking market-derived standards as its own, malpractice law would recognize the existence of two equally valid marketing approaches in the provision of health care. It is true that the economizing incentives of HMOs could lead some of them to "underreduce" some medical risks. There is nothing to indicate, however, that such incentives would be greater than the incentives which cause overspending in the fee-for-service context in attempts to eliminate risks.[114]

Moreover, to create separate and potentially different HMO standards is not to allow HMOs to exist in a vacuum. Insured fee-for-service is the dominant mode of practice, and dissatisfied HMO enrollees can change to other providers and conventional insurance coverage.[115] HMOs thus feel constant competitive pressure to perform as well as fee-for-service providers.[116] The reverse is seldom the case, since HMO care is not a competitive force in most areas. Furthermore, HMO physicians are educated at the same medical schools as other doctors, read the same journals, join the same professional organizations, and are presumably equally humane and desirous of helping their patients—factors which constitute extremely important protection against HMO corner-cutting in evaluating and acting to reduce medical risks. Further, HMO patients (and their relatives) are probably just as demanding of high-quality, low-risk care for a given illness as are others and may be more capable of detecting underservice than others

---

111. The HMO custom rule would apply across the board to all HMOs, not merely procedure by procedure like the reputable minority doctrine. It would also encompass noncustomary practice based upon evaluative disagreements with majority practice, not merely upon differences of opinion over medical effectiveness.

112. HMO divergences from majority custom would be acceptable because of different evaluations and style differences in applying similar methods, but not because of fundamentally conflicting philosophies of healing methods.

113. See generally authorities cited in note 12 *supra*.

114. Overeconomizing, moreover, would not be universal among HMOs, and the general level of care would set the standard.

115. Many HMOs follow a "dual choice" policy. *See, e.g.,* Phelan, Erickson & Fleming, *supra* note 3, at 799-800. Dual choice is also embodied as federal policy in the HMO Act of 1973. 42 U.S.C. § 300e-9 (Supp. III 1973).

116. Lack of subscriber-patient knowledge and understanding may, however, limit competition's effects.

are of resisting overservice.[117] Finally, the integration of services and the centralization of many important medical decisions inherent in the HMO concept enable subscribers to wield substantial influence through grievance procedures, consumer participation on policy boards, and the like.[118] Such efforts are far more difficult in the more fragmented fee-for-service sector, where each hospital, clinic, or medical partnership is independent. Such consumer inputs are imperfect substitutes for well-informed individual patient or subscriber choice, but they are superior to the alternative of nearly total physician discretion in medical decision-making, which creates the customary practice now enforced by malpractice law.

An HMO custom rule would increase emphasis on subscriber choices—and willingness to pay—as determinants of the socially acceptable level of risk in HMO care.[119] It would also shift the perspective of decision-making somewhat away from individual illnesses or crises, the management of which sets the current standard, and toward the more dispassionate focus of a health subscriber's evaluation of hazards from all health-threatening conditions. To the extent that the rationale for a market-oriented negligence standard rests on the assumption that medical custom represents both physician and "customer" views, this is an appropriate shift. To the extent that the medical custom standard simply accepts aggregate physician judgment in lieu of a social judgment on risks, the HMO custom rule would substitute physician judgment constrained by cost considerations for largely unconstrained physician judgment. Finally, a separate HMO custom standard would permit use of different standards as a kind of social

---

117. HMO or insured patients face little cost for extra service and are apt to demand more services rather than less—at least to the extent that they know about possible risk-reducing measures their doctors might provide.

118. *See* Starr, *The Undelivered Health System*, 42 PUB. INTEREST 66, 81-84 (1976).

119. The extent to which agreements on risk reduction between provider and patient or enrollee ought to influence or supersede malpractice standards is an important and difficult question which is seldom considered. (A notable exception is Epstein, *Medical Malpractice: The Case for Contract*, 1976 A.B.F. RESEARCH J. 87.) Particular medical measures, even if more than normally risky, are acceptable where a patient knowledgeably assumes the risk or gives informed consent. More difficult is the case of an HMO which might offer a higher level of risk in medical care in exchange for lower premiums. Here, subscribers, though they could not know in advance exactly what risks are at stake, could rationally choose the general level of care they wish, from Volkswagen to Mercedes, and general regulation could keep quality of care above acceptable minimums. Havighurst & Bovbjerg, *supra* note 19, at 415-16. Thoroughgoing malpractice specification of what care is appropriate obviously would inhibit the making of such choices. Our society generally allows free consumer choice between Volkswagens and Mercedes, without expecting the former to be as safe as the latter, even though consumers are only very poorly able to weigh the exact differences in safety. The law, however, intervenes much more readily in the provision of medical care than in the sale of cars.

experiment, perhaps ultimately generating enough information about both fee-for-service and HMO standards for an independent judicial assessment to be made of both of them.

The objections to an HMO custom standard mirror those against customary practice standards generally.[120] Unfettered HMO discretion in the setting of standards might be abused, given the imperfections of patient influence on medical decision-making generally. Moreover, established HMO practice might, through malpractice law, unduly inhibit others—for example, very innovative new HMOs or an entirely new type of medical organization—from legitimate experimentation with noncustomary methods.

In implementing the proposed HMO custom standard, courts must set forth clearly their rationale; exactly why HMOs are a special case must be understood or the old battle over what schools of practice are legitimate could be reopened: if HMOs set their own standards, why not snake-oil salesmen? Similarly, exactly what constitutes an "HMO" eligible for different standards must be clear; the proposed rule should not serve to legitimate the practice of any group choosing to accept prepayment.[121] Judicial experience with deciding whether a given minority's practice is "reputable" might offer helpful precedent, but the underlying theory of that doctrine is poorly articulated, and the question of the legitimacy of HMO practice generally goes far beyond that of whether a particular noncustomary practice is acceptable in one set of circumstances. The questions here may be difficult and costly to handle under established judicial procedure, as they potentially involve the entire scope of operation of complex institutions. The locality rule in some jurisdictions would also need modification, since there are so few HMOs in most of the country. The law should compare the custom of similarly situated HMOs, so as to avoid grouping together the practices of very disparate organizations, ranging from large urban conglomerates to small rural group clinics, which operate under very different

---

120. This Article has argued that HMOs are less likely than fee-for-service providers to misevaluate risk reduction and costs, to concentrate inappropriately on process standards, or to be subject to other problems stemming from custom-derived standards. See notes 42-102 *supra* and accompanying text.

121. To borrow Prosser's comment on the "school of practice" doctrine, not any "quack, charlatan or crackpot" should be allowed to "set himself up as" an HMO. PROSSER 163. This problem would not be so serious in the HMO case because so many HMOs are clearly reputable and these providers would set the new HMO group's standards of care. Nonetheless, especially where HMOs accept higher risks in one area for the sake of lowering others, see notes 100-02 *supra* and accompanying text, malpractice suits might have to examine practice in both areas, a task for which the case-by-case judicial process is not well suited.

resource constraints. Finally, some HMOs might resist a separate HMO custom standard, fearing that separateness would suggest non-equality to potential enrollees.

Nonetheless, despite theoretical and practical problems with an "HMO custom" malpractice standard, the proposed test makes sense. Allowing HMOs to develop different malpractice standards should help to hold down risk-reducing costs and to maintain a healthy diversity of approaches to medical care—a very desirable goal in an uncertain field.

Conclusion

It should not be expected that unleashing HMOs from the majority medical custom rule will solve all malpractice problems or greatly ease the intractable difficulties of deciding how much medical care is enough and how safe it should be. It is, however, a modest step in the right direction. The capacity of modern medicine to intervene on behalf of human health is immense and growing rapidly, as is the capacity to gather information in deciding whether and how to intervene. But the ability to finance medical procedures is limited, and choices must be made. Medical custom and the law of medical malpractice are important influences on these choices—though perhaps less so than are the organization and financing of health care itself. In any case, finding workable approaches to these problems requires additional attention from the medical and legal communities.

It seems likely that only decision-makers motivated to face up to the harsh fact of limited medical resources can be expected to incorporate cost considerations effectively into their risk-reduction calculations. In theory, patients, third-party insurers, or courts might perform this function, but HMOs offer a unique opportunity to combine the viewpoints of patient, insurer, and provider in determining the proper standard of care. Policed by a malpractice rule of customary HMO practice, and by independent judicial evaluation of standards when feasible, such relative autonomy for HMOs might well be the best solution achievable within the customary practice approach to malpractice law.

COMMENT

AN ANALYSIS OF STATE LEGISLATIVE RESPONSES TO THE MEDICAL MALPRACTICE CRISIS

INTRODUCTION

The recent medical malpractice crisis is the result of the increasing reluctance of insurance companies to write medical malpractice insurance policies and the dramatic rise in premiums demanded by those companies which continue to issue policies. The difficulties in obtaining insurance at reasonable rates have forced many health care providers[1] to curtail or cease to render their services. Such a situation creates obvious dangers to the public welfare, and many state legislatures have attempted to take remedial action. There are two general approaches which such action can take. The first is to establish joint underwriting groups or reinsurance schemes through which health care providers can more easily obtain malpractice insurance. The second is to alter the substantive and procedural rules relating to medical malpractice actions to decrease the liability of health care providers and thereby to make the malpractice risk insurable at a price the health care profession is willing to pay. This Comment will examine the various alternatives which are available under the second approach.[2]

In preparation for this study, correspondence was sent to the legislatures of all fifty states concerning both proposed and enacted

---

THE FOLLOWING CITATIONS WILL BE USED IN THIS COMMENT:
    A. HOLDER, MEDICAL MALPRACTICE LAW (1975) [hereinafter cited as HOLDER];
    D. LOUISELL & H. WILLIAMS, MEDICAL MALPRACTICE (1973) [hereinafter cited as LOUISELL & WILLIAMS];
    W. PROSSER, HANDBOOK OF THE LAW OF TORTS (4th ed. 1971) [hereinafter cited as PROSSER];
    U.S. DEP'T OF HEALTH, EDUCATION AND WELFARE, REPORT OF THE SECRETARY'S COMMISSION ON MEDICAL MALPRACTICE (1973) [hereinafter cited as MEDICAL MALPRACTICE REPORT];
    Waltz & Scheuneman, *Informed Consent to Therapy*, 64 Nw. U.L. REV. 628 (1970) [hereinafter cited as Waltz & Scheuneman];
    Documentary Supplement, Medical-Legal Screening Panels as an Alternative Approach to Medical Malpractice Claims, 13 WM. & MARY L. REV. 695 (1972) [hereinafter cited as *Documentary Supplement*].
    1. The definition of health care provider varies from state to state but generally includes physicians, osteopaths, dentists, and hospitals.
    2. The insurance-oriented approaches were not treated, partially because of a lack of expertise in the area and partially because it is believed that the approaches aimed at changes in the actual resolution of malpractice disputes will determine the extent to which the malpractice crisis is curbed and the sectors of society which will bear the ultimate cost of the malpractice problem.

legislation relating to the malpractice problem.[3] The responses from this survey have been used as the basis of the discussion, although a complete description and evaluation of the measures considered and adopted by each state have not been attempted.[4] Even if spatial considerations would permit such detail, the speed with which current developments in this area are taking place would preclude any pretension to either accuracy or completeness by the time of publication.[5] Instead, common themes have been extracted from the materials. The discussion of these themes is intended to highlight the advantages and disadvantages, both legal and practical, which the various alternatives present. Hopefully, this Comment will act as a general guide to the preparation or evaluation of legislation dealing with the law of medical malpractice.

For convenience, the Comment has been divided into three sections. The first deals with the imposition of direct limits on the amount which can be recovered in a malpractice action. The second discusses various changes in either substantive or procedural law which could act indirectly to reduce damage awards in malpractice cases. The third section is devoted to a special sort of indirect procedural limitation—alterations in the dispute resolution mechanism. This division is artificial since any comprehensive statute will be made up of several components which will interact to some extent. The Comment is not addressed to such potential interactions; however, in considering any given statute they should not be overlooked.

Finally, it must be emphasized that the decision as to what measures should be adopted to meet the malpractice crisis involves very difficult policy considerations. Such decisions are beyond the scope of this Comment, which is designed only to describe the efficacy of alternative attempts to ease this pressing problem

DIRECT LIMITATIONS ON HEALTH CARE PROVIDER LIABILITY

The most straightforward way to alleviate the insurance cost pres-

---

3. The responses are on file in the offices of the *Duke Law Journal*.

4. For a recent comprehensive compilation of the state legislative efforts, see Grossman, *State-by-State Summary of Legislative Activities on Medical Malpractice*, in A LEGISLATOR'S GUIDE TO THE MEDICAL MALPRACTICE ISSUE 12 (D. Warren & R. Merritt eds. 1976). *See also* Rhein, *Malpractice: Grim Outlook for '76*, MED. WORLD NEWS, Jan. 12, 1976, at 71, 72-74; *Survey Shows Gains in Liability Legislation, But Problems Remain*, AM. MED. NEWS, Jan. 12, 1976, at 9.

5. Undoubtedly, many of the proposed measures cited in the Comment will have been enacted, defeated, or amended by the time the Comment is published. The resulting inaccuracies are regretted, but appear to be unavoidable.

sures of the recent medical malpractice crisis is to limit the amount which health care providers can be required to pay in malpractice cases. With an appropriately low ceiling, the risks of negligence in the practice of medicine could be made insurable at a reasonable premium rate. Several states have adopted measures predicated on this idea.[6] At least three general forms of limitations on recovery can be identified. The first is the recovery-limiting statute, which simply places a ceiling on the amount which can be recovered.[7] A variation of this approach imposes a limitation on the liability of individual health care providers as well as a limitation on plaintiff recovery. For example, recent Indiana legislation[8] limits the liability of a qualifying[9] individual health care provider to $100,000 but allows a patient to recover up to $500,000. Any amount due from a judgment or court-approved settlement which exceeds the total combined liability of all liable health care providers is to be paid from a Patients' Compensation Fund which is maintained by annual surcharges on health care providers.[10] A third approach establishes patient compensation boards which would allow recovery up to certain limits in a manner similar to that of workmen's compensation schemes.

In order to be effective, a recovery-limiting approach must necessarily prevent some patients from being fully compensated for their injuries, at least in the sense that a jury would have found full compensation at a higher figure. Moreover, those who are denied receipt of a

---

6. Statutes limiting the liability of health care providers include: Medical Malpractice Reform Act, ch. 75-9, [1975] West's Fla. Sess. Law Service No. 1, at 16 (codified at FLA. STAT. ANN. § 627.353); IDAHO CODE §§ 39-4204, -4205 (Supp. 1975); IND. ANN. STAT. § 16-9.5-2-2(b) (Burns Supp. 1975); Act 817, § 1, [1975] West's La. Sess. Law Service No. 4, at 1383 (codified at LA. REV. STAT. ANN. § 40:1299.42(B)(2)); N.D. CENT. CODE § 26-40-11 (Supp. 1975); ch. 796, § 14, [1975] Ore. Laws 2315; ch. 37, § 10, [1975] West's Wis. Legis. Service No. 1, at 48 (codified at WIS. STAT. ANN. § 655.23(5)).

7. *See, e.g.,* IDAHO CODE §§ 39-4204, -4205 (Supp. 1975) (section 39-4204 limits liability of complying physicians to $150,000 for one patient or $300,000 for two or more patients; section 39-4205 limits liability of complying hospitals to $150,000 for one patient and an aggregate amount equal to the greater of $300,000 or $10,000 times the number of hospital beds); Pub. Act. 79-960, § 4, [1975] Ill. Legis. Service No. 6, at 1617 (codified at ILL. ANN. STAT. ch. 70, § 101) (maximum recovery for any one plaintiff limited to $500,000). It should be noted that both these statutes have been declared unconstitutional by lower state courts. See *Survey Shows Gain in Liability Legislation, supra* note 4, at 10.

8. IND. ANN. STAT. § 16-9.5-2-2(b) (Burns Supp. 1975). See *New Indiana Law Will Cut Negligence Suits, Improve Care,* 17 PHYSICIAN'S LEGAL BRIEF 1 (Fall 1975).

9. A health care provider qualifies for the limited liability by showing financial responsibility in the amount of $100,000 and paying to the Patients' Compensation Fund an annual surcharge of up to ten percent of the cost of maintaining financial responsibility. IND. ANN. STAT. § 16-9.5-2-1 (Burns Supp. 1975).

10. *Id.* § 16-9.5-2-2(c).

total jury award are likely to be the most seriously injured plaintiffs. It can be argued that such legislative abrogation of the common law right to a full damage award constitutes a deprivation of property without due process of law.[11]

The most recent examination of the relationship between the concept of due process and the abolition or modification of common law tort remedies is that made by state courts which have considered the constitutionality of no-fault automobile insurance plans. In their analysis, the courts have asked whether the legislation in question bears a substantial relation to a permissible legislative purpose.[12] If this standard is met, and the legislation is not deemed unreasonable, arbitrary, or capricious, it does not impair due process rights.[13] The Supreme Court applied this test in the 1929 case of *Silver v. Silver*[14] to uphold the validity of automobile guest statutes,[15] which abolish a passenger's cause of action against his host-driver for injuries sustained through the latter's negligence.[16] The Court declared that "the Constitution does not forbid the

---

11. The fourteenth amendment provides: "nor shall any State deprive any person of . . . property, without due process of law." U.S. CONST. amend. XIV, § 1. At this point, a distinction must be made between prospective application of such statutes and retroactive application. Legislation may not be applied retroactively to destroy or to limit vested or accrued causes of action. However, the courts, in a variety of contexts, have approved such legislation when it operates prospectively. In New York Cent. R.R. v. White, 243 U.S. 188 (1917), the Court said, "No person has a vested interest in any rule of law entitling him to insist that it shall remain unchanged for his benefit." *Id.* at 198; *accord*, Silver v. Silver, 280 U.S. 117 (1929) (automobile guest statute); Mountain Timber Co. v. Washington, 243 U.S. 219 (1917) (workmen's compensation plan); Lasky v. State Farm Ins. Co., 296 So. 2d 9 (Fla. 1974) (no-fault automobile insurance plan); Rotwein v. Gersten, 160 Fla. 736, 36 So. 2d 419 (1948) (abolition of common law cause of action for alienation of affections); Pinnick v. Cleary, 360 Mass. 1, 271 N.E.2d 592 (1971) (no-fault automobile insurance plan); Opinion of the Justices, 309 Mass. 571, 34 N.E.2d 527 (1941) (automobile guest statute); Opinion of the Justices, 113 N.H. 205, 304 A.2d 881 (1973) (no-fault automobile insurance plan); Montgomery v. Daniels, 44 U.S.L.W. 2271 (N.Y. Ct. App., Nov. 25, 1975) (no-fault automobile accident compensation law).

12. Lasky v. State Farm Ins. Co., 296 So. 2d 9, 15 (Fla. 1974); Pinnick v. Cleary, 360 Mass. 1, 14, 271 N.E.2d 592, 602 (1971); Opinion of the Justices, 113 N.H. 205, 211, 304 A.2d 881, 886 (1973). This traditional standard of review was first articulated in Nebbia v. New York, 291 U.S. 502, 537 (1934).

13. See cases cited in note 12 *supra*.

14. 280 U.S. 117 (1929).

15. The Court recognized an increase of litigation by ungrateful guests against their host-drivers. *Id.* at 122. In addition, the automobile accident situation created a splendid opportunity for collusion between host and guest to recover from insurance companies. PROSSER § 34, at 187. *But cf.* Brown v. Merlo, 8 Cal. 3d 855, 506 P.2d 212, 106 Cal. Rptr. 388 (1973) (distinguishing *Silver* and holding California guest statute unconstitutional as violation of equal protection).

16. The statutes permit passengers to sue their hosts for acts which are deemed more culpable than mere negligence. *See, e.g.*, ALA. CODE tit. 36, § 95 (1959) (wilful or

creation of new rights, or the abolition of old ones . . . to attain a permissible legislative object."[17] Then, in a passage which seems particularly pertinent in light of the recent malpractice crisis, the Court stated: "Whether there has been a serious increase in the evils of vexatious litigation in this class of cases . . . is for legislative determination and, if found, may well be the basis of legislative action further restricting the liability. Its wisdom is not the concern of courts."[18] Since guest statutes completely eliminate a guest's right of action for his host's merely negligent conduct, they can be viewed as a much more drastic measure than the recovery-limiting statutes, which permit at least some recovery. Thus, if the guest statutes withstand due process objections under the Constitution, it would appear that a recovery-limiting statute should also be valid. This conclusion, however, must be qualified by the fact that guest statutes apply only to drivers who provide gratuitous services,[19] a situation which is seldom found in the provision of health care. Furthermore, a reviewing court could well conclude that forcing the most seriously injured plaintiffs to bear the full cost of the continued availability of medical services is unreasonable, arbitrary, and capricious.[20]

In addition to the rational relationship test, some state courts have adopted a second requirement when passing on the validity of statutes abolishing common law rights: the legislature must provide a reasonable substitute for what it has taken away.[21] Thus, no-fault automobile

---

wanton misconduct); DEL. CODE ANN. tit. 21, § 6101 (1974) (intentional act, or wilful and wanton disregard of rights of others); NEB. REV. STAT. § 39-740 (1968) (intoxication or gross negligence); S.D. COMPILED LAWS ANN., §§ 32-34-1, -2 (1967) (wilful and wanton misconduct); UTAH CODE ANN. § 41-9-1 (1953) (intoxication or wilful misconduct). *See also* 2 F. HARPER & F. JAMES, THE LAW OF TORTS § 16.15 & n.4, at 950-51 (1956).

17. 280 U.S. at 122; *cf.* Carr v. United States, 422 F.2d 1007 (4th Cir. 1970) (abrogating federal employee's common law right of action against government driver not violative of fifth amendment due process clause).

18. 280 U.S. at 123.

19. See statutes cited in note 16 *supra*.

20. The distinction between those patients having small claims who are fully compensated and those with more serious injuries who do not receive a complete recovery may also be a violation of the equal protection clause. *Cf.* Brown v. Merlo, 8 Cal. 3d 855, 506 P.2d 212, 106 Cal. Rptr. 388 (1973); Gutierrez v. Glaser Crandell Co., 388 Mich. 654, 202 N.W.2d 786 (1972). *See generally Developments in the Law— Equal Protection*, 82 HARV. L. REV. 1065, 1077-87 (1969).

21. *See, e.g.*, Lasky v. State Farm Ins. Co., 296 So. 2d 9, 13-14 (Fla. 1974); Pinnick v. Cleary, 360 Mass. 1, 15, 271 N.E.2d 592, 602 (1971). This principle seems to be the product of some dicta contained in New York Cent. R.R. v. White, 243 U.S. 188, 201 (1917), in which the Supreme Court upheld the constitutionality of workmen's compensation legislation:

Nor is it necessary, for the purposes of the present case, to say that a State might, without violence to the constitutional guaranty of 'due process of law,'

insurance legislation has been sustained on the theory that the mutual surrender, by plaintiffs and defendants, of rights and defenses creates a fair alternative to the traditional common law fault system.[22] This same idea provides another point of distinction between recovery-limiting statutes and guest statutes. The latter enactments do give plaintiffs a benefit in that they will be insulated from liability for their own negligence as host-drivers.[23] The recovery-limiting statutes are much more one-sided. The health care provider gives up none of his traditional defenses, and the mutual benefit rationale could be applied only to plaintiffs who are also physicians. Moreover, the plaintiff is not freed from the burden of proving the physician's negligence prior to obtaining any recovery. Therefore, if the reasonable substitute test is applied, it seems quite doubtful that a recovery-limiting approach can be sustained.[24]

A second general group of statutes attempts to reduce health care provider exposure by directly limiting the liability of the provider, rather than recovery by the plaintiff.[25] The operation of these statutes is

---

suddenly set aside all common law rules respecting liability as between employer and employee, without providing a reasonably just substitute . . . . The statute under consideration sets aside one body of rules only to establish another. *Id.*

Whether and under what circumstances the reasonable substitute standard is compelled by the fourteenth amendment is not clear. *See* Pinnick v. Cleary, 360 Mass. 1, 15, 271 N.E.2d 592, 602 (1971). The New York Court of Appeals has recently questioned whether the reasonable substitute test "is any test at all." Montgomery v. Daniels, 44 U.S.L.W. 2271, 2272 (N.Y. Ct. App., Nov. 25, 1975).

22. Lasky v. State Farm Ins. Co., 296 So. 2d 9 (Fla. 1974); Pinnick v. Cleary, 360 Mass. 1, 271 N.E.2d 592 (1971); Opinion of the Justices, 113 N.H. 205, 304 A.2d 881 (1973). It should be noted that no-fault automobile insurance legislation typically provides for tort recovery after a specified threshold of actual economic loss is reached. *See, e.g.*, FLA. STAT. ANN. § 627.737 (1972); KAN. STAT. ANN. § 40-3117 (Supp. 1974); MASS. ANN. LAWS ch. 90, § 34M (1975). This element is not present in the recovery-limiting statutes.

23. Carr v. United States, 422 F.2d 1007, 1011 (4th Cir. 1970).

24. If a legislature is willing to wade into the constitutional problems created by a recovery-limiting statute, it must determine at what level to set the recovery ceiling. Arguably, political pressures would prevent the imposition of extremely low recovery limits. Still, if the ceiling is to be effective in lowering malpractice insurance premiums it must produce some significant reduction in total damage awards. That is, consideration must be given to both the size of individual recoveries and the total number of recoveries. In this connection it should be noted that 1970 figures show that $3000 is the median recovery in medical malpractice actions and that ninety-seven percent of all awards are for less than $100,000. MEDICAL MALPRACTICE REPORT 10 & Table 7, at 11. The figures, of course, are changing rapidly. *See, e.g.*, Steves, *Medical Malpractice in Perspective*, 28 CPCU ANNALS 209, 214-15 (1975).

25. *See* Medical Malpractice Reform Act, ch. 75-9, § 15 [1975] West's Fla. Sess. Law Service No. 1, at 17 (codified at FLA. STAT. ANN. § 627.353) (limits liability of health care provider to $100,000; Patients' Compensation Fund pays excess); ch. 796, §

similar to that of the Indiana legislation.[26] A ceiling is placed on the health care providers' liability and the difference between damage awards—or court-approved settlements—and this limitation is paid from a fund maintained for that purpose. Unlike the Indiana approach, however, there is no direct limit on the patient's total recovery.[27] Thus, the pure liability-limiting approach avoids the constitutional questions which are presented by recovery-limiting schemes.[28] Since patients receive the total compensation awarded by a jury if there is no deficit in the Patients' Compensation Fund, nothing has been taken from them. At the same time, the limitation on the liability of individual health care providers can be structured so as to enable their insurance carriers to continue to write malpractice policies.

Unfortunately, the creation of Patients' Compensation Funds may not be a real solution to the malpractice problem. Since the pure liability-limiting approach does not place a limit on the amount a plaintiff may recover, there is a potential for large annual deficits in the Fund, which may in turn drastically increase surcharges on individual providers. These large surcharges could well have the same effect as the recent rise in malpractice insurance premiums, *i.e.* they might dissuade physicians from providing health care services. Such a tendency appears inevitable if the surcharges are calculated on the basis of the

---

14, [1975] Ore. Laws 2315 (liability limited to amount determined by health care provider's specialty; Medical Excess Liability Fund pays excess); ch. 37, § 10, [1975] West's Wis. Legis. Service No. 1, at 48, 50 (codified at WIS. STAT. ANN. §§ 655.23(5), 655.27(1)) (liability limited to health care provider's insurance coverage; patients' compensation fund pays excess).

26. See note 8 *supra* and accompanying text.

27. Indirect limits on recovery arise from the fact that the Patients' Compensation Funds are funded by health care provider surcharges which generally are not to exceed a set percentage of the cost to the health care provider of establishing financial responsibility. See note 9 *supra*. Deficits in the Patients' Compensation Fund are handled in two ways. Generally, the available funds are prorated among the claims and the unpaid balance is carried over to the following year. *See, e.g.*, IND. ANN. STAT. § 16-9.5-4-1(g) (Burns Supp. 1975). However, the Oregon statute, ch. 796, §§ 17(2)(b), (3), [1975] Ore. Laws 2318, does not provide for carry-over of the unpaid balance after prorating. Thus, that portion of a claimant's recovery which is not paid in the year payment is due is lost.

28. Although the discussion of the due process question focused on the rights of medical malpractice plaintiffs, certain due process objections may also be raised by individual health care providers. If participation in the Patients' Compensation Fund is compulsory, the health care provider might argue that the imposition of annual surcharges is a deprivation of property without due process of law. This argument appears weak, for in most of the plans the health care provider need not participate unless he desires the limitation that the plans impose on his tort liability. *See, e.g.*, Medical Malpractice Reform Act, ch. 75-9, § 15, [1975] West's Fla. Sess. Law Service No. 1, at 17 (codified at FLA. STAT. ANN. § 627.353); IND. ANN. STAT. § 16-9.5-1-5 (Burns Supp. 1975); ch. 796, § 18, [1975] Ore. Laws 2318.

risks encountered by a given specialty. For example, if surgeons are required to contribute large sums to the fund, many doctors may be discouraged from continuing surgery.[29] A pure liability-limiting approach would seem to have a better chance of success if the surcharges were calculated in such a way that high-risk specialties would not be discouraged. The goal of such an approach would be to spread the cost of insuring the high-risk specialists among all health care providers. There can be no guarantee, however, that even this adjustment would be adequate to overcome the problem. Spreading the risk in this manner could instead deter provision of all health care services if the surcharges needed to maintain the system became great enough.[30] Therefore, some limit on recoveries seems necessary if a direct limitation on health care provider liability is to be sure of success.

A third method of limiting recoveries—the patient compensation board—may serve this purpose.[31] This method is modeled after work-

---

29. *But see* Brook, Brutoco & Williams, *The Relationship Between Medical Malpractice and Quality of Care*, 1975 DUKE L.J. 1197. The article suggests that this result is actually beneficial since there is a shortage of general or family practitioners while there is an oversupply of specialists. In addition, unnecessary surgery is a problem in the medical field today, and this unnecessary surgery is proportional to the number of specialists in a geographic area. *See id.* at 1211.

30. A risk-spreading adjustment would produce some inequity in that physicians, and presumably their patients, in low-risk fields would bear a disproportionate share of the cost of maintaining the system. *See generally* Keeton, *Compensation for Medical Accidents*, 121 U. PA. L. REV. 590, 603 (1973). Another way to avoid the problem would be to maintain the compensation fund with tax revenues. Given the present strapped condition of many state budgets, however, this alternative does not seem viable, and no state has yet adopted this approach. To the extent that the state might fund the Patients' Compensation Fund, any deterrent effect provided by the tort system would be negated since the costs of malpractice would be externalized. *Cf.* Havighurst, *"Medical Adversity Insurance"—Has Its Time Come?*, 1975 DUKE L.J. 1233, 1241.

31. Such plans have been proposed in Alabama, Ala. H.B. 300 (1975); Alaska, Alas. H.B. 436 (1975); Georgia, Ga. S.B. 371 (1975); Louisiana, La. S.B. 344 (1975) (not passed); Maryland, Md. H.B. 829 (1975) (not passed); and Pennsylvania, Pa. H.B. 805 (1975) (not approved). The Pennsylvania bill would have established a Patients' Compensation Board with power to make awards within the following limits:
   1. Death of a minor without dependents—up to $25,000, including reasonable value of services (minus maintenance costs), medical expenses, funeral expenses, and the reasonable costs of prosecuting the claim;
   2. Death of adult without dependents—up to $50,000, including the reasonable value of hospital and medical expenses, funeral expenses, and the reasonable costs of prosecuting the claim;
   3. Death of a minor or adult with dependents—up to $100,000, including actual or prospective loss of earnings for the working life expectancy of the deceased during the dependency of the claimant (minus maintenance costs), reasonable medical and funeral expenses, and reasonable costs of prosecuting the claim; and
   4. Bodily injury to an adult or a minor—up to $50,000 for 100 percent impairment, plus up to $50,000 for any and all other injuries, general or specific (including the reasonable cost of prosecuting such claims).

men's compensation legislation and would allow recovery up to certain limits for real economic losses, *e.g.*, loss of earnings, medical expenses, and funeral expenses. Provision would also be made, again within a specified range, for death benefits. However, unlike workmen's compensation schemes, which were upheld as constitutional on the ground of mutual benefit to employee and employer,[32] the patient compensation plans lack reciprocity. While the patient is required to relinquish the possibility of a large jury award in return for a predetermined and often smaller compensation award, the provider gives up few if any of his defenses to the malpractice charges. The patient must still prove, by the preponderance of the evidence, that his injury arose from the provider's negligence.[33] Therefore, the patient compensation schemes, while somewhat analogous to workmen's compensation plans, appear more susceptible to constitutional attack, at least in those states requiring a "reasonable substitute."[34]

Although limitations upon patient recovery and/or provider liability may pass constitutional scrutiny and may reduce the cost of malpractice liability insurance, legislators should be aware that limitations on recovery do not make the societal costs of medical malpractice disappear. Rather these costs are shifted to those severely injured individuals who, but for the limitations, would have received larger recoveries.[35] Legislators should therefore ask themselves whether proposed legislation provides for proper and equitable allocation of societal costs.

INDIRECT LIMITATIONS ON HEALTH CARE PROVIDER LIABILITY

Many states have sought to make the medical malpractice risk insurable by indirectly limiting the liability of health care providers. Unlike the direct recovery or liability ceilings discussed above, the indirect limitations operate on the substantive law of torts or effect procedural changes in ways which make it more difficult for a plaintiff to recover at all in a medical malpractice action. These changes, it is hoped, will eliminate unwarranted recoveries without depriving a deserving patient-plaintiff of compensation; the consequent reduction in

---

32. *Cf.* Mountain Timber Co. v. Washington, 243 U.S. 219 (1917); New York Cent. R.R. v. White, 243 U.S. 188 (1916); Opinion of the Justices, 309 Mass. 571, 34 N.E.2d 527 (1941). See notes 21-24 *supra* and accompanying text.
33. *See, e.g.*, Ala. H.B. 300, § 3 (1975); Md. H.B. 401, § 4 (1975) (not passed); Pa. H.B. 805, § 16 (1975) (not approved).
34. See notes 21-24 *supra* and accompanying text.
35. *See generally* Blum & Kalven, *Ceilings, Costs, and Compulsion in Automobile Compensation Legislation*, 1973 UTAH L. REV. 341 (1974); Keeton, *supra* note 30; *cf.* G. CALABRESI, THE COSTS OF ACCIDENTS: A LEGAL AND ECONOMIC ANALYSIS (1970).

total dollar recoveries then would ease the insurance premium burden. Several mechanisms have been established in recent legislation, and each will be examined in an effort to ascertain its legal and practical implications.

Res Ipsa Loquitur

Res ipsa loquitur is the one legal doctrine most maligned and criticized by the medical profession.[36] This contempt for the rule, however, probably results from misinformation about what the rule provides, rather than from a sincere renunciation of its principles. Though the medical profession apparently fears that *res ipsa* may be applied in all malpractice cases to force the defendant physician to prove he was not negligent,[37] the availability and application of the rule are far more limited.

Literally translated, *res ipsa loquitur* means "the thing speaks for itself."[38] The legal doctrine is invoked only in cases where three conditions are met: (1) the event for which recovery is sought is of a kind that does not normally occur unless someone is negligent; (2) the harm was caused by something within the defendant's exclusive control; and (3) the plaintiff did not contribute to the harm.[39] When these conditions are proven, the plaintiff need not present additional evidence to support his claim.[40] According to the majority view, however, application of the doctrine does not shift the burden of proof to the defendant to prove his non-negligence but merely raises a permissible inference of negligence.[41] The effect is that, unless the defendant is

---

36. *See, e.g.,* MEDICAL MALPRACTICE REPORT 28; Hastings, *Medical Malpractice Background Papers,* in HOUSE COMM. ON INTERSTATE AND FOREIGN COMMERCE, A DISCUSSION OF MEDICAL MALPRACTICE 24 (Comm. Print 1975).

37. *See* Carmody, Res Ipsa Loquitur *In an Ancient Roman Trial,* 2 J. LEGAL MED. 41 (Nov./Dec. 1974). See note 36 *supra.*

38. For the original pronouncement of the doctrine, see Byrne v. Boadle, 159 Eng. Rep. 299, 300 (Ex. 1863) (where a person was hit by a barrel of flour which had fallen from a window, Pollock, C.B., called it a case of which it may be said "res ipsa loquitur").

39. PROSSER 214. A fourth requirement sometimes added by the courts is that evidence of the true explanation be more readily accessible to the defendant than to the plaintiff. *Id.*

40. *See* Comment, *The Application of* Res Ipsa Loquitur *in Medical Malpractice Cases,* 60 Nw. U.L. REV. 852, 853 (1966).

41. PROSSER 217. The practical effects of the rule are: (1) the plaintiff's case, which otherwise would have suffered a directed verdict against it, is allowed to get to the jury, and (2) the defendant, who presumably has a better knowledge of the facts, is encouraged to present evidence of another explanation for the occurrence. The jury is then allowed to attach whatever probative weight it wishes to the inference in weighing

able to rebut the inference of negligence, the plaintiff successfully avoids what would otherwise be a directed verdict for the defendant at the close of plaintiff's case. The defendant, in turn, will not be subject to a directed verdict for the plaintiff, even if he presents absolutely no evidence.[42]

Thus, in the overwhelming majority of jurisdictions, *res ipsa loquitur* is of only limited application and is not allowed as a substitute for proof where specific acts of negligence are alleged. Its application in malpractice litigation has generally been in selected circumstances: when foreign objects are left in the patient's body after surgery, when injuries or burns are suffered while under anesthesia, or where the wrong part of the body, or even the wrong patient, is treated.[43] Thus, the fears of the medical profession are frequently unwarranted. An exception to the general application of the rule is an extension of the doctrine in a few states where satisfaction of the necessary conditions actually shifts the burden of proof, thereby requiring the defendant to establish that he was *not* negligent.[44] Health care providers may fear that this form of the rule will achieve more widespread acceptance. Thus, reform should center not on abandoning or modifying the rule,

---

it against the defendant's testimony. Comment, Res Ipsa Loquitur, *supra* note 40, at 855.

In a few states the rule is varied slightly in that its invocation creates a presumption of negligence. *Id.* The only difference is that the defendant, in order to avoid a directed verdict for plaintiff, must introduce sufficient evidence to rebut the presumption. If the evidence is rebutted, the presumption will have no effect, and the case will go to the jury as if it were only an inference of negligence.

42. The practical effect of such a course of action, however, would probably be a finding against the defendant by the jury. Presumably the defendant would offer some evidence to rebut the inferences.

43. For a collection of such cases, see PROSSER 227-28. In the landmark case applying *res ipsa* to medical malpractice, Ybarra v. Spangard, 25 Cal. 2d 486, 154 P.2d 687 (1944), the plaintiff had been placed under general anesthesia for abdominal surgery. He awoke with a severe shoulder injury and was unable to get a satisfactory explanation from any of the hospital personnel who had treated him. Accordingly, the plaintiff brought actions against everyone connected with his operation, and the California Supreme Court held *res ipsa* appropriate to establish the liability of all such personnel.

44. Alabama, Sellers v. Noah, 209 Ala. 103, 95 So. 167 (1923); Louisiana, Druilhet v. Comeaux, 317 So. 2d 270 (La. App. 1975); New Jersey, Anderson v. Somberg, 67 N.J. 291, 338 A.2d 1, *cert. denied*, 96 S. Ct. 279 (1975); and possibly California, CAL. EVID. CODE § 646, comment (West Supp. 1975), apply this form of the doctrine to malpractice cases. *See* Louisell & Williams, *Res Ipsa Loquitur—Its Future in Medical Malpractice*, 48 CALIF. L. REV. 252 (1960). For a thorough discussion of the procedural effect of this rule, see PROSSER 228-35; Comment, Res Ipsa Loquitur, *supra* note 40; Note, *Recent Development in Wisconsin Medical Malpractice Law*, 1974 WIS. L. REV. 893, 907.

but rather on providing that the rule be applied in its traditional form. So far, suggested reforms have done just the opposite.

At least two states have enacted measures modifying the doctrine in medical malpractice cases.[45] For example, a recent Iowa bill[46] would have permitted a rebuttable inference of negligence in cases where a foreign substance is left in the body, explosions or fires are produced by substances used in medical treatment, and surgery is performed on the wrong organ, limb, or patient. Apparently, the intent of these enactments is to restrict application of *res ipsa* to the enumerated cases, and abolish it for all others. While the majority of medical malpractice cases in which the doctrine has been applied fall within the specified circumstances,[47] this codification will prevent application of the doctrine in some circumstances where it clearly should apply.[48] Moreover, it is difficult to justify the development of a separate *res ipsa* standard for medical malpractice cases without corresponding attention to the use of the doctrine in other tort actions: if its operation is unfair in the medical context, then its use in any situation should be questioned.

At least one state has enacted a statute[49] which would require proof by the plaintiff of the physician's negligence, thereby negating the use of *res ipsa* altogether. Such efforts are misguided since proper application of the doctrine affects relatively few cases,[50] and in those cases absence of the doctrine probably would result in unfairness to the plaintiff.[51]

---

45. These states are Nevada, NEV. REV. STAT. § 41a.100 (1975), and Tennessee, TENN. CODE ANN. § 23-3414 (Supp. 1975). Several other states have considered such proposals. *See, e.g.*, Ill. H.B. 1709 (1975); Iowa H.F. 697 (1975). Washington legislation requires the plaintiff to prove the defendant's failure to exercise the appropriate standard of care, WASH. REV. CODE § 4.24.290 (Supp. 1975), a measure which may be read to eliminate *res ipsa* from medical malpractice actions. *See* Grossman, *supra* note 4, at 20.

46. Iowa H.F. 697 (1975).

47. *See* PROSSER 227-28 (collecting cases).

48. It should be noted that the Iowa bill, Iowa H.F. 697 (1975), would apparently not permit use of *res ipsa* in a case having facts similar to those of Ybarra v. Spangard, 25 Cal. 2d 486, 154 P.2d 687 (1944) (discussed in note 43 *supra*). The Nevada statute would cover such a case by raising the presumption when an injury is suffered during treatment to a part of the body not directly involved in such treatment. NEV. REV. STAT. § 41A.100 (1975).

49. WASH. REV. CODE § 4.24.290 (Supp. 1975). The statute requires a plaintiff to prove by a preponderance of the evidence the negligence of a defendant in a medical malpractice action. The effect of this provision is to negate the doctrine of *res ipsa loquitur* with regard to such actions. *See* Grossman, *supra* note 4, at 20. A proposal having similar consequences was before the Illinois legislature. Ill. H.B. 1709 (1975).

50. Recent statistics show that the doctrine played a part in less than fifteen percent of all medical malpractice cases reaching the appellate level. Dietz, Baird & Berul, *The Medical Malpractice Legal System*, in MEDICAL MALPRACTICE REPORT Appendix 87, 128.

51. *See generally* Ybarra v. Spangard, 25 Cal. 2d 486, 490-91, 154 P.2d 687, 689 (1944) (discussion of situation plaintiff would be in without the doctrine).

Reform is needed only to the extent necessary to ensure that the rule is used solely in its classic form[52] and is not applied discriminatorily against health care providers.

Statutes of Limitations

The primary purpose of a statute of limitations is to prevent the prosecution of stale claims.[53] With the passage of time, evidence may be lost and witnesses may disappear. Thus, to ensure fairness to defendants it has been deemed necessary to place a limit on the time period during which an action may be brought.[54] Under the traditional rule, the time period for the bringing of a tort claim starts to run on the date of the alleged act or omission which forms the basis for the claim, regardless of the plaintiff's knowledge of his injury.[55] Courts following this rule emphasize that it is an act or omission, and not the resulting damage, that gives rise to a cause of action.[56]

The traditional act or omission rule, however, has not been strictly adhered to in the medical malpractice area: the courts have developed a number of exceptions in an attempt to alleviate the harshness of the rule in cases where the plaintiff has in good faith failed to make a timely discovery of his claim. The medical profession contends that these exceptions to the strict application of the limitation period have left physicians vulnerable to the threat of malpractice actions irrespective of when the alleged malpractice took place.[57] In addition, the insurers of health care providers have argued that this perpetual danger of suit forces them to maintain huge reserves, funded by malpractice insurance premiums, to protect themselves from claims brought many years after the date of the injury.[58] The advent of the recent crisis has prompted

---

52. See notes 38-42 *supra* and accompanying text.

53. Note, *Developments in the Law—Statutes of Limitations*, 63 HARV. L. REV. 1177, 1185 (1950). Statutes of limitations also serve to relieve the courts of the burden of adjudicating cases based on tenuous facts and circumstances. *Id.*

54. *See* Railroad Telegraphers v. Railway Express Agency, 321 U.S. 342, 348-49 (1944); New Market Poultry Farms, Inc. v. Fellows, 51 N.J. 419, 425, 241 A.2d 633, 636 (1968).

55. *See, e.g.*, Hill v. Hays, 193 Kan. 453, 395 P.2d 298 (1964); Tantish v. Szendey, 158 Me. 228, 182 A.2d 660 (1962); Peterson v. Roloff, 57 Wis. 2d 1, 203 N.W.2d 699 (1973).

56. *See* Cappuci v. Barone, 266 Mass. 578, 581, 165 N.E. 653, 654-55 (1919).

57. *See* Note, *A Four Year Statute of Limitations for Medical Malpractice Cases: Will Plaintiff's Case be Barred?*, 2 PACIFIC L.J. 663, 668 (1971).

58. *Hearings on S. 482, S. 215, and S. 188 Before the Subcomm. on Health of the Senate Comm. on Labor and Public Welfare*, 94th Cong., 1st Sess. 871 (1975) (Statement of the Nat'l Ass'n of Independent Insurers); Malpractice in Focus: The Problem . . . And Some Solutions 22 (AMA source document prepared by editors of *Prism*, Aug.

physicians and their insurers to ask that state legislatures modify existing statutes of limitations to establish definite periods, preferably short periods, during which a medical malpractice action must be brought.[59] To analyze the effect of changes which have been made, and to evaluate proposed changes, it is necessary to consider both the exceptions which the courts have made to the traditional act or omission rule, and the purpose of a limitation period.

Four different exceptions can be recognized. The first is based on the fact that statutes of limitations for contract actions generally provide for a longer time period than analogous tort statutes of limitations.[60] Accordingly, if the plaintiff is allowed to plead his cause of action as one for breach of contract, he is entitled to take advantage of the longer period.[61] A second exception is applicable where the health care provider had knowlege of the error while treating the patient and fraudulently concealed this error.[62] Under this fraudulent concealment

---

1975); see Note, *Recent Developments in Wisconsin Medical Malpractice Law,* 1974 WIS. L. REV. 893, 896 n.18.

The insurance industry contends that a maximum time limitation should be imposed upon medical malpractice actions to alleviate the problem of the "long tail." "Long tail" is the term used by insurers to describe the difficulty of setting premiums through the use of actuarial techniques which stems from the unpredictability of future inflationary spirals in the cost of medical care and the size of jury awards. *Hearings on S. 482, supra; see* Roddis & Stewart, *The Insurance of Medical Losses,* 1975 DUKE L.J. 1281. A more effective method to counteract the necessity of huge monetary reserves and the actuarial difficulties inherent in the established "occurrence" form of insurance coverage would be the institution of the "claims-made" insurance form. The claims-made form provides that each year's insurance policy covers that policy year's reported incidents rather than future year's claims resulting from this year's medical treatment. *See* MALPRACTICE DIGEST 2 (St. Paul Fire and Marine Ins. Co., Mar./Apr. 1975). With the claims-made form, the "tail's" length will be restricted to one year. At least one malpractice insurance underwriter has found the claims-made form superior to the occurrence form and will write only claims-made policies in the future. *Id.* at 1.

59. 3 AMERICAN MEDICAL ASSOCIATION, STATE HEALTH LEGISLATION REPORT 3 (Oct. 1975).

60. *Compare* ILL. REV. STAT. ch. 83, § 17 (1966) (ten-year limitation period for actions based on written contracts), *with id.* § 15 (two-year limitation period for tort actions).

61. E.g., Sellers v. Noah, 209 Ala. 103, 95 So. 167 (1923). This exception has fallen into disfavor in medical cases for two reasons. First, in a contract action, the plaintiff can only recover tangible damages such as physician and hospital expenses; the plaintiff cannot recover for pain and suffering. 13 SYRACUSE L. REV. 344, 345 n.10 (1961). Second, the vast weight of judicial authority holds that injuries sustained as a result of medical malpractice must lie in tort. *E.g.,* Huysman v. Kirschs, 6 Cal. 2d 302, 57 P.2d 908 (1936); Sales v. Tauber, 27 Ohio N.P. 372 (1929). Furthermore, states are requiring that actions based upon a contract be evidenced by a written contract rather than an oral one. See notes 170-72 *infra* and accompanying text.

62. *See* Comment, *Texas Adopts the Discovery Rule for Limitations in Medical Malpractice Actions,* 1 ST. MARY'S L.J. 77, 78-79 (1969); Note, *Tort Law—Statute of*

exception the statute of limitations is tolled—that is, the limitations period does not continue to run—until the fraud is exposed.[63] The third exception, the "termination rule,"[64] comes into play when the health care provider continues to treat the patient after making an error, but fails to discover it. In such situations the health care provider is deemed negligent both at the time of the malpractice *and* at all subsequent examinations; thus, the limitation period does not commence until the termination of the patient's relationship with the health care provider.[65] The termination rule is frequently applied when a physician negligently leaves a foreign object in a patient's body.[66] The final exception, the discovery rule,[67] is actually a flat rejection of the traditional act or omission rule in the context of medical malpractice cases. Under this exception the statute of limitations does not begin to run until the patient actually discovers the injury or should have discovered

---

Limitations in Medical Malpractice Actions, 1970 WIS. L. REV. 915, 918; 6 AKRON L. REV. 265, 267-68 (1973).

63. *See* 6 AKRON L. REV. 265, 267 n.19 (1973); Annot., 80 A.L.R.2d 368, 401 (1961). The fraudulent concealment theory has been extended by some courts to include constructive fraud. *See* Morrison v. Acton, 68 Ariz. 27, 198 P.2d 590 (1948); Rosane v. Senger, 112 Colo. 363, 149 P.2d 372 (1944). These courts emphasize the fiduciary relationship between the physician and patient which imposes a duty on the physician to disclose material information to his patient, with the failure to do so resulting in concealment.

64. This exception has also been termed the end-of-treatment rule, the continuing treatment exception, and the continuing negligence theory. Note, *Tort Law, supra* note 62, at 918; 6 AKRON L. REV. 265, 268 (1973).

65. The termination rule has been based on one or more of the following rationales: the patient's treatment must not be broken into component parts but must be considered as a whole; the failure to discover and correct the injury is a continuing negligent act giving rise to one claim; while relying on the expertise of the physician, the patient is not under a duty to inquire into the treatment's effectiveness. Lillich, *The Malpractice Statute of Limitations in New York and Other Jurisdictions*, 47 CORNELL L.Q. 339, 361 (1962).
There is a split of authority as to when the statute of limitations should commence to run under this theory. Some courts hold that the statute runs from the end of the particular treatment. *E.g.*, Waldman v. Rohrbaugh, 241 Md. 137, 215 A.2d 825 (1966). Other courts hold that the statutory period commences at the termination of the physician-patient relationship. *E.g.*, Bowers v. Santee, 99 Ohio St. 361, 124 N.E. 238 (1919).

66. *See, e.g.*, Thatcher v. De Tar, 351 Mo. 603, 173 S.W.2d 760 (1943); Sly v. Van Lengen, 120 Misc. 420, 198 N.Y.S. 608 (Sup. Ct. 1923).

67. The discovery rule has been the subject of much legal writing. The more recent contributions include: Comment, *Statutes of Limitations—Malpractice—Discovery Rule Applied to External Injuries—Fraudulent Concealment and the Treating Physician's Duty to Disclose*, 25 RUTGERS L. REV. 711 (1971); Note, *Torts—Statute of Limitations —New Rule for Medical Malpractice Actions*, 23 MERCER L. REV. 697 (1972); Note, *Statute of Limitations—Medical Malpractice—Viability of the Discovery Rule as a Criterion to Determine When a Cause of Action Accrues in Medical Malpractice Actions*, 5 ST. MARY'S L.J. 206 (1973).

it through the exercise of due diligence.[68] The discovery rule has received the most widespread acceptance of all the exceptions.[69]

Prior to the current crisis, the tendency of the courts was to restrict application of the act or omission rule in medical malpractice cases through adoption of the exceptions.[70] Apparently, the judiciary concluded that the danger of stale claims was outweighed by the injustice which would otherwise be visited upon patients who failed to discover their injuries through no fault of their own during the time prescribed by statute.[71] The recent malpractice crisis, however, has caused a legislative reversal of this trend through enactment of shorter limitations periods and the imposition of absolute maximum limits on when a claim may be brought.[72]

The new statutory modifications in statutes of limitations have depended in part upon the interpretation the state courts have placed on

---

68. *E.g.*, Yoshizaki v. Hilo Hosp., 50 Hawaii 150, 433 P.2d 220 (1967); Lipsey v. Michael Reese Hosp., 46 Ill. 2d 32, 262 N.E.2d 450 (1970); Gaddis v. Smith, 417 S.W.2d 577 (Tex. 1967). *See also* Comment, *Malpractice Statute of Limitations in New York: Conflict and Confusion*, 1 HOFSTRA L. REV. 276, 292 n.73 (1973).

69. By 1973, twenty-four jurisdictions had a general discovery rule. Comment, *Malpractice Statute of Limitations, supra* note 68, at 292 n.73.

70. *Compare* Lillich, *supra* note 65, at 357-60, *with* Comment, *Malpractice Statute of Limitations, supra* note 68, at 292-94.

71. *See, e.g.*, Frohs v. Greene, 253 Ore. 1, 452 P.2d 564 (1969). In *Frohs*, the Oregon Supreme Court refused to bar an action brought sixteen years after penicillin had negligently been administered to the plaintiff, a penicillin-allergic patient. The court held that the statutory period commenced on discovery of the injury giving rise to the claim, and the action was brought within two years of the discovery. *Id.* at 4, 452 P.2d at 565.

72. The following statutes have been enacted recently, modifying existing statutes of limitations: Ala. H.B. 300, § 28 (1975); ch. 2, 2d Extra. Sess., § 1.192, [1975] West's Cal. Legis. Service No. 9, at 3809 (codified at CAL. CIV. PRO. CODE § 340.5); Medical Malpractice Reform Act, ch. 75-9, § 7, [1975] West's Fla. Sess. Law Service No. 1, at 13 (codified at FLA. STAT. ANN. § 95.11(4)); Pub. Act. 79-960, § 2, [1975] Ill. L. Service No. 6, at 1617 (codified at ILL. ANN. STAT. ch. 83, § 22.1); IND. ANN. STAT. §§ 16-9.5-3-1, -2 (Burns Supp. 1975); H.F. 803, § 26, [1975] Iowa Legis. Service No. 3, at 327 (codified at IOWA CODE ANN. § 614.1); Act 808, § 1, [1975] West's La. Sess. Law Service No. 4, at 1371 (codified at LA. REV. STAT. ANN. § 9:5628); MD. CTS. & JUD. PRO. CODE ANN. § 5-109 (Supp. 1975); ch. 362, § 5, [1975] Mass. Adv. Legis. Service No. 5, at 324 (codified at MASS. ANN. LAWS ch. 231, § 60D); Pub. Act 142, [1975] West's Mich. Legis. Service No. 3, at 284 (codified at MICH. COMP. LAWS ANN. § 600.5838); NEV. REV. STAT. § 11.400 (1975); N.Y. CIV. PRAC. LAW §§ 203(f), 208, 214(6), 214-a (McKinney Supp. 1975); N.D. CENT. CODE § 28-01-18(3) (Supp. 1975); Amend. Sub. H.B. 682, § 1, [1975] Page's Ohio Legis. Bull. No. 3, at 175 (codified at OHIO REV. CODE ANN. § 2305.11); S.D. COMPILED LAWS ANN. § 15-2-15.1 (Supp. 1975); TENN. CODE ANN. § 23-3415(a) (Supp. 1975). The new Tennessee statute actually liberalizes that state's limitations period for medical malpractice claims. *Compare* Clinaid v. Pennington, 438 S.W.2d 748 (Tenn. App. 1968) (reaffirming strict application of act or omission rule), *with* TENN. CODE ANN. § 23-3415(a) (Supp. 1975).

existing statutes. In Florida, for example, the statutory discovery rule enabled plaintiffs to avoid the two-year statute of limitations indefinitely.[73] Legislation in 1975 altered this situation by placing an absolute maximum four-year limit, computed from the date of the act or omission, on all claims.[74] One exception to this limitation is made where the health care provider fraudulently conceals the injury from the patient: in that event the maximum period during which a claim must be brought is extended to seven years.[75] The legislatures of several other states have taken similar steps to prevent health care providers from being perpetually exposed to suit.[76]

In the determination of a maximum time limit on malpractice claims, a balance must be struck between the interests of the currently hard-pressed medical profession and potential malpractice claimants who are unable to discover an injury within the time limitation. The state legislatures presented with this problem have resolved it by various maximum time limits—ranging from three years[77] to six years.[78] A six-

---

73. *See* FLA. STAT. ANN. § 95.11(4)(a) (Supp. 1974). Prior to 1975 legislative enactments, the state courts of Iowa and Louisiana also permitted circumvention of a short statute of limitations period through the use of the discovery rule. The Iowa Supreme Court interpreted Iowa's accrual of cause of action statute to commence the running of the limitations period only after the negligent act or omission had been discovered. Chrischilles v. Griswold, 260 Iowa 453, 150 N.W.2d 94 (1967), *interpreting* IOWA CODE ANN. § 614.1(2) (Supp. 1974). For a similar holding regarding the pre-1975 one-year limitations period for medical malpractice actions, see Springer v. Aetna Cas. & Sur. Co., 169 So. 2d 171 (La. App. 1964), *interpreting* LA. CIV. CODE ANN. art. 3536 (West 1953).

74. Medical Malpractice Reform Act, ch. 75-9, § 7, [1975] West's Fla. Sess. Law Service No. 1, at 13 (codified at FLA. STAT. ANN. § 95.11). Similar provisions were enacted in 1975 by the Iowa and Louisiana legislatures. H.F. 803, § 26, [1975] Iowa Legis. Service No. 3, at 327 (codified at IOWA CODE ANN. § 614.1) (maximum six-year limit); Act 808, § 1, [1975] West's La. Sess. Law Service No. 4, at 1371 (codified at LA. REV. STAT. ANN. § 9:5628(A)) (three-year maximum).

75. Medical Malpractice Reform Act, ch. 75-9, § 7, [1975] West's Fla. Sess. Law Service No. 1, at 13 (codified at FLA. STAT. ANN. § 95.11(4)(b)).

76. *Compare* Springer v. Aetna Cas. & Sur. Co., 169 So. 2d 171 (La. App. 1964) (discovery rule), *with* Act 808, § 1, [1975] West's La. Sess. Law Service No. 4, at 1371 (codified at LA. REV. STAT. ANN. § 9:5628(A)) (three-year maximum), *and* Wyler v. Tripi, 25 Ohio St. 2d 164, 267 N.E.2d 419 (1971) (termination rule), *with* Amend. Sub. H.B. 682, § 1, [1975] Page's Ohio Legis. Bull. No. 3, at 175 (codified at OHIO REV. CODE ANN. § 2305.11(B)) (four-year maximum).

77. Ch. 2, 2d Extra. Sess., § 1.192, [1975] West's Cal. Legis. Service No. 9, at 3809 (codified at CAL. CIV. PRO. CODE § 340.5); Act 808, § 1, [1975] West's La. Sess. Law Service No. 4, at 1371 (codified at LA. REV. STAT. ANN. § 9:5628(A)). California's three-year maximum time limit is tempered by a number of exceptions. See notes 60-69 *supra*.

78. H.F. 803, § 26, [1975] Iowa Legis. Service No. 3, at 327 (codified at IOWA CODE ANN. § 614.1); N.D. CENT. CODE § 28-01-18(3) (Supp. 1975); S.D. COMPILED LAWS ANN. § 15-2-15(3) (1967).

year maximum time limit represents a reasonable solution[79] if there are additional provisions requiring the timely commencement of actions by plaintiffs who had knowledge, or through the exercise of due diligence should have had knowledge, of a malpractice claim. A tripartite standard requiring an early filing of a complaint if the cause of action is evident upon the act or omission, a limited time period in which to bring an action if the injury is discovered after the initial time limit, and an absolute maximum time limitation[80] should provide the medical profession with a sufficient safeguard against those claimants who have been dilatory in filing a complaint.[81]

In assessing the desirability of a modification in the statute of limitations, however, it should be remembered that the purpose of the statute is to protect defendants from stale claims, and not to insulate them from clearly meritorious ones. Accordingly, a legislature which enacts a maximum limitation period for malpractice claims should also consider certain exceptions to alleviate the harshness of the general rule in compelling cases. The situation which immediately comes to mind is that covered by the fraudulent concealment exception.[82] When a physi-

---

79. A California study of malpractice claims brought between 1951 and 1965 estimated that a four-year limit on malpractice claims, commencing with the negligent act or omission, would bar approximately nine percent of such actions. *See* Note, *A Four Year Statute of Limitations*, supra note 57, at 672. This nine percent includes not only those who have been dilatory in filing complaints, but also those who were unable to discover that they in fact had a complaint. As to the former group, imposition of the bar of the statute of limitations would present no injustice; as to the latter group, a four-year maximum rule would clearly work an injustice. To alleviate, at least partly, unfairness to those claimants who have not discovered negligently caused injuries within four years, the six-year time limit is urged. It should be noted that this limit too would work an injustice on those not discovering injuries within the designated period; however, it is clear that any statute of limitations must produce some degree of injustice. It is submitted that this unfairness to particular individuals is outweighed by the widespread societal benefit to be obtained by making the medical risk more easily insurable. Until empirical evidence is gathered to demonstrate that the injustices inherent in any absolute time restrictions are extremely frequent, such state efforts should not be discouraged.

80. Florida has instituted such a tripartite standard. Medical Malpractice Reform Act, ch. 75-9, § 7, [1975] West's Fla. Sess. Law Service No. 1, at 13 (codified at FLA. STAT. ANN. § 95.11(4)(b)). The statute requires that medical malpractice actions must be commenced within two years if the injury is detectable immediately after the negligent act or omission, or within two years after discovery of the injury, provided that in no event may an action be brought later than four years after the negligent act or omission out of which the cause of action accrued. *Id.*

81. One possible consequence of absolute time limitations could be the filing of contingency suits. In Cook County, Illinois, for instance, two malpractice actions were filed in the spring of 1975 without any knowledge of nor allegation by the plaintiff of negligence. Both cases were filed "on the contingency that a basis for a cause of action might appear at some future date." 2 COMMENTARY No. 6, at 1 (Med. Liability Comm'n, Aug. 1975).

82. See text accompanying notes 62-63 *supra*.

cian knowingly prevents his patients from discovering the negligence within the prescribed period, the physician himself is responsible for the delay in bringing the claim. Thus, it seems neither fair nor logical to allow the doctor to contend under such circumstances that the claim is stale. In this respect, the Florida provision which sets a maximum seven-year period for fraudulent concealment cases[83] is unwise. A statute of limitations should not be structured in such a way that it might be used to perpetrate a fraud. The better solution would be an enactment tolling the running of the limitations period until the fraud was, or should have been, discovered.[84] The heavy burden which a plaintiff must carry to prove fraud[85] is a sufficient limitation on actions of this type.

Another situation in which the imposition of a maximum limitations period seems inappropriate is that which has often resulted in application of the termination rule: *i.e.* where the physician has left a foreign object in the patient's body.[86] In cases of this type, the existence of the foreign body itself provides continuing, direct evidence of negligence.[87] Unlike cases founded on alleged errors in judgment, "foreign object" cases do not create opportunities for fraudulent or frivolous litigation from which physicians should be protected after the lapse of a reasonable time.[88] Accordingly, it would be proper to provide that the statutory period does not commence until the foreign object is, or should have been, discovered by the plaintiff.[89]

---

83. Medical Malpractice Reform Act, ch. 75-9, § 7, [1975] West's Fla. Sess. Law Service No. 1, at 13 (codified at FLA. STAT. ANN. § 95.11(4)(b)).

84. *See* Hinkle v. Hargens, 76 S.D. 520, 81 N.W.2d 888 (1957) (physician's fraudulent concealment of malpractice cause of action is implied exception to statute of limitations and thereby tolled its commencement); ch. 2, 2d Extra. Sess., § 1.192, [1975] West's Cal. Legis. Service No. 9, at 3810 (codified at CAL. CIV. PRO. CODE § 340.5); N.D. CENT. CODE § 28-01-18(3) (Supp. 1975).

85. To prove "affirmative" fraud, a plaintiff must show the representation of a material fact, the representation's falsity, the intent to deceive, a justifiable reliance upon the misrepresentation which induced the plaintiff to act thereon, and an injury sustained by the plaintiff by his reliance on the misrepresentation. Norton v. Curtiss, 433 F.2d 779, 793 (C.C.P.A. 1970). Some courts have alleviated this onerous burden of proof in medical malpractice actions by holding that the patient-physician relationship is confidential, thereby imposing upon the physician the duty of disclosing potential malpractice problems. *See* Hinkle v. Hargens, 76 S.D. 520, 81 N.W.2d 888 (1957).

86. See text accompanying note 66 *supra*.

87. *See* Rothman v. Silber, 90 N.J. Super. 22, 31, 216 A.2d 18, 22-23 (1966).

88. *Cf.* Owens v. White, 380 F.2d 310 (9th Cir. 1967); Young v. Fishback, 262 F.2d 469 (D.C. Cir. 1958) (holding that expert testimony not necessary to establish cause of action where physician left gauze embedded in patient's body); Rothman v. Silber, 90 N.J. Super. 22, 216 A.2d 18 (1966); Easterling v. Walton, 208 Va. 214, 156 S.E.2d 787 (1967). *But see* Note, *Tort Law, supra* note 62, at 921 (arguing that burden of proof imposed on plaintiff makes exception appropriate in negligent diagnosis).

89. The new Tennessee statute of limitations contains both fraudulent concealment

If it is made subject to these appropriate exceptions, the creation of a maximum time limit on the prosecution of medical malpractice claims should help to counteract the present malpractice crisis without doing an injustice to a substantial number of deserving plaintiffs.

Informed Consent

When a physician undertakes to treat a patient, the law requires that certain disclosures be made about that treatment. If the physician fails to make these disclosures, the patient's consent to the procedure may not be deemed "informed," and he may be entitled to recover damages for injuries sustained during the course of treatment.[90] Failure to make the required disclosure is generally regarded as a negligent tort,[91] and an action based on such an omission is independent of any negligence in the performance of the procedure. Thus, if a doctor negligently fails to inform his patient about a certain risk associated with a surgical proce-

---

and foreign body exceptions which indefinitely toll the running of the limitation period. TENN. CODE ANN. § 23-3415(a) (Supp. 1975). These provisions will do much to mitigate the apparent severity of that state's three-year maximum limit on the prosecution of claims not discovered within one year of the negligence. *See id.* See note 84 *supra* and accompanying text.

90. *See, e.g.,* Canterbury v. Spence, 464 F.2d 772 (D.C. Cir.), *cert. denied,* 409 U.S. 1064 (1972); Cobbs v. Grant, 8 Cal. 3d 229, 502 P.2d 1, 104 Cal. Rptr. 505 (1972). *See also* Salgo v. Leland Stanford Jr., Univ. Bd. of Trustees, 154 Cal. App. 2d 560, 317 P.2d 170 (1957); LOUISELL & WILLIAMS ¶ 22.01.

The precise rules used in the application of the informed consent doctrine vary from jurisdiction to jurisdiction, and the doctrine itself has been the subject of a great deal of literature. A thorough review of the doctrine's operation and its underlying objectives is beyond the scope of this Comment. An interested reader, however, will find the following material useful as a starting point for an in-depth study: *Id.* ¶¶ 22.01 -.09; Capron, *Informed Consent in Catastrophic Disease Research and Treatment,* 123 U. PA. L. REV. 340 (1974); Hagman, *The Medical Patient's Right to Know: Report on a Medical-Legal-Ethical, Empirical Study,* 17 U.C.L.A.L. REV. 758 (1970); Shartsis, *Informed Consent: Some Problems Revisited,* 51 NEB. L. REV. 527 (1972); Waltz & Scheuneman; Comment, *A Doctor's Duty to Inform,* Holland v. Sisters of Saint Joseph of Peace, 1974 UTAH L. REV. 851; Note, *Informed Consent and the Dying Patient,* 83 YALE L.J. 1632 (1974); Note, *Restructuring Informed Consent: Legal Therapy for the Doctor-Patient Relationship,* 79 YALE L.J. 1533 (1970).

91. Earlier cases adopted the theory that an intentional tort (i.e. a battery) had taken place. *See generally* Shartsis, *supra* note 90, at 545. Currently, there is some discussion concerning the evolution of a hybrid cause of action for informed consent, complete with its own rules of conduct, causation, and damages. Such a cause of action is analogized to statutory duty cases, *i.e.* where liability can be established by proving breach of a statutory duty by a defendant, and when the statute is "enacted to protect a particular class of persons." Capron, *supra* note 90, at 410. Such a hybrid cause of action appears more likely to occur in the area of experimental treatment, however. *See* 45 C.F.R. § 46 (1975) (sets forth conditions for obtaining informed consent from research subjects).

dure, and that risk materializes, the doctor may be held liable for the consequent harm to the patient, irrespective of his exercise of due care (as measured by a process standard) in the performance of the surgery.[92]

The doctrine of informed consent is grounded on the belief that "[e]very human being of adult years and sound mind has a right to determine what should be done with his own body. . . ."[93] In theory, the doctrine is a salutary one. Its application, however, has led to considerable difficulties since the existence or non-existence of the requisite knowledge has been determined entirely on a case-by-case basis. Because all the decisions are unique, they are uncertain guides to future conduct.[94] Accordingly, health care providers and their patients cannot be sure whether an informed consent has in fact been obtained until a verdict is rendered, a situation which has been most conducive to litigation.

Several state legislatures have recently attempted to clarify the rules relating to informed consent.[95] Perhaps the most appealing solution to the problem is a measure creating a presumption in favor of a written consent which meets specified statutory criteria.[96] In light of the great

---

92. See Shartsis, supra note 90, at 532.
93. Schloendorff v. Society of N.Y. Hosp., 211 N.Y. 125, 129, 105 N.E. 92, 93 (1914).
94. Compare Canterbury v. Spence, 464 F.2d 772 (D.C. Cir.), cert. denied, 409 U.S. 1064 (1972) (evidence that proposed laminectomy involved one percent possibility of ending in paralysis represented jury question as to whether such risk was required to be disclosed by surgeon obtaining consent), with Collins v. Itoh, 160 Mont. 461, 503 P.2d 36 (1972) (risk of hypoparathyroidism following thyroidectomy need not be disclosed in view of fact that only one half of one percent to three percent of patients develop this complication).
95. Medical Malpractice Reform Act, ch. 75-9, § 11, [1975] West's Fla. Sess. Law Service No. 1, at 14 (codified at FLA. STAT. ANN. § 768.132); IDAHO CODE § 39-4304 (Supp. 1975); H.F. 803, § 17, [1975] Iowa Legis. Service No. 3, at 325 (codified at IOWA CODE ANN. § 147); Act 798, [1975] West's La. Sess. Law Service No. 4, at 1354 (codified at LA. REV. STAT. ANN. §§ 1299.40-.46); NEV. REV. STAT. § 41A.110 (1975); N.Y. PUB. HEALTH LAW § 2805-d (McKinney Supp. 1975); Amend. Sub. H.B. 682, § 1, [1975] Page's Ohio Legis. Bull. No. 3, at 176 (codified at OHIO REV. CODE ANN. § 2317.54); TENN. CODE ANN. § 23-3417(a) (Supp. 1975).
96. See, e.g., Medical Malpractice Reform Act, ch. 75-9, § 11, [1975] West's Fla. Sess. Law Service No. 1, at 14 (codified at FLA. STAT. ANN. § 768.132(3)(b)); IDAHO CODE § 39-4304 (Supp. 1975); Act 529, § 1, [1975] West's La. Sess. Law Service No. 3, at 831 (codified at LA. REV. STAT. ANN. § 40:1299.40(A)); Amend. Sub. H.B. 682, § 1, [1975] Page's Ohio Legis. Bull. No. 3, at 176 (codified at OHIO REV. CODE ANN. § 2317.54). The statutory criteria range from the very broad language contained in the Florida statute, "[a] reasonable individual from the information provided by the physician . . . would have a general understanding of the procedure and medically acceptable alternative procedures . . . and substantial risks . . . inherent in the proposed treatment . . . ," Medical Malpractice Reform Act, ch. 75-9, § 11, [1975] West's Fla.

burden which the presumption can place on patient-plaintiffs,[97] however, care should be used in establishing the criteria. If they are such that an adequate disclosure is ensured, health care providers can be protected from litigation without jeopardizing the patient's right to bodily autonomy. Otherwise, the written consent form could operate as a vehicle for fraud and deceit.

Adequate disclosure would seem to require a discussion with the patient concerning at least three groups of facts: the inherent and potential dangers of the proposed treatment; the alternatives to the proposed treatment, if any; and the likely results of foregoing treatment.[98] It is equally important that the disclosure be in layman's terms so that the patient will understand what the doctor is saying.[99] In addition, the patient should be made aware of the legal implications of the consent form before he signs it.[100]

Sess. Law Service No. 1, at 14 (codified at FLA. STAT. ANN. § 768.132(3)(b)), to the very specific criteria of the Ohio statute which requires, among other things, that the consent form set forth the nature and purpose of the procedure along with the known risks of death, brain damage, quadriplegia, and other injuries. Amend. Sub. H.B. 682, § 1, [1975] Page's Ohio Legis. Bull. No. 3, at 176 (codified at OHIO REV. CODE ANN. § 2317.54).

97. Legislation proposed in Arizona, Ariz. H.B. 2418 (1975) (not enacted); Florida, Medical Malpractice Reform Act, ch. 75-9, § 11, [1975] West's Fla. Sess. Law Service No. 1, at 14 (codified at FLA. STAT. ANN. § 768.132(4)(a)); Iowa, H.F. 803, § 17, [1975] Iowa Legis. Service No. 1, at 325 (codified at IOWA CODE ANN. § 147); Nevada, NEV. REV. STAT. § 41A.110 (1975); and Pennsylvania, Pa. H.B. 805, § 13 (1975) (not approved), would create a conclusive presumption as to the validity of the written consent. Such a presumption cannot be overcome by proof to the contrary. See MCCORMICK ON EVIDENCE §§ 340-45 (1972).

98. Canterbury v. Spence, 464 F.2d 772, 787 (D.C. Cir.), cert. denied, 409 U.S. 1064 (1972). See also 2 LOUISELL & WILLIAMS ¶ 22.01 (suggesting six factors appropriate for disclosure); Note, Restructuring Informed Consent, supra note 90, at 1561 (listing nine facts about which disclosure is desirable).

99. Capron, supra note 90, at 413-14; see Amend. Sub. H.B. 682, § 1, [1975] Page's Ohio Legis. Bull. No. 3, at 176 (codified at OHIO REV. CODE ANN. § 2317.54(D)) (attempt to set forth a consent form employing simple language). The Ohio statute also states that a written consent will not be considered valid unless "the person executing the consent was . . . able to communicate effectively in spoken and written English or any other language in which the consent is written." Amend. Sub. H.B. 682, § 1, [1975] Page's Ohio Legis. Bull. No. 3, at 176 (codified at OHIO REV. CODE ANN. § 2317.54). Several other states, including Florida, Medical Malpractice Reform Act, ch. 75-9, § 11, [1975] West's Fla. Sess. Law Service No. 1, at 14 (codified at FLA. STAT. ANN. § 768.132(3)(b)); Georgia, Ga. S.B. 372, § 4 (1975) (not enacted); Illinois, Ill. H.B. 3124, § 3 (1975) (tabled); and North Carolina, N.C.S.B. 902, § 1(b) (1975) (referred to Judiciary Comm.); N.C.H.B. 1239, § 1(b) (1975) (reported unfavorably, referred to Rules Comm.), imply that the physician must make his disclosure in such a manner that a reasonable person would obtain a general understanding of the procedure.

100. Of all the measures examined, both proposed and enacted, only the proposed amendments to the Arizona bill, Ariz. H.B. 2418 (1975), would require the doctor to

Thought should also be given to the circumstances under which a health care provider is not under a duty to disclose. A number of exceptions to the informed consent doctrine are currently recognized. These exceptions include certain emergency treatments,[101] common knowledge,[102] unknown risk,[103] and waiver.[104] For the most part, the need for utility of these exceptions is obvious. More troublesome questions arise when a doctor decides not to disclose information because he believes that such disclosure would be inimical to the patient's well-being.

The latter situation has been referred to as the "therapeutic exception."[105] This exception, however, appears to be subsumed in the test which traditionally has been applied to determine a physician's duty to disclose.[106] That is, the duty to disclose is established by the custom and practice of physicians in the same locality.[107] Recognition of the

---

inform the patient of the nature and implications of the consent form. *See* Arizona Legislative Council, Research Division, Summary Analysis of H.B. 2418 (as Proposed to be Amended, Apr. 18, 1975). See note 97 *supra* and accompanying text.

101. *See* PROSSER § 18; Comment, *Informed Consent for the Terminal Patient*, 27 BAYLOR L. REV. 111, 117 (1975); Note, *Advise and Consent in Medicine: A Look at the Doctrine of Informed Consent*, 16 N.Y.L.F. 863, 874 (1970). Several of the state informed consent measures, as proposed or as enacted, specifically provide for this exception to the informed consent doctrine. *See, e.g.*, Ala. Sub. H.B. 300, § 12 (1975); Ga. S.B. 372, § 3 (1975) (not enacted); IDAHO CODE § 39-4303(c) (Supp. 1975); Act 798, § 1, [1975] West's La. Sess. Law Service No. 4, at 1354-55 (codified at LA. REV. STAT. ANN. § 40:1299.44); NEV. REV. STAT. § 41A.110 (1975).

102. Shartsis, *supra* note 90, at 529; Comment, *A Doctor's Duty to Inform*, *supra* note 90, at 854 & n.22.

103. Waltz & Scheuneman 634. The authors suggest that the threshold question under these circumstances is whether the decision to use an innovative theory with unknown risks was reasonable in light of the physician's level of knowledge. *Id.*

104. Cobbs v. Grant, 8 Cal. 3d 229, 245, 502 P.2d 1, 12, 104 Cal. Rptr. 505, 516 (1972); Hagman, *supra* note 90, at 785. Several of the state informed consent measures, both proposed and enacted, allow the patient to waive his right to disclosure. Ohio, for example, provides for a partial waiver of disclosure in its model consent form; that is, the patient may indicate, after a general disclosure, whether or not he wants a more detailed description of the proposed treatment and its potential hazards. Amend. Sub. H.B. 682, § 1, [1975] Page's Ohio Legis. Bull. No. 3, at 176 (codified at OHIO REV. CODE ANN. § 2317.54(D)). Pennsylvania considered proposals for written waiver of disclosure. Pa. S.B. 907, § 23 (1975) (not approved); Pa. H.B. 1129, § 402 (1975) (not approved).

105. *See* Canterbury v. Spence, 464 F.2d 772, 789 (D.C. Cir.), *cert. denied*, 409 U.S. 1064 (1972); Salgo v. Leland Stanford Jr., Univ. Bd. of Trustees, 154 Cal. App. 2d 560, 578, 317 P.2d 170, 181 (1957); 2 LOUISELL & WILLIAMS ¶ 22.02; Waltz & Scheuneman 642.

106. *See* 2 LOUISELL & WILLIAMS ¶ 22.03.

107. Waltz & Scheuneman 628, 636. A number of the recently proposed or enacted informed consent statutes apply this standard of care. *See, e.g.*, Medical Malpractice Reform Act, ch. 75-9, § 11, [1975] West's Fla. Sess. Law Service No. 1, at 14 (codified at FLA. STAT. ANN. § 768.132(3)(a)); Ga. S.B. 372, § 4 (1975) (not enacted); Ill.

therapeutic exception is essential; however, since each patient's mental and physical condition will differ, it does not seem that a legislature is capable of establishing clear and definite standards as to the circumstances under which a doctor may properly decide to withhold information from his patient. One possible solution to the problem of indefiniteness is to provide that this exception may be raised as a defense only if the physician makes a full disclosure to a relative of the patient and explains to the relative the necessity for not divulging all the facts to the patient. Although a consent obtained from a relative is not a valid consent when the patient is competent to act and has not authorized the relative to act for him, a provision of this sort would operate both to prevent doctors from asserting the exception only as an afterthought and to strengthen the physician's position as to his good faith belief that nondisclosure was necessary.[108]

On a more general level, the traditional "same locality" test for determining the duty of disclosure has been sharply criticized. It has been said that placing the patient's right to be informed entirely within the discretion of the medical profession bypasses any inquiry into the actual importance the undisclosed information would have for the patient.[109] Additional arguments advanced against the same locality rule are that a discernible professional standard of disclosure does not exist and that the rule places a great burden on the plaintiff since it requires the use of expert testimony which may be hard to obtain.[110]

As an alternative to the same locality rule, it has been suggested that the courts should independently examine the patient's expectations and need for information in fixing the health care provider's duty to disclose.[111] Under this alternate approach an objective test would be applied to determine whether particular information should be disclosed.[112] Information would be material (*i.e.* disclosure would be

---

H.B. 3124, § 3 (1975) (tabled); N.C.S.B. 902, § 1(c) (1975) (referred to Judiciary Comm.); N.C.H.B. 1239, § (1c) (1975) (reported unfavorably, referred to Rules Comm.).

108. *Cf.* 2 LOUISELL & WILLIAMS ¶ 22.09, at 594-64; Shartsis, *supra* note 90, at 541, 543; Comment, *Informed Consent of Patient: Duty to Inform Patient to Be Established by Expert Medical Testimony*, 48 WASH. L. REV. 697 (1973).

109. Note, *Legal Therapy, supra* note 90, at 1565-67.

110. Waltz & Scheuneman 637; Comment, *A Doctor's Duty to Inform, supra* note 90, at 853; Note, *A New Standard for Informed Consent in Medical Malpractice Cases—The Role of the Expert Witness*, 18 ST. LOUIS U.L.J. 256, 260 (1973).

111. *See* Waltz & Scheuneman 639-40.

112. One commentator rejects the use of an objective test as irrelevant to the question of the individual's informational needs. He urges that a subjective test is required—what the particular patient, be he rational or irrational, would have wanted to know. Capron, *supra* note 90, at 408-10. While a subjective standard may be better suited to the type of

required) if a reasonable person in the patient's position would attach importance to it in reaching the decision whether or not to submit to the proposed treatment.[113] As far as guidance for a physician's conduct is concerned, the alternative approach does not seem to be a significant improvement over the same locality rule: under the latter the physician must decide whether his decisions are in accord with the professional standards of the community; under the former he must ascertain what information a reasonable patient would desire. Under either approach the answer is not free from doubt. However, application of the "reasonable patient" test would benefit the patient-plaintiff in that he would not be required to present expert medical testimony on the prevailing standard of disclosure in the local medical community. Rather, the question of materiality and reasonableness would be left for the jury.[114] Moreover, using the viewpoint of the reasonable patient as the standard for disclosure could encourage greater communication between doctor and patient, and thus might work indirectly to alleviate the malpractice crisis.[115]

Regardless of the approach to the doctrine of informed consent

---

major and experimental treatment required by catastrophic diseases, the objective standard appears more realistic in the context of routine medical care. See Canterbury v. Spence, 464 F.2d 772, 787 (D.C. Cir.), cert. denied, 409 U.S. 1064 (1972); Cooper v. Roberts, 220 Pa. Super. 260, 267-68, 286 A.2d 647, 650 (1971); Waltz v. Scheuneman 639-40.

A form of the "reasonableness standard" can be found in a Pennsylvania proposal, which provides: "A consent to medical treatment in connection with which is given a general disclosure sufficient to alert a reasonable person as to the nature and hazards of the proposed medical treatment . . . shall be considered a valid medical consent." Pa. S.B. 907, § 23 (1975) (not approved).

113. Waltz & Scheuneman 638-40. The "reasonable patient" test suggested by Waltz and Scheuneman was applied in Canterbury v. Spence, 464 F.2d 772, 787 (D.C. Cir.), cert. denied, 409 U.S. 1064 (1972). See also Fogal v. Genesee Hosp., 41 App. Div. 2d 468, 473, 344 N.Y.S.2d 552, 559 (1973); Wilkinson v. Vesey, 110 R.I. 606, 625, 295 A.2d 676, 688 (1972); Knapp & Huff, *Emerging Trends in the Physician's Duty to Disclose: An Update of* Canterbury v. Spence, 3 J. LEGAL MED. 41 (Jan. 1975). Application of the "reasonable patient" test increases the plaintiff-patient's burden of showing proximate cause: that is, his injury must have resulted from the occurrence of the material undisclosed risk. Waltz & Scheuneman 646.

114. Canterbury v. Spence, 464 F.2d 772, 792, 795 (D.C. Cir.), cert. denied, 409 U.S. 1064 (1972); Fogal v. Genesee Hosp., 41 App. Div. 2d 468, 473, 344 N.Y.S.2d 552, 559 (1973); Wilkinson v. Vesey, 110 R.I. 606, 625-26, 295 A.2d 676, 688 (1972).

115. See generally Capron, supra note 90, at 349 (characterizing the doctrine as a powerful force for "personalization in technical decisions made in the modern medical context"). It has been suggested that the well-informed patient is least likely to sue his physician. Suit is more likely to result where the patient has unrealistic expectations concerning treatment which have not been dispelled. Annas, *Medical Malpractice Litigation Under National Health Insurance: Essential or Expendable?*, 1975 DUKE L.J. 1335.

that is taken by each state legislature, it should be recognized that a balance must be struck between the health care provider's needs for certainty and ease of administration and the patient's need for a full and individualized disclosure. Such a result may be reached by balancing features that favor the health care provider against those that favor the patient, *i.e.* the reasonable patient test could be paired with a presumption in favor of the validity of written consents.[116] Therefore, it appears possible for the legislatures to bring, through thoughtful drafting, greater clarity and certainty to the law of informed consent without creating any substantial injustice to malpractice plaintiffs.

Contingent Fees

The contingent fee system[117] employed by many plaintiff's lawyers has long been a subject of controversy.[118] Its proponents contend that the system enables one with meritorious claims but limited resources to obtain a lawyer who will put forth his best efforts on the client's behalf.[119] Those who oppose the contingent fee system argue that it is debasing to the legal profession,[120] tempts attorneys to become partners to the controversy rather than act as officers of the court,[121] and encourages lawyers to take action adverse to the best interests of their clients.[122]

---

116. The possibilities for intentional and unintentional misuse of written consent forms are enormous. Thus, the well-drawn statute should emphasize not only the certainties that are brought to the law of informed consent but the duties imposed upon the physician to the patient, *i.e.* the duty to explain the risks involved, the alternatives to the proposed treatment, and the consequences of refusing or postponing treatment.

117. A contingent fee is an arrangement by which an attorney is compensated by the receipt of a specified percentage of the recovery. Hence, if there is no recovery the attorney gets no fee. *See generally* F. MACKINNON, CONTINGENT FEES FOR LEGAL SERVICES 62-66 (1964).

118. As early as 1908, the New York State Bar Association considered actions to remedy abuses of the contingent fee system. 31 N.Y. St. B. Ass'n Rep. 99-136 (1908). *See also* Buckley v. Surface Transp. Corp., 277 App. Div. 224, 98 N.Y.S.2d 576 (1950); Radin, *Maintenance by Champertry*, 24 CALIF. L. REV. 48 (1935).

119. *See, e.g.,* Hughes, *The Contingent Fee Contract in Massachusetts*, 43 BOSTON U.L. REV. 1 (1963); Radin, *Contingent Fees in California*, 28 CALIF. L. REV. 587 (1940); Schwartz & Mitchell, *An Economic Analysis of the Contingent Fee in Personal-Injury Litigation*, 22 STAN. L. REV. 1125 (1970). A second argument advanced by proponents of the contingent fee system is that the mechanism permits the client to shift some of the risk of legal expenses to the attorney. *See generally* Hughes, *supra* at 8; Radin, *supra* at 589.

120. F. MACKINNON, *supra* note 117, at 4. *See also* Baruch v. Giblin, 122 Fla. 59, 63, 164 So. 831, 833 (1935).

121. Comment, *Are Contingent Fees Ethical Where Client Is Able to Pay a Retainer?*, 20 OHIO ST. L.J. 329, 339 n.53 (1959).

122. When a lawyer acquires an interest in a lawsuit through a contingent fee, his interest and judgment may conflict with the client's interest over such things as whether

Contingent fees have recently come under fire from physicians who believe them to be a significant contributing factor in the medical malpractice crisis.[123] The physicians maintain that contingent fees prompt lawyers to pursue claims of dubious merit in the hope of securing a large verdict from a sympathetic jury, and to seek irresponsibly high recoveries for legitimate claims.[124]

Some state legislatures have accepted the physicians' arguments and have taken actions designed to limit attorney's fees in malpractice cases.[125] Assuming that some form of regulation is desired,[126] the need

---

to accept an offer of settlement. F. MACKINNON, *supra* note 117, at 5. The attorney may be tempted to settle the case as quickly as possible since this will give him the highest possible ratio of dollars to hours expended. Comment, *Are Contingent Fees Ethical, supra* note 121, at 339 n.53.

123. MEDICAL MALPRACTICE REPORT 2, 32; *see* Bloom, *Malpractice—The Mess That Must be Ended*, 106 READER'S DIGEST 79 (Apr. 1975); Hirsch, *Malpractice Crisis: Fact or Fiction*, 80 CASE & COMMENT 3, 6 (July/Aug. 1975). At least one author has contended that blaming the legal profession for the malpractice crisis is similar to blaming the fire department for arson. Annas, *supra* note 115, at 1344.

124. MEDICAL MALPRACTICE REPORT 33. Some contend that the opposite is true, that the contingent fee structure actually compels attorneys to screen out claims which are spurious or for which recovery appears less than probable. Annas, *supra* note 115, at 1344; *see* Dietz, Baird & Berul, *supra* note 50, at 128.

125. The following statutes regulating attorney contingent fees have been enacted: Medical Injury Compensation Reform Act, ch. 2, 2d Extra. Sess., § 1.185, [1975] West's Cal. Legis. Service No. 9, at 3808 (codified at CAL. BUS. & PROF. CODE § 6146); IDAHO CODE § 39-4213 (Supp. 1975); IND. ANN. STAT. § 16-9.5-5-1 (Burns Supp. 1975); H.F. 803, § 25, [1975] Iowa Legis. Service No. 3, at 327; Amend. Sub. H.B. 682, § 7, [1975] Page's Ohio Legis. Bull. No. 3, at 183; ch. 796, § 25, [1975] Ore. Laws 2319; TENN. CODE ANN. § 23-3419 (Supp. 1975); ch. 37, [1975] West's Wis. Legis. Service No. 1, at 41 (codified at WIS. STAT. ANN. § 655.013).

At least one commentator has argued that measures designed to limit contingent fees violate the fourteenth amendment's guarantees of due process and equal protection. *See* Note, *New Jersey's Maximum Contingent Fee Schedule: The Validity of Rule 1:21-7*, 5 RUTGERS-CAMDEN L.J. 534 (1974). *But see* American Trial Lawyers Ass'n v. New Jersey Supreme Court, 126 N.J. Super. 577, 316 A.2d 19, *aff'd*, 66 N.J. 258, 330 A.2d 350 (1974); Gair v. Peck, 6 N.Y.2d 97, 160 N.E.2d 43, 188 N.Y.S.2d 491 (1959), *cert. denied*, 361 U.S. 374 (1960) (upholding New York's restrictions on contingent fees); *cf.* Yeiser v. Dysart, 267 U.S. 540 (1925) (limits on contingent fees in statutorily created rights of action do not violate fourteenth amendment).

126. A frequently advanced argument for regulation of contingent fees is the apparent overpricing of services of the medical malpractice bar. *See* MEDICAL MALPRACTICE REPORT 32 (feeling of physicians that under contingent fee system lawyers seek irresponsibly high judgments). This argument is fallacious. A study conducted by the Health, Education and Welfare Secretary's Commission on Medical Malpractice compared the hourly fee of medical malpractice defense attorneys with the "effective hourly fee" for plaintiff attorneys. Dietz, Baird & Berul, *supra* note 50, at 115. The authors found the mean fee for defense attorneys to be forty-seven dollars per hour compared to sixty-three dollars per hour for plaintiff attorneys. *Id.* This difference between the hourly rates is not unconscionable when the inherent risk of no recovery and hence no fee is considered. "[T]he results . . . show that the plaintiff lawyers 'effective hourly

to minimize the tendency of the present system to distort malpractice recoveries[127] must be balanced against the need to provide access to the compensatory mechanism for the malpractice plaintiff who is unable to afford the cost of an attorney.

Three approaches have been taken to regulate the use of contingent fees in medical malpractice cases. One is to empower the state courts to determine the reasonableness of attorneys' fees.[128] The advantage of this approach is that it permits an individualized determination of the propriety of each fee by an impartial body which is well acquainted with the details of the particular case. But, without a set of fixed standards, courts are loathe to alter the contingent fee arrangements between lawyers and their clients.[129] Therefore, it is doubtful if this form of regulation can be effective.

A second approach is to promulgate a fixed percentage ceiling for contingent fees in medical malpractice actions.[130] This approach sacri-

---

fee' is *not* excessively large at least in comparison to normal defense lawyer hourly fees . . . ." *Id.* at 116 (emphasis in original).

127. Malpractice recoveries may be distorted in two ways. First is the attorney's overdramatization of a plaintiff's injuries. For example, a malpractice plaintiff with $50,000 in additional medical bills and lost work time and a legitimate pain and suffering claim of $50,000 may receive a jury verdict of $200,000. The $100,000 "premium" may be a result of the attorney's playing upon the jury's emotions. This, of course, is the standard scenario painted by critics of the system. It should be noted, however, that the ascertainment of "legitimate" damages without reference to the jury's findings is extremely difficult.

The second way in which a recovery may be distorted is a jury's conscious inclusion of legal fees in the recovery. This inflated verdict is the result of the increasing popular awareness of the contingent fee arrangement in tort litigation. Morris, *Liability for Pain and Suffering*, 59 COLUM. L. REV. 476, 477 (1959). *But cf.* Kalven, *The Jury, the Law, and the Personal Injury Damage Award*, 19 OHIO ST. L.J. 158, 176-77 (1958). Thus, if the jury believes the plaintiff should receive $100,000 for injuries sustained, it might render a verdict for $150,000 and thereby offset the attorney's presumed one-third fee.

128. *E.g.*, Iowa H.F. 803, § 25, [1975] Iowa Legis. Service No. 3, at 327 (codified at IOWA CODE ANN. § 147).

129. New York courts have exercised control of attorney's fees since 1843 and have been permitted to discipline attorneys who overcharge since 1909. Comment, *Lawyer's Tightrope—Use and Abuse of Fees*, 41 CORNELL L.Q. 683, 693 n.71, 698 (1956). Despite these powers, contingent fees continued to be abused, necessitating the adoption of more objective standards. *See* INSTITUTE OF JUDICIAL ADMINISTRATION, CONTINGENT FEES IN PERSONAL INJURY AND WRONGFUL DEATH ACTIONS IN THE UNITED STATES 11-13 (1957); RESEARCH MEMORANDUM SERIES NO. 10: CONTINGENT FEES IN CLAIMS AND ACTIONS FOR PERSONAL INJURY AND WRONGFUL DEATH (RULE 4) (American Bar Foundation 1956). See authorities collected in note 118 *supra*.

130. *See* IDAHO CODE § 39-4213 (Supp. 1975); ch. 796, § 25, [1975] Ore. Laws 2319. The Tennessee legislature has combined this approach with the first by granting the court power to determine what fee shall be awarded an attorney who represents a medical malpractice claimant on a contingent fee basis, but limiting the maximum fee to one third of the recovery. TENN. CODE ANN. § 23-3419 (Supp. 1975). It seems likely

fices the flexibility of the first and thereby acquires the advantages of simplicity and efficacy. Nevertheless, such ceilings have disadvantages which make them unattractive as a regulatory alternative. The main disadvantage lies in the fact that a flat percentage ceiling will make it quite difficult for those having meritorious small claims to find capable counsel. The amount of work required to secure a recovery bears no direct relation to the size of the recovery.[131] Thus, if lawyers are not allowed to take a larger percentage of small claims, it will be economically infeasible for them to handle such cases.[132] The contingent fee system already operates to discourage the prosecution of meritorious, small-recovery cases.[133] A flat percentage ceiling on the fee a lawyer can charge would only exacerbate this situation. Another disadvantage lies in the size of the fee which would be received by a successful attorney when a large verdict is returned. For example, if $300,000 were awarded in a state having a thirty-three and one-third percent flat ceiling on attorney's fees, the plaintiff's lawyer would receive $100,000. While it might be argued that the prosect of such a fee would stimulate a lawyer to the acme of trial advocacy, the very purpose of the regulation was to prevent compensation of this magnitude. Therefore, flat percentage ceilings are too crude a measure: they fail to provide sufficient compensation in some cases and fail to prevent excessive compensation in others.

The third approach is to adopt a sliding scale which uses the amount of recovery as the factor determining the percentage fee paid to the attorney.[134] The courts of several states have already adopted rules based on this idea to limit contingent fees in all tort actions.[135] For example, in New Jersey an attorney is permitted to receive fifty percent

---

that this measure will operate in the same manner as a flat thirty-three and one-third percent ceiling on contingent fees. Cf. note 129 *supra*.

131. *See* F. MACKINNON, *supra* note 117, at 164, *citing* WASSERVOGEL, REPORT, FINDINGS AND RECOMMENDATION IN THE MATTER OF THE HEARINGS ORDERED BY THE APPELLATE DIVISIONS OF THE SUPREME COURT IN AND FOR THE FIRST AND SECOND JUDICIAL DEPARTMENTS REGARDING A PROPOSED RULE TO LIMIT COMPENSATION OF PLAINTIFFS' ATTORNEYS IN PERSONAL INJURY AND WRONGFUL DEATH ACTIONS (1955).

132. F. MACKINNON, *supra* note 117, at 164.

133. MEDICAL MALPRACTICE REPORT 33. The Secretary's Commission on Medical Malpractice viewed this as "a wholly undesirable and unfair result of the system." *Id.*

134. Such an approach was recommended by the Secretary's Commission on Medical Malpractice. *Id.* at 34-35.

135. See note 136 *infra* and accompanying text. The Ohio General Assembly has directed that state's Supreme Court to promulgate a schedule of "graduated maximum contingent fees" that an attorney representing a medical malpractice plaintiff may recover. Amend. Sub. H.B. 682, § 7, [1975] Page's Ohio Legis. Bull. No. 3, at 183. The legislature also "requested" that no fees in excess of thirty-three and one-third percent be permitted in cases which are not appealed. *Id.*

of the first $1,000 recovered; forty percent of the next $2,000; thirty-three and one-third percent on the next $50,000; and ten percent on any amount over $100,000.[136] Legislation enacted last year in California[137] limits an attorney in a medical malpractice case to forty percent of the first $50,000 recovered, one third of the next $50,000, one fourth of the next $100,000, and ten percent of any recovery in excess of $200,000.[138]

It is apparent that sliding scale limitations remove some of the difficulties which inhere in flat percentage ceilings. The higher percentage for low recoveries will encourage attorneys to accept meritorious small claims. At the same time, the decrease in the percentage which may be charged as the amount of recovery increases prevents excessive compensation: under the New Jersey system a $300,000 damage award will produce $46,967 in attorney's fees. One weakness in a system of this type is that attorneys may be induced to settle malpractice cases for a smaller sum than could be won at trial, thereby securing a higher percentage fee and maximizing profits.[139] The risk of this sort of behavior must be accepted, however, if one wishes to encourage the prosecution of meritorious low-recovery claims.[140] It should not be forgotten that a client who believes his case has been settled in bad faith can bring a malpractice action against his lawyer;[141] a person who

---

136. N.J. Sup. Ct. R. 1:21-7(c) (adopted 1971). Where the amount recovered is for the benefit of an infant or incompetent and the case is settled, the fee on any amount up to $50,000 shall not exceed twenty-five percent. *Id.* The New York courts have also adopted a sliding scale to limit contingent fees. *See* N.Y. COURT RULES § 603.7(e) (McKinney 1975).

Both the New Jersey and New York schedules have been held constitutional. *See* American Trial Lawyers Ass'n v. New Jersey Supreme Court, 126 N.J. Super. 577, 316 A.2d 19, *aff'd*, 66 N.J. 258, 330 A.2d 350 (1974); Gair v. Peck, 6 N.Y.2d 97, 160 N.E.2d 43, 188 N.Y.S.2d 491 (1959), *cert. denied*, 361 U.S. 374 (1960). See note 125 *supra.*

137. Medical Injury Compensation Reform Act, ch. 1, 2d Extra. Sess., § 24.2, [1975] West's Cal. Legis. Service No. 9, at 3789 (codified at CAL. BUS. & PROF. CODE § 6146).

138. *Id.*

139. An example may be helpful to illustrate this point. Under the new California scale, a plaintiff's attorney could retain a $20,000 fee for a $50,000 recovery. On the recovery between $50,000 and $100,000, however, the attorney is entitled only to one third, or a maximum of $16,667. Where a defendant is prepared to settle for $50,000, even a successful continuation of the litigation would yield a lower return to the attorney, and thus his decision whether or not to advise his client to settle may be influenced toward settlement. Of course, a plaintiff's attorney always must balance the expense and risk of proceeding to trial against the certainty of a settlement offer; however, where his own returns are diminished proportionately as recoveries increase, the danger of settlement pressure is greater.

140. *Cf.* Franklin, Chanin & Mark, *Accidents, Money and the Law: A Study of the Economics of Personal Injury Litigation,* 61 COLUM. L. REV. 1, 13-14 (1961).

141. *Cf.* Cohen v. Goldman, 85 R.I. 434, 132 A.2d 414 (1957); Haughey, *Lawyers'*

cannot get a lawyer to handle his case has no recourse whatsoever. In addition, the sliding scale can be structured to reduce the percentages if the case is settled.[142] When a provision of the latter type is included, it would also be wise to allow larger percentages for cases which are appealed. Furthermore, if the attorney can demonstrate to the court that there are extraordinary circumstances which make the scheduled compensation inadequate he should be permitted to charge a higher fee.[143] Such a provision would introduce a degree of flexibility without significantly undercutting the purpose of the schedule.

By adopting a sliding scale of percentage limits on attorney's fees in malpractice cases, a state legislature can thus ensure that patients with meritorious claims will be able to obtain representation while at the same time reducing the possibility that health care providers will continue to be subject to inflated damage recoveries.

Collateral Source Benefits

According to the "collateral source rule," any benefits received by an injured party from sources other than the tortfeasor may not be used to offset the damage recovery.[144] Thus, in the medical malpractice context, a patient-plaintiff is entitled to recover the full amount that a jury considers adequate compensation, without reference to any payments he has received from wage continuation plans, government benefits, insurance proceeds, or gratuitous payments from family and friends. The rule has been accepted by the courts of almost every state,[145] and has been applied both as a rule of evidence and as a rule of damages.[146] Thus, the rule both excludes evidence of collateral source benefits and prevents any reduction of damages because of such payments.

The most common rationale for the collateral source rule is that a reduction in a recovery by the amount of collateral payments would cause the deterrent impact of tort actions to be diminished,[147] or lost

---

Malpractice: A Comparative Appraisal, 48 NOTRE DAME LAW. 888, 902-03 (1973). See generally Annot., 30 A.L.R.2d 944 (1953); Annot., 66 A.L.R. 107 (1930).

142. Such a provision would provide a powerful settlement disincentive to counter the influences noted in text. It would, however, create some of the same problems which the flat percentage fee systems do, *i.e.* discouragement of a settlement where such might be the most suitable course of action for the plaintiff.

143. *Cf.* N.Y. COURT RULES, § 603.7(e)(4) (McKinney 1975).

144. *See, e.g.*, Althorfe v. Wolfe, 22 N.Y. 355 (1860) (wrongful death award not diminished in amount of insurance proceeds); Moceri & Messina, *The Collateral Source Rule in Personal Injury Litigation*, 7 GONZAGA L. REV. 310 (1972).

145. Moceri & Messina, *supra* note 144, at 315.

146. *Id.* at 310.

147. For a discussion of the deterrent aspect of tort law, see PROSSER 23; Williams,

entirely.[148] For certain types of collateral source benefits, *e.g.*, insurance, an additional rationale has been advanced: since the plaintiff has paid for the benefit, his foresight should not lessen the tortfeasor's liability.[149]

The recent medical malpractice crisis has caused some legislatures to re-examine the basis of the collateral source rule,[150] and statutes have been enacted which either make evidence of collateral payments admissible at trial or require a reduction in damages by the amount of such payments.[151] These actions appear to be desirable since serious questions can be raised concerning the reasons for the rule's existence. First, it is most unlikely that anticipation of the abatement of damages by collateral source benefits would seriously weaken the deterrent effect of civil liability.[152] In the context of health care providers, collateral sources are not likely to reduce very large recoveries by any significant degree, and will do nothing to temper the adverse publicity which accompanies malpractice litigation or ease the threat of license revocation.[153] Second, it is likely that one pays for collateral source benefits,

---

The Aims of the Law of Torts, 4 CURRENT LEGAL PROB. 137 (1951). Whether there is a substantial deterrent effect in medical malpractice actions is not certain. *Compare* Brook, Brutoco & Williams, *supra* note 29, at 1220, *with* Havighurst, *supra* note 30, at 1235.

148. *See, e.g.*, Grayson v. Wilkins, 256 F.2d 61, 65 (10th Cir. 1958) (suggesting that a wrongdoer should not be relieved of the full responsibility of his wrongdoing, but should be held fully accountable for the harm he has caused). To say, however, that the wrongdoer should be held liable for the harm he has caused simply begs the question. The very issue in controversy is what constitutes the "harm" to be compensated. *See* Note, *Unreason in the Law of Damages: The Collateral Source Rule*, 77 HARV. L. REV. 741 (1964).

149. Moceri & Messina, *supra* note 144, at 315.

150. *See, e.g.*, Medical Injury Compensation Reform Act, ch. 1, 2d Extra. Sess., § 24.5, [1975] West's Cal. Legis. Service No. 9, at 3790 (codified at CAL. CIV. CODE § 3333.1); IDAHO CODE § 39-4210 (Supp. 1975); Iowa H.F. 803, § 16, [1975] Iowa Legis. Service No. 3, at 325 (codified at IOWA CODE ANN. § 147); N.Y. PUB. HEALTH LAW § 4010 (McKinney Supp. 1975); Amend. Sub. H.B. 682, [1975] Page's Ohio Legis. Bull. No. 3, at 175 (codified at OHIO REV. CODE ANN. § 2305.27); Act 111, § 602, [1975] Purdon's Pa. Legis. Service No. 2, at 301 (codified at PA. STAT. ANN. tit. 43, § 1301.602); TENN. CODE ANN. § 23-3418 (Supp. 1975); *cf.* MEDICAL MALPRACTICE REPORT 34.

151. *See, e.g.*, H.F. 803, § 16 [1975] Iowa Legis. Service No. 3, at 325 (codified at IOWA CODE ANN. § 147) (damages for personal injury shall not include present or future damages to extent reimbursed by certain collateral sources); Amend. Sub. H.B. 682, [1975] Page's Ohio Legis. Bull. No. 3, at 175 (codified at OHIO REV. CODE ANN. § 2307.42(B)) (complaint must list certain collateral source benefits).

152. James, *Social Insurance and Tort Liability: The Problem of Alternative Remedies*, 27 N.Y.U.L. REV. 537, 548 (1952). *See also* Schwartz, *The Collateral-Source Rule*, 41 BOSTON U.L. REV. 348 (1961).

153. The deterrent effect will become more substantial if and when the medical profession adopts more effective means of disciplining members who commit malpractice.

e.g., insurance premiums, not to provide for a double recovery, but rather to provide security for injuries which might befall him.[154] To allow him double recovery is to give him more than his due. Moreover, the objective of a damage award is to restore the plaintiff to the status quo ante.[155] Hence, any recovery in a malpractice action should be the amount necessary to compensate the plaintiff for his losses. These losses do not include the damages for which the plaintiff has already been reimbursed through collateral source benefits.

The validity of the rationale underlying the collateral source rule is, then, questionable at best. In contrast, the loss to society of paying one person twice for the same injury is very real. Thus, some change in the application of the rule seems appropriate in the medical malpractice context. Two alternatives suggest themselves. A state legislature might eliminate the rule, as several have done,[156] and permit the reduction of malpractice recoveries by the amount of first-party insurance or other benefits. Alternatively, the collateral sources themselves might be compensated by the malpractice insurer. Under the latter approach, an injured plaintiff who is awarded a $100,000 recovery would also have the recovery reduced by his collateral source benefits, for example, $20,000. The insurer of the defendant provider, however, would not be relieved of that part of the recovery. Rather, the $20,000 would be payable to the source of the $20,000, typically a first-party medical insurer or disability insurer. Although this approach apparently has not been adopted by statute, it has been urged by commentators.[157]

The choice between the two approaches would depend, of course, on the legislative policy valuation of the deterrent impact of a malprac-

---

A number of states have enacted legislation expanding disciplinary authority in instances of medical malpractice. *See* Brook, Brutoco & Williams, *supra* note 29, at 1224-25 (statutes collected in article).

154. An injured party is not deprived of the benefit of his foresight, because the object of his actions (to shift the risk of loss to a third party) has been realized. To allow recovery both from the collateral source and from the tortfeasor is to grant the injured party more than he had provided for, with the resultant cost of the double recovery being borne by society in the form of increased insurance premiums and higher medical bills.

155. Of course, if the defendant is guilty of wanton or wilful misconduct then punitive damages are appropriate. However, absent this situation, the theory of civil damages is not to punish the tortfeasor. *See generally* Schwartz, *supra* note 152, at 349-50; Note, *Unreason in the Law of Damages*, *supra* note 148. *But cf.* PROSSER 23; Williams, *supra* note 147.

156. See statutes collected in note 150 *supra*.

157. *See* Havighurst & Tancredi, *"Medical Adversity Insurance"—A No-Fault Approach to Medical Malpractice and Quality Assurance*, 51 MILBANK MEMORIAL FUND Q. 125, 129 (1973), *reprinted in* 613 INS. L.J. 69, 72 (1974).

tice suit.[158] It should be recognized that the arguments for altering the collateral source rule are generally applicable in tort actions, and have no special significance in medical cases. Legislators should be encouraged to continue experimentation with changes in the rule, but should be careful to avoid discriminating in favor of the medical profession.

Other Indirect Limitations

Written Guarantees. A physician is not a guarantor of the results of his actions, but is only required to exercise due care in the treatment of his patients.[159] Nevertheless, courts have always respected a doctor's freedom to contract that he will achieve a specific result.[160] As far as malpractice plaintiffs are concerned, a contract action may often be superior to a tort action: breach of contract is generally easier to prove than negligence and contract actions are subject to longer statutes of limitations.[161] If a physician promises a cure or warrants his treatment[162] and there is consideration for this promise,[163] there is no reason to absolve him of his contractual duties. Unfortunately, the courts have not been consistent in determining whether such a guarantee has been made.[164] This problem appears to be especially great when the patient alleges an oral guarantee.[165] The situation is exacerbated by the fact that a physician, wary that he may later be held to have entered into a contract for cure, is reluctant to encourage and offer hope to his patients.[166] The resulting lack of communication may not only have

---

158. See note 147 *supra* and accompanying text.
159. MEDICAL MALPRACTICE REPORT 30.
160. Simonaitis, *Guarantee of Medical Results*, 219 J.A.M.A. 431 (1972); 41 TENN. L. REV. 964, 966 (1974).
161. *See generally* Note, *Contractual Liability in Medical Malpractice*—Sullivan v. O'Connor, 24 DEPAUL L. REV. 212, 220-21 (1974); Note, *Express Contracts to Cure: The Nature of Contractual Malpractice*, 50 IND. L.J. 361, 364 (1975).
162. In Guilmet v. Campbell, 385 Mich. 57, 69, 188 N.W.2d 601, 606 (1971), the Michigan Supreme Court held that a jury could impose liability where there were no express words of warranty but only words which might have been considered a guarantee.
163. Normally, the payment for services constitutes such consideration, but one recent case, Rogala v. Silva, 16 Ill. App. 3d 63, 305 N.E.2d 571 (1973), has required a separate consideration for the warranty.
164. *See* 41 TENN. L. REV. 964, 965-68 (1974). *Compare* Bria v. St. Joseph's Hosp., 153 Conn. 626, 631-32, 220 A.2d 29, 32 (1966) (doctor's statement that he would "take care of everything and would see that whatever was necessary was done" held to be an opinion), *with* Hawkins v. McGee, 84 N.H. 114, 116, 146 A. 641, 642-43 (1929) (doctor's statement that he would "guarantee to make the hand a hundred percent perfect hand" held to be a promise). *See also* Simonaitis, *supra* note 160.
165. MEDICAL MALPRACTICE REPORT 30.
166. *See, e.g.*, McQuaid v. Michou, 85 N.H. 299, 302, 157 A. 881, 883 (1932).

deleterious consequences for the patient's health, but also tends to worsen the malpractice crisis.[167]

For these reasons, it has been suggested that all contracts to cure be declared against public policy, and thus unenforceable.[168] An argument of this nature, however, overlooks the fact that there are some areas of medicine (e.g., cosmetic surgery) in which the patient does have bargaining power and in which the patient's welfare does not require words of reassurance. Also, such a blanket prohibition would destroy the historic ability of a patient to bargain with his doctor.[169] The better solution would be a requirement that guarantees of cure be in writing to be enforceable,[170] an approach which would eliminate the uncertainty caused by alleged oral guarantees, allow contracts for cure to be made, and encourage doctors to make therapeutic reassurances. Of course, some bona fide contracts will be unenforceable because an unsophisticated patient failed to demand a written agreement.[171] Hopefully, the number of meritorious actions lost due to such failures will be low, and, at any rate, the societal need for continued provision of medical services may justify some individual injustice.[172]

Ad Damnum Clauses. The ad damnum clause—that part of the complaint in which the plaintiff sets forth the amount of recovery sought—was an element of common law pleading which was carried over to the United States.[173] Today, the ad damnum serves merely to establish the court's jurisdiction, a purpose which could easily be

---

167. Lack of communication between the physician and his patient is viewed as a major cause of the current crisis. MEDICAL MALPRACTICE REPORT 25. Communication would only be further diminished if doctors are forced to forego therapeutic reassurances to their patients out of fear of liability.

168. *But see* McQuaid v. Michou, 85 N.H. 299, 302-03, 157 A. 881, 883 (1932) (court refused to adopt this policy).

169. See note 160 *supra* and accompanying text.

170. Several states have enacted measures of this type. *See, e.g.,* Medical Malpractice Reform Act, ch. 75-9, § 10, [1975] West's Fla. Sess. Law Service No. 1, at 7, 13-14 (codified at FLA. STAT. ANN. § 725.01); IND. ANN. STAT. § 16-9.5-1-4 (Burns Supp. 1975); Act 817, [1975] West's La. Sess. Law Service No. 4, at 1383 (codified at LA. REV. STAT. ANN. 40:1299.41(c)); Amend. Sub. H.B. 682, [1975] Page's Ohio Legis. Bull. No. 3, at 175 (codified at OHIO REV. CODE ANN. § 1335.05).

171. However, it should be noted that the unenforceability of otherwise meritorious claims is a criticism applicable to all contracts subject to the Statute of Frauds.

172. The policy questions raised by the requirement of written guarantees are similar to those involved with statutes of limitations. See notes 53-89 *supra* and accompanying text.

173. For a discussion of the history of the ad damnum clause, see Morris, *The Ad Damnum Clause* in THE AD DAMNUM CLAUSE: THE PROBLEM AND SOLUTION 2 (Defense Research Institute 1965). The practice has long since been disapproved in England. *Id.*; Ahlers, *The Unsworn Witness,* 27 INS. COUNSEL J. 257, 259 (1960).

achieved by pleading that the amount in controversy exceeds the minimum jurisdictional amount.[174] In addition to its singular lack of utility, the ad damnum produces adverse side effects. It cannot be seriously disputed that the ad damnum is the equivalent of an asking price and frequently bears little resemblance to actual damages.[175] Nevertheless, its insertion in the complaint can condition the public to accept extremely large sums as appropriate measures of damages.[176] Moreover, a large ad damnum can by itself produce a large damage award: two studies have established that, all other factors being equal, a suit for a higher amount will result in a higher verdict.[177]

Surprisingly, most jurisdictions still retain the practice of pleading the ad damnum.[178] The advent of the recent medical malpractice crisis, however, may put an end to this situation. A number of states have recently passed legislation eliminating the ad damnum.[179] It is difficult

---

174. See note 178 *infra.*
175. *See* DesChamps, *The Truth About Ad Damnum* in THE AD DAMNUM CLAUSE: THE PROBLEM AND SOLUTION 8 (Defense Research Institute 1965). *See also* Affett v. Milwaukee & Suburban Transp. Corp., 11 Wis. 2d 604, 614, 106 N.W.2d 274, 280 (1960); REPORT, NEW JERSEY SUPREME COURT'S COMM. ON RULES 14 (1960).
176. It is generally true that when a suit is filed for a relatively large amount of damages, such filing will be reported in the news media, particularly in smaller cities. Thus, the general public is likely to be made aware of suits for large amounts (even if the final award is nowhere near the amount asked), and there develops a general level of expectation concerning damages in certain types of actions (*e.g.*, malpractice actions) which is not based on the actual awards in such cases but rather on the amounts requested in the complaints. *See* Combs, Ad Damnum—*Be Damned*, 24 KY. B.J. 199 (1960).
177. One such study, done by Jury Verdict Research, Inc., concentrated on 246 cases in which plaintiffs had suffered back and neck injuries. The results are reported in 5 PERSONAL INJURY VALUATION HANDBOOK 2001 (1964). The other study was a jury project done by the University of Chicago Law School under a Ford Foundation Grant. *See* Broeder, *The University of Chicago Jury Project*, 38 NEB. L. REV. 744, 759 (1959).
178. The pleading of damages has been restricted in Pennsylvania to setting forth only whether the amount is, or is not, in excess of $10,000. PA. STAT. ANN. tit. 12, R. CIV. P. 1044 (1967); *see* Hileman, *The Pennsylvania Rule,* in THE AD DAMNUM CLAUSE: THE PROBLEM AND SOLUTION 25 (Defense Research Institute 1965). Such pleadings have been eliminated entirely in New Jersey. N.J. Supreme Ct. R. 4:8-1; *see* Lane, *The New Jersey Rule,* in THE AD DAMNUM CLAUSE, *supra* at 29. In Florida, while damage pleading is not prohibited by law, damages are not pleaded as a matter of practice by the bar. See Atkins, *The Florida Rule,* in THE AD DAMNUM CLAUSE, *supra,* at 31, 32.
179. Medical Malpractice Reform Act, ch. 75-9, § 8, [1975] West's Fla. Sess. Law Service No. 1, at 13 (codified at FLA. STAT. ANN. § 768.042); IND. STAT. ANN. § 16-9.5-1-6 (Burns Supp. 1975); H.F. 803, § 27, [1975] Iowa Legis. Service No. 3, at 328 (codified at IOWA CODE ANN. § 619); Act 817, § 1, [1975] West's La. Sess. Law Service No. 4, at 1383 (codified at LA. REV. STAT. 40:1299.41(e)); ch. 362, § 5, [1975] Mass. Adv. Legis. Service No. 5, at 324 (codified at MASS. ANN. LAWS ch. 231, § 60c); Amend. Sub. H.B. 682, [1975] Page's Ohio Legis. Bull. No. 3, at 175 (codified at OHIO REV.

to discern any reason why such action should be discouraged. The ad damnum is a vestige of common-law pleading which is not required to further any present purpose; it should be given a well-deserved legislative burial.[180]

Future Damages. Recoveries in medical malpractice actions often include awards for future damages, *e.g.*, anticipated costs of future health care and loss of earning capacity. Because of the lack of precision in estimating life expectancy and other contingencies which affect the amount of such damages, this portion of the recovery is highly speculative.[181] Thus, a defendant may be forced to compensate a plaintiff for losses which never occur.[182] In addition, there is no assurance that the award will not be squandered by the plaintiff long before his financial needs are met. If such an award is improvidently spent by the imprudent plaintiff, he is likely to become a ward of the state for *his* economic and medical necessities, resulting in a *double cost to society* for his injuries.

Though the inadequacies of the present method of awarding future damages are evident, few proposals for reform have been offered.[183] An

---

CODE ANN. § 2307.42(c)); ch. 37, § 10, [1975] West's Wis. Legis. Service No. 1, at 41 (codified at WIS. STAT. ANN. § 655.009(1)). A Tennessee statute, TENN. CODE ANN. § 23-3416 (Supp. 1975), provides that the amount pleaded will not be disclosed to the jury.

180. *See also* Dornette, *Indiana Adopts Malpractice Legislation*, 3 J. LEGAL MED. 26, 27 (June 1975); Welch, *Medical Malpractice*, 292 NEW ENG. J. MED. 1372, 1374 (1975). Abolition was also recommended by the Secretary's Commission on Medical Malpractice. MEDICAL MALPRACTICE REPORT 38.

181. *See* Richards & Kidner, *Judicial Attitudes Toward Actuarial Evidence*, 124 NEW L.J. 105, 106 (1974).

182. For example, the plaintiff could fall far short of living out his normal life expectancy, either because of an inaccurate estimate of his natural life or as a result of unexpected accidents or illness. The consequence of a plaintiff's failure to live out his life expectancy is an inequitable cost to the paying defendant and an unjustified windfall to the plaintiff's heirs. *See id.*

183. One proffered solution is to require the defendant to buy an insurance annuity policy in an amount sufficient to pay the monthly installments to the plaintiff. *See* Sedgwick & Judge, *Use of Annuities in Settlement of Personal Injury Cases*, 41 INS. COUNSEL J. 584, 586-92 (1974). Under this approach the plaintiff would receive payments for his entire life, even though he lives beyond his life expectancy. But, since the defendant pays a price based on plaintiff's life expectancy, if the plaintiff lives less than his life expectancy, the defendant has paid more than he should. If all defendants were covered by insurance companies this deficiency would work itself out over a period of time, since the insurance company would have some patients die before their life expectancy and others live past their life expectancy. However, in the case of an individual defendant who is bearing the cost of damages himself, there is no built-in equalization device.

Another interesting suggestion is that malpractice plaintiffs should receive compensation in the form of a contract providing them medical care for the remainder of their lives. *See* N.Y. Times, Oct. 14, 1975, at 33, col. 1. Such a proposal would eliminate the

Alabama proposal[184] seeks to ease the malpractice crisis by preventing recoveries for losses which are never realized. Under this bill, awards of future damages would be placed in a trust fund and paid to the plaintiff in monthly increments. Although the language of the proposal is not free from ambiguity, it seems that these monthly payments could not in any event continue beyond the life expectancy of the plaintiff as determined at the time of trial. If the plaintiff dies before reaching that age, the trust fund reverts to the defendant. On the other hand, if the plaintiff lives beyond his life expectancy, he would receive no additional damages.

If the proposal is so contrued, the cost to society of future damage awards would be reduced, since damages would be paid only for the actual life of the plaintiff or his life expectancy, whichever is shorter. Such a construction, however, would make the proposal unfair as applied to persons who outlive their life expectancy.[185] On the other hand, if the proposal is construed as requiring payment to the plaintiff for his actual life, even if he outlives his life expectancy, then such proposal is of less benefit from a societal-cost point of view. In the long run, payments to plaintiffs for their actual lives should average out to be the same as payments to each plaintiff based on his life expectancy.

Thus, the benefit of such a proposal is mostly in terms of fairness to individual defendants, who would pay only the cost of sustaining their particular plaintiffs. In the overall view, society would not benefit except possibly as a result of not having to bear the welfare costs of a plaintiff who squanders his award. In terms of easing the dollar burden

---

"squandering" of awards, but does not deal with either the actuarial problems or other cognizable damages.

184. Ala. H.B. 300, § 13 (1975) provides as follows:
    In all actions for medical malpractice where damages are awarded on the basis of permanent or extended disability, after payment of costs and attorney's fees, the damages awarded for future health care, future maintenance, and lost future earnings shall be placed in a trust fund for the benefit of the plaintiff, with the plaintiff receiving from the fund, on a monthly basis, the amount previously determined as being required to provide for his maintenance, health care, and lost earnings. The provisions of the trust must be approved by the circuit court in which the damages are awarded. The plaintiff shall be entitled to the monthly payments from the trust, but upon his or her death, the corpus of the fund shall revert to the party or parties which established the fund in proportion to the amount they initially contributed.

185. A plaintiff presently receives his award with three possibilities: that (1) he will die earlier than expected, thus leaving an amount to his heirs; (2) he will die when expected, leaving nothing but being entirely provided for; or (3) he will live longer than expected, resulting in the award not being sufficient to provide for his life. Which result will ensue is strictly a matter of chance, the potential costs of the third possibility being balanced by the potential benefit of the first. However, under the interpretation suggested in the text, the plaintiff is left bearing the potential cost of the third possibility while losing the potential benefit of the first.

to society of high medical malpractice awards, the benefits of placing awards in trust seem somewhat attenuated. The interest of finality would appear to outweigh whatever marginal benefits this action would have for the medical profession.

THE DISPUTE RESOLUTION MECHANISM

Hardly anyone is completely satisfied with the jury trial as a dispute resolution mechanism for medical malpractice claims. Among the complaints which have been voiced about the jury system are that its expense increases the cost of malpractice insurance;[186] that its slowness forces patients who desperately need money to pay medical and other bills to settle for less than their claims are worth;[187] and that its lack of predictability makes it difficult to pursue an intelligent settlement strategy.[188] Of course, those same criticisms apply to use of the jury trial in all contexts; however, they are especially pertinent in the medical malpractice area because of the increasing number of claims, the sensitivity and technical complexity of that area, and the large dollar amounts at stake. The recent crisis has led to experimentation with alternative methods of evaluating claims and adjudicating facts. Most of these efforts have been limited to medical malpractice cases; nevertheless, if they prove successful in that area, they could possibly be applied on a broader scale in the future. Therefore, the implications of these alternative dispute resolution mechanisms are quite profound.

The mechanisms discussed in this Comment are strictly procedural, and are primarily directed towards increasing the speed and efficiency of dispute resolution. Prospective alternatives, both those already enacted and those merely proposed, range from simply another stage tacked on to the front of the traditional system to a complete replacement of the traditional system with a simplified, streamlined procedure. The majority of legislative packages which utilize a new dispute resolution mech-

---

186. Estimates of the portion of the insurance dollar paid in which eventually reaches the patient range from eighteen cents to thirty-eight cents. *See* Brook, Brutoco & Williams, *supra* note 29, at 1208 n.54. While part of this loss is attributable to the cost of the insurance mechanism, there can be no doubt that the legal system contributes a great deal to this inefficiency.

187. A study prepared for the Secretary's Commission on Medical Malpractice indicated a mean "case duration" of nineteen months for malpractice suits. Dietz, Baird & Berul, *supra* note 50, at 103 Table III-23. Case duration was defined as "the time from case acceptance until the case is closed." *Id.* at 102.

188. *Id.* at 109. Other impediments to settlement are the defendant-physician's right to refuse settlement, a tendency of malpractice insurers to wait until the last minute before trial to settle, a lack of lawyer preparation, the long wait to trial, plaintiffs' demand for jury trial, unreasonably high award demands, and ineffective pretrial procedures. *Id.*

anism also incorporate various changes in the substantive law and the financing system.[189] Accordingly, the new adjudicatory mechanism may take on special meaning only with reference to other parts of the legislative package.

Screening Panels

The most popular of the alternative adjudicatory devices is the "screening panel."[190] In general, screening panels are intended to provide for a speedy pre-trial review of malpractice claims through the use of some type of simplified procedure. The panel makes specified findings at the conclusion of a hearing, but has no power actually to "screen" malpractice claims since findings are not binding on the parties. Apparently, the theory underlying the use of the panels is that the parties will be better equipped to negotiate a settlement, and under greater pressure to settle, if they are given a preliminary view of the merits of the case; the end result thus should be the same as that yielded by a panel with more extensive powers.[191]

The potentially infinite number of forms which screening panels can assume makes further generalization impossible.[192] Accordingly, to facilitate the examination of current legislation, the discussion will focus on the Indiana plan,[193] which, despite some distinctive features, is fairly representative of the type of legislation currently under consideration in several states.[194] After the basic operation of the plan is summarized,

---

189. The legislative package passed in Indiana is a typical example. It incorporates a screening panel, a high-risk insurance pool, a patient's compensation fund, and several substantive legal changes, including limits on recovery and attorneys' fees and a special statute of limitations. See IND. ANN. STAT. § 16-9.5 (Burns Supp. 1975).

190. Many screening panels are already in operation. However, these existing panels differ in certain aspects from those panels incorporated in recent legislative packages. For a discussion of existing panels, see HOLDER 416-22; Baird, Munsterman & Stevens, *Alternatives to Litigation, I: Technical Analysis*, in MEDICAL MALPRACTICE REPORT Appendix 214, 224-27.

191. *See Arbitration of Malpractice Claims*, 28 ARIZ. MED. 391 (May 1971).

192. The following statutes have implemented screening plans in one form or another. ARK. STAT. ANN. § 34-2602 (Supp. 1975); Medical Malpractice Reform Act, ch. 75-9, § 5, [1975] West's Fla. Sess. Law Service No. 1, at 10-12 (codified at FLA. STAT. ANN. § 768.133); Pub. Act. 79-960, [1975] Ill. Legis. Service No. 6, at 1613-17 (codified at ILL. ANN. STAT. ch. 110, §§ 58.2 -.10); IND. ANN. STAT. § 16-9.5-9 (Burns Supp. 1975); Act 817, [1975] West's La. Sess. Law Service No. 4, at 1387 (codified at LA. REV. STAT. ANN. § 40:1299.47); NEV. REV. STAT. § 41A.020 (1975); N.Y. JUDICIARY LAW § 148-a (McKinney Supp. 1975); Act 111, §§ 301-606, [1975] Purdon's Pa. Legis. Service No. 2, at 297-302 (codified at PA. STAT. ANN. tit. 40, §§ 1301.301-.606); TENN. CODE ANN. § 23-3401-21 (Supp. 1975); ch. 37, § 10, [1975] West's Wis. Legis. Service No. 1, at 42-48 (codified at WIS. STAT. ANN. §§ 655.021-.21).

193. IND. ANN. STAT. § 16-9.5-9 (Burns Supp. 1975).

194. The Indiana plan has been adopted, in modified form, in Louisiana, Act 817,

its major provisions will be analyzed and compared with those contained in other screening plan proposals.

The Indiana plan requires that a malpractice claim be brought before a panel, composed of three physicians and a nonvoting attorney chairman,[195] before it can be filed with a court.[196] The panel is to consider evidence, promptly submitted, in written form only, but such evidence may include despositions, excerpts of treatises, x-rays, "and any other form of evidence allowable by the medical review panel."[197] The panel has authority to request all relevant information and each party has access to any material submitted to the panel. At any time after submission of all the evidence and before issuance of the panel report, the panel may be convened by any party upon ten days notice. At any such meeting, the parties shall have the right to question panel members "concerning any matters relevant to issues to be decided."[198] After reviewing the evidence, the panel is to render its opinion within thirty days[199] in the form of *one or more* of four specified findings relating to negligence, proximate cause, and the need for expert testimony.[200] No findings are made as to damages. The report of the opinion,

---

[1975] West's La. Sess. Law Service No. 4, at 1387-89 (codified at LA. REV. STAT. ANN. § 40:1299.47), and has been proposed in several other states.

195. IND. ANN. STAT. § 16-9.5-9-3 (Burns Supp. 1975). "All physicians engaged in the active practice of medicine" are available for selection. Each side of the litigation has the right to select one panel member, and these two will then select the third member. There are further provisions for challenging members for cause and for selection in case of two such successful challenges. The attorney member of the panel is to be selected by agreement of the parties or, if no agreement can be reached, by alternately striking names from a list of five attorneys drawn at random by the clerk of the state supreme court. *Id.*

196. IND. ANN. STAT. § 16-9.5-9-2 (Burns Supp. 1975). The Louisiana plan, which is otherwise identical to that of Indiana, provides that use of the panel may be waived upon consent of both parties. Act 817, [1975] West's La. Sess. Law Service No. 4, at 1387-89 (codified at LA. REV. STAT. ANN. § 40:1299.47(B)). The filing of the request for review of a claim shall toll the Indiana statute of limitations until ninety days following the issuance of the panel opinion. IND. ANN. STAT. § 16-9.5-9-8 (Burns Supp. 1975).

197. IND. ANN. STAT. § 16-9.5-9-4 (Burns Supp. 1975).

198. *Id.* § 16-9.5-9-5.

199. *Id.* § 16-9.5-9-7. It would seem from the language that the panel is to render its opinion within thirty days "[a]fter reviewing all evidence and after any examination of the panel by counsel," but that interpretation puts no pressure on the panel to review the evidence quickly. This could impair the value of the panel.

200. The four findings are as follows:

(1) The evidence supports the conclusion that the defendant or defendants failed to comply with the appropriate standard of care as charged in the complaint.

(2) The evidence does not support the conclusion that the defendant or defendants failed to meet the applicable standard of care as charged in the complaint.

(3) That there is a material issue of fact, not requiring expert opinion, bearing on liability for consideration by the court or jury.

which is to be prepared by the attorney member of the panel, will be admissible as evidence in a subsequent trial of the action but is not conclusive of any issue.[201] Any party shall have the right to call, at his cost, any member of the panel as a witness.[202]

Perhaps the most significant feature of the plan is that utilization of the panel is mandatory.[203] Many defense attorneys are of the opinion that screening panels serve merely as discovery devices for plaintiffs; hence, if use of the panel is made optional, insurers will not permit their policyholders to appear.[204] This practice would obviously eliminate the benefits the panel is designed to provide. Despite the problem with optional screening panels, a few legislative packages still allow a party to opt against the panel's use.[205] Certainly, if one is serious about the rationalization for screening panels, provisions making their use optional should be regarded as mistakes.[206]

---

(4) The conduct complained of was or was not a factor of the resultant damages. If so, whether the plaintiff suffered: (1) any disability and the extent and duration of the disability, and (2) any permanent impairment and the percentage of the impairment. *Id.*

201. *Id.* § 16-9.5-9-9.

202. *Id.* All panel members are entitled to compensation for their service on the panel—$25.00 per day, not to exceed $250.00, plus travel expenses. Panel fees are to be paid "by the side in whose favor the majority opinion is written." *Id.* § 16-9.5-9-10.

203. Indiana requires that the panel decision be rendered before a formal complaint can be filed. Other proposals would simply use the filing of the complaint to trigger the screening process. *See, e.g.*, Pub. Act. 79-960, [1975] Ill. Legis. Service No. 6, at 1613-17 (codified at ILL. ANN. STAT., ch. 110, §§ 58.2-.10); ch. 362, [1975] Mass. Adv. Legis. Service No. 5, at 322 (codified at MASS. ANN. LAWS ch. 231, § 60B); Amend. Sub. H.B. 682, § 1, [1975] Page's Ohio Legis. Bull. No. 3, at 177 (codified at OHIO REV. CODE ANN. § 2711.21). The former procedure seems preferable in that publicity is more easily avoided; the request for a panel hearing need not be a public document as is the formal complaint.

204. Most of the existing screening panels are optional. *See* HOLDER 416. This feature apparently was used by insurers to avoid panel appearances by their policyholders. *See Documentary Supplement.*

205. ARK. STAT. ANN. § 34-2603 (Supp. 1975) ("Any person . . . *may* submit his or her claim . . . to a hearing panel. . . .") (emphasis added); Act 817, [1975] West's La. Sess. Law Service No. 4, at 138 (codified at LA. REV. STAT. ANN. § 40:1299.47(B)) ("By agreement of both parties, the use of the medical review panel may be waived."). The waiver permitted by the Louisiana statute is the only materially distinguishing feature between it and the Indiana plan. See note 196 *supra* and accompanying text.

206. *See Documentary Supplement* 715-17. It can be argued that malpractice defendants will not exhibit a significantly higher or faster settlement rate if forced to utilize the panel. That is, defendants may simply "endure" the panel procedure and go through the proceeding on a pro forma basis, hoping perhaps to wear down the plaintiff's mental or economic endurance. This argument, however, merely illustrates the need for putting some teeth into the panel's decision, *e.g.*, by making it admissible at a subsequent trial of the case. See notes 220-27 *infra* and accompanying text.

Some have maintained that mandatory utilization of the panel is unconstitutional as violative of due process and equal protection. HOLDER 419-20. While such constitution-

A second important feature of the Indiana plan is that the specified findings may be made only by the physician members of the panel.[207] On the one hand, this procedure reflects the need for expertise in dealing with the complicated technical aspects of the typical malpractice claim.[208] On the other hand, the all-physician makeup of the panel's voting segment could be viewed as an attempt to reduce the number of decisions favoring the plaintiff. Despite attempts to create an impartial selection process,[209] the natural tendency of physicians will be to empathize with the defense. It has been argued that this problem can be avoided by diversification of decision-making segments of the panel.[210] Most legislative advocates of screening panels have apparently accepted this argument: the majority of proposed screening panels are to consist of one health care provider,[211] one attorney, and a third person, either a judge or layman.[212] Whether the results will justify the use of a diversified panel has yet to be determined.[213]

Another distinctive feature of the Indiana plan is that only written

---

al arguments may be valid as applied to *binding* panel proceedings, see notes 246-54 *infra* and accompanying text, it is doubtful that they will be found meritorious with regard to mandatory *utilization* of the panel. In view of both the peculiar and severe nature of the malpractice crisis and the "nonsuspect" nature of the classification involved, the courts are likely to uphold procedural remedies which are reasonably adapted to alleviate that crisis.

207. In some respects this provision represents a carryover from the first malpractice screening panels which were established by local medical societies to provide guidance to physicians as to the merits of claims against them. Baird, Munsterman & Stevens, *supra* note 190, at 224-25.

208. In some plans the expertise concept has been carried one step further. Particularly where panel membership is diversified, see notes 210-13 *infra* and accompanying text, the physician member of the panel is often required to be of the same medical specialty as the defendant. *See, e.g.*, Medical Malpractice Reform Act, ch. 75-9, [1975] West's Fla. Sess. Law Service No. 1, at 10 (codified at FLA. STAT. ANN. § 768.133(1)(a)); ch. 362, [1975] Mass. Adv. Legis. Service No. 5, at 322 (codified at MASS. ANN. LAWS ch. 231, § 60B) (where the defendant health care provider is not a physician, but, for example, a dentist, the physician's position on the panel shall be replaced by a dentist). This seems desirable where it is feasible to do so, *i.e.* where there is available a sufficient number of specialists in each field.

209. The defendant and the plaintiff are each allowed to pick one physician member of the panel, who, in turn, will select the third member. See note 195 *supra*.

210. *See* HOLDER 419.

211. If the defendant is a dentist, the panel member will be a dentist, etc. See note 208 *supra*.

212. *See, e.g.*, Medical Malpractice Reform Act, ch. 75-9, [1975] West's Fla. Sess. Law Service No. 1, at 10 (codified at FLA. STAT. ANN. § 768.133(1)); ch. 362, [1975] Mass. Adv. Legis. Service No. 5, at 321 (codified at MASS. ANN. LAWS ch. 231, § 60B); Minn. S.F. 1723 (1975).

213. One preliminary study in Arizona has suggested that results achieved under the diversified panel may be similar to those achieved with a jury. Baird, Munsterman & Stevens, *supra* note 190, at 248-53.

evidence will be considered by the panel. There is no provision for oral testimony or argument of any kind. Instead, the parties are limited to questions directed to panel members,[214] and, presumably, written argument. These limitations reduce the cost and difficulty of preparing an appearance before the panel. In contrast, other plans provide for full-dress hearings, complete with oral testimony, cross-examination, and oral argument.[215] Some plans even go so far as to allow the parties to use the full range of civil discovery devices.[216] Even assuming that the procedure followed before the panels will be rather informal,[217] it would seem that a full-dress hearing would be nearly as expensive and time consuming as a formal jury trial. Despite these drawbacks, however, the additional procedural trappings would arguably produce more correct findings: to this extent, the likelihood of pre-trial settlement would be enhanced. Thus, in determining how closely the procedure of the panel is to parallel that of traditional adjudicatory mechanisms, it is necessary to balance the desire for speed and economy against the benefits provided by the panoply of rights associated with a jury trial.

The Indiana screening panel is not designed to deal at all with the damage issue, but is required to make more detailed findings as to liability than are panels under other plans.[218] This approach has two advantages. First, by ignoring damages, attorneys are able to avoid spending a great deal of time and money in preparing for an appearance before the panel. Second, the detailed liability findings, coupled with an attorney-written opinion, help counsel to locate the precise strengths and weaknesses of their respective cases, thereby providing a firmer basis for settlement.

A great number of proposed plans require the panel to make findings as to damages.[219] Although this means that the procedure will

---

214. See note 197 *supra* and accompanying text.
215. *See, e.g.*, ARK. STAT. ANN. § 34-2604 (Supp. 1975); Cal. A.B. 11 (2d Extra. Sess. 1975); Medical Malpractice Reform Act, ch. 75-9, [1975] West's Fla. Sess. Law Service No. 1, at 11-12 (codified at FLA. STAT. ANN. § 768.133(7)); Pub. Act. 79-960, [1975] Ill. Legis. Service No. 6, at 1615 (codified at ILL. ANN. STAT. ch. 110, § 58.6).
216. *See* Medical Malpractice Reform Act, ch. 75-9, [1975] West's Fla. Sess. Law Service No. 1, at 11 (codified at FLA. STAT. ANN. § 768.133(6)).
217. While many plans do specifically provide that the procedure will be informal, others simply declare that screening panel procedures shall be in accordance with the state's rules of civil procedure and its rules of evidence, sometimes with a provision allowing modification in the interests of justice.
218. See note 200 *supra* and accompanying text.
219. *See, e.g.*, ARK. STAT. ANN. § 34-2605 (Supp. 1975); Pub. Act 79-960, [1975] Ill. Legis. Service No. 6, at 1615 (codified at ILL. ANN. STAT. ch. 110, § 58.7(1)); Ill. H.B. 2769 (1975) (returned to committee for interim study).
Other states, notably Florida, are considering the idea that panels should not be

be more time-consuming and expensive, it may be beneficial where only the amount of damages is in serious dispute. Again, however, the wider the scope of the duties of the panel, the closer is the approximation both as to form and as to time and expense between the panel proceeding and a jury trial.

The more important point with regard to panel findings is their admissibility at a subsequent jury trial. Without provisions for admissibility, the panel is a great deal less effective as a screening device. It is too tempting in those circumstances for a losing plaintiff or defendant, where a great deal of money is involved, to gamble on achieving a different result at trial. Criticism by insurers that the panel is nothing more than a discovery tool for plaintiffs takes on a great deal more validity in this context,[220] for it is difficult to argue that all attorneys will feel morally bound to honor panel decisions.[221] Nevertheless, there are a few recent legislative proposals which expressly provide for the nonadmissibility of panel findings.[222] This approach has to be considered a

---

required to make damage findings but should be authorized to do so at the option of the parties once a finding as to liability is made. The panel would assume the role of mediator in such proceedings. *See, e.g.,* Medical Malpractice Reform Act, ch. 75-9, [1975] West's Fla. Sess. Law Service No. 1, at 12 (codified at FLA. STAT. ANN. § 768.133(9)). It should also be noted that a number of states have prohibited the pleading of the amount of damages in a medical malpractice action. See notes 173-80 *supra* and accompanying text.

220. See notes 203-06 *supra* and accompanying text.

221. One study has concluded that, without provision for admissibility, the success of the panel depends primarily upon the good working relationship between the legal and medical professions in the particular locale involved. Where it exists, attorneys will accord a great deal of respect to panel decisions by virtue of the social and professional pressures involved, *e.g.,* pressure from the bar associations themselves. Where it does not exist, as is usually the case in very large metropolitan areas, the panels are generally unsuccessful. *See Documentary Supplement* 715, 720.

New Mexico and Arizona take a slightly different, but more direct, approach. After an adverse panel decision, the claimant's attorney is prohibited from filing suit "unless personally satisfied that strong and overriding reasons compel such action." *See* HOLDER 418.

222. *See, e.g.,* Pub. Act 79-960, [1975] Ill. Legis. Service No. 6, at 1616 (codified at ILL. ANN. STAT. ch. 110, § 58.8(4)); Ill. H.B. 2769 (1975) (returned to committee for interim study). Some plans make panel findings admissible at trial only upon a finding by the trial judge that they have been made in accordance with law and are not clearly erroneous. See note 223 *infra.* It is also common that only findings as to liability are admissible. *See* Ill. H.B. 3124 (1975) (tabled). Apparently this proposal stems from a view that the panel's expertise extends only to the issue of liability. The strongest provision to be proposed would permit the admissibility at trial of findings as to damages, but not as to liability. *See* Minn. S.F. 1723 (1975). It is not clear how this bill would permit consideration by the jury of the damage findings without affecting its deliberations on the liability issue, unless the issues are tried separately. Most of the existing plans do not provide for admissibility. *See Documentary Supplement* 720.

weakness of those plans, for without admissibility there is much less motivation to settle.[223]

The Indiana plan also provides that either party may call any of the three physician panel members as expert witnesses at trial.[224] This provision is apparently a response to the "conspiracy of silence" problem, *i.e.* the alleged tendency of physicians to decline to testify against their colleagues and associates, thereby making it difficult for plaintiffs to locate expert witnesses.[225] Many states have addressed the problem in a fashion similar to that of Indiana.[226] Thus, a plaintiff who secures favorable findings from the panel will presumably be able to obtain favorable expert testimony. If the plaintiff does not prevail before the panel he may encounter difficulty in finding an expert witness. In either event, the pressure to settle would be increased, thus enhancing the likelihood that the panel would in fact operate so as to "screen" malpractice claims.[227]

---

223. Under a proposed plan in Ohio, certain safeguards are added so as to ensure that the admission of such findings is not unfairly prejudicial. The decision will be admissible at trial only
> if the court conducts a review of the arbitration decision and any other relevant information submitted by the parties and concludes that:
> (1) the findings of fact by the arbitration board were not clearly erroneous;
> (2) the decision is in accordance with applicable law;
> (3) the procedures required for conducting the hearing and rendering the decision were followed fairly and properly without prejudice to either party.
> Amend. Sub. H.B. 682, [1975] Page's Ohio Legis. Bull. No. 3, at 177 (codified at OHIO REV. CODE ANN. § 2711.21(c)).

For nearly identical language, see Cal. A.B. 2287 (1975). This type of provision seems to be a wise one if the court has *absolute* discretion in making this determination. Otherwise, it would simply provide one more source of appeal and delay.

224. IND. ANN. STAT. § 16-9.5-9-9 (Burns Supp. 1975).

225. *See* MEDICAL MALPRACTICE REPORT 36-37.

226. *See, e.g.*, Pub. Act. 79-960, [1975] Ill. Legis. Service No. 6, at 1616 (codified at ILL. ANN. STAT. ch. 110, § 58.8(5)) (the panel will provide an expert to the party who abides by its decision, *i.e.* the non-appealing party); NEV. REV. STAT. § 41A.030 (1975) (the Nevada panels consist of three attorneys and three physicians); *cf.* ch. 362, [1975] Mass. Adv. Legis. Service No. 5, at 322-23 (codified at MASS. ANN. LAWS ch. 231, § 60B) (if panel appoints its own expert, his testimony may be admissible at trial—this should have nearly the same practical effect as appointment of expert specifically for trial).

227. Irrespective of the benefits of increased pressure to settle, the provision of expert testimony only after a successful panel appearance may be a futile gesture. Despite the relative informality of the proceedings and the presence of experts on the panel, it seems beyond doubt that the plaintiff's chances of success before the panel will be reduced if he is unable to obtain expert assistance, especially where the panel procedure itself takes on many of the trappings of a formal trial. New Mexico has responded to this problem by providing for access to expert advice before submission to the panel. *See Documentary Supplement* 719. One proposal in California would also provide the claimant with a choice of experts prior to the hearing before the panel. Cal. A.B. 25 (2d Extra. Sess. 1975).

Unlike several other proposed plans,[228] the Indiana plan contains no provision requiring that panel records be kept private. Such privacy provisions have much to recommend them,[229] but they will also operate to impede predictability and uniformity of decision. Availability of prior panel determinations might enhance the settlement process, one of the goals of the screening panel device.[230] The ideal compromise between predictability and privacy would seem to be apparent: panel reports could be published without using the names of the parties. Unfortunately, this idea has yet to be proposed in a malpractice legislation package.

If the screening panel can be structured to be efficient, swift, and economical, it will have much to recommend it. Whether or not the number of claims filed will actually be reduced is a matter of speculation, and may depend on other factors.[231] Even more speculative is whether use of screening panels will reduce the total societal cost of the malpractice problem. In any event, it certainly seems worthwhile to continue experimentation with such procedural devices.[232]

Arbitration

Arbitration is another alternative adjudicatory procedure which has been proposed for resolution of medical malpractice disputes. For purposes of this Comment, arbitration is defined to mean any nonjudicial mechanism which is binding upon the parties.[233] The advantages of arbitration over the jury trial in this context are basically the same as those of the screening panel: speed, informality, and the use of a sophisticated decision-maker in a matter of technical complexity.[234]

---

228. *See, e.g.*, La. S.B. 344 (1975).
229. See the discussion of ad damnum clauses at notes 173-80 *supra* and accompanying text.
230. If panel reports are published, the standard of care will eventually be influenced by them. The effect may be very similar to that of various "decisions" made by government agencies in their rulemaking and adjudicative capacities.
231. *See Documentary Supplement* 714-17, 721.
232. *See* MEDICAL MALPRACTICE REPORT 91.
233. There are a great number of legislative proposals which utilize the term "arbitration" but which, in effect, are just a species of the mechanism denominated "screening panel." Their common feature is the provision for a trial de novo following the hearing by the screening or arbitration panel. For a discussion of arbitration of malpractice cases, see Bergen, *Arbitration of Medical Liability*, 211 J.A.M.A. 175 (1970).
234. For more extended treatment of the various advantages of arbitration, see Averbach, *A Plaintiff's Attorney Says: Malpractice Cases Don't Belong in the Courts!*, HOSP. PHYSICIAN 56 (Jan. 1969); Coulson, *The Malpractice Mess: Is Arbitration the Answer?*, 99 MED. TIMES 131 (Oct. 1971); Ludlam & Hassard, *Arbitration*, 114 CAL. MED. 102 (May 1971); *Arbitration of Malpractice Claims, supra* note 191.

The distinction, of course, is that the decisions of an arbitration panel are final, at least as to conclusions of fact, a characteristic which could be quite significant in regard to time and cost savings.

Under the laws of most states, parties to an existing dispute can agree to submit it to arbitration and enforce the decision of the arbitrator.[235] More significantly, parties about to enter into a contract or course of conduct can agree to arbitrate any dispute that may arise in the future out of such contract or course of conduct.[236] Even where such laws exist, however, such an agreement will not be enforced if it is shown that the contract to arbitrate was not knowingly and voluntarily entered into, or that it was one of adhesion.[237] Arbitration agreements relating to health care are particularly susceptible to these defenses,[238] since the patient signing the agreement to arbitrate future disputes may be in no condition to understand what he is signing, or because the hospital requires the patient to sign as a precondition to admission.

A few states have responded to this problem by specifically authorizing health care providers to enter into contracts to arbitrate malpractice claims;[239] by establishing guidelines as to the terms and conditions of such agreements;[240] and by setting forth a sample contract designed

---

235. At least thirty-five states have arbitration statutes of some form. D. DOBBS, HANDBOOK ON THE LAW OF REMEDIES 937-38 (1973). The Uniform Arbitration Act provides for the validity of a written agreement to submit an existing controversy to arbitration. UNIFORM ARBITRATION ACT § 1.

236. UNIFORM ARBITRATION ACT § 1; MEDICAL MALPRACTICE REPORT 94. The Report recommends that *all* states adopt legislation upholding the enforcement of agreements to arbitrate. *Id.*

237. *See, e.g.*, Commercial Factors Corp. v. Kurtzman Bros., 131 Cal. App. 2d 133, 280 P.2d 146 (1955); Arthur Philip Export Corp. v. Leatherstone, Inc., 275 App. Div. 102, 87 N.Y.S.2d 665 (1949). The Uniform Arbitration Act provides that agreements to arbitrate are enforceable "save upon such grounds as exist at law or in equity for the revocation of any contract." UNIFORM ARBITRATION ACT § 1.

238. These problems are extensively explored by Professor Henderson, the leading writer in this area, in *Alternatives to Litigation, III: Contractual Problems in the Enforcement of Agreements to Arbitrate Medical Malpractice*, in MEDICAL MALPRACTICE REPORT Appendix 321.

239. *See, e.g.*, Ala. H.B. 300 (1975); Cal. A.B. 32 (2d Extra. Sess. 1975); Cal. S.B. 14 (2d Extra. Sess. 1975) (validity to be judged in accordance with *existing* standards); Cal. S.B. 15 (2d Extra. Sess. 1975); Cal. A.B. 926 (1975); Act 371, [1975] West's La. Sess. Law Service No. 3, at 651 (codified at LA. REV. STAT. ANN. § 9:4232) (validity to be judged in accordance with existing Louisiana arbitration law); Md. H.B. 401 (1975) (arbitration "encouraged"); Amend. Sub. H.B. 682, [1975] Page's Ohio Legis. Bull. No. 3, at 177 (codified at OHIO REV. CODE ANN. § 2711.22). Wisconsin permits the parties appearing before the nonbinding pretrial review board to agree that the findings will be binding. Ch. 37, [1975] West's Wis. Legis. Service No. 1, at 42 (codified at WIS. STAT. ANN. § 655.07).

240. *See, e.g.*, Ala. H.B. 300 (1975); Cal. A.B. 32 (2d Extra. Sess. 1975); Cal. A.B. 926 (1975); Medical Injury Compensation Reform Act, ch. 1, 2d Extra. Sess., [1975]

to pass muster under the guidelines.[241] In nearly every case, the patient is given the option of voiding the contract for a certain period of time after execution[242] or after discharge from the hospital or termination of the physician-patient relationship.[243] While the use of such agreements seems desirable, several factors make it questionable whether they will ever achieve widespread acceptance.[244] First, a physician may be reluctant to take the time and effort required to explain such contracts to each and every one of his patients and "persuade" them to sign, though presumably that function could be fulfilled by a secretary, nurse, or other personnel. Second, there can be little certainty as to enforceability, inasmuch as a successful attack on the agreement might be made on a number of grounds.[245]

The other possible use of arbitration is to impose it legislatively upon the parties as a complete substitute for a jury trial, and such a proposal has been made in more than one instance.[246] The difficulty with this straightforward approach is that there are three different types

---

West's Cal. Legis. Service No. 9, at 3795-96 (codified at CAL. CIV. PRO. CODE §§ 1295(a)-(b)); Amend. Sub. H.B. 682, [1975] Page's Ohio Legis. Bull. No. 3, at 177 (codified at OHIO REV. CODE ANN. § 2711.23).

241. *See, e.g.,* Ala. H.B. 300 (1975); Act 371, [1975] West's La. Sess. Law Service No. 3, at 651 (codified at LA. REV. STAT. ANN. § 9:4231); Amend. Sub. H.B. 682, [1975] Page's Ohio Legis. Bull. No. 3, at 177-78 (codified at OHIO REV. CODE ANN. § 2711.24); Pub. Act 140, [1975] West's Mich. Legis. Service No. 3, at 274 (codified at MICH. COMP. LAWS ANN. § 600.5041(3)-(6)); *cf.* Md. H.B. 401 (1975) (did not pass) ("the Legislature requests the Court of Appeals to promulgate . . . standard forms of arbitration agreement").

242. *See, e.g.,* Ala. H.B. 300 (1975) (voidable within thirty days after execution); Cal. A.B. 32 (2d Extra. Sess. 1975) (forty-five days); Medical Injury Compensation Reform Act, ch. 1, 2d Extra. Sess., [1975] West's Cal. Legis. Service No. 9, at 3796 (codified at CAL. CIV. PRO. CODE §§ 1295(c)-(d)) (thirty days); Act 371, [1975] West's La. Sess. Law Service No. 3, at 652 (codified at LA. REV. STAT. ANN. § 9:4235(1)).

243. *See, e.g.,* Cal. A.B. 926 (1975) (can be rescinded within thirty days after completion of services for which contract was signed); Amend. Sub. H.B. 682, [1975] Page's Ohio Legis. Bull. No. 3, at 177 (codified at OHIO REV. CODE ANN. § 2711.23(B) (within sixty days after discharge from the hospital or termination of the physician-patient privilege).

244. At present, these agreements are apparently being utilized in very few places. *See* HOLDER 422-31.

245. Of necessity, standards of enforceability will vary from patient to patient, depending upon such matters as the physical and mental condition, and the general intelligence level of the patient.

246. *See* Ala. H.B. 436 (1975) (all factual determinations of the Medical Injuries Compensation Board are conclusive and remedy is exclusive); Cal. A.B. 31 (2d Extra. Sess. 1975) (no trial de novo following determination of claim by California Medical Malpractice Commission); Cal. S.B. 2 (2d Extra. Sess. 1975); Md. H.B. 429 (1975) (patient can elect to sue at law rather than utilize the Compensation Commission if the injury was caused intentionally).

of potential constitutional limitations on its use. First, federal due process may require that the parties have the right to present evidence and to cross-examine witnesses.[247] Second, the equal protection clause of the fourteenth amendment would prevent the drawing of discriminatory lines between those types of cases which are entitled to jury trial and those that are not. Inasmuch as there is no federal right to a jury trial in state court,[248] however, it would seem that such classifications need only be reasonable or rational ones in order to avoid the constitutional prohibition.[249] Thus, it should be permissible to single out malpractice cases for arbitration both because of their unique complexity and because of the current crisis, which is caused at least in part by the unavailability of a more efficient claims-handling procedure.[250] Similarly, it would also seem legally nondiscriminatory to require arbitration of claims for less than a certain dollar amount.[251] This particular variation is especially appealing as at least a partial solution insofar as it provides a practicable method of handling small claims.

The most substantial objection to binding, compulsory arbitration is the state-guaranteed right to jury trial, which is contained in the constitutions of forty-eight states.[252] Proposals in two different states would help to overcome this obstacle by permitting the patient to reject the provisions of the new bill before the health care which results in injury is rendered.[253] In the case of emergency care, the patient is apparently entitled to reject the act and go to trial if he does so within a

---

247. *See* HOLDER 424-25.
248. The seventh amendment right to jury trial applies only to the federal courts. It does not apply, through the fourteenth amendment, to the states. *See* Olesen v. Trust Co. of Chicago, 245 F.2d 522 (7th Cir.), *cert. denied*, 355 U.S. 896 (1957).
249. *See* Adams & Bell, *Alternatives to Litigation, II: Constitutionality of Arbitration Statutes,* in MEDICAL MALPRACTICE REPORT Appendix 315, 317.
250. *Id.* at 318.
251. HOLDER 425; Adams & Bell, *supra* note 249, at 317. Many counties in Pennsylvania have, pursuant to statute, adopted a requirement that all claims for less than $3,000 be first subjected to arbitration. *See* Wadlington, *Alternatives to Litigation, IV: The Law of Arbitration in the U.S.,* in MEDICAL MALPRACTICE REPORT Appendix 346, 402. This statute was upheld against constitutional attack in the case of *In re Smith,* 381 Pa. 223, 112 A.2d 625, *appeal dismissed,* 350 U.S. 858 (1955). It should be noted, however, that under this statute both parties have the right to insist upon a jury trial de novo. The state-guaranteed right to jury trial is another problem. See notes 252-54 *infra* and accompanying text. In addition, requiring arbitration of claims below a certain dollar amount will only encourage the plaintiff to increase the amount of his claim in order to avoid compulsory arbitration. See notes 173-80 *supra* and accompanying text.
252. *See* Adams & Bell, *supra* note 249, at 318. Only Louisiana and Colorado do not have such a constitutional provision for civil cases.
253. La. S.B. 344 (1975); Pa. H.B. 805 (1975).

reasonable time.²⁵⁴ Whether or not these escape valves will be judged sufficient is questionable: it seems clear that, in most instances, patients will be totally unaware of their jury-trial rights and any action required to enforce them. Thus, a strong argument can be made that this procedure will not satisfy the constitutional requirements.

The number of legislative proposals which include binding, compulsory arbitration is relatively small and, as yet, none has been enacted. Presumably, this is a result of state constitutional restrictions on dispute resolution in civil cases. The alternative, of course, is to adopt screening panels. In the short run, it is far more likely that compulsory screening panels and other nonbinding mechanisms will be resorted to in an attempt to alleviate the crisis.²⁵⁵ In the long run, however, binding arbitration would seem to hold greater potential by virtue of both its finality and its streamlined procedures.²⁵⁶ Therefore, continued efforts in that direction should be encouraged. If the malpractice crisis continues to deepen, it may even be feasible to propose state constitutional amendments, thus paving the way for a thoroughgoing overhaul of the traditional dispute resolution mechanism.

Conclusion

The legislative responses to the current medical malpractice crisis are varied and complex. These responses effect many changes which will prove crucial, not only to the medical and legal professions, but to the entire American populace as consumers of health care. While the many proposals and enactments deal with a broad array of substantive and procedural issues in the handling of malpractice claims, it is clear that there is a common goal: making the malpractice risk insurable at reasonable rates. Toward that end, state assemblies have placed ceilings on the potential liability of health care providers, altered rules of law in an effort to make large malpractice recoveries more difficult to obtain, and established new procedural mechanisms designed to simplify and speed up the resolution of claims. More radical solutions to the malpractice problem—for example, no-fault approaches, basic shifts in medical liability insurance coverage, or a restructuring

---

254. La. S.B. 344 (1975).
255. If this approach is adopted, the compulsory screening panel process will have to be limited in scope or it will merely add another expensive stage to the current jury trial process. *Cf.* Baird, Munsterman & Stevens, *supra* note 190, at 215 (present arbitration plan reduces court dockets by only 0.7 percent of the total volume of malpractice claims).
256. *See* HOLDER 423.

of the entire system to incorporate outcome (as opposed to process) standards and market-oriented incentives for better care—are left to scholarly commentary. Whether the legislative steps taken thus far will be adequate or will prove only stop-gap measures until sterner approaches are devised to reduce the frequency and severity of treatment-related injuries remains to be seen. It can be said with confidence, however, that the experimentation now being conducted in fifty state laboratories will surely serve as guideposts along the road toward the fairest and most efficient resolution of the malpractice crisis.